RETHINKING ENVIRONMENTAL LAW

This book has been published with the contribution of the research project "Climate change and plastic waste: legal challenges of the circular economy as a paradigm for the protection of planetary health and justice" with reference PID2020-115551RA-I00, funded by MCIN/ AEI/10.13039/501100011033.

This book has been published with the contribution of the Industrial Doctorate Programme of the Generalitat de Catalunya.

The editors are members of the Research Group 'Territory, Citizenship and Sustainability' of the Universitat Rovira i Virgili, supported by the Research and Universities Department of the Generalitat de Catalunya (2021 SGR 00162).

European Environmental Law Forum Series, Volume 9

RETHINKING ENVIRONMENTAL LAW

Connectivity, Intersections and Conflicts in the Global Environmental Crisis

Edited by
Endrius COCCIOLO
Jordi JARIA-MANZANO
Aitana DE LA VARGA-PASTOR
Maria MARQUES-BANQUE

INTERSENTIA
Cambridge – Antwerp – Chicago

Intersentia Ltd
8 Wellington Mews
Wellington Street | Cambridge
CB1 1HW | United Kingdom
Tel: +44 1223 736 170
Email: contact@larcier-intersentia.com
www.larcier-intersentia.com

Distribution for the UK and
Rest of the World (incl. Eastern Europe)
NBN International
1 Deltic Avenue, Rooksley
Milton Keynes MK13 8LD
United Kingdom
Tel: +44 1752 202 301 | Fax: +44 1752 202 331
Email: orders@nbninternational.com

Distribution for Europe
Lefebvre Sarrut Belgium NV
Hoogstraat 139/6
1000 Brussels
Belgium
Tel: +32 (0)2 548 07 13
Email: contact@larcier-intersentia.com

Distribution for the USA and Canada
Independent Publishers Group
Order Department
814 North Franklin Street
Chicago, IL 60610
USA
Tel: +1 800 888 4741 (toll free) | Fax: +1 312 337 5985
Email: orders@ipgbook.com

Rethinking Environmental Law. Connectivity, Intersections and Conflicts in the Global Environmental Crisis

Image on cover: JLBvdWOLF / Alamy Stock Photo

ISBN 978-1-83970-447-5
D/2024/7849/45
NUR 828

British Library Cataloguing in Publication Data. A catalogue record for this book is available from the British Library.

CONTENTS

LIST OF AUTHORS

Eva Balounová is a postdoctoral researcher at the Centre for Climate Law and Sustainability Studies at the Institute of State and Law of the Czech Academy of Sciences, where she focuses on international and European climate change law. Eva graduated as a Master of Law at the Charles University in Prague, and as a Master of Natural Resources Law and International Environmental Law at the University of Iceland. Since 2015, Eva has been working as a legal consultant in the Chamber of Deputies of the Czech Parliament. In 2019, Eva received her PhD from the Charles University in Prague.

Camille Bertaux is a PhD candidate at the UCLouvain Saint-Louis Brussels, working under the supervision of Professor Delphine Misonne. She graduated from the Université Libre de Bruxelles, in Public and International Law (Bachelor's and Master's degrees), and pursued her studies with an LLM in International Environmental Law at Queen Mary University of London. Her area of research focuses on the role of World Health Organization guidelines in environmental law, specifically in water quality and air quality law. Besides writing her doctoral thesis, she works at the Université Libre de Bruxelles, as a teaching assistant in public international law.

An Cliquet is an international environmental and biodiversity law professor at Ghent University, Belgium. Her research covers international and EU biodiversity law. In recent years, she has focused more specifically on ecological restoration law, and topics like climate change and biodiversity, gender and biodiversity, health and biodiversity, protection of urban biodiversity, and protected areas. She teaches courses on international and European environmental and biodiversity law, international law and sustainability, and marine nature conservation law and public international law.

Endrius Cocciolo is an administrative and energy law associate professor at the Public Law Department of Universitat Rovira i Virgili (Tarragona, Catalonia, Spain). He is a researcher at the Tarragona Centre for Environmental Law Studies (CEDAT) and the University Institute for Research in Sustainability, Climate Change and Energy Transition (IU-Rescat). Endrius is member of the URV consolidated research group 'Territory, Citizenship and Sustainability', recognised by the Generalitat de Catalunya. He has also served as co-chair of the research committee at the International Union for Conservation of Nature Academy of Environmental Law (IUCN AEL), and is a member of the managing board of the European Environmental Law Forum (EELF). He is currently the coordinator of a Horizon MSCA Doctoral Network project (THERESA) on hydrogen regulation, and the principal investigator of an interdisciplinary project founded by the Spanish Ministry of Innovation, on energy communities (ComEnerSys).

Aitana De la Varga-Pastor is an administrative and environmental law associate professor at the Public Law Department of the Universitat Rovira i Virgili (Tarragona, Catalonia, Spain). She is a researcher at the Tarragona Centre for Environmental Law Studies (CEDAT) and the University Institute for Research in Sustainability, Climate Change and Energy Transition (IU-Rescat). Aitana is a member of the URV consolidated research group 'Territory, Citizenship and Sustainability', recognised by the Generalitat de Catalunya. She is the principal investigator of the R+D+I project 'Climate change and plastic waste: legal challenges of the circular economy as a paradigm for the protection of planetary health and justice' (JustCircular), and has had several publications on environmental law in high-impact reviews. Her current lines of research are climate change law, human rights defenders, circular economy, waste prevention and management, and soil protection.

Martijn van Gils is a PhD candidate at the Utrecht University Centre for Water, Oceans and Sustainability Law (UCWOSL), in the Netherlands. His research focuses on the legal aspects of soil subsidence in peatlands in the Netherlands, including the use of legal instruments to implement measures to reduce soil subsidence and/or the adverse effects thereof, such as CO2 emissions. Martijn's research is conducted within the multidisciplinary 'Living on Soft Soils' research programme, funded by the Dutch Research Council (NWO), which is aimed at researching the causes, physical processes and consequences of soil subsidence in Dutch peatlands, and arranging new strategies to cope with (the consequences of) subsidence in peatlands (https://nwa-loss.nl/).

Tilak Ginige is an environmental law senior lecturer at Bournemouth University's Faculty of Science & Technology. His research interests include renewable energy, mining waste, the Water Framework Directive, environmental liability and sustainable development law.

Carola Glinski is an environmental law professor at Trier University of Applied Science, Germany, and an associate professor at the University of Copenhagen. Her research focuses on environmental law, EU law, international economic law and private governance. Currently, she co-leads a Biodiversa+ network project on biodiversity protection in transnational value chains ('BioTrade').

Jordi Jaria-Manzano is Serra Húnter Fellow of Constitutional and Environmental Law at the Public Law Department of the Universitat Rovira i Virgili (Tarragona, Catalonia, Spain) and a researcher at the Tarragona Centre for Environmental Law Studies (CEDAT) and at the Research Institute in Sustainability, Climate Change and Energy Transition (IU-RESCAT). He is chief editor of the *Revista d'Estudis Autonòmics i Federals/Journal of Self-Government)* and currently leads a research project on sustainability in the digital domain, funded by the Spanish Ministry of Economic Affairs and Digital Transformation.

Matija Kajić is a PhD candidate at Utrecht Centre for Regulation and Enforcement in Europe (RENFORCE) and the Utrecht Center for Water, Oceans and Sustainability Law (UCWOSL), at Utrecht University, in the Netherlands. She is conducting interdisciplinary research on the legal and institutional challenges shaping the governance of the EU's circular economy for the biowaste and wastewater streams. Her current employment at Triodos Bank has diversified her research interests to include the broader circular economy and energy transitions, and the role financial institutions play in driving them forward.

Francesca Leucci is an environmental law lecturer at Wageningen University, in the Netherlands. She was previously a PhD candidate at Bologna, Rotterdam and Hamburg Universities (European Doctorate in Law and Economics). She gained her first legal degree in Italy, and her LLM in Economic Analysis of European Law at the College of Europe in Bruges. Her fields of interest include environmental laws, the economic analysis of environmental liability laws, and remedies for environmental damage. She is also a temporary expert for Eklipse, working on the impact assessments of projects on biodiversity (no net loss) through the concept of ecosystem services.

Maria Marques-Banque is a criminal law associate professor at the Public Law Department of the Universitat Rovira i Virgili (Tarragona, Catalonia, Spain). She is a researcher at the Tarragona Centre for Environmental Law Studies (CEDAT) and the University Institute for Research in Sustainability, Climate Change and Energy Transition (IU-Rescat). Maria is a member of the URV consolidated research group 'Territory, Citizenship and Sustainability', recognised by the Generalitat de Catalunya. She is the director of the Department of Public Law and the director of the Environmental Law Clinic. Her research focuses on environmental crime, wildlife crime, transnational crime, EU criminal law, sentencing, and Spanish domestic criminal law.

Sophie Melchers is a PhD candidate at the Utrecht Centre for Water, Oceans and Sustainability Law (UCWOSL) of Utrecht University, in the Netherlands. She graduated in 2021, in the field of international and European law, at Tilburg University. Before that, she completed two undergraduate degrees in social psychology and data science, and in global law, also at Tilburg University. Her research is connected with the AquaConnect project, and is part of the UCWOSL research group. She researches the role of the law in innovations in freshwater management, particularly with regard to droughts and the climate and circularity goals.

Alba Nogueira López is an administrative law professor at the Universidade de Santiago de Compostela, Spain. Her research in the field of environmental law deals with the choice of regulatory and policy instruments, the circular economy, and the interface between environmental protection and market/economic regulation. Alba is a member of the scientific boards of several environmental journals, the Spanish Observatory of Environmental Policies, and the Tarragona Centre for Environmental Law Studies (CEDAT).

Lissia Queiroz de Menezes is a practising Brazilian lawyer who has been working in the field of public law, specifically in the port sector. She graduated in Law from Universidade de Fortaleza (UNIFOR), has been a member of the Brazilian Bar Association since 2010, and has a postgraduate degree in Brazilian Tax Law. She obtained her Master's degree (LLM) in International Commercial Law from Bournemouth University. Her research focuses on corporate and environmental law, connecting Environmental, Social and Governance (ESG), sustainability, the renewable energy market, and corporate purpose, in the new Green Industrial Revolution context.

Leonie Reins is a public law and sustainability professor at the Erasmus University Rotterdam, in the Netherlands. Leonie's research focuses on the intersections of energy and environmental law. She is particularly interested in the regulation of new technologies capable of contributing to climate change mitigation and adaptation efforts.

Albert Ruda-Gonzalez is a private law associate professor and dean at the Faculty of Law of the University of Girona, Spain. He is also a member of the Institute of European and Comparative Private Law of the same university, the European Centre of Tort and Insurance Law (ECTIL, Vienna), the Instituto Brasileiro de Estudos de Responsabilidade Civil (IBERC), and the Institute of Iberoamerican Law (IDIBE), research fellow of the Utrecht Centre for Accountability and Liability Law (UCALL), founding member and chair of the European Law Institute (ELI) Spanish Hub, chair of the ELI Special Interest Group on Global Private Law, and member of the Commission of Codification of Catalonia. He is also a former scholar of the Japan Foundation, and a former van Calker scholar of the Swiss Institute of Comparative Law.

Gonzalo Vial Fourcade is a PhD candidate at the University of Cambridge, under a scholarship from the Cambridge Trust and the Chilean government. He is a lawyer from Universidad Católica, and holds an LLM from Stanford Law School (Fulbright scholarship). Previously, he was a partner at a Chilean dispute resolution boutique firm. He has taught civil procedure, civil law and arbitration at Universidad Adolfo Ibáñez and Universidad Católica. He was a visiting scholar at the University of Sydney, and an intern at the Australian Disputes Centre, the Australian Centre for International Commercial Arbitration, AMPLA Brazil, and Carey. He has several publications on dispute resolution and energy disputes.

Jiri Vodicka is an assistant professor at the Department of Environmental Law and Land Law at Masaryk University in Brno, Czech Republic. He has worked as a lawyer at the Czech Competition Authority, gaining valuable experience in the regulatory aspects of law, and as an environmental and EU law advisor at the Czech Supreme Administrative Court. Jiri focuses on environmental and regulatory aspects of the automotive industry, climate, and other environmental law themes. He has authored several publications and scientific articles on these topics, and regularly presents at academic conferences and events.

Ida Mae de Waal is a PhD candidate at the Utrecht Centre for Water, Oceans and Sustainability Law (UCWOSL) of Utrecht University, in the Netherlands. Her research focuses on the interaction and coherence between EU chemicals legislation, product legislation and waste legislation, in light of the transition towards a circular economy in the EU.

INTRODUCTION

Rethinking Environmental Law

Endrius Cocciolo, Jordi Jaria-Manzano,
Aitana De la Varga-Pastor and Maria Marques-Banque

The human footprint on the planet is growing rapidly. In the beginning, environmental law focused on local phenomena. However, over time, it has raised awareness of the comprehensiveness and complexity of the anthropic impact on the Earth system, as the climate emergency makes clear. Different physical processes are connected at the planetary level, producing a blurred picture of interactions, and the gigantic size of human activity in the system acquires a geological dimension, as stated by the Anthropocene narrative. A holistic view seems to appropriately describe the planet's evolution while the biosphere is becoming a complex mix of life and technology. This poses enormous challenges for the disciplines related to the study of the different aspects of the environment, because none of them can offer a complete and sufficient view.

We are confronted with an emerging understanding of the connectivity of environmental realities, which impacts on our knowledge. These interactions challenge the traditional legal parochialism, centred in clearly delimited sectors of law and specific territories of jurisdiction, and demand new exchanges between different legal disciplines, as well as advancing into interdisciplinarity beyond legal knowledge. Complexity not only produces connectivity and raises intersections, but also gives rise to conflicts. Environmental law is, accordingly, becoming a complex field of knowledge, where different legal disciplines flow in, and where connections with non-legal disciplines are, growingly, required. The sectorialisation of legal knowledge and the fragmentation of legal practice can no longer be held back.

Connections are the routine reality of the environmental crisis, and demand an environmental law adjusted to this intersected state of affairs. These connections are manifold: climate and land use, food security and energy, waste and marine protection, trade and biodiversity, and many more combinations. Legal scholars and practitioners cannot be confined to securing provincial borders of specialised knowledge, nor can they ignore the need to advance into the troubled waters of interdisciplinary exchange. They must also acknowledge the importance of conflict as a source of legal imagination, and as an expression of the complexity of the intertwined network of life and technology in the Anthropocene. Ultimately, environmental law needs to be rethought, to confront the challenges raised by the complex structure of the biosphere, and the pervasiveness of the human footprint on it.

The 9th European Environmental Law Forum, held in Tarragona, in September 2022, confronted this tricky situation of intersections and conflicts – of connectivity and complexity. Several contributions were presented there, and some of these have been elaborated into the chapters of this book, which tries to capture the richness of the conference debates, and to give a sample of the different problems addressed by the attendees. Therefore, in these pages, the reader can discover some of the most significant debates regarding the challenges raised by the complexity of the Earth system, for contemporary environmental law. This a vibrant and creative field of knowledge whose scholars are trying to help design the tools and maps to navigate the global environmental crisis, which plausibly marks the transition to a new geological era.

With such a broad scope, we have been confronted, as editors, with a significant multiplicity of views, themes and approaches, giving a sample of the manifoldness of current environmental law research. While the reader can consult each chapter individually, we have tried to incorporate some kind of narrative when ordering the chapters, providing a path for readers to follow when exploring the volume as a whole. We have divided the contributions into two main parts: those centred on connections, and those centred on conflicts. Within each part, we have grouped the contributions according to their respective focuses.

The volume starts with a chapter by An Cliquet, who examines one of the most significant intersections in the current global environmental crisis: that of climate change and biodiversity loss. The author underlines how such an important connection is mostly being missed in the legal regimes regarding both fields, and how this affects biodiversity protection. In so far as the equilibrium of existent ecosystems is essential in the managing of the climate emergency, the author stresses the need for new binding targets.

Thereafter, also regarding biodiversity loss, Carola Glinski emphasises how inefficient the current legal framework has been in providing protection against this. The author explores a particularly significant aspect of the complexity of biodiversity protection, i.e. the role of due diligence in the field of business, as it is clear that transnational value chains impact on biodiversity. This contribution shows how the inclusion of transnational private standardisation schemes could bring solutions in this field.

Air pollution has been a traditional concern of environmental law. The two following chapters approach different aspects of this area. First, Camille Bertaux analyses how a soft law document, the World Health Organization guidelines regarding air quality, influences EU Law. This is a case of how epistemic authority can define legal standards. This phenomenon is becoming common in the context of the global environmental crisis, where scientific knowledge provides not only relevant information, but also counsel and guidance in the decision-making process.

Thereafter, Jiri Vodicka addresses a very controversial issue: how to regulate vehicle circulation, as a significant source of air pollution (the most important in urban areas), in light of the different implications – legal as well as economic – which such restrictions might imply. The attempts of several municipalities to impose car restrictions have been implemented under the shadow of their compatibility with EU law, particularly vehicle type-approval regulation. This chapter explores the possibilities of regulation in this area, and stresses the problems in combining different fields of law that have different goals.

After these contributions, there is a block of chapters devoted to different aspects of energy law, beginning with the contribution by Endrius Cocciolo and Leonie Reins, on the implications of the Energy Charter Treaty for the prevention of plastic production. Beyond being a significant source of pollution, particularly impacting on marine biodiversity, plastics also pose a proven threat to planetary boundaries. Employing an Earth System Law framework, the authors elucidate how intricate interactions within the biosphere reverberate in the manner in which certain transnational regimes, initially designed to address specific sectors of human activity, transcend their original scope, and extend their influence into diverse facets of anthropogenic impact on the planet.

Subsequently, Gonzalo Vial Fourcade approaches the interface between climate change, electricity systems and the law of contracts, drawing from a particular real-life case concerning the Chilean electricity system. The author concludes that climate principles should be incorporated into the regulatory frameworks of electricity systems, as energy markets are a key factor in the production of greenhouse gases (GHGs). This should also raise the awareness of energy consumers about the climate change implications of their decisions.

The following chapter, authored by Lissia Queiroz de Menezes and Tilak Ginige, presents a comparative analysis between the United Kingdom and Brazil, specifically examining the political and legal frameworks that promote the production of green energy, with a primary emphasis on the hydrogen framework. The conclusion is that each jurisdiction must develop a regulatory framework that suits its specific circumstances. Furthermore, the chapter stresses the potential for Brazil to be a major actor in energy innovation, which will be a pivotal aspect for the adaptation of states and societies to planetary constraints, in the context of the global environmental crisis.

Adapting to these circumstances and producing a sustainable society is the goal of a circular economy, which is the subject of the three following chapters. The first one of these, by Alba Nogueira, focuses on the right to repair, a key legal aspect of the circular economy, which is confronted with some limitations, under existing regulations. As the author emphasises, the influence of corporate interests in decision-making processes relating to the circular economy at the EU level, along with the presence of substantial areas of corporate law that lack sensitivity towards sustainability and consumption restraint, impede suitable solutions in this field.

Chapter 9, by Ida Mae de Waal, is devoted to how the EU legislation on plastic packaging addresses a real transition, in terms of the circularity of plastic use in the packaging chain. According to the author, the relationship between the current legislation governing the life cycle of plastic packaging, on the one hand, and the transition to a circular economy, on the other, is mostly weak, although some improvements seem imminent, and these could contribute to decreasing the impact of material consumption, by implementing a more circular plastic packaging chain.

The last chapter of Part I of the book is focused on how to balance competence and circularity. In this contribution, Matija Kajić analyses, in particular, the incentive for the recovery of valuable resources from biowaste. From a particular case study about Den Haag, in the Netherlands, the author concludes that the transition to a circular agri-food system needs an appropriate balancing of the interests of different actors, both private and public, beyond the obviously necessary technological innovation.

Part II of the book focuses on conflicts and frictions deriving from the multifaceted and complex nature of environmental issues. The first contribution in this part addresses potential friction between technological innovation and legal constraints, in the domain of freshwater management. The author, Sophie Melchers, underlines that technological innovations need an adequate legal framework, but that this framework should take account of interests other than technology, in managing any sector. Accordingly, if legal systems help to manage uncertainty created by innovations, they should also provide enough flexibility to facilitate technological developments to confront the global environmental crisis.

The following chapter shows, with a case study, the gap between the interconnectedness of the environment and the fragmentation of the legal and institutional reality. Martijn van Gils shows that this gap makes the implementation of effective environmental policies, by public authorities, very difficult. Attempts to reduce oxidation and GHG emissions in Dutch peatlands provide a clear example of how these difficulties are present in real-life politics. However, the author stresses that public authorities can use their policy and legal instruments to bridge the aforementioned gap.

Thereafter, Francesca Leucci focuses on the tricky question of compensation for environmental damage. According to the author, environmental liability laws can prevent and remedy environmental damages. However, this depends, among other factors, on how accurately the loss is measured, and how the compensation is calculated. Habitat equivalency is the area chosen by the author to pursue her analysis, in order to unveil hidden loopholes that result in incomplete compensation.

The last two chapters are centred on climate litigation – probably the most salient aspect of current environmental law conflicts. Eva Balounová's contribution focuses on future generations' rights, considering the increase in cases in which young people are litigating for their rights regarding climate change. The chapter distinguishes between this type of case and those cases where young plaintiffs are not pleading the rights of future generations. This analysis leads to a review of how the law should consider intergeneration justice.

Albert Ruda authors the final chapter, and addresses a crucial issue regarding complexity: causation and liability. The contribution focuses on climate change litigation. According to the author, with the rise of climate litigation, and in leading cases such as *Urgenda*, causation, although it is traditionally the legal foundation for liability, is hardly analysed. Poor causal analyses seem to be unacceptable from a legal point of view. The author proposes the use of pollution-share liability to circumvent the problems of indeterminate causation, and to reinforce the legal consistency of judicial decisions on liability regarding climate change.

All in all, this book includes contributions addressing a very diverse range of issues, to show the complexity of contemporary environmental law, and the need to rethink its borders, contents and goals. We are becoming increasingly aware of the dimensions of our environmental footprint, as a global society, on the very material basis of our lives. With this awareness, we are also becoming familiar with the complexity of the phenomenon of life, and the multiple interactions determining the evolution of the planet. Environmental law is one of our major tools, as a society, to confront the planetary change we are causing; we need to redesign it according to our growing knowledge about the supercomplexity of the Earth system. We hope that this volume will help in the process of rethinking environmental law.

PART I

CONNECTIVITY AND INTERSECTIONS

LINKAGES BETWEEN BIODIVERSITY AND CLIMATE CHANGE

Twin Crises Need Twin Solutions

An CLIQUET

ABSTRACT

Biodiversity and climate change are linked in three ways: biodiversity helps to mitigate climate change, through carbon sinks; it helps people to adapt to the impact of climate change; and biodiversity is under threat from climate change, and needs to become more resilient. The interconnection between the climate and biodiversity crises is recognised in international climate law and biodiversity law, albeit that the attention for biodiversity in the climate regime has only emerged recently, and has focused predominantly on forests as carbon sinks, neglecting other ecosystems such as peatlands. The implementation of both regimes falls short in sufficiently protecting and restoring biodiversity. As restored and healthy ecosystems are an essential part of facing the climate crisis, additional legally binding targets are required. The European Union (EU) Nature Restoration Law proposal could be a game-changer in the EU, and serve as an inspiration at the global level.

1. INTRODUCTION

It is increasingly clear from scientific literature that the biodiversity and climate crises are intertwined.[1] The linkages between biodiversity and climate change are threefold: firstly, biodiversity plays a crucial role in the mitigation of climate change, as many ecosystems are natural carbon sinks; secondly, biodiversity helps with adaptation to the effects of climate change, as ecosystems perform many functions, such as flood regulation and buffering against the impact of extreme weather events; thirdly, biodiversity is under increased pressure from the effects of climate change. These aspects are all strongly interrelated: to fulfil the functions of mitigation and adaptation, biodiversity and ecosystems need to be resilient, but climate change, in many instances, aggravates the already dire state many ecosystems are in, decreasing the capacity of ecosystems to fulfil their role in these functions.[2]

The linkages between biodiversity and climate change (further explored in section 2 below) have been recognised in international and European Union (EU) law, both in climate law and biodiversity law (discussed in section 3).[3] There are, however, still several issues regarding the linkages between biodiversity and climate change in law, which boil down to an insufficient protection of biodiversity

1 See, e.g. H.O. Pörtner et al., 'Overcoming the coupled climate and biodiversity crises and their societal impacts', *Science*, 2023 (380/eabl4881).

2 See also, on linkages between biodiversity and climate change in international law, A. Telesetsky, A. Cliquet and A. Akhtar-Khavari, *Ecological Restoration in International Environmental Law*, Routledge, 2017, ch. 11, on climate change and ecological restoration, pp. 263–283; A. Cliquet, 'Wetlands, Climate Change, and International Law' in R. Gardner et al. (eds.), *Wetlands and International Environmental Law: The Evolution and Impact of the Ramsar Convention*, Edward Elgar (in press).

3 On the interlinkages between climate and biodiversity in international law, see also H. Van Asselt, F. Sindico and M. Mehling, 'Global Climate Change and the Fragmentation of International law', *Law and Policy*, 2008 (30), pp. 427–432; J. Verschuuren, 'Regime interlinkages: examining the connections between transnational climate change and biodiversity law' in V. Heyvaert and L.-A. Duvic-Paoli (eds.), *Research Handbook on Transnational Environmental Law*, Edward Elgar, 2020, pp. 179–197.

as a solution to the climate crisis, especially when it comes to ecosystems such as wetlands (sections 4 and 5). The present author advocates for a faster and better protection of ecosystems, which can serve as a win-win for helping to cope with both the biodiversity and climate crises. Two recent developments at the international and EU levels will be examined: at the international level, the Kunming-Montreal Global Biodiversity Framework, which was adopted in Montreal, in December 2022, will be discussed; at the EU level, the proposal for a Nature Restoration Law, by the Commission, in June 2022, will be examined (section 6).

2. BIODIVERSITY AND CLIMATE CRISES: INTERCONNECTED AND MUTUALLY REINFORCING

2.1. CLIMATE MITIGATION

Ecosystems, such as forests, peatlands, grasslands, wetlands and marine ecosystems, are important reservoirs of CO^2 and other greenhouse gases.[4] As a result of the destruction or degradation of ecosystems (for example, clearing of forests, peat mining, draining of wetlands), greenhouse gases are released, and natural storage capacity for greenhouse gases is lost. According to a 2019 report from the Intergovernmental Panel on Climate Change (IPCC), agriculture, forestry and other land use (AFOLU) accounted for 23 per cent of total net anthropogenic greenhouse gas emissions.[5] The connection between biodiversity and climate change is, thus, a double-edged sword: well-functioning ecosystems help mitigate climate change, whereas degraded ecosystems will intensify climate change.[6]

Protecting remaining ecosystems, such as ancient forests and peatlands, is imperative to preventing further emissions, and restoring ecosystems can restore storage capacity. The 'One Earth Initiative' proposes three pillars to meet the goals of the Paris Agreement:[7] 100 per cent renewable energy, the protection and restoration of 50 per cent of land and sea, and a transition to

---

4 C. Epple et al., *Managing ecosystems in the context of climate change mitigation: A review of current knowledge and recommendations to support ecosystem-based mitigation actions that look beyond terrestrial forests*, Technical Series No. 86, Secretariat of the Convention on Biological Diversity, 2016.

5 IPCC, *Climate Change and Land: An IPCC Special Report on climate change, desertification, land degradation, sustainable land management, food security, and greenhouse gas fluxes in terrestrial ecosystems – Summary for Policymakers, Approved Draft*, IPCC, 2019, p. 7, https://www.ipcc.ch/site/assets/uploads/2019/08/4.-SPM_Approved_Microsite_FINAL.pdf.

6 See also R. Scholes et al. (eds.), *Summary for policymakers of the assessment report on land degradation and restoration of the Intergovernmental Science-Policy Platform on Biodiversity and Ecosystem Services*, IPBES secretariat, 2018.

7 Paris Agreement to the United Nations Framework Convention on Climate Change, Paris, 12 December 2015, ILM, 2016 (55), p. 740.

regenerative agriculture.[8] More and more, 'nature-based solutions' or 'natural climate solutions' are being put forward as a strategy in the fight against climate change. Such nature-based solutions can, potentially, contribute a third of the total mitigation needed to stay below a global temperature increase of 2 degrees Celsius.[9] However, nature-based solutions alone will not be sufficient to stop further climate change: ambitious emission reductions from industry, agriculture, transport, etc., through technological mitigation measures, are also imperative, as the rate to mitigate climate change and effectiveness of nature-based solutions is constrained by the degree of warming.[10]

2.2. CLIMATE ADAPTATION

Ecosystems and biodiversity are also important in climate adaptation, and to help people adapt to the effects of climate change.[11] That the effects of climate change are not in the distant future, but are already having an impact now, has increasingly been demonstrated, in recent years, by exceptional and severe weather phenomena, such as heavy rainfall, floods, droughts, heatwaves, and an increase in the frequency and severity of hurricanes, storms and wildfires, which are having socio-economic impacts and affecting human health.[12] An example of where protection and restoration can play a role in adaptation is through buffering against floods, by restoring mangroves and coral reefs and wetlands.[13] Another example is expanding natural areas in and around cities, which can provide cooling, and reduce the heat effect in cities.[14]

---

8 One Earth, 'Below 1.5°C: a breakthrough roadmap to solve the climate crisis', https://www.oneearth.org/below-1-5-c-a-breakthrough-roadmap-to-solve-the-climate-crisis/; see also S. Teske (ed.), *Achieving the Paris Climate Agreement Goals. Global and Regional 100% Renewable Energy Scenarios with Non-energy GHG Pathways for +1.5°C and +2°C*, Springer Open, 2019.

9 See, e.g. B.W. Griscom et al., 'Natural climate solutions', *PNAS*, 2017 (114/44), pp. 11645–11650; A. Cécile et al., 'Nature-based solutions can help cool the planet – if we act now', *Nature*, 2021 (593), pp. 91–194.

10 H.O. Pörtner et al., 'Overcoming the coupled climate and biodiversity crises and their societal impacts', *Science*, 2023 (380/eabl4881).

11 See, on nature-based solutions for climate change adaptation, European Environment Agency, *Nature-based solutions in Europe: Policy, knowledge and practice for climate change adaptation and disaster risk reduction*, EEA Report No. 01/2021, 2021; V. Kapos et al., 'Nature-based solutions for adaptation' in United Nations Environment Programme (UNEP), *Adaptation Gap Report 2020*, UNEP, 2021, pp. 43–76, https://wedocs.unep.org/handle/20.500.11822/34754.

12 World Meteorological Organization, *State of the Global Climate 2022*, WMO, 2023; World Meteorological Organization, *State of the Climate in Europe 2021*, WMO, 2022; European Environment Agency, *Climate change, impacts and vulnerability in Europe 2016: An indicator-based report*, EEA Report No. 1/2017, 2017.

13 See Secretariat of the Convention on Biological Diversity, *Connecting Biodiversity and Climate Change Mitigation and Adaptation: Report of the Second Ad Hoc Technical Expert Group on Biodiversity and Climate Change*, Technical Series No. 41, 2009.

14 See N. Kabisch et al. (eds.), *Nature-based Solutions to Climate Change Adaptation in Urban Areas: Linkages between Science, Policy and Practice*, Springer, 2017.

2.3. CLIMATE-PROOFING OF BIODIVERSITY

Climate change will have an impact on biodiversity, and will often aggravate the already degraded state nature is in due to other causes, such as over-exploitation, changes in land and sea use, pollution and invasive species.[15] Climate change will lead to species shifts and biodiversity loss. Nature will have to adapt to the effects of climate change. Biodiversity can be better protected from the effects of climate change if ecosystems are in a good state of conservation, and are more resilient and robust. Resilience means the ability of a system to recover from perturbations.[16] Ecosystems should be made more resilient, to be able to withstand the additional pressure from climate change, as resilient systems will probably be able to continue functioning. Restoration of ecosystems and ecosystem functions, and recovery of species, are seen as important strategies for increasing ecosystems' resilience to the adverse effects of climate change.[17]

Despite increasing knowledge on the interlinkages between the climate and biodiversity crises and their reciprocal impact, the awareness of these interlinkages, amongst a larger public, is still only emerging,[18] and both crises are still underestimated at the political level.[19]

3. LINKAGES BETWEEN BIODIVERSITY AND CLIMATE CHANGE IN INTERNATIONAL LAW: A ONE-SIDED LOVE?

Although the biodiversity and climate crises are inextricably connected, they have been dealt with separately in law and policy, and are also perceived differently amongst the public. The climate crisis has received much attention, both in the general media, and at the political level, through the UN Framework Convention on Climate Change (UNFCCC).[20] In turn, the yearly climate Conferences of

---

15 Intergovernmental Science-Policy Platform on Biodiversity and Ecosystem Services (IPBES), *Summary for policymakers of the Global Assessment Report on Biodiversity and Ecosystem Services*, IPBES Secretariat, 2019.

16 J. Lawler, 'Climate Change Adaptation Strategies for Resource Management and Conservation Planning', *The Year in Ecology and Conservation Biology*, 2009 (1162), p. 81.

17 See J. Mawdsley, R. O'Malley and D. Ojima, 'A Review of Climate-Change Adaptation Strategies for Wildlife Management and Biodiversity Conservation', *Conservation Biology*, 2009 (23), pp. 1080–1089; N. Heller and E. Zavaleta, 'Biodiversity management in the face of climate change: a review of 22 years of recommendations', *Biological Conservation*, 2009 (142), p. 4.

18 M. Benato, '2021: when the link between the climate and biodiversity crises became clear', *The Guardian*, 20 December 2021.

19 C.J.A. Bradshaw, 'Commentary: Underestimating the Challenges of Avoiding a Ghastly Future', *Frontiers in Conservation Science*, 2021, https://doi.org/10.3389/fcosc.2021.666910.

20 United Nations Framework Convention on Climate Change, Rio de Janeiro, 9 May 1992, ILM, 1992 (31), p. 849.

Parties (COPs) attract a lot of attention. The IPCC was established in 1988, and has provided policymakers with various assessment reports on climate change.

The biodiversity crisis is less well known amongst the public,[21] and the meetings of the Biodiversity Convention receive less attention,[22] although the Biodiversity Convention was concluded in the same year as the UN Climate Change Convention. The Intergovernmental Science-Policy Platform on Biodiversity and Ecosystem Services (IPBES), the scientific counterpart of the IPCC, was established in 2012. In December 2020, a joint workshop took place between the IPCC and IPBES.[23]

Also, attention to biodiversity in the climate change regime seems less well developed than attention to climate change in biodiversity law. It is possible to speak of a one-sided love: in biodiversity law, attention to climate change has existed for a considerable time, and much attention has been granted to the relationship between biodiversity and climate change; in the climate change regime, attention to this relationship has been rather limited, and has only emerged more recently.[24]

3.1. ATTENTION TO BIODIVERSITY IN CLIMATE LAW

As already indicated, ecosystems play a key role in climate change mitigation and adaptation. The role of ecosystems for mitigation has been recognised in international climate law. Conservation and enhancement of 'sinks' was included in the UNFCCC,[25] and is also mentioned in the Paris Agreement.[26] From 2005 onwards, the REDD+ (Reducing Emissions from Deforestation and Forest Degradation in Developing Countries) programme on forests has been developed, under the UNFCCC (see section 4 below).

Adaptation policies were also developed in the context of climate policy under the UNFCCC, and were given a formal legal basis in the Paris Agreement, which

---

21 S. Poole, 'Biodiversity: the word no one used – until it began to vanish', *The Guardian*, 10 May 2019; B. Keim, 'Many people don't know what biodiversity means', *Anthropocene*, 24 July 2019.

22 See C. Einhorn, 'The most important global meeting you've never heard of is now', *New York Times*, 14 October 2021; I. Bourke, 'Cop15: the most important summit you've never heard of', *New Statesman*, 5 December 2022.

23 See the outcome report: H.O. Pörtner et al., *Scientific outcome of the IPBES-IPCC co-sponsored workshop on biodiversity and climate change*, IPBES Secretariat, 2021.

24 See also J. Verschuuren, 'Regime interlinkages: examining the connections between transnational climate change and biodiversity law' in V. Heyvaert and L.-A. Duvic-Paoli (eds.), *Research Handbook on Transnational Environmental Law*, Edward Elgar, 2020, p. 195.

25 Art. 4, UNFCCC.

26 Art. 5(1), Paris Agreement: 'Parties should take action to conserve and enhance, as appropriate, sinks and reservoirs of greenhouse gases as referred to in Article 4, para. 1 (d), of the Convention, including forests.'

mentions building the resilience of socio-economic and ecological systems, including through economic diversification and sustainable management of natural resources.[27]

Despite the above-mentioned elements, the attention for biodiversity as such, and its crucial importance for climate change mitigation and adaptation, has only recently emerged. Whereas in the UNFCCC text biodiversity was missing, the Paris Agreement refers to it in its preamble: '*Noting* the importance of ensuring the integrity of all ecosystems, including oceans, and the protection of biodiversity, recognized by some cultures as Mother Earth, and noting the importance for some of the concept of "climate justice", when taking action to address climate change'.[28]

Biodiversity, including forests and grasslands, has been one of the priority areas under the Nairobi work programme on impacts, vulnerability and adaptation to climate change, since 2018.[29] An expert group was established on biodiversity and climate change adaptation, which led, amongst other things, to a briefing paper on biodiversity and climate change adaptation and the role of forest and grassland ecosystems,[30] and a technical brief on promoting synergies between climate change adaptation and biodiversity through the national adaptation plan and national biodiversity strategy and action plan processes.[31]

COP26 (November 2021) in Glasgow had specific attention for biodiversity. The Glasgow Climate Pact,[32] which was the most important decision of COP26, emphasises 'the importance of protecting, conserving and restoring nature and ecosystems to achieve the Paris Agreement temperature goal, including through forests and other terrestrial and marine ecosystems acting as sinks and reservoirs of greenhouse gases and by protecting biodiversity, while ensuring social and environmental safeguards'.[33] Also at this COP, the Glasgow Leaders' Declaration on Forests and Land Use[34] was signed by 143 states and the EU.

---

27 Art. 7(9), Paris Agreement.

28 Preamble, Paris Agreement.

29 Report of the Subsidiary Body for Scientific and Technological Advice on the first part of its forty-eighth session, held in Bonn from 30 April to 10 May 2018, FCCC/SBSTA/2018/4, para. 21.

30 Briefing paper. Biodiversity and climate change adaptation: the role of forest and grassland ecosystems, Nairobi work programme on impacts, vulnerability and adaptation to climate change, https://unfccc.int/sites/default/files/resource/NWP_Biodiversity_BP.v06%20%281%29.pdf.

31 A. Terton, J. Qi, and G. Zúñiga, *Promoting Synergies Between Climate Change Adaptation and Biodiversity Through the National Adaptation Plan (NAP) and National Biodiversity Strategies and Action Plan (NBSAP) Processes*, UNFCCC, CBD, IISD, GIZ, UNEP and SwedBio, United Nations Climate Change Secretariat, 2022.

32 Decision 1/CMA.3, FCCC/PA/CMA/2021/10/Add.1.

33 Ibid., para. 38.

34 Glasgow Leaders' Declaration on Forests and Land Use, 2 November 2021, https://webarchive.nationalarchives.gov.uk/ukgwa/20230418175226/https://ukcop26.org/glasgow-leaders-declaration-on-forests-and-land-use/.

Subsequent COPs have also addressed biodiversity more prominently, including the organisation of a 'Biodiversity day' at COP27 in Sharm el-Sheikh in 2022 and a Nature, Land Use and Ocean Day at COP28 in Dubai in 2023, the latter leading to a Joint Statement that was signed by the CBD COP15 Presidency and UFCCC COP28 Presidency, and several states.[35] The role of biodiversity is mentioned in several decisions of the Conference of the Parties serving as the meeting of the Parties to the Paris Agreement (CMA).[36]

Although there is an overwhelmingly clear relationship between biodiversity and climate change, and a clear role played by biodiversity in climate mitigation and adaptation, this does not seem to be clear to everyone,[37] nor has it been sufficiently translated into action to protect and restore biodiversity.

The Paris goal of staying below a global temperature increase of 1.5 degrees Celsius is implemented through the Nationally Determined Contributions (NDCs). Analysis of the NDCs shows an increased attention over time for nature-based solutions. However, the focus is more on mitigation rather than adaptation, and there is a focus on afforestation and tree-planting[38] (see also section 4 below). The revised climate pledges, made in 2021, show an increased attention to nature-based solutions. However, not all nature-based solutions in the NDCs are measurable against deadlines and quantitative targets.[39] In spite of the increase in attention to nature-based solutions, there is still a lot of unlocked potential for such solutions, in the NDCs.[40] This was also concluded in an evaluation from 2023, which concluded that nature-based solutions are not yet

---

35 COP28 Joint Statement on Climate, Nature and People, https://www.cop28.com/en/joint-statement-on-climate-nature.

36 See for example at COP27: Decision 1/CMA.4. Sharm el-Sheikh Implementation Plan; Decision 3/CMA.4. Glasgow–Sharm el-Sheikh work programme on the global goal on adaptation referred to in decision 7/CMA.3, FCCC/PA/CMA/2022/10/Add.1; at COP28: Decision -/CMA.5. Glasgow–Sharm el-Sheikh work programme on the global goal on adaptation referred to in decision 7/CMA.3.

37 See, e.g. the Belgian prime minister, who wanted to pause the adoption of the EU Nature Restoration Law (see section 6 below), as adding new rules would possibly undermine reaching the climate goals. The prime minister stated: 'Don't overload the wagon with issues that, strictly speaking, have nothing to do with global warming.' See: Belga News Agency, 'Belgian PM wants to hit pause on EU nature restoration law', 24 May 2023. This led to fierce reactions from other politicians, NGOs and scientists (see, e.g. L. Baeten et al., 'Pauze indrukken? De premier vergist zich van knop: het is tijd om te fastforwarden', *De Standaard*, 25 May 2023).

38 For an analysis of nature-based solutions in the NDCs, see N. Seddon et al., 'Global recognition of the importance of nature-based solutions to the impacts of climate change', *Global Sustainability*, 2020 (3/e15), pp. 1–12.

39 Nature-Based Solutions Initiative, 'Revised climate pledges show enhanced ambition for nature-based solutions', 22 February 2022, https://www.naturebasedsolutionsinitiative.org/news/nbs-policy-platform-ndc-submissions/.

40 See also recommendations by the World Wide Fund for Nature, in WWF, *NDCs – A Force for Nature? (4th ed.): Nature in enhanced NDCs*, WWF, 2021.

a mainstream measure. Moreover, the scientific foundations of the nature-based solutions are undervalued,[41] and financing for nature-based solutions should increase substantially.[42]

3.2. ATTENTION FOR CLIMATE CHANGE IN BIODIVERSITY LAW

Although explicit mention of 'climate change' is absent from the texts of most multilateral and regional biodiversity legislation, the link between biodiversity and climate change has been addressed in the framework of these laws.[43] Attention to the linkage of biodiversity and climate change can be found in the three linkages identified at the beginning of this contribution: (1) the role of biodiversity in mitigation; (2) the role of biodiversity in adaptation; and (3) the impact of climate change on biodiversity, and the need to make ecosystems more resilient to the effects of climate change. Also, the need to make ecosystems more resilient is not only seen as beneficial for biodiversity as such, but also for their increased potential for climate mitigation and adaptation. Overall, the linkages recognised in biodiversity law are more holistic than the somewhat narrower focus on ecosystems as 'sinks' for greenhouse gases, in international climate law. Some examples of the linkages in biodiversity law are given below.

3.2.1. Biodiversity Convention

Under the Convention on Biological Diversity (CBD) – or short Biodiversity Convention[44] – the link between biodiversity and climate change is a cross-

41 H. Zhai, B. Gu and Y. Wang, 'Evaluation of policies and actions for nature-based solutions in nationally determined contributions', *Land Use Policy*, 2023 (131/106710).

42 UN Climate Change News, 'Finance for Nature-Based Solutions Must Triple by 2030', 18 October 2022, https://unfccc.int/news/finance-for-nature-based-solutions-must-triple-by-2030; see also UNEP, *State of Finance for Nature – Time to act: Doubling investment by 2025 and eliminating nature-negative finance flows*, UNEP, 2022, https://wedocs.unep.org/20.500.11822/41333.

43 See also A. Trouwborst, 'International Nature Conservation Law and the Adaptation of Biodiversity to Climate Change: a Mismatch?', *Journal of Environmental Law*, 2009 (21), pp. 419–442; A. Cliquet et al., 'Adaptation to climate change: legal challenges for protected areas', *Utrecht Law Review*, 2009 (1), pp. 158–175; A. Trouwborst, 'Conserving European Biodiversity in a Changing Climate: The Bern Convention, the European Union Birds and Habitats Directives and the Adaptation of Nature to Climate Change', *Review of European Community and International Environmental Law*, 2011 (20), pp. 62–77; A. Trouwborst, 'Transboundary Wildlife Conservation in A Changing Climate: Adaptation of the Bonn Convention on Migratory Species and Its Daughter Instruments to Climate Change', *Diversity*, 2012 (4), pp. 258–300; A. Cliquet, 'International and European law on protected areas and climate change: need for adaptation or implementation?', *Environmental Management*, 2014 (54), pp. 721–722.

44 Convention on Biological Diversity, 5 June 1992, ILM, 1992 (31), p. 818.

cutting thematic issue.[45] Linkages between biodiversity and climate change are also discussed in several reports and other information documents under this Convention.[46]

There have been several COP decisions on this link,[47] from 2004 onwards. The COP decisions address the different interlinkages between biodiversity and climate change. A first link is the impact of climate change on biodiversity. In COP decisions, guidance is given on assessing the impacts of climate change on biodiversity, as well as on reducing the impacts of climate change on biodiversity and biodiversity-based livelihoods.[48] More recent decisions point to the value of investing in actions to reduce biodiversity loss, and to the cost of inaction.[49]

A second link that is recognised is the role that ecosystems can play in climate change mitigation and adaptation. At the same time, states are asked to increase positive and reduce negative impacts of climate change mitigation and adaptation measures on biodiversity.[50] An important element is the ecosystem-based approach that is put forward in both climate mitigation and adaptation.[51] In 2018, voluntary guidelines for the design and effective implementation of ecosystem-based approaches to climate change adaptation and disaster risk reduction were adopted.[52] The role of protected areas and other effective area-based conservation measures, as cost-effective instruments for climate change adaptation and mitigation, as well as for disaster risk reduction, is recognised.[53] Also, ecosystem restoration is increasingly recognised, in the context of climate change.[54]

The COP decisions on biodiversity and climate change mention several types of ecosystems, going beyond the role of forests. The roles of other ecosystems, such as wetlands and peatlands, are also mentioned. For example, a COP Decision of 2018 encouraged parties to collaborate on the conservation, restoration and wise/sustainable use of wetlands, so that their importance, within the context of climate change and disaster risk reduction, is recognised.[55]

---

45 Climate Change and Biodiversity, https://www.cbd.int/climate/.

46 See: Climate Change and Biodiversity. Resources, https://www.cbd.int/climate/resources.shtml.

47 For an overview, see: Biodiversity and Climate Change Decisions, https://www.cbd.int/climate/decision.shtml.

48 See, e.g. Decision X/33. Biodiversity and climate change, UNEP/CBD/COP/DEC/X/33, 2010.

49 Decision XIII/4. Biodiversity and climate change, CBD/COP/DEC/XIII/4, 2016, para. 8(a).

50 Decision X/33. Biodiversity and climate change, UNEP/CBD/COP/DEC/X/33, 2010, paras. 8(u)–(x).

51 See, e.g. in Decision X/33. Biodiversity and climate change, UNEP/CBD/COP/DEC/X/33, 2010.

52 Decision 14/5. Biodiversity and climate change, CBD/COP/DEC/14/5, 2018, Annex, Voluntary guidelines for the design and effective implementation of ecosystem-based approaches to climate change adaptation and disaster risk reduction.

53 Decision XIII/4. Biodiversity and climate change, CBD/COP/DEC/XIII/4, 2016, para. 8(f).

54 See, e.g. Decision 14/5. Biodiversity and climate change, CBD/COP/DEC/14/5, 2018, para. 4(c).

55 Ibid., para. 8.

The parties to the Biodiversity Convention have also paid attention to forest restoration activities for climate change mitigation, and the need to implement safeguards for biodiversity under REDD+.[56] When designing, implementing and monitoring afforestation, reforestation and forest restoration activities for climate change mitigation, parties are asked to consider conservation of biodiversity and ecosystem services. This can, for example, include prioritising local and acclimatised native tree species when selecting species for planting.[57]

COP decisions also ask for coherence of the biodiversity regime with the climate regime. In 2008, an Ad Hoc Technical Expert Group (AHTEG) on Biodiversity and Climate Change was established, to develop scientific and technical advice on biodiversity and its relation to climate change, and to provide biodiversity-relevant information to the UNFCCC.[58] States were asked to promote synergies between biodiversity and climate change policies and measures.[59] In 2018, parties were asked to integrate ecosystem-based approaches when updating their NDCs under the Paris Agreement.[60]

The link between biodiversity and climate change is reflected in the Strategic Plan for 2011–2020, including the Aichi Targets.[61] An explicit link to climate change is made in Target 10: 'By 2015, the multiple anthropogenic pressures on coral reefs, and other vulnerable ecosystems impacted by climate change or ocean acidification are minimized, so as to maintain their integrity and functioning.' Aichi Target 15 explicitly refers to mitigation and adaption: 'By 2020, ecosystem resilience and the contribution of biodiversity to carbon stocks has been enhanced, through conservation and restoration, including restoration of at least 15 per cent of degraded ecosystems, thereby contributing to climate change mitigation and adaptation and to combating desertification.' Neither target was achieved.[62] The current Global Biodiversity Framework, adopted in 2022, also addresses climate change (see section 6 below).

---

56 Decision XI/19. Biodiversity and climate change related issues: advice on the application of relevant safeguards for biodiversity with regard to policy approaches and positive incentives on issues relating to reducing emissions from deforestation and forest degradation in developing countries; and the role of conservation, sustainable management of forests and enhancement of forest carbon stocks in developing countries, UNEP/CBD/COP/DEC/XI/19, 2012; The Convention on Biological Diversity (CBD) Secretariat also provided technical advice on REDD+: see Secretariat for the Convention on Biological Diversity, *REDD-plus and Biodiversity*, CBD Technical Series No. 59, 2011.

57 Decision X/33. Biodiversity and climate change, UNEP/CBD/COP/DEC/X/33, 2010, para. 8(p)(ii).

58 Decision IX/16. Biodiversity and climate change, UNEP/CBD/COP/DEC/IX/16, 2008, para. B, 12(b) and Annex III.

59 Decision XI/21. Biodiversity and climate change: integrating biodiversity considerations into climate-change related activities, UNEP/CBD/COP/DEC/XI/21, 2012, para. 6(c).

60 Decision 14/5. Biodiversity and climate change, CBD/COP/DEC/14/5, 2018, para. 5(b).

61 Decision X/2. The Strategic Plan for Biodiversity 2011–2020 and the Aichi Biodiversity Targets, UNEP/CBD/COP/DEC/X/2, 2010.

62 Secretariat of the Convention on Biological Diversity, *Global Biodiversity Outlook 5*, CBD, 2020.

3.2.2. *Ramsar Convention*

Interlinkages between biodiversity and climate change have been recognised by the Conference of Parties of the Ramsar Convention.[63] The link between climate change and wetlands has also been addressed in various other documents in the framework of the Ramsar Convention, including in briefing notes,[64] policy briefs,[65] technical reports,[66] and the *Global Wetland Outlook* reports.[67] The different linkages have also been addressed in this framework, including, firstly, the impact of climate change on wetlands, and the need to make wetlands more resilient against the impact of climate change, and, secondly, the role of wetlands in climate mitigation and adaptation.

On the link between climate change and its impact on wetlands, the parties under the Convention recognise that climate change may substantially affect the ecological character of wetlands and their sustainable use.[68] They are asked to manage wetlands to increase their resilience to climate change and extreme climatic events.[69] Several resolutions point to the need to restore wetlands, to increase their resilience, and help them cope with the effects of climate change.[70]

Parties are also asked, when taking climate measures under the UNFCCC – including revegetation, and forest management, afforestation and reforestation – to ensure that implementation of such measures does not lead to serious damage to the ecological character of their wetlands, by using, where appropriate, strategic and other forms of environmental impact assessment and risk assessment.[71]

---

63 Convention on Wetlands of International Importance especially as Waterfowl Habitat, Ramsar, 2 February 1971, ILM, 1972 (11), p. 963.

64 See, for instance, Ramsar Convention Secretariat, 'Ramsar Briefing Note 10. Wetland Restoration for Climate Change Resilience', 2018, https://www.ramsar.org/sites/default/files/documents/library/bn10_restoration_climate_change_e.pdf.

65 Ramsar Convention Secretariat, 'Ramsar Policy Brief 5. Restoring drained peatlands: A necessary step to achieve global climate goals', 2021, https://www.ramsar.org/sites/default/files/documents/library/rpb5_restoring_drained_peatlands_e.pdf.

66 See, for instance, H. Gitay, C.M. Finlayson and N.C. Davidson, *A Framework for assessing the vulnerability of wetlands to climate change*, Ramsar Technical Report No. 5/CBD Technical Series No. 57, Ramsar Convention Secretariat & Secretariat of the Convention on Biological Diversity, 2011.

67 R.C. Gardner and C.M. Finlayson, *Global Wetland Outlook: State of the World's Wetlands and their Services to People 2018*, Ramsar Convention Secretariat, 2018; M. Courouble et al., *Global Wetland Outlook: Special Edition 2021*, Ramsar Convention Secretariat, 2021.

68 COP 8, Resolution VIII.3. Climate change and wetlands: impacts, adaptation, and mitigation, 2002, para. 1.

69 Ibid., para. 14; COP 10, Resolution X.24. Climate change and wetlands, 2008, para. 28.

70 See, e.g. COP 10, Resolution X.24. Climate change and wetlands, 2008, paras. 30–31; COP 11, Resolution XI.14. Climate change and wetlands: implications for the Ramsar Convention on Wetlands, 2012, para. 26; COP 14, Resolution XIV.17. The protection, conservation, restoration, sustainable use and management of wetland ecosystems in addressing climate change, 2022.

71 COP 8, Resolution VIII.3. Climate change and wetlands: impacts, adaptation, and mitigation, 2002, para. 17.

The role of wetlands in climate mitigation and adaptation has been recognised in several Ramsar resolutions. Resolution VIII.3 on climate change and wetlands, from 2002, addressed both climate mitigation and adaptation, and called on states:

> to take action to minimize the degradation, as well as promote restoration, and improve management practices of those peatlands and other wetland types that are significant carbon stores, or have the ability to sequester carbon and are considered as mitigation factors, as well as to increase the adaptive capacity of society to respond to the changes in these ecosystems due to climate change.[72]

In 2008, the parties acknowledged the increasing evidence that some types of wetlands play important roles as carbon stores, but were also concerned that this was not yet fully recognised by international and national climate change response strategies, processes and mechanisms. The parties recognised, in a resolution, the significant progress that had been made since Ramsar COP8 (2002), with respect to peatland inventory, and awareness of the carbon storage function of wetlands such as peatlands.[73] The resolution urged contracting parties to reduce the degradation of, promote the restoration of, and improve management practices of peatlands and other wetland types that are significant GHG sinks.[74] In the same resolution, the parties recognised the contribution of the wise use and restoration of wetlands to adapting human populations to climate change impacts.[75]

In 2012, Resolution XI.14 pointed to the fact that the continuing degradation and loss of some types of wetlands causes the release of large amounts of stored carbon, and thus exacerbates climate change.[76] The COP recognised that degradation and loss is occurring more rapidly in wetlands than in other ecosystems, and that it will likely be exacerbated by climate change, which will further reduce the mitigation and adaptation capacity of wetlands. As the conservation and wise use of wetlands has the potential to halt this degradation, the designation of Ramsar sites, and the effective management of Ramsar sites and other wetlands, can play a vital role in carbon sequestration and storage.[77] Parties are urged to sequester and store carbon, for climate change mitigation, through the maintenance and enhancement of the ecological functions of wetlands, as well as to reduce or halt the release of stored carbon from the

72 Ibid., para. 15.
73 COP 10, Resolution X.24. Climate change and wetlands, 2008, paras. 8–9.
74 Ibid., para. 32.
75 Ibid., para. 18.
76 COP 11, Resolution XI.14. Climate change and wetlands: implications for the Ramsar Convention on Wetlands, 2012, para. 12.
77 Ibid., para. 13.

degradation and loss of wetlands. Parties should also promote the ability of wetlands to contribute to nature-based climate change adaptation.[78] In 2022, the role of wetlands was again recognised, this time using an explicit reference to 'nature-based solutions'. Nature-based solutions being delivered by wetlands is seen as an important approach that can contribute significantly to climate action, while simultaneously providing biodiversity and human well-being benefits and addressing other social, economic and environmental challenges.[79] States are encouraged to use these wetland nature-based solutions in their national plans and strategies.[80]

The Ramsar COPs have given attention to climate change and different wetland ecosystems, including urban wetlands,[81] mountain wetlands[82] and coastal wetlands.[83] Peatlands are gradually getting more specific attention in the COP resolutions. In 1999, in a recommendation on the wise use and management of peatlands, parties to the Convention were already aware of the need to include all wetland carbon sinks and sequestration initiatives as key issues in the global discussion concerning the Kyoto Protocol under the UNFCCC.[84] The importance of peatlands to the maintenance of global diversity, and for the storage of water and carbon, a function vital to the world's climate system, was recognised.[85]

A resolution of 2015 encouraged parties to consider limiting activities that lead to the drainage of peatlands.[86] In 2018, the guidance for identifying peatlands as Ramsar sites was revised to include the designation of peatlands as Ramsar sites for global climate change regulation, as an additional argument to the existing Ramsar criteria.[87] In 2018, a specific resolution was dedicated to the restoration of peatlands for climate mitigation and adaptation. The resolution encouraged parties to develop or improve legislation on restoration and rewetting of degraded peatlands, as well as on the protection and sustainable

78 Ibid., para. 26.

79 COP 14, Resolution XIV.17. The protection, conservation, restoration, sustainable use and management of wetland ecosystems in addressing climate change, 2022, para. 5.

80 Ibid., para. 8.

81 COP13, Resolution XIII.16. Sustainable urbanization, climate change and wetlands, 2018.

82 COP 8, Resolution VIII.12. Enhancing the wise use and conservation of mountain wetlands, 2002.

83 COP 13, Resolution XIII.14. Promoting conservation, restoration and sustainable management of coastal blue-carbon ecosystems, 2018.

84 COP 7, Recommendation 7.1. A global action plan for the wise use and management of peatlands, 1999.

85 COP 8, Resolution VIII.17. Guidelines for Global Action on Peatlands, 2002.

86 COP 12, Resolution XII.11. Peatlands, climate change and wise use: Implications for the Ramsar Convention, 2015, para. 21.

87 COP 13, Resolution XIII.12. Guidance on identifying peatlands as Wetlands of International Importance (Ramsar Sites) for global climate change regulation as an additional argument to existing Ramsar criteria, 2018.

use of peatlands in general.[88] It also encouraged parties to conserve and restore degraded peatlands, in order to contribute to climate change mitigation, adaptation, biodiversity conservation and disaster risk reduction.[89] Peatland conservation and restoration measures were seen as a way to contribute to the NDCs under the Paris Agreement.[90]

The Fourth Ramsar Strategic Plan 2016–2024[91] sees the importance of wetlands for climate change mitigation and adaptation as one of its priority areas. Target 12 of the Strategic Plan states: 'Restoration is in progress in degraded wetlands, with priority to wetlands that are relevant for biodiversity conservation, disaster risk reduction, livelihoods and/or climate change mitigation and adaptation.' Annex 1 to the Strategic Plan includes baselines and indicators for the various targets. The baseline for Target 12 shows that 68 per cent of parties have identified priority sites for restoration, and 70 per cent of parties have implemented restoration or rehabilitation programmes. Indicators to assess the implementation of Target 12 are twofold: the percentage of parties that have established restoration plans (or activities) for sites, and the percentage of parties that have implemented effective restoration or rehabilitation projects (based on National Reports).[92] The Ramsar Strategic Plan refers to synergies with the CBD Aichi Targets: Target 12 of the Ramsar Strategic Plan corresponds to Aichi Target 15.

3.2.3. Other Conventions

Other global biodiversity conventions have also addressed climate change, albeit that mention of climate change is absent from the convention texts themselves.

The World Heritage Convention[93] considers climate change one of its core focuses of activity, as climate change poses a serious threat to World Heritage sites.[94] The work under the World Heritage Convention focuses on adapting World Heritage sites to the effects of climate change.[95] Parties to the World

---

88 COP 13, Resolution XIII.13. Restoration of degraded peatlands to mitigate and adapt to climate change and enhance biodiversity and disaster risk reduction, 2018, para. 23.

89 Ibid., para. 24.

90 Ibid., para. 32.

91 COP 12, Resolution XII.2. The 4th Strategic Plan 2016–2024, 2015.

92 Ibid., Annex 1: Ramsar Goals and Targets with Relevant Tools, Actors, Baselines and Indicators.

93 Convention Concerning the Protection of the World Cultural and Natural Heritage, Paris, 16 November 1972, ILM, 1972 (11), p. 1358).

94 Climate Change and World Heritage, https://whc.unesco.org/en/climatechange/; E. Osipova et al., *IUCN World Heritage Outlook 3: A conservation assessment of all natural World Heritage sites*, IUCN, 2020, pp. 25–26.

95 Guidance is given to contracting parties in several reports, see, e.g. Policy Document on the Impacts of Climate Change on World Heritage Properties, Document WHC-07/16.GA/10, adopted by the 16th General Assembly of States Parties to the World Heritage Convention,

Heritage Convention consider that world heritage may be 'in danger' because of certain causes, including serious fires, landslides, changes in water levels, floods and tidal waves.[96] Climate change is not mentioned in the Convention text, but the above-mentioned events can be consequences of global climate change. The Operational Guidelines contain criteria for the inscription of sites on the List of World Heritage in Danger. In 2008, the World Heritage Committee amended these criteria, and agreed that the emphasis on corrective measures for World Heritage sites that are in danger due to climate change should be on 'adaptation' rather than 'mitigation'.[97] The criteria in the Operational Guidelines now include the 'threatening impacts of climatic, geological or other environmental factors'.[98] World Heritage sites under threat from climate change impacts, including sites on the List of World Heritage in Danger, can become subject to reactive monitoring. If climate change fundamentally alters characteristics of a site that formed the basis of its inclusion in the World Heritage List, that site could be removed from the list.[99]

Natural World Heritage sites can also play a role in climate mitigation, as several sites, such as forests, serve as carbon sinks,[100] but these are under pressure.[101] World Heritage sites can also play a role in adaptation to climate change, through the prevention of disasters, such as floods.[102] As the World Heritage Convention includes obligations to take necessary measures to protect World Heritage sites, this would, in principle, mean that, based on the World Heritage Convention, states have to take measures to mitigate the drivers of climate change; however, in practice, this is not the case.[103]

2007; A. Colette, *Climate Change and world heritage: report on predicting and managing the impacts of climate change on world heritage and Strategy to assist States Parties to implement appropriate management responses*, World Heritage Report No. 22, UNESCO World Heritage Centre, 2007; J. Perry and C. Falzon, *Climate Change Adaptation for Natural World Heritage Sites: A Practical Guide*, World Heritage Paper Series No. 37, UNESCO, 2014.

96 Art. 11(4), World Heritage Convention.

97 World Heritage Committee, Decision 32COM 7A.32 (2008).

98 UNESCO, Operational Guidelines for the Implementation of the World Heritage Convention, WHC.21/01, 2021, paras. 179–180.

99 Although various World Heritage sites are under threat from climate change (see some examples in A. Colette, *Climate Change and world heritage: report on predicting and managing the impacts of climate change on world heritage and Strategy to assist States Parties to implement appropriate management responses*, World Heritage Report No. 22, UNESCO World Heritage Centre, 2007, pp. 20–24), no sites have yet been removed from the list because of climate change.

100 E. Osipova et al., *The Benefits of Natural World Heritage: Identifying and assessing ecosystem services and benefits provided by the world's most iconic natural places*, IUCN, 2014.

101 T. Carvalho Resende et al., *World Heritage forests: Carbon sinks under pressure*, UNESCO, WRI & IUCN, 2021.

102 E. Osipova et al., *The Benefits of Natural World Heritage: Identifying and assessing ecosystem services and benefits provided by the world's most iconic natural places*, IUCN, 2014.

103 For an analysis, see K. Lafrenz Samuels and E. Platts, 'Global Climate Change and UNESCO World Heritage', *International Journal of Cultural Property*, 2022 (29), pp. 409–432.

In the framework of the Convention on Migratory Species,[104] as well as in its daughter agreements, attention has been paid to climate change.[105] Several resolutions from the COPs have addressed the link between climate change and migratory species.[106] The focus is on protecting migratory species against the impact of climate change. A programme of work on climate change and migratory species, containing measures to facilitate species adaptation in response to climate change, was adopted in 2014,[107] and revised in 2021.[108] States are called upon to improve the resilience of migratory species and their habitats to climate change. But assisted colonisation, including translocation, can also be considered for those migratory species most severely threatened by climate change. States should develop general guidelines for climate change mitigation and adaptation projects, to ensure that these are not harmful to migratory species.

Under the United Nations Desertification Convention (UNCCD),[109] the link with climate change is twofold: on the one hand, good stewardship of the land is vital to climate change mitigation, and to help to meet the Paris Agreement targets, and, on the other, UNCCD's goal is to make land-based ecosystems and communities more resilient and better able to adapt to the effects of climate change.[110] In its Strategic Framework 2018–2030, Strategic objective 4 is to generate global environmental benefits through effective implementation of the UNCCD. The expected impact is that 'sustainable land management and the combating of desertification/land degradation [will] contribute to the conservation and sustainable use of biodiversity and addressing climate change'.[111]

The land degradation neutrality goal, which has been established as a Sustainable Development Goal,[112] is one of the key actions within the Desertification Convention, and state parties have been asked to formulate

---

104 Convention on the Conservation of Migratory Species of Wild Animals, Bonn, 23 June 1979, ILM, 1979 (19), p. 15.

105 For an analysis, see A. Trouwborst, 'Transboundary Wildlife Conservation in A Changing Climate: Adaptation of the Bonn Convention on Migratory Species and Its Daughter Instruments to Climate Change', *Diversity*, 2012 (4), pp. 258–300.

106 UNEP/CMS/Resolution 12.21. Climate change and migratory species, 2017.

107 UNEP/CMS/Resolution 11.26. Programme of work on climate change and migratory species, 2014.

108 Annex to Resolution 12.21. Programme of work on climate change and migratory species, 2017.

109 United Nations Convention on Combating Desertification, Paris, 17 June 1994, ILM, 194 (33), p. 1328.

110 Climate Change, https://www.unccd.int/land-and-life/climate-change/overview.

111 Decision 7/COP.13. The future strategic framework of the Convention, 2017, Annex. The UNCCD 2018–2030 Strategic Framework.

112 The land degradation neutrality goal has been accepted under the Sustainable Development Goals (Goal 15.3): 'By 2030, combat desertification, restore degraded land and soil, including land affected by desertification, drought and floods, and strive to achieve a land degradation-neutral world.'

voluntary targets to achieve land degradation neutrality.[113] Countries have committed to restoring about 450 million hectares, across various forms of land restoration, and according to national needs and circumstances, through the land degradation neutrality national voluntary target-setting programme.[114] Although the target of land degradation neutrality can certainly play a role in achieving climate goals, more synergies between these different regimes are recommended.[115] The questions are whether voluntary targets will be sufficient, and if not, whether more binding laws are necessary (see section 6 below).

3.2.4. *EU Biodiversity Law*

The core EU biodiversity legislation, the Birds and Habitats Directives,[116] also do not refer explicitly to climate change in their texts.[117] But, as with the international conventions, the conservation and restoration of protected areas, under these directives, can help protect ecosystems that are important for climate mitigation and adaptation. In 2013, the Commission issued guidelines on climate change and Natura 2000.[118] It focused both on the role of Natura 2000 sites in climate change mitigation and adaptation, and on the impact of climate change on species and habitats. It dealt extensively with management measures for the Natura 2000 network, including issues such as relocation of species as an adaptive strategy.

In EU biodiversity policy, attention has been paid to climate change in both the Biodiversity Strategy to 2020[119] and the Biodiversity Strategy for 2030.[120] In

---

113 Decision 3/COP.12. Integration of the Sustainable Development Goals and targets into the implementation of the United Nations Convention to Combat Desertification and the Intergovernmental Working Group report on land degradation neutrality, 2015.

114 PBL Netherlands Environmental Assessment Agency, *The global potential for land restoration: Scenarios for the Global Land Outlook 2*, PBL, 2022, p. 37.

115 M. Akhtar-Schuster et al., 'Unpacking the concept of land degradation neutrality and addressing its operation through the Rio Conventions', *Journal of Environmental Management*, 2017 (195/1), pp. 4–15.

116 Directive 2009/147/EC of the European Parliament and of the Council on the conservation of wild birds, OJ 2010 L 20/7; Directive 92/43/EEC on the conservation of natural habitats and of wild fauna and flora, OJ 1992 L 206/7.

117 For an analysis, see A. Trouwborst, 'The Habitats Directive and Climate Change: Is the Law Climate Proof?' in C.-H. Born et al. (eds.), *The Habitats Directive in its EU Environmental Law Context: European Nature's Best Hope?*, Routledge, 2015, pp. 303–324.

118 European Commission, *Guidelines on climate change and Natura 2000: Dealing with the impact of climate change on the management of the Natura 2000 network of areas of high biodiversity value*, Technical Report 2013-068, 2013.

119 European Commission, Communication from the Commission to the European Parliament, the Council, the Economic and Social Committee and the Committee of the Regions – Our life insurance, our natural capital: an EU biodiversity strategy to 2020, COM(2011) 244 final, 2011.

120 European Commission, Communication from the Commission to the European Parliament, the Council, the European Economic and Social Committee and the Committee of the

the latter strategy, there is an explicit recognition not only that the biodiversity and climate crises are linked, but that the solutions to both crises are too:

> Nature is a vital ally in the fight against climate change. Nature regulates the climate, and nature-based solutions, such as protecting and restoring wetlands, peatlands and coastal ecosystems, or sustainably managing marine areas, forests, grasslands and agricultural soils, will be essential for emission reduction and climate adaptation.[121]

The Strategy commits to protecting at least 30 per cent of the EU's land and sea area by 2030. Within this protection, there should be a specific focus on areas of very high biodiversity value or potential. These are the areas most vulnerable to climate change, and they should be granted special care in the form of strict protection. At least one-third of the protected areas – representing 10 per cent of EU land, and 10 per cent of EU sea – should be strictly protected. According to the Strategy, all the EU's remaining primary and old-growth forests should be strictly protected. But '[s]ignificant areas of other carbon-rich ecosystems, such as peatlands, grasslands, wetlands, mangroves and seagrass meadows should also be strictly protected, taking into account projected shifts in vegetation zones.'[122] Member States have until the end of 2023 to demonstrate significant progress in legally designating new protected areas. The Commission will assess, by 2024, whether stronger actions, including further legislation, are needed. A second part of the Strategy takes the form of an EU Nature restoration plan,[123] including commitments for binding restoration targets (see section 6 below), and commitments for different ecosystems. In several of those commitments, for example in relation to agricultural land, soil and forests, the link with climate change is made explicit.

Overall, in international and EU biodiversity law, attention has been paid to the different linkages between biodiversity and climate change. The protection of ecosystems plays a key role in both climate mitigation and adaptation. All instruments discussed above pay attention to the impact of climate change on biodiversity, and suggest measures to increase the adaptation of biodiversity to the additional effects of climate change, through, for instance, increasing resilience. The climate regime took much more time to pay attention to biodiversity, although lately this has changed. However, there are still a few issues, which will be dealt with in the following sections. Firstly, there is an imbalance in the level of attention given to different ecosystems that can serve as carbon sinks, in policy and law, and disproportionate attention is paid to forests. Secondly, the

Regions – EU Biodiversity Strategy for 2030: Bringing nature back into our lives, COM(2020) 380 final, 2020; endorsed by the Council, 23 October 2020; welcomed by the European Parliament in a Resolution of 9 June 2021.

121 Ibid., s. 1.

122 Ibid., s. 2.1.

123 Ibid., s. 2.2.

protection of biodiversity that can help in climate mitigation and adaptation is often based on voluntary commitments; considering the combined biodiversity and climate crisis, the question is whether this is sufficient.

4. MAY THE FOREST BE WITH YOU

In the international climate regime, attention on biodiversity has been predominantly focused on forests. For instance, under UNFCCC, the REDD mechanism was developed. REDD is a mechanism to provide developing countries with financial resources for climate mitigation activities and sustainable forest management. REDD initially focused on reducing emissions from deforestation and forest degradation, but was broadened to include the role of conservation, sustainable management of forests, and increasing forest carbon stocks in developing countries (known as REDD+). REDD+ covers several activities, including increasing forest carbon stocks, which can include forest restoration. REDD was first introduced at the 2005 Conference of the Parties to the Convention, and reappeared at subsequent COPs.[124] The 2015 Paris Agreement gives a formal legal basis to COP decisions related to REDD+.[125]

Besides UNFCCC, other international initiatives have been taken regarding forest restoration, partly with a view to mitigating climate change. On the initiative of Germany and the International Union for Conservation of Nature (IUCN), the so-called 'Bonn Challenge' was adopted in 2011.[126] The Bonn Challenge calls for the restoration of 150 million hectares of deforested and degraded land by 2020. The Bonn Challenge is not a new global commitment, but, rather, a practical means to realise other existing international commitments, including Aichi Target 15, the UNFCCC REDD+ target, and the land degradation neutrality goal. In 2016, the 'Bonn Challenge Barometer' was developed, to track progress on forest restoration commitments.[127] By 2021, the Restoration Barometer had been updated to include all terrestrial ecosystem types, including coastal and inland waters.[128] According to the Bonn Challenge website, commitments have been made to restore 210.12 million hectares of forests. However, it is not clear how many of the pledges have been realised in practice. Furthermore, an analysis

124 For the COP decisions relating to REDD, see UNFCCC Secretariat, key decisions relevant for reducing emissions from deforestation and forest degradation in developing countries (REDD+), June 2014, http://unfccc.int/files/land_use_and_climate_change/redd/application/pdf/compilation_redd_decision_booklet_v1.1.pdf.

125 Art. 5, Paris Agreement.

126 Bonn Challenge, https://www.bonnchallenge.org/.

127 Progress reports on the Bonn Challenge: R. Dave et al., *Bonn Challenge Barometer of Progress: Spotlight Report 2017*, IUCN, 2017; R. Dave, et al., *Second Bonn Challenge progress report: Application of the Barometer in 2018*, IUCN, 2019.

128 *IUCN Restoration Barometer 2022 Report*, IUCN.

shows that part of the 'restoration' consists of plantations of commercial trees, which are much less efficient than natural forests for storing carbon.[129]

In 2014, the New York Declaration on Forests[130] made the commitment to restore 200 million hectares by 2030, on top of the 150 million hectares of the Bonn Challenge. The Declaration was signed by several governments, companies, civil society organisations and indigenous organisations. Like the Bonn Challenge, it is a non-legally binding document. The 2019 progress report shows that big pledges are being made, but that implementation is lagging behind.[131]

While the increased focus on forest restoration certainly has its merits, there are some possible negative side effects, or even perverse outcomes.[132] If the conservation and restoration of forests are seen exclusively as ways to enhance carbon stocks, this can disregard biodiversity and other ecosystem services that are provided by forests and other ecosystems.[133] The REDD+ mechanism, for example, has been criticised for its focus on enhancement of forest carbon stocks, as there is a possibility that other services and social issues could be adversely affected,[134] while it is clear that monocultures provide far fewer benefits than restored natural forests.[135] Also, recent policy initiatives, such as the EU Biodiversity Strategy for 2030, include tree-planting initiatives, raising concerns that this might lead to inappropriate afforestation.[136] Furthermore, having (non-binding) commitments to restore forests, on the one hand, and continuing deforestation, on the other,[137] is fighting a running battle. The implementation of the various voluntary pledges and commitments are far from enough to help reach the climate goals.[138]

---

129 S.L. Lewis et al., 'Restoring natural forests is the best way to remove atmospheric carbon', *Nature*, 2019 (568/25).

130 New York Declaration on Forests, https://forestdeclaration.org/.

131 Climate Focus (coordinator and editor), *Protecting and Restoring Forests: A Story of Large Commitments yet Limited Progress*, NYDF Assessment Partners, 2019; New York Declaration on Forests, *Five-Year Assessment Report*, NYDF Assessment Partners, 2020.

132 See also A. Cliquet, 'International Law and Policy on Restoration' in S. Allison and S. Murphy (eds.), *Routledge Handbook of Ecological and Environmental Restoration*, Routledge, 2017, pp. 387–400.

133 A. Telesetsky, A. Cliquet and A. Akhtar-Khavari, *Ecological Restoration in International Environmental Law*, Routledge, 2017, p. 270.

134 J.M. Bullock et al., 'Restoration of ecosystem services and biodiversity: conflicts and opportunities', *Trends in Ecology and Evolution*, 2011 (26), pp. 541–549.

135 S. Alexander et al., 'Opportunities and Challenges for Ecological Restoration within REDD+', *Restoration Ecology*, 2011 (19), pp. 683–689; see also A. Di Sacco et al., 'Ten golden rules for reforestation to optimize carbon sequestration, biodiversity recovery and livelihood benefits', *Global Change Biology*, 2021 (27), p. 1328.

136 C. Tölgyesi et al., 'Urgent need for updating the slogan of global climate actions from "tree planting" to "restore native vegetation"', *Restoration Ecology*, 2021 (30/e13594).

137 See M. Weisse, E. Goldman and S. Carter, 'Tropical Primary Forest Loss Worsened in 2022, Despite International Commitments to End Deforestation', World Resources Institute, https://research.wri.org/gfr/latest-analysis-deforestation-trends.

138 UNEP, *Making Good on the Glasgow Climate Pact: A Call to Action to Achieve One Gigaton of Emissions Reductions from Forests by 2025*, UNEP, 2022.

The focus on forests is to the detriment of other ecosystems, such as peatlands and wetlands, that also play a key role in climate mitigation and adaptation.[139] The role of these ecosystems is still too much misunderstood. Moreover, there is the danger of unwanted effects of afforestation, for example by planting trees in ecosystems such as grasslands, which are ecologically unsuitable for them, thereby causing a decline in the functioning and biodiversity of grasslands.[140] There are, therefore, calls from scientific quarters to broaden the Bonn Challenge to other ecosystems, and to move towards landscape restoration.[141]

In the NDCs, the most commonly mentioned ecosystems are forests and woodland habitats, followed by marine and coastal habitats. Other ecosystems, like grasslands, are less commonly mentioned.[142] But even for forests, an analysis of updated NDCs found that their quantitative targets fell short of forests' economic mitigation potential.[143]

5. POWER TO THE PEATLANDS

While wetlands play a particularly key role in both climate change mitigation and adaptation, and this role has increasingly been recognised in both international climate change law and international biodiversity law, it seems this attention is too little, too late.

Many of the initiatives are soft law, or are voluntary or political commitments. For instance, the resolutions from the Ramsar COPs are legally non-binding, albeit that they can be seen as interpretations of the Convention text.[144] Also, the language of the different Ramsar resolutions remains soft, by 'urging' or 'encouraging' states to protect and restore wetlands. The question can be asked whether the Ramsar Convention framework is showing sufficient teeth to stop

139 See M. Strack (ed.), *Peatlands and Climate Change*, International Peat Society, 2008.

140 J.W. Veldman et al., 'Tyranny of trees in grassy biomes', *Science*, 2015 (347), pp. 484–485.

141 V.M. Temperton et al., 'Step back from the forest and step up to the Bonn Challenge: how a broad ecological perspective can promote successful landscape restoration', *Restoration Ecology*, 2019 (27), pp. 705–719.

142 Nature-based Solutions Initiative, 'Revised climate pledges show enhanced ambition for nature-based solutions', 22 February 2022, https://www.naturebasedsolutionsinitiative.org/news/nbs-policy-platform-ndc-submissions/; H. Zhai, B. Gu and Y. Wang, 'Evaluation of policies and actions for nature-based solutions in nationally determined contributions', *Land Use Policy*, 2023 (131/106710).

143 Climate Focus (coordinator and editor), *Taking Stock of National Climate Action for Forests*, NYDF Assessment Partners, 2021, www.forestdeclaration.org.

144 J. Verschuuren, 'Ramsar soft law is not soft at all: Discussion of the 2007 decision by the Netherlands Crown on the Lac Ramsar site on the island of Bonaire', 2008, https://www.ramsar.org/sites/default/files/documents/library/wurc_verschuuren_bonaire.pdf.

further degradation, and to restore wetlands, to contribute to climate change mitigation and adaptation.

Much will depend on the willingness of states to act at the national level. Many initiatives exist, for example the Scottish government's Climate Change Plan 2018–2032 update, which aims to restore at least 250,000 hectares of degraded peatland by 2030,[145] or the National Peatland Action Programme in Wales.[146] But for national initiatives, the question also arises as to whether the initiatives taken so far are sufficient, and whether the challenges are being sufficiently addressed.[147] Voluntary initiatives, mostly driven by non-governmental organisations (NGOs), also exist, including large initiatives such as the Global Peatlands Initiative[148] and the Global Mangrove Alliance.[149] However, the lack of concrete and/or binding obligations for restoration, the often predominantly quantitative targets, and the lack of guidance, lead to the demand for better policies, laws and standards.[150]

Considering the urgency of tackling both the climate and biodiversity crises, there is a pressing need for immediate and strong protection for wetlands; primarily, remaining wetlands, such as peatlands, should be protected and restored, through strong legally binding norms. An immediate non-deterioration obligation for all remaining wetlands is vital. Examples of such non-deteriorating clauses, applicable in protected areas, can be found in EU law, most importantly in Article 6(2) of the Habitats Directive, but this should be expanded to other areas outside Natura 2000 sites (see section 6 below).

---

145 Scottish Government, Update to the Climate Change Plan 2018–2032. Securing a Green Recovery on a Path to Net Zero, December 2020, https://www.gov.scot/publications/securing-green-recovery-path-net-zero-update-climate-change-plan-20182032/pages/12/.

146 See Natural Resources Wales, National Peatland Action Programme, 2020–2025, 27 November 2020, https://naturalresources.wales/evidence-and-data/maps/the-national-peatland-action-programme/?lang=en; see also V. Jenkins and J. Walker, 'Maintaining, Enhancing and Restoring the Peatlands of Wales: Unearthing the Challenges of Law and Sustainable Land Management', *Journal of Environmental Law*, 2022 (34), pp. 163–193.

147 R. Andersen et al., 'An overview of the progress and challenges of peatland restoration in Western Europe', *Restoration Ecology*, 2017 (25), p. 271; I. Brown, 'Challenges in delivering climate change policy through land use targets for afforestation and peatland restoration', *Environmental Science & Policy*, 2020 (107), p. 36.

148 The Global Peatlands Initiative is an effort to save peatlands, as the world's largest terrestrial organic carbon stock, and to prevent carbon being emitted into the atmosphere. It was formed by experts and institutions at the UNFCCC COP in Marrakech in 2016: see https://www.globalpeatlands.org/.

149 The Global Mangrove Alliance seeks to increase global mangrove cover by 20%, by 2030. It is a collaboration between NGOs, governments, industry, local communities and funders, and was launched in 2017: see https://www.mangrovealliance.org/.

150 See, e.g. S.Y. Lee et al., 'Better restoration policies are needed to conserve mangrove ecosystems', *Nature Ecology and Evolution*, 2019 (3), p. 870; see also A. Cliquet et al., 'Upscaling ecological restoration: toward a new legal principle and protocol on ecological restoration in international law', *Restoration Ecology*, 2021 (30/e13560).

6. STRENGTHENING THE LINKAGES BETWEEN BIODIVERSITY AND CLIMATE CHANGE

Although there are interlinkages between biodiversity and climate change, and attention to these is increasing, both crises and their interlinkages have been insufficiently addressed. There is a need for stronger interlinkages. Two recent developments will be discussed here.

6.1. KUNMING-MONTREAL GLOBAL BIODIVERSITY FRAMEWORK

The Kunming-Montreal Global Biodiversity Framework, under the Biodiversity Convention, was approved at COP15 in December 2022, in Montreal.[151] The Global Biodiversity Framework should provide a response to the failed Aichi Targets. It has an overall vision, with a time frame to 2050,[152] and a mission for the period up to 2030.[153] It has four overall goals for 2050, and twenty-three global action-oriented targets for measures to be taken up to 2030.

Some targets refer explicitly to climate change. Target 8 is the most relevant of these, and reads as follows:

> Minimize the impact of climate change and ocean acidification on biodiversity and increase its resilience through mitigation, adaptation, and disaster risk reduction actions, including through nature-based solutions and/or ecosystem-based approaches, while minimizing negative and fostering positive impacts of climate action on biodiversity.

This target has a dual function: on the one hand, it is about reducing the impact of climate change on biodiversity; on the other, it is about the impact that climate actions can have on biodiversity.

Target 8 falls under the category of actions aimed at reducing the threats to biodiversity. Several other targets in this group are also relevant, even if they do not mention climate change. For instance, the aim of Target 2 is to ensure that at least 30 per cent of areas of degraded terrestrial, inland water, and marine and coastal ecosystems are under effective restoration by 2030, in order to enhance biodiversity and ecosystem functions and services, ecological integrity and connectivity. Target 3 seeks to increase protected areas, or other effective area-based conservation measures, to 30 per cent of both terrestrial and marine

151 Annex to Decision 15/4. Kunming-Montreal Global Biodiversity Framework, CBD/COP/DEC/15/4, 2022.
152 Ibid., para. 10.
153 Ibid., para. 11.

areas, which should be 'effectively conserved and managed'. These targets should contribute to Goal A, which is that the 'integrity, connectivity and resilience of all ecosystems are maintained, enhanced, or restored, substantially increasing the area of natural ecosystems by 2050'.[154] As more resilient and well-connected ecosystems are better protected against the negative impacts of climate change, all these targets and goals are most relevant for protecting biodiversity against the impact of climate change.

A second group of targets is on meeting people's needs through sustainable use and benefit-sharing. Target 11 refers to climate. It aims to:

> Restore, maintain and enhance nature's contributions to people, including ecosystem functions and services, such as the regulation of air, water and climate, soil health, pollination and reduction of disease risk, as well as protection from natural hazards and disasters, through nature-based solutions and/or ecosystem-based approaches for the benefit of all people and nature.

A third group of targets includes tools and solutions for implementation and mainstreaming. Target 19 seeks to:

> Substantially and progressively increase the level of financial resources from all sources, in an effective, timely and easily accessible manner, including domestic, international, public and private resources, in accordance with Article 20 of the Convention, to implement national biodiversity strategies and action plans, mobilizing at least $200 billion per year by 2030, including by: ... (e) Optimizing co-benefits and synergies of finance targeting the biodiversity and climate crises.

These targets on implementation, as well as providing for financial means, are probably the biggest difference between the Global Biodiversity Framework and its predecessor, the Aichi Targets. The Framework, furthermore, includes measures that should support its implementation, including the responsibility for parties to the Biodiversity Convention to implement mechanisms for planning, monitoring, reporting and review,[155] as well as measures for communication, education and awareness.[156] The Global Biodiversity Framework is supported by several other decisions, such as on the monitoring framework of the Global Biodiversity Framework,[157] on planning, monitoring, reporting and review;[158] on

---

154 Ibid., para. 12, Goal A.
155 Ibid., ss. I–J.
156 Ibid., s. K.
157 Decision 15/5. Monitoring framework for the Kunming-Montreal Global Biodiversity Framework, CBD/COP/DEC/15/5, 2022.
158 Decision 15/6. Mechanisms for planning, monitoring, reporting and review, CBD/COP/DEC/15/6, 2022.

resource mobilisation;[159] and on capacity-building.[160] This is an improvement, and will allow for a better follow-up, but the Framework is based on a COP decision, which means that binding targets and deadlines are, again, lacking.

Another issue is that the targets of the Global Biodiversity Framework are global targets, and each party to the Convention has to contribute to attaining the goals and targets in accordance with their national circumstances, priorities and capabilities.[161] This entails the risk that states will only do the minimum required, and that the sum of their actions will not add up to reaching the overall goals.

Although the link with climate change has been made, a specific focus on wetlands is absent from the Global Biodiversity Framework. Given their significant role for both biodiversity and climate change mitigation and adaptation, wetlands should have received specific attention in the Framework.[162]

6.2. EU NATURE RESTORATION LAW PROPOSAL

A more holistic approach, and a clear link between biodiversity and climate change, have been included in the European Commission proposal for a Nature Restoration Law.[163] This proposal follows the commitment that was made in the EU Biodiversity Strategy for 2030, in which it was agreed to propose legally binding targets for restoration. It is an essential element of the EU Green Deal. Although the existing EU legislation already contains several restoration obligations, it is considered necessary to have binding and concrete restoration obligations.[164]

This new EU law on restoration, which will take the form of a regulation, was proposed by the Commission on 22 June 2022. The Nature Restoration Law proposal has a threefold aim: recovery of nature, helping climate change mitigation and adaptation, and meeting international commitments.[165]

---

159 Decision 15/7. Resource mobilization, CBD/COP/DEC/15/7, 2022.

160 Decision 15/8. Capacity-building and development and technical and scientific cooperation, CBD/COP/DEC/15/8, 2022.

161 Kunming-Montreal Global Biodiversity Framework, para. 7(d).

162 See also Wetlands International, *Policy Brief: Ensuring the Global Biodiversity Framework prioritises measures to safeguard wetlands and wetland biodiversity*, Wetlands International, 2022, https://www.wetlands.org/publications/ensuring-the-global-biodiversity-framework-prioritises-measures-to-safeguard-wetlands-and-wetland-biodiversity/.

163 European Commission, Proposal for a Regulation of the European Parliament and of the Council on nature restoration, COM(2022) 304 final, 2022/0195 (COD), Brussels, 22 June 2022, https://environment.ec.europa.eu/publications/nature-restoration-law_en (hereinafter 'Nature Restoration Law proposal').

164 Explanatory Memorandum of the Nature Restoration Law Proposal, COM(2022) 304 final, 2022/0195 (COD), Brussels, 22 June 2022, https://environment.ec.europa.eu/publications/nature-restoration-law_en, s. 3.

165 See Art. 1(1), Nature Restoration Law proposal.

There are two groups of restoration obligations: the first group is the obligations for habitats listed in Annex I and II of the proposal; a second group is additional obligations for different ecosystems. The annex-related targets are ambitious, and include quantitative and qualitative elements, as well as clear deadlines. For terrestrial, coastal and freshwater ecosystems, restoration measures are necessary for Annex I habitat types that are not in good condition. The deadlines for putting in place these restoration measures are at least 30 per cent by 2030, at least 60 per cent by 2040, and at least 90 per cent by 2050.[166] The Member States must also take restoration measures to re-establish habitats in areas not covered by those habitats, in order to reach the 'favourable reference area'[167] for each group of Annex I habitat types (at least 30 per cent by 2030, 60 per cent by 2040, and 100 per cent by 2050).[168] Areas where restoration measures are taken must show a continuous improvement until a good condition is reached, and should not deteriorate.[169] In areas where Annex I habitats occur, there is also a non-deterioration clause.[170] The proposal not only contains targets for taking restoration measures, but also has a result obligation that there must be an increase of habitat area in good condition for Annex I habitat types, until at least 90 per cent is in good condition, and until the favourable reference area for each habitat type is reached.[171] Very similar provisions exist for marine habitats (listed in Annex II).[172] There are exceptions for the restoration obligations and non-deterioration clauses in Articles 4 and 5. Both inside and outside Natura 2000 sites, one of the exceptions is 'unavoidable habitat transformations which are directly caused by climate change'.[173]

For the specific ecosystems, additional restoration obligations are included for urban ecosystems,[174] rivers,[175] pollinator populations,[176] agricultural ecosystems[177] and forests.[178] Especially important for climate mitigation is the obligation, under agricultural ecosystems, to take restoration measures for

166 Ibid., Art. 4(1).
167 A 'favourable reference area' is defined as 'the total area of a habitat type in a given biogeographical region or marine region at national level that is considered the minimum necessary to ensure the long-term viability of the habitat type and its species, and all its significant ecological variations in its natural range, and which is composed of the area of the habitat type and, if that area is not sufficient, the area necessary for the re-establishment of the habitat type' (Ibid., Art. 3(5)).
168 Ibid., Art. 4(2).
169 Ibid., Art. 4(6).
170 Ibid., Art. 4(7).
171 Ibid., Art. 4(10).
172 Ibid., Art. 5.
173 Ibid., Arts. 4–5, (8)–(9), (b).
174 Ibid., Art. 6.
175 Ibid., Art. 7.
176 Ibid., Art. 8.
177 Ibid., Art. 9.
178 Ibid., Art. 10.

drained peatlands in agricultural use. For those peatlands, restoration measures must be in place in accordance with the following minimum standards: 30 per cent of such areas by 2030, of which at least a quarter should be rewetted; 50 per cent by 2040, of which at least half should be rewetted; and 70 per cent by 2050, of which at least half should be rewetted.[179]

The implementation of these targets must be done through national restoration plans. The proposal contains details of both the preparation and the contents of these plans.[180] The plans will be assessed by the Commission, and must be reviewed at least every ten years. The proposal also includes obligations on monitoring and reporting.[181]

The Nature Restoration Law proposal contains many explicit references to climate change, in the Explanatory Memorandum, in the considerations, and in several articles of the proposal itself. According to the Explanatory Memorandum, it is recognised that restoring nature will contribute significantly to the EU's climate mitigation and adaptation objectives, to prevent and mitigate the impact of natural disasters. The considerations of the proposal confirm that securing biodiverse ecosystems and tackling climate change are intrinsically linked.[182]

Climate change is explicitly mentioned in the objective of Article 1; in the exception to fulfilling the restoration obligations because of climate change, in Articles 4 to 5; and in several Articles on the preparation, contents and review of the national restoration plans.[183] Although this strong interlinkage with climate change is very commendable, some suggestions for improvement may be made. On the exception to fulfilling the obligations, there is some concern that this is formulated in a rather broad and vague way, which could be abused to avoid fulfilling the obligations. The Nature Restoration Law must make clear that the exception only applies where habitat changes are not the result of action or inaction by Member States. It has been, therefore, suggested that the following text be added to each of Articles 4(8)(b) and 5(8)(b): 'in so far as these transformations are not the result of action or inaction by the Member States'.[184]

If this proposal becomes a law, this will result in the most detailed and binding obligations, in international law, for restoration that addresses both the biodiversity and climate crises. The proposal has the potential to be a game-changer for protection and restoration in the EU, and could also be a source of inspiration outside the EU, for commitments at the international and national levels.

---

179 Ibid., Art. 9(4).
180 Ibid., Arts. 11–16.
181 Ibid., Arts. 17–18.
182 Ibid., Consideration 15.
183 Ibid., Arts. 11, 12 and 15.
184 SERE Legal Working Group, 'Legal assessment of the Proposal for an EU Nature Restoration Law', 2023, p. 10, https://chapter.ser.org/europe/.

The adoption of the proposal led to positive reactions from international organisations,[185] NGOs,[186] scientists,[187] environmental lawyers[188] and the business sector.[189] But, closer to the voting in both the European Parliament and the Council, a negative campaign started from certain stakeholders, followed by objections by some Member States.[190] Although some concerns, and the necessity for clarifications, are legitimate, the Nature Restoration Law proposal ended up in a storm of misinformation. Some of this was due to certain stakeholders who feared implications for their sectors,[191] but another explanation was that the proposal was the victim of political games at EU level,[192] and upcoming 'election fever'.[193]

185 UNEP, 'European Union proposes law to bring back nature', 29 June 2022, https://www.unep.org/news-and-stories/story/european-union-proposes-law-bring-back-nature.

186 European Environmental Bureau, 'EU nature restoration law: Huge opportunity to fight biodiversity and climate crises – NGO reaction', 22 June 2022, https://eeb.org/eu-nature-restoration-law-huge-opportunity-to-fight-biodiversity-and-climate-crises-ngo-reaction/.

187 European Chapter of the Society for Ecological Restoration, 'Declaration on the European Commission Proposal for a Regulation on Nature Restoration', Alicante, 9 September 2022, https://chapter.ser.org/europe/declaration-on-eu-nature-restoration-law-2022/; G. Pe'er et al., 'Scientists support the EU's Green Deal and reject the unjustified argumentation against the Sustainable Use Regulation and the Nature Restoration Law' (supported by 6,000 scientists), (Full Version 9.07.2023 (pre-print)). Zenodo. https://doi.org/10.5281/zenodo.8128624.

188 N. Hoek, 'A Critical Analysis of the Proposed EU Regulation on Nature Restoration: Have the Problems Been Resolved?', *European Energy and Environmental Law Review*, 2022 (31), pp. 320–333; SERE Legal Working Group, 'The EU Nature Restoration Law: Providing legal certainty in tackling the biodiversity and climate crisis', May 2023, https://chapter.ser.org/europe/.

189 Heidelberg Materials, 'Statement for an ambitious EU Nature Restoration Law', 17 April 2023, https://www.heidelbergmaterials.com/en/statement-for-an-ambitious-eu-nature-restoration-law; Business for Nature, 'CEOs and executives from more than 80 companies and financial institutions urge the EU to adopt environmental legislation to address the nature and climate crises together', 6 July 2023, https://www.businessfornature.org/news/euenviroregulation; Wind Europe, 'Nature restoration and wind energy go hand in hand', 6 June 2023, https://windeurope.org/newsroom/press-releases/nature-restoration-and-wind-energy-go-hand-in-hand/#:~:text=It%20aims%20to%20restore%2030,expansion%20go%20hand%20in%20hand.

190 Z. Weise and L. Guillot, 'How repairing nature became the EU's most contentious green project', *Politico*, 25 May 2023, https://www.politico.eu/article/how-repairing-nature-became-the-eus-most-contentious-green-project/.

191 See objections by farmers' lobby groups, e.g. COPA-COGECA, 'Nature Restoration Law. Priority List', Ref. EN(23)03076[2]; counter-arguments in SERE Legal Working Group, 'Legal assessment explaining why COPA-COGECA's objections against the Nature Restoration Act proposal are misleading', 6 July 2023, https://chapter.ser.org/europe/.

192 I. Please, '"Bullied into voting": EPP chief accused of blackmailing MEPs over nature restoration law', *The Brussels Times*, 14 June 2023, https://www.brusselstimes.com/551552/bullied-into-voting-epp-chief-accused-of-blackmailing-meps-over-nature-restoration-law; D. Draulans and K. Vermeylen, 'Waarom de strijd tegen de natuurherstelwet een ideologische oorlog is', *Knack*, 26 June 2023.

193 K. Decleer and A. Cliquet, 'Nature restoration: proposed EU law under threat', Correspondence, *Nature*, 11 July 2023; L. Guillot and B. Brzeziński, 'EPP pitches itself as farmers' party ahead of 2024 European election', *Politico*, 4 May 2023, https://www.politico.eu/article/european-peoples-party-farmer-rural-interest-2024-european-election/.

Many of the arguments against the Commission proposal are preposterous. A striking example is that some opponents have claimed that the Nature Restoration Law will make it impossible to reach climate goals, as nature restoration will make it more difficult, or impossible, to get permits, for instance for renewable energy installations. This is surprising, as several links with climate change are present in the Commission proposal,[194] not least in the objectives of the proposal. The proposal provides exceptions to the restoration and non-deterioration obligations, which allow specifically for climate measures. The proposal includes alignment of, and a win-win for, biodiversity and renewable energy and climate measures, in the national restoration plans.[195] The proposal has also received support from the industrial sector, including the wind energy sector.[196]

In spite of this broad support, the proposal has been rejected by the Agricultural, Fisheries and Environmental Committees in the European Parliament.[197] The proposal was accepted in the plenary meeting of the European Parliament,[198] however, with numerous amendments that reduced the proposal largely to an empty box. After trilogue negotiations between Commission, Council and Parliament, a compromise was reached in November 2023. The trilogue compromise text is closer to the original Commission proposal, although in several instances it still has been weakened. One example of weakening of the proposal, which is particularly relevant for climate change, is lowering the targets for restoration of peatlands and providing exceptions on the obligations to restore peatlands in agricultural use.

The compromise was approved by a majority of EU Member States and the Environmental Committee of the Parliament in November 2023. This compromise was also approved by the plenary session in Parliament in February 2024. It still needs a final formal approval by Member States, scheduled for April 2024. If the Nature Restoration Law would ultimately not be approved, this would have grave implications at EU and global levels. Without restoration, it will be impossible

---

194 In Arts. 1(b), 4 & 5(8)(b), 4(9)(b), 11(5)(a), 12(2)(j–k) and 15 (1).

195 See also SERE Legal Working Group, 'The EU Nature Restoration Law: Providing legal certainty in tackling the biodiversity and climate crisis', May 2023; SERE Legal Working Group, 'Infographic – EU Nature Restoration Law: myths and misconceptions debunked by the SER Legal Working Group', May 2023; both documents available at https://chapter.ser.org/europe/.

196 L. Guillot, 'Business slams EU conservatives' anti-nature crusade', *Politico*, 8 June 2023, https://www.politico.eu/article/business-slams-eu-conservatives-anti-nature-crusade-epp-renewables/; Wind Europe, Nature restoration and wind energy go hand in hand, 6 June 2023, https://windeurope.org/newsroom/press-releases/nature-restoration-and-wind-energy-go-hand-in-hand/.

197 European Parliament, 'No majority in committee for proposed EU Nature Law as amended', 27 June 2023, https://www.europarl.europa.eu/news/en/press-room/20230626IPR00847/no-majority-in-committee-for-proposed-eu-nature-restoration-law-as-amended.

198 European Parliament, Amendments adopted by the European Parliament on the proposal for a regulation of the European Parliament and of the Council on nature restoration, COM(2022)0304 – C9-0208/2022–2022/0195(COD), 12 July 2023.

to solve the biodiversity and climate crises, and to meet EU and international commitments. It will also have implications beyond the EU: the EU risks losing its leading role and credibility as an environmental player in the international sphere. How can other nations, like Brazil, Congo and Indonesia, be convinced to protect their vulnerable carbon sinks if Europe fails to restore just a small fraction of all the nature that has been lost on our continent over the centuries?[199]

7. CONCLUSION

Science point to interlinkages between the biodiversity and climate crises, with both reinforcing each other. But not only the crises themselves are linked: the solutions are too. Ecosystems are important carbon sinks, and are crucial in helping people to adapt to the impacts of climate change. But this requires healthy ecosystems, for the sake of biodiversity itself, and for the sake of humans. Without healthy, restored ecosystems, the Paris Agreement climate goals of staying well below a temperature increase of 2 degrees Celsius, or preferably 1.5 degrees Celsius, will not be reached. Opportunities to help humans cope with the impact of climate change will be lost.

Although these linkages are clear in science, and increasingly in law and policy, it seems they are not clear for everyone. When certain politicians agree with climate laws but want to press the pause button for biodiversity,[200] they seem not to grasp that both are inextricably linked to each other.

International biodiversity laws have not been able to stop or reverse the trend of biodiversity loss. Protecting what is left of biodiversity will not suffice. Restoring ecosystems on a massive scale will be required as a solution for the climate and biodiversity crises. Both the biodiversity and climate legal regimes need to strengthen their commitments in this regard. Stronger commitments are necessary for all ecosystems, not just for forests. There is a need for legally binding, concrete quantitative and qualitative targets for protecting and restoring biodiversity. Considering the urgency of both the climate and biodiversity crises, binding deadlines are essential. Legislation needs to have a comprehensive approach in which climate and biodiversity measures are mutually reinforcing. The EU Nature Restoration Law proposal from the European Commission fulfilled all those requirements to a very large extent. Although this proposal has been weakened during the political process and still needs final approval by the Council, it still can serve as an example of a law in which biodiversity and climate change are explicitly and strongly linked.

---

199 SERE Legal Working Group, 'Legal assessment explaining why COPA-COGECA's objections against the Nature Restoration Act proposal are misleading', 6 July 2023, https://chapter.ser.org/europe/.

200 See note 37 above.

BIODIVERSITY PROTECTION IN TRANSNATIONAL VALUE CHAINS

Carola GLINSKI*

ABSTRACT

Mankind faces an ongoing loss of biodiversity, which multilateral environmental agreements have not been able to halt, and which is closely linked to transnational value chains. The European Union (EU) has been, and is now, adopting a number of unilateral frameworks, which refer to international agreements, addressing biodiversity protection in European value chains via business 'due diligence' duties. However, as concrete biodiversity-related requirements that could be

* This research has been conducted within the Bio-Trade network project, with partners from the Finnish Environment Institute, the Raoul Wallenberg Institute (Sweden), and the University of Bern, funded by BiodivERsA and the Innovation Fund Denmark.

(directly) applied by private actors are lacking in international law, the challenge is to concretise these requirements. Thus, this chapter analyses the intersections of due diligence laws with international environmental and trade law, and with transnational private governance instruments, such as standardisation and certification schemes, and explores the resulting challenges and consequences for legitimate and effective biodiversity protection requirements in transnational value chains.

1. INTRODUCTION: THE REGULATORY CHALLENGE

We face a global biodiversity crisis, with biodiversity being one of the planetary boundaries where mankind has already gone beyond safe operating space. The main drivers of biodiversity loss are unsustainable agricultural and forestry practices, which are closely linked to transnational value chains. Approximately, more than 50 per cent of the European Union (EU)'s biodiversity footprint is caused abroad, and EU imports have been responsible for as much as 16 per cent of tropical deforestation in some previous years.[1]

Thirty years of multilateral environmental agreements, in particular the Convention on Biological Diversity of 1992 (CBD), have not been able to mitigate these developments. Multilateral environmental approaches suffer from decreasing international consensus, and from their framework character, which lacks concretisation[2] and ambitious implementation in relevant matters and regions. Many biodiversity-rich countries show deficiencies concerning their protection laws, and their implementation or control.[3] At the same time, transnational economic activities and actors, as major drivers of global environmental degradation, are not (directly) addressed. Attempts to codify binding environmental duties for transnational corporations have failed,[4] or

1 See, e.g. WWF, *Stepping Up? The Continuing Impact of EU Consumption on Nature Worldwide*, 2021, https://wwfeu.awsassets.panda.org/downloads/new_stepping_up___the_continuing_impact_of_eu_consumption_on_nature_worldwide_fullreport.pdf.

2 E.g. the protection of forests is still limited to declarations of intent, such as in the CBD's Aichi Targets of 2020, or the UNFCC's Glasgow Declaration of 2021, according to which the Glasgow leaders 'commit[ted] to working collectively to halt and reverse forest loss and land degradation by 2030'.

3 See the deforestation activities in Brazil, under the Bolsonaro government: BBC News, 'Brazil: Amazon sees worst deforestation levels in 15 years', 19 November 2021, bbc.com/news/world-latin-america-59341770.

4 E.g. the Draft Code of Conduct on Transnational Corporations, UN Doc. E/1988/39; see P. Muchlinski, *Multinational Enterprises and the Law* (2nd ed.), Oxford University Press, 2007, pp. 660 ff. The Human Rights Council has, since 2014, been working on turning the UN Guiding Principles into a binding international treaty: see Human Rights Council, 'Elaboration of an International Legally Binding Instrument on Transnational Corporations and Other Business Enterprises with Respect to Human Rights', UN Doc. A/HRC/26/L.22/Rev.1 (2014). The current draft dates from 2021: see https://www.ohchr.org/sites/default/files/Documents/HRBodies/HRCouncil/WGTransCorp/Session6/LBI3rdDRAFT.pdf.

remained soft law,[5] such as the United Nations (UN) Guiding Principles for Business and Human Rights.[6]

Therefore, a certain turn to unilateralism can be observed, with a number of European legislative acts being adopted that aim at the protection of biodiversity in European value chains, including the Renewable Energy Directive;[7] the Timber Regulation;[8] the Deforestation Regulation,[9] which replaces the Timber Regulation with effect from 30 December 2024; and the EU Commission's proposal for a Directive on Corporate Sustainability Due Diligence.[10]

These value chain sustainability 'due diligence' regulations connect private business duties to (EU and) public international law requirements, which poses challenges for the concretisation of biodiversity-related requirements. Whereas the intersection between business due diligence duties and human rights frameworks also leads to (relatively) clear substantive requirements for private actors, and the same applies to clearly defined environmental duties, such as the prohibitions or restrictions of certain dangerous substances, for example those provided for in the Stockholm Convention on Persistent Organic Pollutants, the situation is far more complicated with a broader approach to biodiversity due diligence. Here, clear international duties and prohibitions, which could be applied (directly) by private actors, are lacking.

Thus, the challenge is either to codify such duties and prohibitions directly, or to refer to more concrete requirements elsewhere, in order to achieve legitimate, coherent, fair and effective biodiversity protection requirements in transnational value chains, and to control compliance with them effectively.

In fact, the various legal value chain instruments take different approaches as to which obligations should be met (for details, see section 2 below). The Timber Regulation requires legality in the production state, whereas the Renewable Energy Directive and the Deforestation Regulation set up their own criteria for the prevention of land-use changes, or for deforestation-free commodities, with the former to be concretised by private systems. The EU Commission's proposal for a Directive on Corporate Sustainability Due Diligence, finally, refers to the very general Article 10(b) of the CBD, with the role of private schemes and certification not yet clarified.

---

5 E.g. the OECD Guidelines for Multinational Enterprises, 2011, http://www.oecd.org/corporate/mne/48004323.pdf.

6 J. Ruggie, 'Guiding Principles on Business and Human Rights: Implementing the United Nations "Protect, Respect and Remedy" Framework', UN Doc. A/HRC/17/31 (2011).

7 Directive (EU) 2018/2001 on the promotion of the use of energy from renewable sources (recast), OJ 2018 L 328/82 (RED II).

8 Regulation (EU) No. 95/2010 laying down the obligations of operators who place timber and timber products on the market, OJ 2010 L 295/23.

9 Regulation (EU) 2023/1115 on the making available on the Union market and the export from the Union of certain commodities and products associated with deforestation and forest degradation, OJ 2023 L 150/206.

10 COM(2022) 71 final.

These approaches pose different challenges as to their legitimacy, effectiveness and control. Jurisdictional constraints, limited legislative and administrative resources, and limited expertise and knowledge of the situation abroad confine the concretisation and control of requirements for the codifying state. Thus, the (unilateral) setting of concrete European or Member State requirements might be inadequate, or face legality or legitimacy concerns with respect to international trade law. References to the legal requirements in the production state only rule out enforcement deficits, but not regulatory deficits. Therefore, the inclusion of transnational private standardisation and certification schemes, and business 'best practices', plays an important role, yet this, again, poses legal and practical challenges relating to the legitimacy, adequacy and reliability of such schemes and practices.

This chapter analyses the intersections of unilateral due diligence laws with international environmental and trade law, and transnational private governance instruments, such as standardisation and certification schemes, and explores the resulting challenges and consequences for legitimate and effective biodiversity protection in transnational value chains.

The chapter is structured as follows: first, it provides a short overview of the different regulatory approaches of European supply chain laws embracing biodiversity protection (section 2), before it analyses intersections with public international law and trade law, and the consequences for the legality and legitimacy of the concretisation of supply chain law requirements (section 3). It then turns to the effectiveness of existing regulatory approaches towards biodiversity protection (section 4), before providing suggestions as to how supply chain laws and interconnections to private standardisation and certification schemes could be drafted in order to include transnational participatory elements (section 5), and then conclusions (section 6).

2. REGULATORY APPROACHES: OVERVIEW

2.1. RENEWABLE ENERGY DIRECTIVE 2018/2001/EU (RED II)

In order to prevent the promotion of renewable energies from contributing to unsustainable land-use changes and unsustainable forestry, the sustainability criteria of the Renewal Energy Directive (RED II) require that biofuels, biomass fuels and bioliquids from agro-biomass have not been obtained from sources grown on formerly biodiversity-rich land, such as forests or protected areas, or 'biodiversity-rich' land such as wetlands or grasslands (Article 29(3)–(5)); and, for biofuels, biomass fuels and bioliquids from forest biomass, that their sources have been harvested legally and sustainably, and that protected areas have been respected (Article 25(6) and (7)). For implementation purposes, economic operators have to join a national standardisation system,[11] or a private 'voluntary' standardisation system which has been recognised by the Commission on the basis of certain structural and procedural requirements, and which concretises the requirements of the Directive and entails regular controls by certification bodies (Article 30). Business initiatives are admissible, as well as multi-stakeholder systems. With this, EU regulation of renewable energies has established an elaborate transnational multi-level governance system, although this has shown a number of weaknesses, which have led to several amendments.

2.2. TIMBER REGULATION (EU) 995/2010 (EUTR)

The Timber Regulation prohibits operators from placing illegally logged timber and timber products on the internal market (Article 4(1)). It requires operators to carry out due diligence, and ensure traceability throughout the supply chain (Articles 4(2), 5 and 6). To this end, operators may use established due diligence systems, for example those established by monitoring organisations recognised by the European Commission, (Articles 4(3) and 8). Operators that already use systems that comply with the Regulation are not required to set up new systems.[12] Mainly due to the lengthy recognition process on the part of the European Commission, only few monitoring organisations have used this possibility.[13] Other supervision or certification systems may be used as part of due diligence and risk control, but these do not remove due diligence obligations or liability from operators.[14] Thus, certification by, for example, the Forest Stewardship Council (FSC) is not regarded as proof of compliance by authorities, but only as a good starting point for a sufficient compliance system.[15] In practice, however, neither the FSC nor the PEFC,[16] which both adapted their systems to the Timber Regulation, have experienced a significant increase in membership following the Regulation.[17]

---

11 These are not subject of this chapter.

12 Recital 18, RED II.

13 Another reason was that the systems themselves were reluctant to guarantee compliance: see European Commission, 'Fitness Check on Regulation (EU) No. 995/2010', p. 23.

14 Ibid., p. 7.

15 Thus, according to Art. 6(1)(b), assurance of compliance with applicable legislation, which may include certification or other third-party-verified schemes which cover compliance with applicable legislation, can be an element of the risk assessment and, therefore, of the due diligence system. See also L. Walker, *Umweltbezogene Sorgfaltspflichten*, Nomos, 2022, pp. 207 *et seq.*; T. Häbe, U. Malessa and V. Kopp, 'EU-Holzhandelsverordnung: So geht's mit FSC!', *Holzzentralblatt*, 2012 (44), pp. 1123 *et seq.*

16 Programme for the Endorsement of Forest Certification Schemes.

17 See Walker, supra, note 15, pp. 207, 209, with further references; L. Gulbrandsen, 'Public sector engagement with private governance programs: interactions and evolutionary effects in forest and fisheries certification' in J. van Erp et al. (eds.), *Smart Mixes for Transboundary*

2.3. DEFORESTATION REGULATION (EU) 2023/1115

The Deforestation Regulation replaces the Timber Regulation with effect from 30 December 2024. It prohibits the placing on the market of products made from palm oil, soy, wood, cocoa, coffee or beef, unless they have been produced legally and deforestation-free, which means that they have not been produced on land which was subject to deforestation, and have been harvested without inducing forest degradation (Article 3). This prohibition does not, however, include valuable ecosystems other than forests, such as grasslands, savannahs or wetlands, which could lead to an increased risk of destruction of other valuable ecosystems; the risk of indirect land-use changes has not been addressed either.

These provisions are accompanied by detailed due diligence obligations for operators and traders (Articles 4, and 8 to 11), and reporting requirements (Article 12). A number of risk-assessment criteria are provided for, as well as the possibility to use information supplied by certification schemes, and other third-party-verified schemes, including voluntary schemes recognised by the European Commission under RED II, which should not, however, substitute the operators' due diligence responsibility (Article 10). The regulation foresees a complaints procedure for any natural or legal person (Article 31), and access to justice for any natural or legal person having sufficient interest (Article 32). It also requires frequent controls by authorities, which cover due diligence systems, commodities, spot checks in third countries, Earth observation data, cooperation with other authorities, and sanctions (Articles 16 *et seq.* and 21 *et seq.*).

Stakeholder inclusion is not an explicit part of due diligence. The Regulation, however, also provides for the European Commission to cooperate with third countries. In that case, as well as for evaluation, stakeholder participation is foreseen.[18]

2.4. PROPOSED CORPORATE SUSTAINABILITY DUE DILIGENCE DIRECTIVE

The proposed Corporate Sustainability Due Diligence Directive will impose due diligence duties on European companies, as well as for products accessing the European market (Articles 4 to 11). The due diligence duties follow the UN

Environmental Harm, Cambridge University Press, 2019, pp. 211, 224; I. Gavrilut et al., 'The Interaction between FSC Certification and the Implementation of the EU Timber Regulation in Romania', *Forests*, 2016 (7), pp. 3, 4, with further references; S. Leipold, 'How to move companies to source responsibly? German implementation of the European Timber Regulation between persuasion and coercion', *Forest Policy and Economics*, 2017 (82), pp. 41, 44.

18 See Recitals 27, 29 and 69, and Art. 30(2).

Guiding Principles on Business and Human Rights, and include identification, prevention and mitigation of potential adverse human rights and environmental impacts, allocation of responsibilities, monitoring, public communication, and a complaints procedure.

Adverse environmental impacts are defined as resulting from a violation of a (listed) provision of an international environmental convention, such as the Convention on International Trade in Endangered Species of Wild Fauna and Flora (CITES), the Minamata Convention on Mercury, the Stockholm Convention on Persistent Organic Pollutants, or the Basel Convention on Transboundary Movements on Hazardous Wastes (Article 3(b), with Annex, Part II). Regarding biodiversity, the proposed directive requires, with reference to Article 10(b) of the CBD, the adoption of measures relating to the use of biological resources, to avoid or minimise adverse impacts on biological diversity.

Stakeholder inclusion, standardisation and certification schemes are mentioned several times. The European Commission and the Member States may facilitate joint stakeholder initiatives, to help companies fulfil their obligations (Article 14(3)). Companies may rely on appropriate industry schemes and multi-stakeholder initiatives to support the implementation of their obligations, while the Commission and Member States may facilitate the dissemination of information on such schemes and the Commission may issue guidance for assessing their adequacy (Article 14(4)). For the purposes of verifying compliance, a company may refer to suitable industry initiatives or independent third-party verification (Articles 7(4) and 8(5)).

The proposal foresees supervision by authorities, the possibility to submit substantiated concerns, and sanctions (Articles 17 to 21). Also, the European Commission wants to impose civil liability on companies, in cases where non-compliance with due diligence duties has led to damage (Article 22). The proposal contains a limited 'safe harbour' clause, according to which liability for indirect business partners would be excluded in the event that compliance had been verified by a suitable industry initiative, or through independent third-party verification (Article 22(2)). This provision, however, is still subject to discussion.

3. INTERSECTIONS WITH PUBLIC INTERNATIONAL LAW AND TRADE LAW: LEGALITY AND LEGITIMACY THROUGH CONSENSUS, COHERENCE AND PARTICIPATION

As supply chain regulation addresses production conditions abroad, intersections with public international law and with international trade law need to be considered.

Firstly, transnational biodiversity protection faces jurisdictional constraints. Public international law basically reduces the national right to regulate to territorial and personal jurisdiction. This leaves the EU only with indirect links to biodiversity protection abroad, namely by addressing its own value chains via companies domiciled in the EU (personal jurisdiction), or via access to its markets (territorial jurisdiction). Due to the interrelation of supply chain laws with domestic production and consumption patterns, as well as with global environmental degradation, supply chain laws can also be justified by the effects doctrine.[19] As the supply chain laws of EU countries respect these constraints, they are generally considered to be in line with public international law.[20] The right to enforce is generally limited to a state's own territory, and thus requires either agreements with other states or the use of private actors.

Due to their impact on production conditions abroad, supply chain laws should, nevertheless, and in line with the public international law principles of comity and cooperation, be based on international consensus as far as possible, to enhance their legitimacy. While supply chain due diligence aiming at environmentally sound production conditions abroad is necessary to embed transnational value chains environmentally,[21] production requirements imposed by importing countries are regularly criticised, by countries of the Global South, as extraterritorial, eco-imperialist or disguised protectionist measures.[22]

Supply chain laws reflect consensus-oriented approaches, through their rooting in the UN Guiding Principles on Business and Human Rights,[23] as well

---

19 See E.V. Henn and J. Jahn, *Zulässigkeit und Gegenstand umweltbezogener Sorgfaltspflichten in einem Lieferkettengesetz*, BUND/Greenpeace/Deutsche Umwelthilfe, 2020, https://www.business-humanrights.org/documents/6124/handel_lieferkettengesetz_rechtsgutachten.pdf, pp. 29 *et seq.*, with further references.

20 See, e.g. E. Hoffberger-Pippan, 'Ein Lieferkettengesetz für Deutschland zur Einhaltung der Menschenrechte – Eine Ersteinschätzung aus völkerrechtlicher Sicht', *Archiv des Völkerrechts*, 2020 (58), pp. 400, 418 *et seq.*

21 See only J. Ruggie, 'Taking Embedded Liberalism Global: The Corporate Connection' in D. Held and M. Koenig-Archiburgi (eds.), *Taming Globalization: Frontiers of Governance*, Cambridge University Press, 2003, pp. 93 *et seq.*; S. Bernstein and E. Hannah, 'Non-State Global Standard Setting and the WTO: Legitimacy and the Need for Regulatory Space', *Journal of International Economic Law*, 2008 (11), pp. 575 *et seq.*; C. Vidal-Léon, 'Corporate Social Responsibility, Human Rights and the World Trade Organisation', *Journal of International Economic Law*, 2013 (16), pp. 893 *et seq.*

22 See, e.g. the Joint letter by Indonesia and Brazil on the European Union proposal for a Regulation on deforestation-free products, WTO Doc. G/AG/GEN/213 of 29 November 2022; more generally, see M. Joshi, 'Are Eco-Labels Consistent with World Trade Organization Agreements?', *Journal of World Trade*, 2004 (38), pp. 69, 72. See also Vidal-Léon, supra, note 21, pp. 899 *et seq.*; M. Du, 'Permitting Moral Imperialism? The Public Morals Exception to Free Trade at the Bar of the World Trade Organisation', *Journal of World Trade*, 2016 (50), pp. 675, 694 *et seq.*

23 So-called 'process and production methods' (PPMs). Following the Appellate Body's rulings in *Tuna Dolphin II*, WT/DS381/AB/R, and *EC – Measures Prohibiting the Importation and Marketing of Seal Products*, WT/DS/400/AB/R, WT/DS 401/AB/R, PPMs are now regarded

as through their references to international human rights and environmental agreements. However, as the devil lies in the detail, the concretisation of biodiversity protection requirements should be consensus-oriented as well (or at least participatory), in order to enhance their legitimacy (and effectiveness).

With regard to international trade, the law of the World Trade Organization, and current bilateral trade agreements, reflect these principles more clearly.[24] The General Agreement on Tariffs and Trade (GATT) as the centrepiece of WTO law requires imported products to be treated no less favourably than products originating from other countries (Article I:1), or 'like products' of national origin (Article III:4), and prohibits unnecessary restrictions on trade (Article XI). These rules cover product requirements, as well as production-related requirements with extraterritorial implications. Due to their impact on production conditions abroad, supply chain requirements might constitute production-related requirements which treat imported products less favourably.[25] According to Article XX lit. (a), (b) and (g), such measures can, among others, be justified in the event that they are necessary to pursue: the protection of public morals; the protection of human, animal or plant life or health; or relate to the conservation of exhaustible natural resources.[26] These justifications would most likely apply to supply chain requirements, as extraterritorial protection aims can nowadays be regarded as, in principle, admissible.[27]

---

as generally admissible: see, e.g. C. Glinski, 'CSR and the Law of the WTO – The Impact of *Tuna Dolphin II* and *EC–Seal Products*', *Nordic Journal of Commercial Law*, 2017, pp. 120, 124 *et seq.*, with further references.

24 See, e.g. the Comprehensive Economic and Trade Agreement (CETA) between the EU and Canada, and the EU–Singapore Free Trade Agreement.

25 Thereby, any negative impact on the competitive opportunities of imported products could be regarded as prohibited *de facto* discrimination: see *EC – Seal Products*, supra, note 23, para. 5.90. For an analysis, see, e.g. R. Howse, J. Langille and K. Sykes, 'Pluralism in Practice: Moral Legislation and the Law of the WTO after *Seal Products*', *New York University School of Law, Public Law and Legal Theory Research Paper Series*, Working Paper No. 15-05, 2015, pp. 81, 132 *et seq.*, 146.

26 For (a), see *EC – Seal Products*, supra, note 23, paras 5.167 and 5.173; Howse, Langille and Sykes, supra, note 26, pp. 124 *et seq.* For the protection of animal or plant life or health, see *Tuna Dolphin II*, supra, note 23, which did not address the issue of extraterritoriality at all; see also J. Pauwelyn, '*Tuna*: The End of the PPM distinction? The Rise of International Standards?', *International Economic Law and Policy Blog*, 29 May 2017, http://worldtradelaw.typepad.com/ielpblog. For Art. XX(g), see, e.g. S. Charnovitz, 'The Law of Environmental "PPMs" in the WTO: Debunking the Myth of Illegality', *Yale Journal of International Law*, 2002 (27), pp. 59, 92 *et seq.*; see also Glinski, 'CSR and the Law of the WTO', supra, note 23, p. 137.

27 Nevertheless, the sustainability requirements of the RED have been challenged before the WTO dispute settlement mechanism, by Argentina: see *European Union and certain Member States – Certain Measures on the Importation and Marketing of Biodiesel and Measures Supporting the Biodiesel Industry*, WT/DS459.

However, ultimately, admissibility depends on the concrete (production) requirements. Here, no less trade-restrictive measures must be available,[28] and requirements must not be applied or concretised in a manner which constitutes 'a means of arbitrary or unjustifiable discrimination' or 'a disguised restriction on international trade' (the so-called 'chapeau' clause, in Article XX). In general, it is helpful, in this regard, to refer to international standards for concretisation, and to pursue a consistent policy (also with regard to internal measures).[29] The requirement to base (technical) regulations, labels and standards on international standards is even more clearly codified in the Agreement on Technical Barriers to Trade of the WTO (Articles 2.4 and 2.5 TBT).

Not only international environmental agreements, but also private biodiversity standards, could provide for 'international standards' in the terms of Articles 2.4 and 2.5 TBT, as the example of the International Organization for Standardization (ISO)[30] shows. According to Annex 1, No. 4 of the TBT Agreement, an 'international standard' has to be approved 'by an "international standardising body" whose membership is open to the relevant bodies of at least all Members'. Thereby, it is not necessary to have an 'organization', but the development of a single standard could be enough.[31] In addition, the procedural requirements of transparency, openness, impartiality, consensus, effectiveness, relevance, coherence, and of addressing the concerns of developing countries, have to be safeguarded.[32] These principles are open for acceptance for all standardising bodies, be they governmental or non-governmental, local, national, regional or international.[33] Standards development must 'take place transparently and with wide participation' of 'all interested parties', which also aims at stakeholders,[34] and 'must not privilege any particular interests'.[35] In fact, a number of private standardisation organisations, like the FSC or Fairtrade, have adapted their structures and procedures accordingly. Thus, the use of private standards could add legitimacy to (concretised) supply chain due diligence requirements.

---

28 In *EC – Seal Products*, supra, note 23, paras 7.637, and 7.496 ff., labelling requirements were regarded as less effective, compared with prohibitions.

29 See S. Charnovitz, 'The Moral Exception in Trade Policy', *Virginia Journal of International Law*, 1998 (38), pp. 689, 717 and 742; Howse, Langille and Sykes, supra, note 26, pp. 117 ff.

30 The ISO, as *the* example of an international standardisation organisation, is a private organisation under Swiss law.

31 *Tuna Dolphin II*, supra, note 23, paras 349 ff., in particular para. 359.

32 Decision of the Committee on Principles for the Development of International Standards, Guides and Recommendations with relation to Articles 2, 5 and Annex 3 of the Agreement, Second Triennial Review of the Operation and Implementation of the Agreement on Technical Barriers to Trade, Annex IV, G/TBT/9, 13 November 2000, s. A. 24–26.

33 Annex 3 of the TBT Agreement.

34 *Tuna Dolphin II*, supra, note 23, para. 379.

35 Ibid., para. 384.

Finally, international environmental law requires the participation of civil society, and of those concerned, to enhance the legitimacy of environmental decisions. Generally, participation options are regarded as an element of deliberative democracy,[36] which enhances rational discourse.[37] Two prominent agreements codifying participatory rights are the Aarhus Convention,[38] and the Escazú Agreement[39] between Latin American and Caribbean states. Both agreements require information, public participation and access to justice, in environmental matters. These requirements reflect the experience that environmental concerns are structurally under-represented in traditional (administrative) decision-making, and need particular representation, for example through non-governmental organisations (NGOs). Participation in environmental matters also reflects democratic and human rights concerns.[40] In this regard, the Escazú Agreement, in particular, explicitly links the three aforementioned rights to democracy, and 'to the right of every person of present and future generations to live in a healthy environment and to sustainable development'.[41] Another important aspect of the Escazú Agreement is its protection of the rights of 'human rights defenders in environmental matters',[42] as defending environmental concerns is enormously dangerous in Latin America, as well as in other parts of the world.

Thus, cooperative and participatory instruments enhance the legitimacy of concretised value chain requirements, in a horizontal as well as a vertical perspective.[43] This also applies to transnational standardisation schemes. At the same time, particular protection of environmental stakeholders is also required by international environmental law.

---

36 See, e.g. A. Fisahn, *Demokratie und Öffentlichkeitsbeteiligung*, Mohr Siebeck, 2002, pp. 335 ff.; G. Lübbe-Wolff, 'Europäisches und nationales Verfassungsrecht', *Veröffentlichungen der Vereinigung der Deutschen Staatsrechtslehrer*, 2001 (60), pp. 246, 279 *et seq*. Deliberative elements are, however, not meant to replace democratic representation, but only to complement representative legitimacy chains: see W. Hoffmann-Riem, 'Öffentliches Recht und Privatrecht als wechselseitige Auffangordnungen – Systematisierung und Entwicklungsperspektiven' in W. Hoffmann-Riem and E. Schmidt-Aßmann (eds.), *Öffentliches Recht und Privatrecht als wechselseitige Auffangordnungen*, Nomos, 1996, pp. 261, 320 *et seq*.; C. Möllers, *Gewaltengliederung*, Mohr Siebeck, 2005, pp. 189 *et seq*.

37 See, in particular, J. Habermas, 'Die postnationale Konstellation und die Zukunft der Demokratie' in J. Habermas, *Die postnationale Konstellation*, Suhrkamp, 1998, p. 166.

38 Convention on Access to Information, Public Participation in Decision-making and Access to Justice in Environmental Matters (Aarhus Convention) of 25 June 1998.

39 Regional Agreement on Access to Information, Public Participation and Justice in Environmental Matters in Latin America and the Caribbean of 4 March 2018 (hereinafter 'Escazú Agreement').

40 The right to a clean, healthy and sustainable environment, as a human right, was recognised by the UN General Assembly in 2022, with Resolution A/76/L.75 (2022).

41 Art. 1 of the Escazú Agreement.

42 Ibid., Art. 9.

43 With regard to the considerably more important role of civil society at transnational level, as compared with the national level, see, e.g. E. Rehbinder, 'Forest Certification and

4. EFFECTIVENESS OF THE INCLUSION OF PRIVATE SCHEMES

Initial results regarding the effectiveness of the regulatory approaches described above, with a view to substantive requirements, as well as to control and enforcement, can mainly be derived from experiences with the RED, the Timber Regulation and private biodiversity schemes.

Here, the implementation and concretisation of requirements by different schemes varied enormously.[44] Typically, business schemes have less strict requirements than multi-stakeholder schemes.[45] Often, they only apply the bare minimum requirements, whereas multi-stakeholder schemes apply additional social or environmental requirements, or address consequences of (indirect) land-use changes.[46] But also multi-stakeholder systems interpret key concepts like 'deforestation' very differently, and some of them only cover CO_2-neutrality of forest management, allow the conversion from natural forests to plantations, or cover only primary forests but not secondary forests. Similar considerations apply to different categories of land and their importance for biodiversity protection.[47] The reasons for this are that supply chain laws codify relevant sustainability criteria in very broad terms, such as 'highly biodiverse grassland' in Article 29(3)(d) of RED II,[48] and often

---

Environmental Law' in E. Meidinger, C. Elliott and G. Oesten (eds.), *Social and Political Dimensions of Forest Certification*, Forstbuch, 2003, pp. 331, 334. See also V. Haufler, *A Public Role for the Private Sector: Industry Self-Regulation in a Global Economy*, Carnegie, 2001, pp. 23, 41 *et seq.*, 119 *et seq.*

44 For detailed analysis, see J. Hamelmann, '*Certification of biofuels within the Directive 2009/28/EC: A comparative analysis of certification schemes*', Bachelor thesis, University of Twente, 2016, pp. 3 *et seq.*; Y. Naiki, 'Trade and Bioenergy: Explaining and Assessing the Regime Complex for Sustainable Bioenergy', *European Journal of International Law*, 2016 (27), pp. 129, 138 ff.

45 See also, generally, on this phenomenon, P. Verbruggen, 'Tort Liability for Standards Development in the United States and European Union', Tilburg Private Law Working Paper 12/2018, p. 3.

46 For details, see A. Schmeichel, *Towards Sustainability of Biomass Importation: An Assessment of the EU Renewable Energy Directive*, Europa Law Publishing, 2014, pp. 167 ff.; C. Glinski, 'Certification of the Sustainability of Biofuels in Global Supply Chains' in P. Rott (ed.), *Certification – Trust, Accountability, Liability*, Springer, 2019, pp. 163, 172 ff.; European Commission, Directorate-General for Environment/Preferred by Nature, *Study on Certification and Verification Schemes in the Forest Sector and for Wood-based Products – Report*, EU Publications Office, 2021 (hereinafter 'Preferred by Nature'), https://op.europa.eu/en/publication-detail/-/publication/afa5e0df-fb19-11eb-b520-01aa75ed71a1/language-en, pp. 140 *et seq.*

47 See, e.g. Preferred by Nature, supra, note 46, pp. 141 *et seq.*, 156 *et seq.*, for a comparison of the Roundtable on Sustainable Palm Oil (RSPO), the Round Table on Responsible Soy Standard (RTRS) and UTZ (cocoa).

48 For critique, see European Court of Auditors, *The EU system for the certification of sustainable biofuels*, Special Report 18/2016, 2016, pp. 25 *et seq.* See also S. Romppanen, 'The EU's Biofuels: Certified as Sustainable?', *Renewable Energy Law and Policy Review*, 2012 (3), pp. 173, 177; Schmeichel, supra, note 46, pp. 167 ff. Concretising Acts by the Commission,

lack clear standards for good environmental or agricultural practice, or leave out important issues such as indirect land-use changes.[49]

Another reason lies in the functioning of private schemes, and even multi-stakeholder schemes with high state-of-the-art procedural safeguards, such as the FSC,[50] have developed unsustainable biodiversity standards.[51] Here, structural power imbalances between stakeholders play a crucial role. Due to their economic power, business interests regularly prevail in decision-making processes, while environmental stakeholders often lack financial and personal resources, and access to information.[52]

In relation to the monitoring of compliance, there are, again, huge differences between schemes, and between certifiers, concerning the intensity and transparency of controls. Here, once again, business-driven schemes have been found to be less transparent and less ambitious than multi-stakeholder schemes.[53] But even ambitious multi-stakeholder systems with, in principle, good governance systems, such as the Roundtable on Sustainable Palm Oil (RSPO), have revealed methodological monitoring shortcomings in details such as stakeholder inclusion and stakeholder interviews in safe spaces.[54] At the same time, high state-of-the-art

---

such as the Communication on voluntary schemes and default values in the EU biofuels and bioliquids sustainability schemes, [2010] OJ C 160/1, the Communication on the practical implementation of the EU biofuels and bioliquids sustainability scheme and on counting rules for biofuels, [2010] OJ C 160/8, and the Commission note on Verification of the chain of custody of biofuels made from waste and processing residues (10 October 2014), https://ec.europa.eu/energy/sites/ener/files/documents/2014_letter_wastes_residues.pdf, came relatively late, and still left much room for interpretation.

49 This applies to the Timber Regulation, as well as to RED I, which required respective practices only within the EU. For critique, see European Court of Auditors, supra, note 48, p. 35.

50 These safeguards include transparency, independence, participation and public input, based upon the ISEAL Code of Good Practice for Setting Social and Environmental Standards, 2004, p. 5, and the ISO definition for consensus, ISO/IEC Guide 2:1996, 3.1.

51 E.g. in Nordic forests, only 5% of trees had to be maintained, in order to safeguard habitats; on this insufficiency, see M. Elbakidze et al., 'How does forest certification contribute to boreal biodiversity conservation? Standards and outcomes in Sweden and NW Russia', *Forest Ecology & Management*, 2011 (262), pp. 1983 *et seq*. In tropical rainforests, single trees may be harvested; on the negative impacts, see, e.g. A. Arbainsyah et al., 'Structure, composition and diversity of plant communities in FSC-certified, selectively logged forests of different ages compared to primary rain forest', *Biodiversity Conservation*, 2014 (23), pp. 2445 *et seq*.

52 On the difficulty of applying an ecologic perspective at the concretising level, and on other difficulties with fair and equal representation of the various stakeholders, see H. Garrelts and M. Flitner, 'Governance Issues in the Ecosystem Approach: what lessons from the Forest Stewardship Council?', *European Journal of Forest Research*, 2011 (130), pp. 395, 396 *et seq*., 400 *et seq*. On the prevailing economic rationale of forestry companies, see also J. Johansson, 'Towards democratic and effective forest governance? The discursive legitimation of forest certification in northern Sweden', *Local Environment*, 2014 (19), pp. 803, 812 ff. On ISO, see, J. Clapp, 'The Privatization of Global Environmental Governance: ISO 14000 and the Developing World', *Global Governance*, 1998 (4), pp. 302 *et seq*. See also H. Schepel, *The Constitution of Private Governance*, Hart Publishing, 2005, pp. 185 ff.

53 For the schemes under RED I, see European Court of Auditors, supra, note 48, p. 27.

54 See European Center for Constitutional and Human Rights (ECCHR), Brot für die Welt and Misereor, *Human rights fitness of the auditing and certification industry?*, ECCHR, 2021,

procedural requirements for control and certification that are meant to prevent bias, fraud or bribery, such as interdisciplinary control teams (for example, composed of biologists, foresters and social scientists), stakeholder consultations and expert peer reviews,[55] do not necessarily, in practice, prevent unsustainable production methods from being certified. Common problems are that local certifiers lack the competence to reveal fraud, or that they cooperate with enterprises or forest owners, or get bribed, threatened, or even killed.[56] Further, NGOs regularly criticise the fact that they do not have access to certification procedures.[57] The structural proximity between certifiers and controlled enterprises, as the latter pay the former, provides another problem.[58]

While private systems often provide for complaints mechanisms and sanctions for non-adherence, in most cases sanctions are not imposed. An important reason for this is that private schemes fear that business members could leave their systems and join a less ambitious scheme.[59]

Therefore, other main points of critique regarding the system of inclusion of private schemes in the RED refer to insufficient codification of minimum structural, procedural and methodological requirements for private schemes and certification, in supply chain laws; lacking recognition;[60] lack of control (after recognition); and lacking public complaints systems, without which irregularities remain unknown, and do not lead to derecognition.[61] As a

---

pp. 55 *et seq.*; Preferred by Nature, supra, note 46, pp. 141 *et seq.*, 156 *et seq.* Similar problems were found with the Round Table on Responsible Soy Standard (RTRS).

55 For the governance structure of the FSC, see E. Meidinger, 'Multi-Interest Self-Governance through Global Product Certification Programmes' in O. Dilling, M. Herberg and G. Winter (eds.), *Responsible Business, Self-Governance and the Law in Transnational Economic Transactions*, Nomos, 2008, pp. 259 *et seq.*; K. Nowrot, 'Forest Stewardship Council', in C. Tietje and A. Brouder (eds.), *Handbook of Transnational Economic Governance Regimes*, Brill, 2009, pp. 865 *et seq.*

56 Again, the FSC provides an illustration: see Deutsche Welle, 'Die Ausbeutung der Urwälder', 2019, https://www.youtube.com/watch?v=b3vvomF3KEY. The FSC's unreliability even led to the foundation of an NGO called FSC-Watch: see https://fsc-watch.com/about. See also M. Du, 'Clearing the fog: Forest Stewardship Council labelling and the World Trade Organization', *Review of European, Comparative & International Environmental Law (RECIEL)*, 2021, pp. 81, 91 *et seq.*, with further references. For a comparison of different forest certification schemes, see Preferred by Nature, supra, note 49.

57 See Johansson, supra, note 52, p. 816.

58 See also G. Wagner, 'Marktaufsichtshaftung produktsicherheitsrechtlicher Zertifizierungsstellen', *Juristenzeitung*, 2018, pp. 130, 135 *et seq.*; C. Glinski and P. Rott, 'Regulating certification bodies in the field of medical devices: The PIP breast implants litigation and beyond', *European Review of Private Law*, 2019, pp. 403, 423 *et seq.*

59 See E. Meidinger, 'The Administrative Law of Global Private-Public Regulation: The Case of Forestry', *European Journal of International Law*, 2006 (17), pp. 47, 53.

60 European Court of Auditors, supra, note 48, pp. 28 *et seq.* Under RED I, certifiers were neither approved nor controlled.

61 See European Court of Auditors, supra, note 48, p. 25; S. Romppanen, 'New governance in context: Evaluating the EU biofuels regime', Dissertation, University of Eastern Finland, 2015, p. 49; Schmeichel, supra, note 46, pp. 136 *et seq.*

consequence of imprecise supply chain frameworks and insufficient control mechanisms, comparatively ambitious voluntary systems continuously lose members to less ambitious systems.[62]

At the same time, not least with a view to effectiveness, the inclusion of private standardisation and certification schemes provides advantages. As mentioned above, multi-stakeholder systems often go beyond legal requirements, and thus provide for additional sustainability benefits. They promote standardised requirements that facilitate coherent implementation and comparability, and produce fewer frictions, as compared with a situation where each enterprise develops its own requirements. From a cost–benefit perspective, the inclusion of private systems provides the most efficient method for risk assessment, prevention and mitigation, for economic operators as well as authorities. Due to the lack of in-house expertise and financial means, an all-encompassing individual risk assessment and prevention is regarded as almost impossible for many enterprises, in particular in longer supply chains.[63] Thus, the use of private standardisation schemes and certification provides far more reliability concerning proper risk management, corruption and fraud control, traceability, and so on, than purely internal due diligence systems, although none of the schemes is perfect.[64]

5. DESIGN OF INTERCONNECTIONS

As is clear from the foregoing, supply chain laws need to strike a balance between the advantages of including private schemes, and their legitimacy, effectiveness and risks.

5.1. CONCRETISATION OF REQUIREMENTS

Firstly, in concretising requirements towards the protection of biodiversity, supply chain laws need to address the tension between the reference to international standards detailed by participatory systems, which ensures the legitimacy and adequacy of standards, and the codification of encompassing legal requirements with a high degree of concretisation, which prevents highly divergent and inadequate implementation, and a 'race to the bottom' between biodiversity standards, as the implementation of the RED I has shown.

62 This happened, e.g., to the German national system: see C. Glinski, 'Certification of the Sustainability of Biofuels in Global Supply Chains', supra, note 46, pp. 178 *et seq.*
63 See Walker, supra, note 15, p. 285, with further references; Preferred by Nature, supra, note 46, pp. 5 *et seq.*, 150 *et seq.*
64 See Preferred by Nature, supra, note 46, pp. 5 *et seq.*

Technically, broad general clauses, while being open to regional implementation, and adaptation to progressing knowledge, could be concretised by rule examples, and guidelines and comments to guide interpretation, as well as by minimum requirements with limited possibilities for deviation and compensation. Another possibility would be a public register for (questions and) clarifications.[65] In this regard, the reference to the very broad Article 10(b) of the CBD, in the upcoming Corporate Sustainability Due Diligence Directive, needs further concretisation. Similar considerations concerning the clearness of criteria and requirements apply at the next level of concretisation, by private schemes, in order to ensure their adequacy and certifiability. Important aspects of this are a clear focus on targets,[66] local input, and a feedback system with certifiers.[67]

At the same time, supply chain laws must be aware of their side effects and limitations with regard to complex socio-economic resource-use and sustainability issues, and, in particular, to indirect land-use changes. The RED II, for example, is based on this insight, and phases out the promotion of biomass with a high risk of land-use changes by 2030.[68] In this regard, the focus of the Deforestation Regulation on forests only might cause major risks for other valuable ecosystems.

5.2. STRUCTURAL AND PROCEDURAL REQUIREMENTS FOR STAKEHOLDER INCLUSION AND PRIVATE STANDARDISATION

Further, a clear procedural framing is needed to structure the legitimising and competent participation of local expertise and local stakeholders in additional standard-setting by private actors. Different possibilities for the inclusion of private schemes exist. Adherence to private standards could either be accepted as compliance with legal requirements,[69] as a (rebuttable) presumption, or as a mere indication of compliance.[70] A mere indication, however, does not provide a legal incentive to use the advantages of private schemes[71] concerning

65 Ibid., p. 153.

66 ISEAL Code of Good Practice for Setting Social and Environmental Standards, supra note 50.

67 Interview with a certifier on 30 December 2022.

68 Arts. 25 and 26, RED II.

69 Examples are the RED II, and also Regulation (EU) 2017/821 laying down supply chain due diligence obligations for Union importers of tin, tantalum and tungsten, their ores, and gold originating from conflict-affected and high-risk areas, OJ 2017 L 130/1. Of course, the exact scope of application must be clearly codified.

70 Examples are the Deforestation Regulation and the proposal for a Corporate Sustainability Due Diligence Directive.

71 For the FSC, see section 2.2. above.

sustainability, legitimacy, effectiveness and efficiency, either for economic operators or authorities, nor does it incentivise the private systems to adapt their provisions to the legal requirements. Thus, academic authors and stakeholders prefer a rebuttable presumption.[72] This would lead to a graded threefold control system, consisting of private schemes, enterprises and authorities. Identified weaknesses or gaps in private systems could be completed by (modified) due diligence measures, controlled by authorities.[73]

Depending on the extent of the inclusion of private schemes into a supply chain law, preconditions for the concretisation of their requirements must be codified. The standardisation mandates to the European Committee for Standardization (CEN) and the European Electrotechnical Committee for Standardization (CENELEC) provide examples of how (far-reaching) references are usually drafted.[74]

Laws that accept the use of private schemes as valid implementations usually require an official recognition or accreditation of such schemes,[75] which would also be helpful in the case of a (rebuttable) presumption of valid implementation. In that case, registration, jurisdiction and applicable law, as well as structural and procedural requirements for the schemes, should be codified. The recognition procedure should be transparent and accessible, including for NGOs. Recognition should be temporary, and recognised systems should be controlled regularly.[76] The recognising authorities should run a complaints or whistle-blower system.[77]

Structural and procedural requirements for private systems, to ensure their legitimacy, include plural participation of those (interests) concerned, accessibility, transparency, early publication, reasons, and the possibility to articulate concerns or objections.[78] Consensus requirements according to ISO,[79]

---

72 This was common ground in a stakeholder workshop of the German Federal Ministry of Labour and Social Affairs, on 19 January 2023.

73 Preferred by Nature, supra, note 46, pp. 5 *et seq.*, 150 *et seq.*

74 See Regulation (EU) No. 1025/2012 on European standardisation, OJ 2012 L 316/12.

75 See, in particular, RED I and II.

76 Therefore, a continuous monitoring process for standardisation and certification systems has been suggested: see P. Gailhofer and C. Glinski, *Haftungsrechtlicher Rahmen für Zertifizierungen in textilen Lieferketten*, Öko-Institut e.V., 2021, https://www.vzbv.de/sites/default/files/2021-12/10122021_VZBV_Gutachten_Zertifizierer_final.pdf, pp. 64 *et seq.*; Preferred by Nature, supra, note 49, p. 154.

77 Concerning the respective weaknesses in the RED I in this regard, see European Court of Auditors, supra, note 48, pp. 25 *et seq.*, 28 *et seq.*

78 See, e.g. M. Schmidt-Preuß, 'Private technische Regelwerke – Rechtliche und politische Fragen' in M. Kloepfer (ed.), *Selbst-Beherrschung im technischen und ökologischen Bereich*, Duncker und Humblot, 1998, pp. 89, 96; G. Lübbe-Wolff, 'Verfassungsrechtliche Fragen der Normsetzung und der Normkonkretisierung im Umweltrecht', *Zeitschrift für Gesetzgebung*, 1991 (6), pp. 219, 242 *et seq.* These principles are also reflected in the respective ISO and ISEAL standards, supra, note 50.

79 'Consensus: General agreement, characterized by the absence of sustained opposition to substantial issues by any important part of the concerned interests and by a process seeking

veto rights, or objection rights concerning the next level of procedure, could safeguard the input of less powerful stakeholders, such as those representing social or environmental interests.[80] The inclusion of experts representing different disciplines and opinions, and selected according to their qualifications, independence and reliability, contributes to the substantial correctness of standards. The same applies to elements of output control, such as third-party comments, external evaluation, openness to revision in case of shortcomings, and accessible complaints procedures.[81]

For codification, references to ISO[82] or ISEAL[83] standards could be complemented by further procedural requirements reflecting sector-specific problems and the transnational multi-level system.

While multi-stakeholder initiatives (can) meet the requirements for plural input and representation of non-economic interests, industry schemes are particularly problematic in this regard. As a consequence, their inclusion and legal impact could be linked to the extent of their inclusion of stakeholders. An implementing regulation to the RED II, the Commission Implementing Regulation (EU) 2022/996 on rules to verify sustainability and greenhouse gas emissions saving criteria and low indirect land-use change-risk criteria,[84] for example, while still accepting industry schemes in principle, now requires a balanced inclusion of stakeholders, namely from science, agriculture and forestry, indigenous peoples and local communities (Article 3(1) to (3)). In addition, certification schemes have to prove sufficient legal and technical expertise, and, where possible, include external expertise.

Another option would be an increased focus on output correctness, based upon extensive expertise, high substantive requirements and best practices, and inclusion of stakeholders in encompassing monitoring and control mechanisms. A formal recognition of standards (and their concrete outreach) would add state-based output control.[85]

In addition, under Implementing Regulation (EU) 2022/996, private systems should provide for clear consequences for non-compliant economic operators (Article 4), rules strictly limiting the possibilities for economic operators to

---

to take into account the views of interested parties, particularly those directly affected, and to reconcile any conflicting arguments. Note – Consensus need not imply unanimity.' (ISO/IEC Guide 2:1996: 3.1).

80 See, e.g. E. Denninger, *Verfassungsrechtliche Anforderungen an die Normsetzung im Umwelt- und Technikrecht*, Nomos, 1990, pp. 170 *et seq.*

81 See, e.g. Hoffmann-Riem, supra, note 36, pp. 320 *et seq.*

82 ISO/IEC Guide 59 Code of good practice for standardization: ISO/IEC Guide 59: 2019.

83 ISEAL Standard-Setting Code of Good Practice, Version 6.0, 2014, currently under revision, https://www.isealalliance.org/sites/default/files/resource/2017-11/ISEAL_Standard_Setting_Code_v6_Dec_2014.pdf.

84 OJ 2022 L 168/1.

85 At the same time, this would fulfil constitutional legitimacy requirements, e.g. under German law, in the event that adherence to the standard is recognised as compliance with the law.

change systems (Article 7), internal monitoring systems (Article 5(1) and (2)), accessible complaints mechanisms (Article 5(3)), and far-reaching transparency requirements (Articles 5(4) and (5), and 6).

Should membership of a private scheme, or adherence to a private standard, only be regarded as an indication that due diligence is being carried out, a (non-binding) list of adequate schemes or standards, or guidance with relevant criteria, at least, would be helpful.

5.3. REQUIREMENTS FOR CERTIFICATION BODIES

Private certification could either be regarded as full proof of adherence, as a rebuttable presumption, or as a mere indication. To this end, certification could either be part of a private scheme, as in the RED system, or required independently, as in certain areas of EU product safety law.[86] In both cases, certification bodies should be accredited. In order to safeguard the quality of controls abroad, the accountability of the accredited standardisation or certification body for its subsidiaries and subcontractors should be codified.[87] Certification bodies should be controlled regularly, and their accreditation should be time-limited. Authorities should run a complaints or whistle-blower system.[88]

Structural requirements for certification bodies relate to their independence, impartiality, expertise and sufficiency of resources.[89] Expertise must include biodiversity- and land-use-specific methods. Protection against contract termination by the economic operator,[90] maximum contract length, and mandate allocation systems or rotation mechanisms, provide safeguards for independence.[91] Control methods should (as minimum requirements) be codified precisely and consistently, and be supplemented by a general clause which refers to best practices, and requires an investigative risk- oriented application of these methods. The minimum requirements are unannounced

86 E.g. in medical devices law: see Glinski and Rott, supra, note 58.

87 Examples are Regulation (EU) 2017/745 on medical devices, OJ 2017 L 117/1, Annex VII, 3.4.; Regulation (EC) 2009/391 on common rules and standards for ship inspection and survey organisations, OJ 2009 L 131/11, Annex I, B.7; Bundesministerium für Wirtschaft und Entwicklung, Grüner Knopf – Zertifizierungsprogramm 4.0 (2022), https://www.gruener-knopf.de/media/672/download, 6.2.2.

88 For a positive example, see Grüner Knopf – Zertifizierungsprogramm 4.0, supra, note 87, 4.1.2.

89 See, e.g. Regulation (EC) No. 765/2008 setting out the requirements for accreditation and market surveillance relating to the marketing of products, OJ 2008 L 218/30; Commission Decision No. 768/2008/EC on a common framework for the marketing of products, OJ 2008 L 218/82; and Regulation (EU) 2017/745 on medical devices, as relevant European frameworks on (product safety) certification.

90 See, e.g. Grüner Knopf – Zertifizierungsprogramm 4.0, supra, note 87, 4.1.4.2.

91 See, e.g. Arts. 3(4) to (6), Implementing Regulation (EU) 2022/996.

visits; identification and inclusion of stakeholders, in safe spaces; and a review procedure.[92]

Again, Implementing Regulation (EU) 2022/996 to the RED provides for important elements of the state of the art. Thereunder, certifiers have to be accredited according to ISO 17021 or 17065, and the highest level of independence must be secured through rotation mechanisms and other best practices (Article 3(4) to (6)). Voluntary systems have to ensure that their auditors have the necessary competence, and are trained regularly (Article 11). Audits have to be carried out in accordance with ISO 19011 and other detailed requirements (Articles 10 and 12), amongst them the control of waste management, CO_2 emissions, and biodiversity requirements (Articles 13 to 16). The Regulation also contains provisions concerning the control of economic operators, private schemes and certification bodies by the Member States, and by the Commission (Article 17).

5.4. ADDITIONAL SAFEGUARDS

In order to be effective, supply chain laws should pay particular attention to (far-reaching) transparency requirements, not only for economic operators, but also for standardisation and certification schemes. Transparency eases assessments by accreditation authorities, and informed decisions concerning the outreach and reliability of systems by economic actors and authorities, and strengthens control by stakeholders and the general public.[93]

Also, legal empowerment of stakeholders is of major importance. This encompasses accessible and effective complaints mechanisms, not only within private systems, but also within authorities, to ensure effective remedies. Additional safeguards are access to justice for those concerned, and for NGOs, as well as a liability regime for economic operators and certifiers.[94] Ideally, those legal safeguards should be accompanied by financial and other support to social and environmental representatives in the Global South.

---

92 Concerning the breast implants scandal around the French producer PIP, see Glinski and Rott, supra, note 58. See also ECCHR, Brot für die Welt and Misereor, supra, note 54, pp. 24, 31 *et seq.*

93 See, e.g. Art. 6, Implementing Regulation (EU) 2022/996.

94 See ECCHR, Brot für die Welt & Misereor, supra, note 54, p. 24; Gailhofer and Glinski, supra, note 76, pp. 73 *et seq.* For the area of ship certification, see C. Glinski, 'The public–private governance regime on sustainable ship recycling: An in-depth analysis', *Review of European, Comparative & International Environmental Law (RECIEL)*, 2022, pp. 268 *et seq.*; and C. Glinski, 'Liability of shipowners and classification societies for environmental damage and unsafe working conditions at recycling yards', *Review of European, Comparative & International Environmental Law (RECIEL)*, 2022, pp. 468 *et seq.*

6. CONCLUSION

Biodiversity protection through supply chain laws has to address a number of challenges of legitimacy and effectiveness which derive from the transnationality of the subject matter. While the reference to international standards, and the participation of those concerned, provides legitimacy (and also adequacy) to these laws, there are no generally applicable, sufficiently precise, biodiversity protection standards in international law which could simply be 'picked up' and applied by economic actors. The inclusion of transnational private standardisation schemes could provide a solution, while certification could bridge jurisdictional borders, in terms of control. However, experience has shown that there are serious risks concerning the adequacy of these standards and their reliability.

Thus, the inclusion of these instruments needs to be drafted wisely. Firstly, the concretisation of requirements needs to be guided thoroughly, through clear minimum requirements, rule examples and interpretation guidance. Secondly, schemes should be recognised and controlled, and should adhere to encompassing structural and procedural requirements. Thirdly, schemes should neither replace the due diligence duties of economic operators, nor the control by authorities, but should constitute only one element in a three-level governance and control system. Inclusion and legal empowerment of stakeholders is of major importance.

EXPLORING THE LINKS BETWEEN THE WORLD HEALTH ORGANIZATION GUIDELINES AND THE EU AIR QUALITY LAW

Scientific Authority and the Lawmaking Process

Camille BERTAUX

ABSTRACT

The European Environment Agency recently underlined that air pollution is still one of the largest environmental health issues in the European Union (EU). In the field of air quality, the World Health Organization (WHO) guidelines infuse EU legislation: not only are they taken into consideration by the Ambient Air Quality Directive, but the 2022 Proposal for a recast of the Directive on ambient air quality and cleaner air in the European Union also aims at a closer alignment with the guidelines. These non-binding norms tend to have significant influence in the EU lawmaking process, based on the authority they bear. This contribution aims to demonstrate that the analysis of the guidelines' development process enables a better understanding of how air quality standards are constructed. Such an analysis could be better reflected within the EU lawmaking process.

1. INTRODUCTION

In Europe, air pollution is the biggest environmental health-related risk. In April 2023, the European Environment Agency published a briefing on the current status of pollutant concentration in ambient air, for the years 2021 and 2022, in relation to the 2021 World Health Organization (WHO) Global Air Quality Guidelines levels and the European Union (EU) air quality applicable standards.[1] The Agency not only uses the EU legally binding standards, but also the non-binding levels published by the WHO, as a reference for citizens' health.

The EU lawmaking process relating to air quality also relies on the standards published by the Organization. The second recital of the EU Ambient Air Quality Directive recognises the WHO air quality standards as *appropriate* for the adoption of air quality objectives 'to protect human health and the environment as a whole'. By initiating the recast of the EU Ambient Air Quality Directive in 2021, the European Commission aims to align the Directive more closely with the WHO guidelines on air quality.[2]

Altogether, the scientific argument has a significant role in environmental law. It is frequently debated amongst scholars and before courts.[3] For instance, attribution science related to climate change[4] is decisive in the adjudication of climate litigation. In *Urgenda v. Government of the Netherlands*, the national jurisdiction relied 'heavily' on scientific recommendations issued by the

---

1 EEA, 'Europe's air quality status 2023', 24 April 2023, https://www.eea.europa.eu/publications/europes-air-quality-status-2023; European Parliament and Council Directive on Ambient Air Quality and Cleaner Air for Europe, OJ 2008 L 152; WHO, *Global air quality guidelines*, WHO, 2021.

2 EC, 'Revision of the Ambient Air Quality Directives', https://ec.europa.eu/environment/air/quality/revision_of_the_aaq_directives.htm.

3 The French Council of State ruled against a ministerial order partly due to the absence of scientific knowledge relating to brown bear conservation: see State Council of France, *Association Ferus – Ours, loup, lynx and others*, 25 April 2022, 442676 and 442769, para. 15; Civil Tribunal of Bruxelles, *Klimaatzaak*, 17 June 2021, 2015/4585/A, paras 63–65; Administrative Tribunal of Paris, *L'affaire du Siècle*, 14 October 2021, 1904967, 1904968, 1904972, 1904976/4-1, para. 16; J. Moore et al., 'Towards linking environmental law and science', *FACETS Journal*, 2018(3), pp. 375–391.

4 Attribution science explores the links between human activities and climate change. It studies how human activities are linked to 'changes in the climate system and corresponding impacts

International Governmental Panel on Climate Change (IPCC), to establish the percentage reduction of greenhouse gas emissions the government would need to reach in order to deter forthcoming dangers linked to climate change.[5] Although the relationship between the IPCC and climate change law is well established, interactions between international organisations and other environmental law areas have been sparsely explored within the literature. In environmental health-related laws and case law, the WHO could play a similar role, health and environmental concerns being interconnected.[6] Scientific recommendations seem to respond to a vacuum, as they feed the normative content.

The WHO's recommendations are frequently mobilised on the legal spectrum,[7] yet they do not have a compulsory nature. According to the UN Environmental Programme (UNEP) Guide on Regulating Air Quality, WHO air quality guidelines' values 'reflect a high degree of scientific consensus, giving them global authority'.[8] These guidelines appear to have a scientific authority[9] upon which environmental law stakeholders might construct stronger objectives challenging established legal standards.

After a preliminary analysis, this chapter explores the potential epistemic force a non-legal instrument issued by the WHO may have, based on the links between the environment and the Organization's normative powers. The WHO has fuelled discussions on air quality standards with a view to bettering human health globally.[10] This observation leads to question how the Organization, by

on natural and earth systems': M. Burger, J. Wentz and R. Horton, 'The Law and Science of Climate Change Attribution', *Columbia Journal of Environmental Law*, 2020 (43), p. 66. In the United States, the US Supreme Court held that the State of Massachusetts and other plaintiffs could file a lawsuit against the US Environmental Protection Agency, based on scientific knowledge (establishing a link between climate change and local flood disasters): Supreme Court of The United States, *Massachusetts v. EPA*, 2 April 2007, 549 US 497.

5 J. Setzer and L. Vanhala, 'Climate change litigation: A review of research on courts and litigants in climate governance', *Wiley Interdisciplinary Reviews*, 2019 (10), p. e589; Rechtbank Den Haag, *Urgenda v. Government of the Netherlands*, confirmed in appeal, 24 June 2015, ECLI:NL:RBDHA:2015:7145.

6 S.J. Turner et al. (eds.), *Environmental Rights: The Development of Standards*, Cambridge University Press, 2019, p. 3.

7 Regarding the case law, see Administrative Tribunal of Paris, *Les amis de la terre*, 2 July 2021, 1920927/4-3 and 1921120/4-3, and C. Cass., *Belgian State v. A.T.*, 3 January 2008, C.06.0322.N/1, para. 60. Regarding the law, see Ambient Air Quality Directive, supra, note 1, and the Recast of the Proposal for a European Parliament and Council Directive on ambient air quality and cleaner air for Europe (recast), 26 October 2022, COM(2022) 542.

8 E. Scotford and D. Misonne, *Regulating Air Quality: the First Global Assessment of Air Pollution Legislation*, UNEP Guide, 2021, p. 5.

9 The WHO 'is widely regarded as the preeminent international authority on health and scientific matters': T. Das, 'Basically a house of experts: the production of World Health Organization information', *African Health Sciences*, 2010 (10), p. 390.

10 WHO (Resolutions and Decisions of the World Health Assembly), Sixty-Eighth Session of the World Health Assembly, 18–26 May 2015, WHA68/2015/REC/1, pp. 20–24; WHO,

issuing non-binding guidelines – the 2021 *WHO Global Air Quality Guidelines* – has, in some ways, affected EU law and, more specifically, the 2022 Proposal for a recast of the Directive on ambient air quality and cleaner air in the European Union.

2. WHO AND THE ENVIRONMENT: A MUTUAL DEPENDENCE

Environment and health interact in many ways. In 2020, Dr Tedros Adhanom Ghebreyesus, the WHO's director-general, relevantly asserted that:

> The pandemic is a reminder of the intimate and delicate relationship between people and planet. Any efforts to make our world safer are doomed to fail unless they address the critical interface between people and pathogens, and the existential threat of climate change that is making our earth less habitable.[11]

For decades, the WHO considered underlying determinants of health, such as the environment, to be fully part of the right to health.[12] In 1989, the WHO called on states to 'adopt appropriate legislation, regulating anthropogenic influences on ecological systems'.[13]

According to the 2020 *WHO Global Strategy on Health, Environment and Climate Change*, 'the environment is essential for good health and development'.[14] Avoidable environmental risks are causing 13 million deaths per year: air pollution is responsible for 'seven million preventable deaths';[15] over 2 billion people suffer from poor water quality, causing important diseases, including cholera and diarrhoea;[16] climate change and land uses are sources of vector-borne

---

'Health and the environment: Draft road map for an enhanced global response to the adverse health effects of air pollution', 2016, A69/18.

11 WHO, Address by Dr Tedros Adhanom Ghebreyesus, Director-General, 18 May 2020, A73, p. 2.

12 The WHO's Constitution 'defines health as a state of complete physical, mental and social well-being and not merely the absence of disease or infirmity, and declares that the enjoyment of the highest attainable standard of health is one of the fundamental rights of every human being without distinction of race, religion, political belief, economic or social condition': WHO (World Health Assembly Plenary Meeting), 'Strengthening WHO preparedness for and response to health emergencies', 31 May 2021, WHA74.7.

13 WHO (Resolution of the World Health Assembly), 'WHO's contribution to the international efforts towards sustainable development', 19 May 1989, WHA42.26, para. 3(4).

14 WHO, *Global Strategy on Health, Environment and Climate Change*, WHO, 2020, pp. 4–5.

15 WHO (Report by the Director-General), 'Health, Environment and Climate Change', 5 December 2018, EB/144/15.

16 WHO, 'Drinking-water', factsheet, 21 March 2022, https://www.who.int/news-room/fact-sheets/detail/drinking-water.

diseases;[17] while many people die due to long exposure to chemicals.[18] In addition, climate change is the biggest 'health challenge of the 21st Century', pressuring all aspects of human society, and adversely impacting on basic needs such as water, air, food and shelter.[19] In the WHO's *COP 24 Special Report*, the Organization underlined this tight connection: 'the greater the warming, the greater the risks for human health'.[20]

The 2020 *WHO Global Strategy on Health, Environment and Climate Change* seeks to create a new approach that better covers environmental risks, climate change and health, and reduces adverse environmental impacts on health.[21] It calls for actions at 'the root causes of disease', the sole 'focus on the treatment of individual diseases ... be[ing] insufficient to tackle modern environmental health challenges'.[22] Similarly, in 2021, the WHO, jointly with the UN Development Programme (UNDP), published a compendium aiming to better advise policymakers and practitioners on the environmental risks to health.[23]

Environmental concerns are shaping the WHO's response to disease in many different ways. It is, therefore, unsurprising that environmental law plays a part in enhancing the right to health, as a better environment is key to better health. According to the Organization, the Paris Agreement is potentially one of this century's 'strongest' agreements for health.[24] Collaborating with the Secretariat of the Convention on Biological Diversity, the WHO also guarantees that interlinkages between health and biodiversity are properly taken into consideration.[25] The WHO works with several environmental actors, through memorandums of understanding, to reduce environmental and health-related

---

17 A.M. Sheela et al., 'Assessment of relation of land use characteristics with vector-borne diseases in tropical areas', *Land Use Policy*, 2017 (63), pp. 369–380; C. Caminade, K. McIntyre and A. Jones, 'Impact of recent and future climate change on vector-borne diseases', *Annals of the New York Academy of Sciences*, 2019 (1436), pp. 157–173.

18 WHO, *The Public Health Impact of Chemicals: Knowns and Unknowns*, WHO, 2016 and Data Addendum for 2019, 2019.

19 The Organization also points out emerging challenges causing environmental, climate and health damage (such as nanoparticles, toxic and electronic wastes, etc.): WHO, *COP24 Special Report: Health and Climate Change*, WHO, 2018, pp. 9 and 14; E. Maibach et al., 'Health professionals, the Paris agreement, and the fierce urgency of now', *The Journal of Climate Change and Health*, 2021(1), p. 2.

20 *WHO COP 24 Special Report*, supra, note 19, p. 14.

21 *WHO Global Strategy on Health, Environment and Climate Change*, supra, note 14, p. 4.

22 Ibid., p. 3.

23 WHO, UNDP and UNICEF, *Compendium of WHO and other UN guidance on health and environment*, WHO/UNDP/UNICEF, 2021.

24 UNFCCC, 'WHO: Health Benefits Far Outweigh Costs of Meeting Paris Goals', 5 December 2018, https://unfccc.int/news/who-health-benefits-far-outweigh-costs-of-meeting-paris-goals; UNFCCC, 'The Paris Agreement is a Health Agreement – WHO', 3 May 2018, https://unfccc.int/news/the-paris-agreement-is-a-health-agreement-who.

25 CBD and UNEP, 'Biodiversity and Health', 9 April 2021, CBD/SBSTTA/24/9.

threats.[26] Finally, in cooperation with the UN Environment Programme, the World Organisation for Animal Health, and the Food and Agriculture Organization, the WHO has developed the One Health Initiative. The One Health Initiative is an integrated approach that seeks 'to sustainably balance and optimise the health of people, animals and ecosystems'.[27] The initiative acknowledges the tight connections between human and animal health, and the dangers of disease to society. According to Mackenzie and Jeggo, a cross-disciplinary approach is vital in responding to emerging and resurging illnesses.[28]

There are close connections between environmental concerns, the law and the WHO. These connections on the legal spectrum are not frequently explored within the literature, and require more attention, especially since the WHO guidelines tend to infuse policies, lawmaking processes and case law in the fields of air and water pollution.[29] It is, therefore, important to first understand the WHO's normative powers, as an organisation that generates a large variety of instruments.

3. THE NORMATIVE POWERS OF THE WHO: A VARIETY OF INSTRUMENTS

Constituted in 1948, the WHO seeks to reach the highest possible level of health for all people. According to the Organization, health 'is a state of complete physical, mental and social well-being and not merely the absence of disease or infirmity'.[30] Brought to the fore during the COVID-19 pandemic, the WHO is a United Nations specialised agency that coordinates, and provides leadership on international health issues.[31] The WHO may adopt a large variety of instruments, as formulated in its Constitution. Although the organisation

---

26 Jointly with UNEP, the WHO launched a memorandum to 'support health and environment sectors to engage in cross-sectoral dialogue, so that selected policy options achieve sustainable development objectives – enhancement of health and wellbeing, environmental protection and economic development': UNEP and WHO, *Managing the Linkages for Sustainable Development*, WHO, 2008, p. 11; 'UN Climate Change and WHO Team Up to Protect Health from Climate Change at COP23', online, https://www.who.int/news/item/12-11-2017-un-climate-change-and-who-team-up-to-protect-health-from-climate-change-at-COP23; FAO, OIE and WHO, 'Memorandum of Understanding between the United Nations Food and Agriculture Organisation and the World Organisation for Animal Health and the World Health Organization regarding cooperation to combat health risks at the animal-human-ecosystems interface in the context of the one health approach and including antimicrobial resistance', 2017.

27 WHO, 'One health', https://www.who.int/health-topics/one-health#tab=tab_1.

28 J. Mackenzie and M. Jeggo, 'The One Health Approach – Why Is It So Important?', *Tropical Medicine and Infectious Disease*, 2019 (4), p. 1.

29 See section 3.2.3 below.

30 Preamble of the Constitution of the World Health Organization, New York, 1946.

31 Art. 2 of the WHO Constitution.

may produce binding agreements and regulations, its main activities rely on non-binding norms.

3.1. BINDING NORMATIVE POWERS

The WHO has a constitutional mandate to address and endorse internationally binding agreements or regulations relating to health matters.[32] Under Articles 19 and 20 of the WHO Constitution (the Constitution), the World Health Assembly (WHA) may adopt, on a two-thirds vote, any agreements or conventions within the WHO's constitutional competence. Considering the WHO's broad objective, and the wide-encompassing definition of health, the provisions establish a 'treaty-making power of virtually limitless potential'.[33] The WHA, composed of Member States' representatives, has the power to establish mandatory conventions applicable to signatory parties, following internal ratification.[34] In 2003, the WHA adopted the first and (to date) sole binding international convention of the WHO. The Framework Convention on Tobacco Control aims to reduce tobacco consumption. While there may have been difficulties around the enactment of this convention, its adoption was feasible because it regulates 'the only lawful product that is uniformly harmful'.[35]

Under Article 22 of the Constitution, the WHA may also adopt, on a simple majority, international regulations that are directly binding on Member States once voted on.[36] There are two regulations in force: nomenclature regulations that classify morbidity and mortality and compare them statistically,[37] and international health regulations aiming to control global disease spread.[38]

Considering these powerful mandates, the 'WHO has the widest ranging legal authority to address global public health concerns'.[39] Yet, it does not

---

32 Arts. 19 and 21 of the WHO Constitution.

33 K. Klock, 'The Soft Law Alternative to the WHO's Treaty Powers', *Georgetown Journal of International Law*, 2013 (44), p. 827; D. Fidler, 'The Future of the World Health Organization: What Role for International Law?', *Vanderbilt Journal of Transnational Law*, 1998 (31), p. 1087.

34 F. Kastler, *Le Rôle Normatif de l'Organisation Mondiale de la Santé*, L'Harmattan, 2019, pp. 252–253.

35 L. Gostin, D. Hougendobler and D. Sridhar, 'The normative authority of the World Health Organization', *Public Health*, 2015 (129), p. 858; Banque Mondiale, *Maîtriser l'épidémie: L'État et les aspects économiques de la lutte contre le tabagisme*, Banque Mondiale, 1999.

36 Except for Member States that notify their rejection or reservations to the WHO's director-general (Arts. 21, 22 and 60 of the WHO Constitution).

37 WHO Nomenclature Regulations, 1967, Art. 2; G.L. Burci and C.-H. Vignes, *World Health Organization*, Kluwer Law International, 2004, p. 132.

38 WHO International Health Regulation, 2nd ed., 2005, Art. 2; Burci and Vignes, supra, note 37, p. 135.

39 B.M. Meier et al., 'The World Health Organization in Global Health Law', *The Journal of Law, Medicine & Ethics*, 2020 (48), p. 797.

frequently exercise such mandates. The broad compelling powers of the WHO are challenged by states' sovereignty: 'Article 22 was one of the most debated [provisions] during the drafting of the Constitution, as it was perceived by some delegations as an infringement of state sovereignty'.[40] Member States' reluctance towards the WHO's binding authority does not, however, prevent the Organization from adopting other non-compulsory instruments.

3.2. NON-BINDING NORMATIVE POWERS

The WHO has the normative capacity to establish, under Articles 2(k) and 23 of its Constitution, non-binding instruments called recommendations. Recommendations are 'invitation[s] to adopt a precise behaviour, addressed by an international body to an external recipient'.[41] Recommendations are based on technical and scientific advice, and are the most successful and prolific activity of the WHO.[42] These recommendations seek to regulate precise health issues rather than producing a general policy.[43] After a preliminary analysis, recommendations refer to a generic term covering different types of non-binding norms formulated by the WHO, including guidelines.[44] Interestingly, the WHO seems to produce two types of recommendations: on the one hand, the organisation formulates technical-based instruments; on the other, it issues science-based and policy guidelines. The two types of instruments are further discussed in the subsections below.

3.2.1. *Technical-Based Instruments*

The technical recommendations seek to inform on a specific scientific subject, publishing the latest scientific information for experts and stakeholders in the field.[45] The abundance of scientific recommendations reflects the historical

---

40 K. Lee, 'World Health Organization' in J. Sperling (ed.), *Handbook of Governance and Security*, Edward Elgar Publishing, 2014, p. 18; see also Klock, supra, note 33 at p. 827; D. Fidler, 'The Future of the World Health Organization: What Role for International Law', supra, note 33, pp. 1090–1091; A. Taylor, 'Making the World Health Organization work: a legal framework for universal access to the conditions for health', *American Journal of Law & Medicine*, 1992 (18), p. 329.

41 Originally written in French: 'la recommandation est une invitation à observer un comportement déterminé, adressée par un organe international à un destinataire qui lui est extérieur': A. Virally, 'La valeur juridique des recommendations des organisations internationales', *Annuaire Français de Droit International*, 1956, p. 94.

42 Burci and Vignes, supra, note 37, p. 141.

43 Ibid., p. 142.

44 Yet, within the guidelines, experts do produce recommendations on the adoption of certain practices.

45 For illustration, the Toolkit for Clinical Care for Severe Acute Respiratory Infection seeks to inform 'clinicians working in acute care, managing adult and paediatric patients with acute

purpose of the WHO. The Organization, initially constituted to exercise its powers through technical expertise, kept technical and science-based work as a pre-eminent activity.[46] The WHO is mainly composed of 'Hippocratic society' members, uniting experts, including physicians, doctors and medical scientists.[47] This traditional institutional culture created an approach focusing on sanitary issues that are medically and technically oriented.[48] Aside from WHO's historical traditions, multiple reasons explain the choice to rely on these technical instruments. First, the non-compulsory nature of these instruments enables better flexibility and adaptability to local circumstances, and facilitates integration into national policies.[49] Second, their adoption follows a lightened procedure that does not require the political consensus of all Member States, and which also facilitates their later updating.[50] Third, according to the WHO, they result from a scientific adoption process based on reliable scientific evidence, insulating them from political and/or commercial pressure.[51]

Because they are flexible, recommendations permit the WHO to expand its field of action, ranging from the establishment of a *Codex Alimentarius* relating to food consumption,[52] to the adoption of a practical toolkit aiming to guide clinicians working with patients affected by severe respiratory infections.[53] Aside from technical recommendations, the WHO has somehow extended its normative powers towards a more political and/or judicial role, with the formulation of guidelines.[54]

3.2.2. Science and Policy-Based Instruments

At this stage of exploration, and because the WHO produces a large variety of different instruments, it seems that guidelines seek to inform public policy and formulate political guidance, based on scientific evidence. Compared with

---

respiratory infection': WHO, *Clinical Care for Severe Acute Respiratory Infection: Toolkit*, WHO, 2022, p. vii.

46 L. Gruszczynski and M. Melillo, 'The Uneasy Coexistence of Expertise and Politics in the World Health Organization', *International Organizations Law Review*, 2022, pp. 6–7.

47 D. Fidler, 'International Law and Global Public Health', *University of Kansas Law Review*, 1999 (48), p. 23.

48 Ibid.

49 Ibid.

50 Kastler, supra, note 34, p. 447.

51 Burci and Vignes, supra, note 37, p. 150.

52 The *Codex Alimentarius* collects standards, guidelines and practices issued by the Codex Alimentarius Commission, relating to consumer health and fair trade practices in the food market. The list of standards, guidelines and practices can be found at https://www.fao.org/fao-who-codexalimentarius/codex-texts/all-standards/en/.

53 WHO, *Clinical Care for Severe Acute Respiratory Infection: Toolkit*, supra, note 45; the variety of subjects encompassed by the WHO, and the multitude of instruments, may nevertheless affect the general cohesion of its actions: Kastler, supra, note 34, p. 456.

54 Kastler, supra, note 34, p. 465.

technical recommendations, guidelines appear to extend the expert advisory aspect of a recommendation to the production of guidance that informs policy and lawmaking.[55]

3.2.2.1. Definition, Purposes and Development Process of the Guidelines

The WHO defines guidelines as any WHO documents issuing recommendations for clinical practice or public health policy.[56] Such recommendations 'help the user of the guideline to make informed decisions on whether to undertake specific interventions, clinical tests or public health measures, and on where and when to do so'.[57] The WHO guidelines serve as a basis to elaborate national recommendations, and offer a flexible model on a specific health issue, guiding national policies and/or legislations.[58] They are hybrid in nature, as they are developed on science-based expertise, while their primary objective is to offer political and/or judicial guidance on health matters. They therefore go beyond expertise, to offer policy guidance on a selected health-related topic.[59] The technical and science-based aspect is reflected in the stringent development process applied to the guidelines.

In trying to produce highly qualitative guidelines, the WHO establishes strict methods of development, based on independent review evidence that adequately considers conflicts of interest.[60] The organisation underlines how essential these methods are 'to ensur[ing] that the ... recommendations are independent, evidence-based and unbiased'.[61] The guideline development hence follows several principles. According to the *WHO Handbook for Guideline Development*, guidelines seek to address a need for advice on uncertain issues while also reflecting the right to health – the WHO's core value. Their elaboration must be clear and transparent, and include relevant experts and stakeholders, as the process must be multidisciplinary.[62] The risk of bias must be

55 Please note that the distinction is not always straightforward, as some instruments partly inform policymakers but are not titled under the *guidelines* terminology. For illustration, the Global Breast Cancer Initiative Implementation Framework seeks 'to provide evidence-based recommendations for a phased approach to implementing interventions focused on improving early detection, diagnosis, treatment, and supportive services', while it is 'intended for dissemination to a broad target audience, including ministries of health, other governmental and allied policy-makers, [and] nongovernmental organizations (NGOs)': WHO, *Global Breast Cancer Initiative Implementation Framework*, WHO, 2023, pp. xvi and 10.

56 WHO, *Handbook for Guideline Development*, 2nd ed., WHO, 2014, p. 1.

57 Ibid.

58 Kastler, supra, note 34, pp. 464–465.

59 Ibid., p. 466.

60 WHO, 'WHO guidelines: development and governance, Report by the Secretariat', 20 May 2015, EB137/5, para. 4.

61 Ibid.

62 WHO, *Handbook for Guideline Development*, supra, note 56, p. 2.

taken into consideration, and reduced, during the whole development process, while recommendations have to be 'based on a systematic and comprehensive assessment of the balance of a policy's or intervention's potential benefits and harms and explicit consideration of other relevant factors'.[63] All evidence that served the development of the guidelines must be made publicly available. Finally, if recommendations can be adapted to local peculiarities, guidelines should be addressed to the targeted audience (for example, policymakers, healthcare providers, the general public, etc.).[64]

The Guideline Review Committee, composed of WHO staff members and external experts, reviews the planning proposal, and make sure the required methodology and development processes are being respected, and are homogeneous.[65] To ensure that guidelines are in conformity with the best current practice, the *WHO Handbook for Guideline Development* dictates the criteria and process to be followed.[66] WHO Member States intervene during guideline development on two occasions: upstream, they call for the adoption of guidelines on a certain topic, and participate in setting priority questions, and downstream, they have the authority to implement and adapt the guidelines produced.[67] The intervention of Member States during the development process indicates that guidelines are not based solely on technical expertise.

3.2.2.2. Beyond Technical Expertise

The frequent reliance by the WHO on these non-binding instruments is seen, in the literature, as an extension of the Organization's powers: guidelines not only seek to advise on a sole scientific basis, but also pursue a more political objective, aiming to guide policymakers and lawmakers.[68] In some ways, these non-binding instruments are more convenient for the WHO, as they produce international health policy guidance, conciliating Member states' interests when there is no possible international consensus on a common binding framework.[69] The WHO has a policy that values states' accountability over compulsory compliance with the guidelines.[70] Still, in the absence of legal obligations, lawmakers and judges decide whether or not to implement and enforce the guidelines.

---

63 WHO, 'WHO guidelines: development and governance', supra, note 60, para. 5.

64 WHO, *Handbook for Guideline Development*, supra, note 56, pp. 165–167.

65 Ibid., p. 11; D. Sinclair et al., 'World Health Organization guideline development: an evaluation', *PLoS One*, 2013 (8), p. e63715.

66 WHO, *Handbook for Guideline Development*, supra, note 56.

67 WHO, 'WHO guidelines: development and governance', supra, note 60, para. 5.

68 Kastler, supra, note 34, pp. 464–467; Gostin, Hougendobler and Sridhar, supra, note 35, p. 5; Gruszczynski and Melillo, supra, note 46, pp. 11–12; Sinclair et al., supra, note 65, p. e63715; Das, supra, note 9, p. 392.

69 Kastler, supra, note 34, p. 465; L. Gostin and D. Sridhar, 'Global Health and the Law', *The New England Journal of Medicine*, 2014 (370), p. 1737.

70 Gostin and Sridhar, supra, note 69, p. 1739; Kastler, supra, note 34, p. 465.

The normative powers of WHO instruments stem not only from national implementations by lawmakers, but also, more directly, from their use by national jurisdictions. For illustration, in 2008, the Belgian Court of Cassation considered the WHO *Guidelines for Community Noise*[71] as having authority, 'even if [originally] non-binding', where national noise pollution standards were missing.[72] Conversely, in the Netherlands, the Civil Tribunal was required to assess the level of protection offered by national standards, compared with the higher protection defined in the 2005 WHO Air Quality Guidelines (2005 WHO AQG).[73] The Tribunal refused to apply the stricter standards in the 2005 WHO AQG, on the basis that '[t]he mere fact that the WHO standards ... offer better protection [than the respected national standards] is insufficient'[74] to establish violation of the rights to life, and private life and family.[75] In each case, the judges opted for different applications of the guidelines. In Belgium, the absence of existing national standards could explain the reliance on the guidelines to interpret a duty of care.[76] Thus, the guidelines fulfilled one of their main objectives: addressing 'an area of uncertainty and an unmet need for guidance'.[77]

WHO guidelines appear frequently within legislation and policies.[78] For illustration, in the EU, WHO guidelines and recommendations are mentioned multiple times within the Directive on the Quality of Water Intended for Human

71 WHO, *Guidelines for Community Noise*, WHO, 1999.

72 *'Bien qu'elles ne soient pas obligatoires, ces lignes directrices peuvent être prises en considération et faire autorité lors de l'examen de la question de savoir si l'administration agit ou non de manière irrégulière'*: see *Belgian State v. A.T.*, supra, note 7, para. 60.

73 Rb (Den Haag), *Milieudefensie and Stichting Adem*, 27 December 2017, ECLI:NL:RBDHA:2017:15380, confirmed in appeal, Gh (Den Haag), *Milieudefensie and Stichting Adem*, 7 May 2019, ECLI:NL:GHDHA:2019:915.

74 *Milieudefensie and Stichting Adem*, 2017, para. 4:89.

75 According to the Tribunal, if a balance must be exercised between the individual's interests and the interests of the Community as a whole, it does not mean that human rights must always prevail. In this case, the Tribunal applied the state's 'margin of appreciation', in relation to Arts. 2 and 8 of the European Convention of Human Rights. It concluded that, by respecting the legal standards imposed by Directive 2008/50, and working towards the WHO AQG standards, the authorities had respected their obligations. The Tribunal stated that the 'treaty provisions do not require that the human rights protected by them always – by definition – take precedence over the other relevant interests': *Milieudefensie and Stichting Adem*, 2017, paras 4.85–4.86.

76 According to the Court of Cassation, the WHO guidelines may be used as a reference when national regulatory standards are missing: see *Belgian State v. A.T.*, supra, note 7, para. 74.

77 WHO, 'WHO guidelines: development and governance', supra, note 60, para. 5.

78 For illustration, when determining the maximum concentration for aluminium in drinking water, '[t]he Canadian guideline value differs from the WHO's health-based value because Canada takes into consideration advancements in science since 2010', while it stays consistent with the WHO Drinking Water Quality Guidelines for the maximum concentration for Escherichia coli in drinking water: WHO, *Guidelines for Drinking-water Quality*, 4th ed., 2017; Health Canada, *Guidelines for Canadian Drinking Water Quality, Technical Document on Aluminum iii*, 2021, and *Guideline Technical Document on Escherichia coli*, 2020.

Consumption.[79] Article 13 of the Directive establishes an obligation to consider WHO scientific research when updating the watch list of water pollutants endangering human health. The Directive also obliges the Commission to take WHO recommendations into account when evaluating the Directive in the future.[80] Regarding air quality, Recital 2 of the Ambient Air Quality Directive underlines the relevance of the 'World Health Organization standards, guidelines and programmes' when establishing 'appropriate' ambient air quality objectives. Even if EU lawmakers are not legally obliged to consult the WHO guidelines, they appear as an 'authority' to refer to when they are establishing *appropriate* legal air and water quality objectives. As with judges, the reliance on the guidelines relates to the guidelines' primary objective in aiming to respond to a need for guidance on health-related subjects.

Considering recent developments on the EU Air Quality Framework, it is interesting to further analyse how the guidelines and EU air quality law interact, as the non-binding guidelines tend to infuse the law and compulsory norms.

4. CASE STUDY: INTERACTIONS BETWEEN WHO AIR QUALITY GUIDELINES AND FUTURE EU AIR QUALITY LAW

References to the WHO 2021 Global Air Quality Guidelines (AQG), within the 2022 Proposal for a recast of the Directive on ambient air quality and cleaner air in Europe (the Proposal), are significant.[81] The Organization appears to have a special authority, derived from science and expertise reflected in the rigorous development process of the WHO AQG. The interaction between the AQG and the Proposal presents an interesting case study regarding the integration of non-binding guidelines within the lawmaking process.

---

79 Recitals 5, 6, 14, 15, 19, 29, 33 and 45 and Arts. 13 and 19 of the European Parliament and Council Directive (EU) 2020/2184 on the quality of water intended for human consumption, OJ 2020 L 435/1.

80 Art. 19, §4 of the Directive on the quality of water intended for human consumption, supra, note 79; please note that, regarding water, the WHO guidelines might not always be optimal and protective enough: E. Southerland and L.S. Birnbaum, 'What Limits Will the World Health Organization Recommend for PFOA and PFOS in Drinking Water?', *Environmental Science & Technology*, 2023 (57), pp. 7103–7105; World Health Organization. PFOS and PFOA in Drinking-water: Background document for development of WHO Guidelines for Drinking-water Quality, 2023, https://www.who.int/teams/ environment-climate-change-and-health/water-sanitation-and-health/chemical-hazards-in-drinking-water/per-and-polyfluoroalkylsubstances.

81 See proposed Recitals 2, 4, 5, 11, 15, 18 and 22 and suggested Arts. 3, 7, 8, 12 and 22 of the Proposal for a European Parliament and Council Directive on ambient air quality and cleaner air for Europe, supra, note 7.

4.1. EU AIR QUALITY LAW RECAST AND WHO AIR QUALITY GUIDELINES

Following the WHO's publication of updated air quality guidelines, in 2021, the European Commission announced, the same week, its intention to revise the 2008 Ambient Air Quality Directive, 'to align the EU air quality standards more closely with the new recommendations of the World Health Organization'.[82] The 2021 WHO Global Air Quality Guidelines seek to produce 'quantitative health-based recommendations for air quality management, expressed as long- or short-term concentrations for a number of key air pollutants',[83] namely particulate matter (PM2.5 and PM10), sulphur dioxide, nitrogen dioxide, carbon monoxide and ozone. These guidelines aim to 'provide WHO member states with an evidence-based tool that they can use to inform legislation and policy'.[84] The reduction of air pollution and related health burdens worldwide is the Guidelines' ultimate objective. The AQG establish, for each pollutant, levels above which adverse health impacts have been scientifically verified.[85] AQG levels are expressed with reference to long-term (on an annual basis or the highest six-month average) and/or short-term (24-hour) health effects.[86] The guidelines also contain good practice statements for certain types of pollutants that affect health, but where information is insufficient to issue AQG levels, namely ultrafine particles, black carbon or elemental carbon, and particles arising from sand and dust storms.[87]

The 2022 Proposal for a recast of the Directive on ambient air quality and cleaner air in Europe refers frequently to the recommendations of the 2021 WHO AQG. The close alignment with the WHO AQG is reiterated as the first objective of the revision, and the expertise of the WHO, amongst others, has been used in the proposal's development.[88] The standards suggested by the WHO AQG serve

---

82 WHO, *Global air quality guidelines*, supra, note 1; European Commission (DG Environment), 'European Green Deal: Commission launches public consultation for cleaner air', 23 September 2021, https://environment.ec.europa.eu/news/european-green-deal-commission-launches-public-consultation-cleaner-air-2021-09-23_en; this declaration comes from a previous commitment issued in the Green Deal – see Communication from the Commission to the European Parliament, the European Council, the Council, the European Economic and Social Committee and the Committee of the Regions on the European Green Deal, 11 December 2019, COM(2019) 640, p. 14.

83 WHO, *Global air quality guidelines*, supra, note 1, p. 3.

84 Ibid.

85 Ibid., pp. 32 and 59.

86 'Long-term effects were considered for all-cause and cause-specific mortality' and 'short-term effects were considered for all non-accidental and cause-specific mortality' (ibid., p. 74).

87 Proposal for a European Parliament and Council Directive on ambient air quality and cleaner air for Europe, supra, note 7, p. 4.

88 Ibid., pp. 3 and 7. At the time of the writing, the institutions have reached an agreement, not yet published, on the revision of the EU Ambient Air Quality Directive. If the standards

as a starting reference to propose updated air quality standards, applicable in the EU, for 2030. From a post-2030 perspective, the Proposal seeks to reach a full alignment with the guidelines, and aims to get 'on track toward alignment also with future WHO [g]uidelines'.[89]

The proposed Article 3 would require the Commission to review the scientific evidence of air pollution impacts on human health and the environment, considering, *inter alia*, the WHO AQG, and with a view to aligning with the related standards. Another significant reference to the AQG lies in the Proposal's assessment thresholds for air quality modelling and monitoring, set out in Annex II. These thresholds, identical to the WHO AQG standards, are to be used for the assessment of the concentrations of air pollutants (sulphur dioxide, nitrogen dioxide, particulate matter, carbon monoxide, and ozone in ambient air) in certain locations, as per the suggested Articles 7 and 8.

New air pollutants included in the WHO Guidelines' good practice statements are also included in the part of the Proposal that aims to introduce sampling points for new air pollutants of rising concern, including ultrafine particles and black carbon.[90] The significant references to the Guidelines, within the future EU air quality law, raise questions regarding the authority and production of the WHO guidelines. The next section, therefore, tries to understand the authority attached to the guidelines.

4.2. THE EPISTEMIC AUTHORITY OF THE WHO'S NON-BINDING INSTRUMENTS

The reliance on science, and the authority that emanates from the knowledge produced, is related to the WHO's epistemic authority. An epistemic authority refers to the idea that 'science as a virtual institution has the ability to provide true beliefs and to avoid false beliefs about … the topics of a discipline'.[91] International organisations may draw authority from experts' knowledge in a given domain, and produce documents relying on such technical and scientific expertise. International organisations that issue recommendations thus hold their legitimacy from the very technical and scientific knowledge upon which

are less protective than the one proposed by the WHO, revisions are planned with a view to aligning with the WHO AQG, see European Council, 'Air Quality: Council and Parliament Strike Deal to Strenghten Standards in the EU', 20 February 2020, https://www.consilium.europa.eu/en/press/press-releases/2024/02/20/air-quality-council-and-parliament-strike-deal-to-strengthen-standards-in-the-eu/.

89 Ibid., p. 8 and proposed Recital 4.

90 Ibid., proposed Recital 11 and Art. 10.

91 R. Bromme, R. Jucks and D. Kienhues, 'Sealing the gateways for post-truthism: Reestablishing the epistemic authority of science', *Educational Psychologist*, 2020 (55), p. 144.

their decisions are based.[92] Hence, they may utilise experts' knowledge to confer an epistemic authority on their decisions.[93]

The WHO relies on experts and science to inform and guide policy, and draw legitimacy and authority. As reflected in the WHO Constitution, the organisation was created to exercise its authority through technical expertise.[94] Under Article 2 of the WHO Constitution, the Organization's functions include furnishing 'appropriate technical assistance', establishing 'administrative and technical services', and promoting 'cooperation among scientific and professional groups'. Additionally, the *WHO Handbook for Guideline Development* recognises that the 'WHO's legitimacy and technical authority' lie in 'its rigorous adherence to the systematic use of evidence as the basis for all policies'.[95] Expertise may, hence, be 'conceptualised ... as a resource available for [international organisations] to enhance their input and output legitimacy'.[96]

In line with its purpose, the WHO nurtures a self-image that depicts the Organization as science-based, with science being central to every action it takes.[97] Most of the WHO's work is devoted to non-legal instruments,[98] and considering that the WHO's main activity to fulfil its leadership on health takes the form of guidelines,[99] the authority of these instruments must be analysed in light of their epistemic power. The guidelines' authority may rely on, or be exercised on the basis of, epistemic elements: knowledge and science. According to Klabbers, this 'knowledge informs policy-making which in turn gets translated into proper, generally recognized legal instruments: conventions, resolutions, declarations'.[100]

For illustration, Article 3 of the Proposal for the new Ambient Air Quality Directive would establish an obligation to review the Directive with the

---

92 C. Boswell, 'The Role of Expert Knowledge in International Organizations' in A. Littoz-Monnet (ed.), *The Politics of Expertise in International Organizations*, Routledge, 2017, p. 31.

93 A. Littoz-Monnet, *The Politics of Expertise in International Organizations*, Routledge, 2017, p. 7.

94 Gruszczynski and Melillo, supra, note 46, p. 6.

95 WHO, *Handbook for Guideline Development*, supra, note 56, p. 1.

96 M. Louis and L. Maertens, *Why International Organizations Hate Politics: Depoliticizing the World*, Routledge, 2021, p. 4.

97 In the WHO's Thirteenth General Programme of Work for 2019–2023, the WHO's status is described 'as a science- and evidence-based organisation that sets globally applicable norms and standards ... vital in a rapidly changing world': WHO, 'Thirteenth General Programme of Work 2019–2023', 2018, WHO/PRP/18.1, 3.

98 E. Granziera and R. Koskenmäki, 'L'Organisation Mondiale de la Santé' in J.-M. Thouvenin and A. Trebilcock (eds.), *Le Droit International Social*, Routledge, 2013, p. 294.

99 According to the WHO, the 'Guidelines are the fundamental means through which the Organisation fulfils its technical leadership in health': WHO, *Handbook for Guideline Development*, supra, note 56, p. 1.

100 J. Klabbers, 'The Normative Gap in International Organizations Law: The Case of the World Health Organization', *International Organization Law Review*, 2019 (272), p. 279; for an

objective of aligning 'the World Health Organization … Air Quality Guidelines and the latest scientific information', while the 'latest scientific information from WHO' would feature in the review. The perception of WHO guidelines' authority affects EU Member States' reliance on the guidelines, since they seem to acquire the status of a scientific reference, for the purposes of law revision. Yet, the guidelines are not solely based on technical expertise; they also seek to offer policy guidance. The rigorous development process of the AQG may help understand the important role played by science, and how it reinforces the Organisation's legitimacy and (epistemic) authority.

4.3. WHO AIR QUALITY GUIDELINES: DEVELOPMENT PROCESS, SCIENCE AND LAW

The 2021 WHO AQG are an update of previous AQG, published in 2005.[101] The rigorous procedure applied to the 2021 AQG, following the *Handbook for Guideline Development*, and the development process explained transparently in a full chapter thereof, illustrates the WHO's need for legitimacy,[102] as an organisation that produces science. Taking into consideration the substantial scientific studies strengthening the evidence base for key air pollutants, the scientific community, echoed by WHO Member States, called for 'updated air quality guidelines in 2015, recognizing their utility as an effective instrument to help decision makers confront the air pollution problem'.[103] In line with the *Handbook for Guideline Development*, the AQG revision followed a five-step process, enabled by groups of individuals tasked with well-defined roles.[104]

The WHO steering group comprised WHO staff members with relevant expertise in air quality, and they intervened at different stages of the process, including planning guidelines, selecting other groups, evaluating evidence, drafting recommendations, and managing peer review.[105] Selected by the WHO steering group, the Guideline Development Group (GDG) was composed of experts chosen for their technical skills, and on the basis of their geographical

illustration of the WHO 'as a norm-setter even when it has not meant to take on this role', see Klock, supra, note 33, p. 838.

101 WHO, *Air Quality Guidelines: Global Update*, WHO, 2005.

102 P.E. Alexander et al., 'World Health Organization recommendations are often strong based on low confidence in effect estimates', *Journal of Clinical Epidemiology*, 2014 (67), p. 630.

103 R. Pérez and D. Jarosińska, 'Update of the WHO global air quality guidelines: Systematic reviews – An introduction', *Environment International*, 2022 (170), p. 2; WHO (Plenary Meeting of the World Health Assembly), 'Health and the environment: addressing the health impact of air pollution', 2015, WHA68.8.

104 WHO, *Global air quality guidelines*, supra, note 1, p. 26; WHO, *Handbook for Guideline Development*, supra, note 56.

105 WHO, *Global air quality guidelines*, supra, note 1, p. 27.

locations, as necessary for the development of global guidelines. It evaluated the evidence, formulated recommendations, assisted in the guidelines' scope determination, defined key review questions, and chose the critical health results.[106] Formed of experts in environmental and clinical epidemiology, selected on the basis of their publications and their fields of expertise, the Systematic Review Team led the systematic review of evidence, to inform the recommendations.[107] Finally, the External Review Group was composed of technical experts, chosen on the basis of their expertise, gender and geographical origins, and stakeholder representatives (including patient organisations, environmental non-governmental organisations, industry coalitions and scientific organisations). Its missions consisted of providing information on precise topics, evaluating and translating scientific articles, peer-reviewing the evidence base, and giving inputs on the draft guidelines.[108]

Annex I of the WHO AQG identifies the experts and stakeholders, and specifies their positions, affiliations or departments, whereas Annex II sets out the experts' declared interests. The identification of declared interests seeks to avoid conflicts of interest, as the WHO considers that these 'can undermine the credibility of a guideline'.[109]

The guideline development procedure is divided into five stages, in line with a rigorous process. First, the scope of the guidelines and review questions is determined. This stage was critical as it determined the air pollutants that required attention, and identified their related health effects, in terms of duration and exposure.[110] For the 2021 AQG, experts identified 32 air pollutants of relative importance, but, considering the resources available, the GDG gave priority to particulate matter (PM2.5 and PM10), sulphur dioxide, nitrogen dioxide, carbon monoxide and ozone, in establishing air quality levels. Due to insufficient clear quantitative evidence on health effects, the GDG elaborated good practice statements for black and elemental carbon, sand and dust storms, and ultrafine particles.[111] Finally, it defined questions to retrieve evidence necessary for the development of appropriate AQG levels.

Second, to address these questions, the Systematic Review Team reviewed and synthesised air quality and health systematic reviews existing in the scientific

---

106 Ibid., p. 28.

107 Ibid.

108 In addition, the Methodological Working Group was an *ad hoc* group that adapted the systematic review methods and the guidelines adoption process to the air quality and health field. It was composed of the methodologist that established the risks of bias, and other experts: WHO, *Global air quality guidelines*, supra, note 1, pp. 28–29.

109 Ibid., p. 29; A full chapter of the *Handbook for Guideline Development* is devoted to conflict of interest management: '[t]he declaration and management of conflicts of interest is essential to the development of unbiased and credible recommendations and guidelines', WHO, *Handbook for Guideline Development*, supra, note 56, p. 97.

110 WHO, *Global air quality guidelines*, supra, note 1, p. 30.

111 Ibid., p. 32.

literature. Two reviewers independently analysed the papers' content to ensure the criteria of the questions are met. Should these reviewers disagree, a third reviewer would assist them in resolving the discussion. The reviewers also take into consideration the studies' risks of bias.[112]

Third, the certainty level of the body of evidence derived from the systematic reviews was determined.[113] The working group assessed studies with moderate to high certainty of evidence, based on the Grading of Recommendations Assessment, Development and Evaluation (GRADE) approach.[114] Followed by many other organisations,[115] 'GRADE is an explicit, comprehensive, transparent, and pragmatic approach to guideline development that … provides detailed guidance on how to rate the confidence in estimates of effect (quality of evidence) and how to develop recommendations based on evidence'.[116] It gives information on the quality and the reliability of the review. For the AQG, moderate and high evidence form the basis on which panelists make strong recommendations. The evidence rating is important because lawmakers or policymakers who 'view WHO guidelines as authoritative' rely on strong recommendations to establish policies and laws.[117] If strong recommendations were based on low confidence in effect, they 'may feel that, in the face of such strong recommendations, they should put aside concern that the recommendation may not be optimal,'[118] and adopt policies or laws based on uncertainty.

Fourth, the GDG formulated appropriate air quality levels, based on epidemiological evidence. Long-term air quality guideline levels are 'the lowest exposure level of an air pollutant above which the GDG is confident that there

---

112 Ibid., p. 54.

113 Ibid., pp. 55–58.

114 The GRADE approach was adapted to include other criteria: see WHO (Working Group on Certainty of Evidence Assessment), 'Approach to assessing the certainty of evidence from systematic reviews informing WHO global air quality guidelines', WHO, 2020. Please note that the appropriateness of the use of GRADE by guidelines panellists was criticised in 2014 and 2016 studies, based on guidelines from 2007 to 2012, before the publication of the second *WHO Handbook for Guideline Development*: Alexander et al., 'World Health Organization recommendations are often strong based on low confidence in effect estimates', supra, note 102, p. 633, and P.E. Alexander et al., 'World Health Organization strong recommendations based on low-quality evidence (study quality) are frequent and often inconsistent with GRADE guidance', *Journal of Clinical Epidemiology*, 2016 (67), p. 99.

115 GRADE Working Group, https://www.gradeworkinggroup.org.

116 'GRADE does not seek to eliminate subjective judgments – such judgments are an inevitable part of rating evidence and making or grading recommendations – but rather to make judgments transparent and explicit': P.E. Alexander et al., 'World Health Organization strong recommendations based on low-quality evidence (study quality) are frequent and often inconsistent with GRADE guidance', supra, note 114, p. 99.

117 'When guideline panelists make strong recommendations, they are suggesting that front line decision makers need not consider the issue any further and should simply implement the suggested course of action', ibid., pp. 103–104.

118 Ibid., pp. 103–104.

is an increase in adverse health effects'.[119] Considering the current scientific knowledge cautiously, the GDG estimated that these levels are not thresholds below which there is *no* effect: they are levels below 'which there is less certainty of the existence of an effect'.[120] Short-term guideline levels are a high percentile of daily value distribution, equivalent to a few days a year exceeding this value. The short-term levels identify peaks of pollution that may harm specific groups, such as asthmatics or coronary disease heart patients.[121]

The last step concerned the establishment of interim targets and good practice statements. Interim targets seek to permit air quality ameliorations, in locations where air pollution levels are high, as a step towards achieving AQG levels.[122] Good practice statements provide guidance for pollutants considered harmful to health, but where there is a lack of clear quantitative evidence for this.[123]

The development process of the guidelines followed a well-determined procedure that clearly identified groups of actors and the different stages of creation, in accordance with the *WHO Handbook for Guideline Development*. In light of the development process, the 2021 WHO AQG are the product of scientific standards based on published relevant articles selected by experts in relevant scientific fields. Yet, the guidelines are not solely a reflection of scientific systematic reviews; they also include political aspects. Indeed, the call for updated AQG was not only a demand from the scientific community, but was also from WHO Member States. The formulation of long-term AQG levels was equally affected by scientific and political considerations. When establishing a threshold above which the 'GDG is confident that there is at least moderate certainty evidence for adverse health effects',[124] the GDG avoided the double uncertainty of political and scientific concerns. On the one hand, the formulation of 'accepted levels of risk' could contravene national air quality legislation that does not accept the adverse health effects of air pollution, such as the US National Ambient Air Quality Standards.[125] On the other hand, the GDG wanted to avoid creating a 'safe' level of exposure, since the available scientific evidence cannot identify exposure levels that are free of risk.[126]

---

119 WHO, *Global air quality guidelines*, supra, note 1, p. 59.
120 Ibid., p. 64.
121 Ibid., p. 66.
122 Ibid., p. 70.
123 Ibid., p. 71.
124 Ibid., p. 59.
125 Ibid., p. 60; 'Any national secondary ambient air quality standard prescribed under subsection (a) shall specify a level of air quality the attainment and maintenance of which in the judgment of the Administrator, based on such criteria, is requisite to *protect* the public welfare *from any known or anticipated* adverse effects associated with the presence of such air pollutant in the ambient air' (US National primary and secondary ambient air quality standards, 42 U.S.C. 70409(a)).
126 WHO, *Global air quality guidelines*, supra, note 1, p. 60.

More generally, non-binding instruments, including guidelines, are the most successful activity of the WHO because their flexibility responds to the same two uncertainties. The first uncertainty concerns the absence of political consensus. It is easier to negotiate non-compulsory agreements with Member States, since, in the absence of obligations, they are more likely to agree with higher norms.[127] Second, with science evolving, there is a need for the guidelines to adapt rapidly to the evolution of the scientific consensus. As explained by Kastler, producing binding instruments would enable stronger compliance, yet, practically, it would also burden the adoption procedures, and hence slow the WHO's response to ongoing health issues.[128] The guidelines are a hybrid instrument at the interface of pure scientific recommendations and political advice, with sufficient flexibility to adapt easily to the constraints of each area.

The WHO has epistemic authority, and seems to be seen as a scientific reference, as illustrated above in relation to the proposed Articles 3, 7 and 8 of the recast Ambient Air Quality Directives. It should not, however, relieve policymakers and lawmakers from questioning the guidelines' adoption process, especially since they are not a reflection of pure science, and could influence the future EU air quality law. In this case study, the WHO took a full book chapter to explain the development process, and how it adapted its approach to the specific field of air quality. This well-elaborated and transparent WHO AQG development process should provide strong confidence in the guidelines' legitimacy.

5. CONCLUSION

The WHO's main normative activity is devoted to its non-binding powers, due to the organisation's historical position, the flexibility offered by non-binding instruments, and the technical advice the WHO produces. Extending its non-binding powers, the WHO also issues guidelines that go beyond technical expertise, as they might also inform judges, lawmakers and policymakers.

In the Proposal for a recast of the Directive on ambient air quality and cleaner air in Europe, the WHO guidelines' authority does not seem to be questioned, as EU Member States aim to align with future – not yet produced – WHO guidelines. The non-binding guidelines could, however, have significant influence, since they lie at the origin of the recast, and are frequently mentioned not only in its preamble, but also within Articles imposing consultation of the WHO AQG in relation to future reviews, or assessment of air quality each time

127 Nevertheless, being of a non-compulsory nature, governments 'can largely ignore' the guidelines and refuse to apply the standards: Gostin and Sridhar, supra, note 69, p. 1739.

128 Kastler, supra, note 34, p. 752.

AQG levels are exceeded. EU lawmakers' reliance on the WHO seems to be based on the scientific information provided by the organisation (illustrated in the proposed Article 3 of the Proposal), and the epistemic authority that emanates from it.

However, the AQG are not exempt from political influence, and the WHO does not shy away from the political aspects, since the guidelines include, within their objectives, the information and guidance for lawmakers and policymakers.[129] The AQG also follow a rigorous development process, governed by the *Handbook for Guideline Development*, which seems transparent, disclosing experts' names, declared interests and institutions. In addition, the use of moderate to high certainty of evidence during the scientific literature review, by two independent scientists, with a third one to resolve any conflicts of view emerging, and the disclosure of potential conflicts of interest, also show the technicity and legitimacy of the evidence.

On first analysis, it seems that, thanks to their epistemic authority, based on knowledge and science, the guidelines are to be used as a reference for EU lawmakers in the establishment of recast Ambient Air Quality Directives. Considering the role played by the WHO guidelines in the Proposal, and the political aspect of the guidelines, the EU lawmaker could better discuss the development process and the certainty of the guidelines' recommendations, during the creation of the law. Briefly explaining the reliance on WHO guidelines in the preparatory work could be a first step, especially given the rigorous procedure, seriousness and transparency of the guidelines' development process.

---

129 WHO, *Global air quality guidelines*, supra, note 1, p. 3.

EU AIR QUALITY AND VEHICLES

An Incompatible Pair?

Jiri Vodicka

ABSTRACT

Despite the current emphasis on climate change, the air quality is still subpar or insufficient in many parts of Europe. The primary source of air pollution in cities is vehicle emissions. Although some communities have sought to impose car restrictions to enhance air quality, recent legal arguments and instances of non-compliance have demonstrated how challenging such restrictions are to implement. Further complicating the situation, and limiting the options open to municipalities and Member States, is a recent Court of Justice of the European Union (CJEU) case *Ville de Paris and Others*.[1] To improve air quality, it has become necessary to strike a balance between legal responsibilities and political choices. This chapter's objective is to examine the tools that the current European Union (EU) air quality legislation (Directive 2008/50) provides

1 Judgment of the Court (Fifth Chamber) of 13 January 2022, C-177/19 P, *Ville de Paris and Others*.

to regulate vehicles, and the degree to which local governments can impose restrictions on vehicles without violating the Vehicle Type-approval Regulation (Regulation 2018/858).

1. INTRODUCTION

Air quality has a direct impact on human health. This relationship has already been analysed in tens of scientific studies, and is still being studied. The adverse effects of polluted air can contribute to neurodegenerative diseases, cancer, high blood pressure, diabetes and premature deaths, and even lower IQs.[2] According to the World Health Organization (WHO)'s air quality standards, which were introduced in 2005, almost 90 per cent of the world's population, in 2019, lived in areas with inadequate air quality.[3] Additionally, the WHO, in 2021, introduced new, stricter quality standards that aim to protect human health.[4]

The current European Union (EU) air quality legislation (Directive 2008/50 on ambient air quality and cleaner air for Europe[5] (AQD)) has been in effect for about 15 years, has helped to reduce emissions of several air pollutants, and has, in general, increased air quality.[6] Despite this, exceedances of limit values of air pollutants still pose a significant problem for EU Member States. Currently, the most problematic air pollutants (according to infringement proceedings under Article 258 of the Treaty on the Functioning of the European Union (TFEU)) are nitrogen dioxide and soot particles (PM10).[7] These pollutants can be attributed to several sectoral sources, and among these, the most significant is the transport sector.[8]

The transport sector accounts for about a minimum of 10 per cent of all emissions in the EU.[9] Therefore, reduction of air pollutants is vital if the Member

---

2 I. Manisalidis et al., 'Environmental and Health Impacts of Air Pollution: A Review', *Frontiers in Public Health*, 2020(8). p. 1.

3 World Health Organization, 'New WHO Global Air Quality Guidelines aim to save millions of lives from air pollution', 22 September 2021, https://www.who.int/news/item/22-09-2021-new-who-global-air-quality-guidelines-aim-to-save-millions-of-lives-from-air-pollution.

4 Ibid.

5 Directive 2008/50/EC of the European Parliament and of the Council of 21 May 2008 on ambient air quality and cleaner air for Europe, OJ 2008 L 152.

6 European Environment Agency, 'National air pollutant emissions data viewer 2005–2020', https://www.eea.europa.eu/data-and-maps/dashboards/necd-directive-data-viewer-6.

7 According to the European Commission's infringement database: https://ec.europa.eu/atwork/applying-eu-law/infringements-proceedings/infringement_decisions/index.cfm?lang_code=EN&typeOfSearch=true&active_only=1&noncom=0&r_dossier=&decision_date_from=&decision_date_to=&DG=ENV&title=air&submit=Search.

8 Even though air pollutants have decreased significantly in the transport sector, since 1990: European Environment Agency, 'Emissions of air pollutants from transport', https://www.eea.europa.eu/data-and-maps/indicators/transport-emissions-of-air-pollutants-8/transport-emissions-of-air-pollutants-8.

9 Ibid.

States are to reach ambient air quality. The urgent need to reduce air pollution is being further bolstered by the current revision of Directive 2008/50, and the subsequent introduction of a proposal that promises new and stricter air pollution limits.[10]

It might be said that the need to lower air pollutants to reduce negative impacts on health, and avoid infringement proceedings, constitutes a solid incentive for Member States to actively seek solutions within their own and the EU's legal frameworks, to reduce air pollutants. However, even if the Member State is active in this field, other obstacles may arise, making the implementation of efficient measures nearly impossible. This is also the case for limiting air pollutants from the transport sector, especially from vehicles, because they are primarily subjected to legislation other than AQD. This specific regulation of vehicles can hinder any attempt to limit vehicles as sources of air pollutants.

The chapter aims to ascertain whether the current EU air quality legislation (mainly Directive 2008/50) offers instruments to regulate vehicles (and improve air quality and protect human health), and how much local authorities can restrict vehicles without infringing any provisions in Regulation 2018/858 (Vehicle Type-approval Regulation),[11] as was partially shown in case *Ville de Paris and Others*. In other words, the chapter shows synergies and discords between the AQD and type-approval legislation.

This chapter is divided into several sections. The first section focuses on determining whether Directive 2008/50 contains relevant instruments (and provisions) that could be used to regulate vehicles, and thus their emissions, which would be beneficial to air quality.

The second section of the chapter introduces Regulation 2018/858 and Regulation No. 715/2007,[12] and considers whether these Regulations contain any instruments to regulate traffic (vehicles) and curb possible inadequate air quality in urban areas. However, the analysis of the Regulations is not comprehensive, and focuses only on relevant principal (environmental) provisions. Furthermore, the analysis provides a basic framework for subsequent examination of case law.

The third section of the chapter looks for possible synergies and obstacles arising between Directive 2008/50 and type-approval legislation. The section

---

10 European Commission, 'Air quality – revision of EU rules', https://ec.europa.eu/info/law/better-regulation/have-your-say/initiatives/12677-Air-quality-revision-of-EU-rules_en.

11 Regulation (EU) 2018/858 of the European Parliament and of the Council of 30 May 2018 on the approval and market surveillance of motor vehicles and their trailers, and of systems, components and separate technical units intended for such vehicles, amending Regulations (EC) No. 715/2007 and (EC) No. 595/2009 and repealing Directive 2007/46/EC, OJ 2018 L 151.

12 Regulation (EC) No. 715/2007 of the European Parliament and of the Council of 20 June 2007 on type approval of motor vehicles with respect to emissions from light passenger and commercial vehicles (Euro 5 and Euro 6) and on access to vehicle repair and maintenance information, OJ 2007 L 171.

focuses primarily on the case law of the Court of Justice of the European Union (CJEU) that has interpreted the legislation (such as *Ville de Paris and Others* case, and the preceding decision of the General Court (*Ville de Paris v. Commission*)[13] and the Opinion of Advocate General Bobek).

2. DIRECTIVE 2008/50 AND RELEVANT INSTRUMENTS

The main question is whether the Directive contains provisions that could be used directly to limit or regulate vehicles, to improve air quality, or whether other mechanisms or instruments could be used instead.

The Directive mentions vehicles in Article 24(2), on short-term action plans. The Directive states only that one of the measures adopted under a short-term action plan can be the suspension of motor-vehicle traffic, providing that it is an activity contributing to the exceedance of limits. The provision does not suggest or list specific measures connected with traffic restriction.

However, one must look into the previous paragraph of Article 24, because short-term action plans do not have to be drawn up. Member States enjoy quite a large margin of appreciation when drawing up short-term action plans. The Directive states that Member States have to draw up these plans if there is a risk that the levels of pollutants will exceed one or more of the alert thresholds specified in Annex XII.[14] On the other hand, if there is no such risk (this can be proved by air quality monitoring), Member States do not have to draw up short-term action plans.[15] For example, the legal code of the Czech Republic does not contain such an instrument. However, the Czech Air Protection Act contains a similar instrument, on the smog situation, which is similar to short-term action plans, but with particular distinctions.[16]

Other provisions directly referring to vehicles, traffic or transport can be found in the Annexes of the Directive. Nevertheless, these provisions mostly stipulate conditions and requirements for the assessment of ambient air quality, and sampling points for various air pollutants.[17]

---

13 Judgment of the general court (Ninth Chamber, Extended Composition) of 13 December 2018, T-339/16, *Ville de Paris v. Commission*.

14 Art. 24(1) of Directive 2008/50/EC of the European Parliament and of the Council of 21 May 2008 on ambient air quality and cleaner air for Europe, OJ 2008 L 152.

15 Although under the CJEU Case C-237/07, *Janecek*, of 25 July 2008, Member States should be prepared to draw up action plans if there are persons directly concerned by possibility of exceedances: K. Pedrosa and B. Vanheusden, 'EU Air Pollution Law: Comprehensive but Insufficient' in M. Peeters and M. Eliantonio (eds.), *Research Handbook on EU Environmental Law*, Edward Elgar Publishing, 2020, pp. 309–310.

16 S. 10 of Act No. 201/2012 Coll. on Air Protection.

17 Annexes I, III, IV, V and VIII of Directive 2008/50.

The unexpressed possibility to limit traffic can be inferred from Article 23, on air quality plans. The differences between measures adopted under Article 24 and Article 23 lie in their urgency and aims. Article 24 aims at measures that can be adopted in the short term, and thus temporarily reduce exceedances, whereas Article 23 aims for the time period of exceedances of limit values to be as short as possible, and therefore the measures do not have to be as strict and draconian. Even though Article 23 does not contain specific measures to restrict vehicles or traffic, Member States usually adopt some measures restricting traffic, under their national air quality plans. Therefore, it is up to the Member States and local authorities to develop measures that are effective enough to lower or limit exceedances caused by the transport sector.

On the other hand, the provision has to be read in accordance with Annex XV. The Annex stipulates an obligation to include, *inter alia*, information about the origin of pollution (including traffic), details of those factors responsible for the exceedance (vehicles), and details of possible measures for the improvement of air quality.[18] Thus, the Annex does not provide any specific suggestions about possible measures in air quality plans, but only sets an obligation to provide information.

Even though it contains only a few mentions of vehicles or traffic or transport, this does not necessarily mean that Directive does not influence the Member States and their traffic regulation. The Directive's limits and thresholds for air pollutants can be identified as indirect tools through which Member States ought to limit air pollutants to achieve ambient air quality. In other words, to prevent exceeding defined values of air pollutants (stipulated in the Directive), the Member State has to introduce measures that are effective, and these measures can, *inter alia*, be aimed at traffic.[19] Thus, regulation of certain polluting activities does not have to be explicitly stipulated in the Directive, because it sets only the general aim of air quality, and leaves room for Member States to choose the most suitable regulation methods. The method can vary from Member State to Member State: a state can introduce low- or zero-emission zones, introduce an access toll/congestion charge, create an emergency air pollution scheme, or introduce incentives for buying new vehicles.[20]

---

18 Ibid., Annex XV, Section A, (5) and (6).

19 Judgment of the Court (Grand Chamber) of 10 November 2020, C-644/18, *Commission v. Italy*, ECLI:EU:C:2020:895; Judgment of the Court (Tenth Chamber) of 28 April 2022, C-286/21, *Commission v. France*, ECLI:EU:C:2022:319.

20 Urban Access Regulations in Europe, 'What are Urban Vehicle Access Regulations (UVARs)?', https://urbanaccessregulations.eu/userhome/what-are-access-regulations-uvars-or-urban-vehicle-access-regulations.

3. A BRIEF INTRODUCTION TO VEHICLE EMISSION REGULATIONS

As vehicles are a dominant pollution source in cities, one must look at legislation other than the AQD to ascertain whether vehicle emission footprints can be regulated differently, or via different legislation. A possible solution is to ascertain whether technical legislation (type-approval legislation) protects the environment as a whole or only some parts of it (for example, air and water), and whether there is a relationship between type-approval legislation and the AQD.

First, it must be stated that the overall aim of type-approval legislation is not the protection of air quality (or the environment); the main aim of such legislation is to harmonise technical requirements within the EU, to allow for the free movement of goods. This was particularly distinct in previous type-approval legislation (namely Directive 2007/46).[21] However, the current shift in society is towards higher environmental protection, and Regulation 2018/858 has put more emphasis on environmental protection. Nevertheless, it must be noted that protecting the environment (and air quality) is still mainly a secondary aim of the legislation.

3.1. REGULATION 2018/858

Regulation 2018/858 forms a basis for a process known as a type-approval procedure, i.e. a procedure in which goods have to be tested as to whether they fulfil legal-technical requirements set in EU law to be allowed to enter the internal market. Specific technical requirements are set in regulatory Acts, such as Regulation No. 715/2007 (Euro 5 and 6).

According to the Recitals,[22] environmental protection is one of the Regulation's aims. This is embodied in several provisions that, to some extent, protect the environment in various ways. An example of such a provision could be a safeguard clause under Article 51, because if it is believed of a vehicle that it 'presents a serious risk to the health or safety of persons or to other aspects of the protection of public interests covered by [Regulation 2018/858] or does not comply with the requirements laid down in [Regulation 2018/858]', the relevant authority can adopt a corrective or restrictive measure. Even though the protection of the environment is not expressly stated, it can be inferred, *inter*

---

21 Directive 2007/46/EC of the European Parliament and of the Council of 5 September 2007 establishing a framework for the approval of motor vehicles and their trailers, and of systems, components and separate technical units intended for such vehicles (Framework Directive), OJ 2007 L 263.

22 E.g. Recitals 5–11 of Regulation 2018/858.

alia, from the recitals, Article 5 (technical requirements), Article 13 (general obligations of manufacturers), Article 53(2)(a), and regulatory Acts (Annex II), that the protection of the environment is protected by public interest under Regulation 2018/858.

A provision that could have a substantial environmental impact would be a provision concerning *defeat devices*. These devices alter a vehicle's behaviour, to allow it to pass the type-approval laboratory tests. If the devices tamper with the vehicle's emissions systems,[23] their use can have an adverse effect on local air quality and human health. Regulation 2018/858 does not explicitly ban these devices. However, Article 13(5) contains a general ban on 'vehicles, systems, components and separate technical units ... designed to incorporate strategies or other means that alter the performance exhibited during test procedures in such a way that they do not comply with [Regulation 2018/858] when operating under conditions that can reasonably be expected in normal operation'. The use of such devices could also be caught under a broader category stated in Article 84(2)(a) of the Regulation. For specific bans, regulatory Acts have to be analysed.

3.2. REGULATION NO. 715/2007 (EURO 5 AND 6) AND IMPLEMENTING ACTS

Regulation No. 715/2007 sets specific requirements during the type-approval procedure. It defines specific steps that must be undertaken, and pollutant limits that cannot be exceeded, during the type-approval procedure: so-called Euro emission norms. It should be noted that the Regulation is further implemented by Commission regulations that contain particularities.

Even though the Regulation does not explicitly mention ambient air quality or Directive 2008/50, it contains references to air quality in its recitals (as a part of the Clean Air for Europe programme), and suggests that EU air quality objectives are also the aims of the Regulation.[24]

Within the text of the Regulation, there are no references to ambient air quality. However, it contains definitions of environmentally friendly technologies, for example a hybrid vehicle,[25] alternative fuel vehicle,[26] and biofuels,[27] that have an impact on air quality, as well as a definition of *defeat device*,[28] and, under Article 5(2), a general ban on the use of such a device. The issue here is that the provision also contains exemptions, i.e. specific situations in which a defeat

23 As in Volkswagen's 'dieselgate' scandal.
24 Recitals 4–6 of Regulation No. 715/2007.
25 Ibid., Art. 3(1).
26 Ibid., Art. 3(17).
27 Ibid., Art. 3(16).
28 Ibid., Art. 3(10).

device can be used.[29] It must be reiterated that the unregulated use of exemptions may have an adverse effect on local air quality.

The Regulation also allows Member States to provide financial incentives. Incentives can be applied for selling new vehicles that comply with emission limits, retrofitting in-use vehicles with new technology to comply with the Regulation, and scrapping vehicles that do not comply with the Regulation. Even though the provision mainly aims at the renewal of car fleets (and, in a sense, causes more sales of cars and helps manufacturers), it can help to boost sales of new, more environmentally friendly vehicles, and increase the protection of the environment (and local air quality).

4. SYNERGIES AND DISCORDS

The main question is whether any synergies exist between the analysed pieces of legislation. The analysis conducted above showed that ambient air quality legislation and type-approval legislation have different primary aims, even though a few provisions can be found in type-approval legislation that should protect the environment. Other differences between these pieces of legislation can be found in their legal forms (directive and regulation) and addressees (directives address only Member States, whereas regulations address a large group of entities and undertakings).

However, one synergy can be found in thresholds and limits set for specific air pollutants. Under the Directive 2008/50, regulated and measured or assessed air pollutants are NO_2, NO_X, PM10, PM2.5, Pb, benzene, CO, O_3, and SO_2,[30] whereas, under the Type-approval Regulation, regulated (measured) air pollutants are CO, NO_X, PM (mass of particulate matter), PN (number of particles), NMHC (mass of non-methane hydrocarbons), THC (mass of total hydrocarbons), and THC + NO_X.

From the list above, it can be noticed that several of the air pollutants covered by the Directive and the Regulation are the same: NO_X, CO, and PM. Does this mean there is a synergy in their ways of regulating them? The answer is no, because both pieces of legislation are aimed at different addressees, and coexist with each other. The instruments through which the air pollutants are regulated are different, with different aims.

However, analysing both pieces of legislation in more detail, some faint connections can be inferred, especially in connection with air quality plans (Article 23 of the Directive 2008/50). According to Directive, Member States shall adopt measures that curb air pollution. The Directive does not specify

29 Ibid., Art. 5(2).
30 Art. 5(1) of Directive 2008/50.

measures, but one of the most efficient ways to increase air quality is to adopt some kind of traffic restrictions, in the form of low-emission zones or urban road tolls.[31] Specific requirements set under the adopted measures can be linked to Euro emission norms. For example, the entrance into low-emission zones can be conditional on the type-approved Euro emission norm of the vehicle.

Therefore, it can be concluded that a small synergy is present in this sense. However, the relationship between these pieces of legislation is not as straightforward as it would seem, as was shown in cases *Ville de Paris v. Commission* and *Ville de Paris and Others*, analysed below.

4.1. CASE LAW: TYPE-APPROVAL AND THE AQD

4.1.1. Ville de Paris v. Commission[32]

Even though this judgment concerns the interpretation of Directive 2007/46 (the preceding legislative Act to Regulation 2018/858), the conclusions drawn also apply to the current legislation. The judgment of the General Court[33] is a significant ruling for two reasons: the first reason is the admissibility of the actions for annulment, and the second concerns a direct connection to vehicle emissions regulation.

The admissibility issue is due to the fact that the applicants were municipalities that needed to meet the criteria stated in the fourth paragraph of Article 263 TFEU: 'any … legal person may … institute proceedings against an act addressed to that person or which is of direct and individual concern to them, and against a regulatory act which is of direct concern to them and does not entail implementing measures'.

The first requirement of Article 263 TFEU is a regulatory Act. This requirement was fulfilled, since the legislative Act (Commission regulation) in question was adopted based on Regulation No. 715/2007.[34]

The second requirement is connected to the applicability of the legal Act, i.e. that the Act does not need any implementing measure. The contested legislative Act did not require any implementation, since it was a Commission regulation based on Regulation No. 715/2007.[35]

---

31 See Urban Access Regulations in Europe, https://urbanaccessregulations.eu/.

32 This section is inspired by Chapter 4 of author's book, *Vehicle Type-approval and Emission Regulation in the EU: Environmental Perspective* (in publishing process).

33 Judgment of the General Court (Ninth Chamber, Extended Composition) of 13 December 2018, Joined Cases T-339/16, T-352/16 and T-391/16, *Ville de Paris, Ville de Bruxelles and Ayuntamiento de Madrid v. European Commission*, ECLI:EU:T:2018:927.

34 Ibid., para. 38.

35 Ibid., para. 40.

The third criterion requires the Act to be of direct concern to applicants (this provision can be further explained as directly affecting the applicant's legal situation, and leaving no discretion to implement the Act).[36] The Court analysed Article 4(3) of Directive 2007/46 because the Commission argued that this provision left discretion to national authorities to limit or restrict vehicles, and thus this requirement was not satisfied. The term in question that had to be interpreted was 'circulation on the road of vehicles'.

According to the Court's interpretation, infra-state bodies cannot impose restrictions on vehicle circulation if vehicles comply with the emission limits of the regulation that is in force.[37] Based on the Court's interpretation, such restrictions could violate the free movement of goods.[38] Furthermore, the Court stated that the provision could not be limited in essence, i.e. a possible restriction on the use of vehicles would impede legal certainty and practical usage of vehicles (drivers would not know whether they could use their vehicles normally).[39] The Court highlighted that the intended use of a vehicle (or goods) cannot be opposed if the product satisfies harmonised requirements, otherwise the practicality of such harmonisation would be in vain.[40]

The Court stated that the infra-state bodies could restrict the circulation of vehicles in general (for example based on their fuel), or restrict vehicles on criteria outside of Directive 2007/46 and regulatory Acts (for example, restrict Euro 4 vehicles).[41] The Court summarised its thoughts in point 76 of the judgment:

> The literal, teleological and contextual interpretations of Directive 2007/46, and more specifically of the second subparagraph of Article 4(3) thereof, are therefore along the same lines, that is to say that that directive actually prevents the public authorities of the Member States, without affording them any discretion, from prohibiting, restricting or impeding the circulation on the road of vehicles on grounds related to aspects of their construction and functioning covered by the directive if they satisfy the requirements of the latter, which means that, on account of the adoption of the contested regulation, the applicants may not, as they claim, actually limit, within the context of a targeted measure taking into account the pollutant emission levels of vehicles, the circulation of those vehicles which during the RDE [Real Driving Emissions] tests do not comply with the emission limits for oxides of nitrogen laid down in the Euro 6 standard, but which do nevertheless comply during those tests

36 Ibid., para. 41.
37 Ibid., para. 59.
38 Ibid., para. 64.
39 Ibid., point 67.
40 Ibid., point 69.
41 Ibid., points 68 and 74.

with the NTE [Not-To-Exceed] values for emissions of oxides of nitrogen defined in that regulation, which are higher than the emission limits.

Therefore, the applicants fulfilled all criteria stated in Article 263 TFEU, so the actions were admissible.

The judgment's connection to vehicle emissions regulation and ambient air quality was achieved through the Court's interpretation of conformity factors for NO_X during the type-approval procedure. The issue was whether the Commission could define the final conformity factor and temporary conformity factor for NO_X,[42] as part of the comitology regulatory review procedure (via Commission Regulation No. 692/2008, as amended by Commission Regulation 2016/646),[43] and set more lenient values for NO_X emissions[44] than those under Regulation No. 715/2007.[45] This would be problematic because such type-approved vehicles could emit more NO_X and directly contribute to the exceedances of polluting substances in the air.

The Court ruled that Regulation No. 715/2007 does not explicitly state that the Commission can amend the values of NO_X.[46] The Court also inferred that Euro 6 limit values for NO_X are an essential part of the regulation and, therefore, these values can be changed only through the ordinary legislative procedure. Accordingly, the Court ruled that the Commission lacked competence, and had exceeded its powers,[47] and therefore annulled points 2.1.1 and 2.1.2 of Annex IIIA of Commission Regulation No. 692/2008, as amended by Commission Regulation 2016/646.[48]

This judgment is seminal because it defines the relationship between type-approval legislation and air quality legislation. The Court explained that there is a public interest in adequate air quality (which can be realised through possible legislative measures stated in the AQD); however, this public interest is limited by the public interest in free, properly type-approved goods in circulation on the internal market.

---

42 Paras. 2.1.1 and 2.1.2, Annex IIIA of Commission Regulation (EC) No. 692/2008 of 18 July 2008 implementing and amending Regulation (EC) No. 715/2007 of the European Parliament and of the Council on type-approval of motor vehicles with respect to emissions from light passenger and commercial vehicles (Euro 5 and Euro 6) and on access to vehicle repair and maintenance information, OJ 2008 L 199.

43 Commission Regulation (EU) 2016/646 of 20 April 2016 amending Regulation (EC) No. 692/2008 as regards emissions from light passenger and commercial vehicles (Euro 6), OJ 2016 L 109.

44 NTE (not-to-exceed) values (which consist of conformity factors), introduced by Commission Regulation 2016/646, were set higher than limit values for Euro 6, in Regulation No. 715/2007.

45 T-339/16, supra, note 30, para. 1 of verdict.

46 Ibid., para. 119.

47 Ibid., paras. 126–134.

48 Ibid., para. 1 of verdict.

4.1.2. Ville de Paris and Others – Advocate General's Opinion[49]

In 2019, Germany, Hungary and the Commission appealed the judgment of the General Court in *Ville de Paris v. Commission.*

As the case is essential to the type-approval legislation, the Opinion of Advocate General (AG) Bobek,[50] and the judgment, are examined in more detail here.

The AG reached the same conclusions as the General Court in *Ville de Paris v. Commission*, and dismissed all appeals. However, the AG disagreed with the General Court on the admissibility of the actions by municipalities, and presented his own view on the admissibility of these actions (even though both the Court and the AG admitted the actions).

The AG disagreed with the Court's interpretation of Article 4(3) of Directive 2007/46. The AG viewed the Directive as defining standards for new vehicles. Therefore, 'circulation on the road' cannot mean possible restrictions of type-approved vehicles in use.[51] Furthermore, the AG stated that the General Court had not interpreted the provision as a whole. Therefore, according to the AG, the Court's interpretation was incorrect.[52] The AG also rejected the Court's notion that the infra-state body could not adopt rules restricting the use of Euro 6 vehicles because this could have constituted a measure having an equivalent effect to quantitative restrictions.[53]

On the other hand, the AG introduced his view on the criteria stated in Article 263 TFEU. According to the AG:

> [the] Court's test should be regarded as granting standing to local or regional entities when a *direct cause and effect relationship* between the contested EU act and the exercise of a *specific autonomous legal power* of a local entity can be identified. That relationship exists when the EU act is the *determining factor* which either precludes the local or regional authorities from using their powers at all, or compels them to act, while significantly altering the manner in which they can lawfully make use of those powers.[54]

Overall, the AG did not try to interpret Article 4(3) of Directive 2007/46. However, he tried to give logical reasoning for his above-stated test. The AG admitted that cities and municipalities retained the right to regulate local traffic

49 This section is inspired by Chapter 4 of author's book, *Vehicle Type-approval and Emission Regulation in the EU: Environmental Perspective* (in publishing process).
50 Opinion of the Advocate General Bobek from 10 June 2021, C-177/19 P, *Allemagne – Ville de Paris and Others v. Commission*, ECLI:EU:C:2021:476.
51 Ibid., paras. 48 and 69.
52 Ibid., para. 61.
53 Ibid., paras. 67–71.
54 Ibid., para. 86 (emphasis added).

(they can ban Euro 6 and introduce their own Euro standard).[55] However, at the same time, he added that no one could reasonably expect the cities to do so. Furthermore, the AG indirectly criticised the Commission for the fact that cities cannot currently rely on established Euro emission standards[56] (air pollution from traffic stagnates or worsens, even with strict Euro standards), and therefore have to create their own solutions, which do not have to be publicly accepted.[57]

The AG ended his Opinion on this issue with three reasons that supported his interpretation of Article 263 TFEU. The first reason for broader access to EU justice was the possibility of contesting numerous obligations imposed by EU law.[58] The narrow interpretation could contradict the constitutional principles stipulated in Article 4(2) and (3) of the Treaty on European Union (TEU).[59]

The second reason concerned the inability to challenge the EU Acts that affected the exercise of powers entities enjoy on a constitutional level.[60]

The last reason questioned the current rigid judicial structure relating to access to the EU Courts. The AG pointed out that the rigid structure limits the possible actions of interested stakeholders, which end up at the EU Courts anyway, because of the preliminary ruling procedure, but years later, and at high cost.[61] Therefore, a broader view of Article 263 TFEU should ensure broader access to justice.

The AG dismissed the interpretation of Article 4(3) of Directive 2007/46 by the General Court. However, one must remember that Regulation No. 715/2007 (and subsequent regulatory Acts) and Directive 2007/46 are intertwined. Therefore, it is crucial to interpret whether the provision in question can fulfil the criteria of Article 263 TFEU. Another debatable notion of the AG is whether municipalities could introduce their own (stricter) emissions regulation when vehicle type-approval is fully harmonised (or even unified, due to Regulation 2018/858).

It must be concluded that the General Court reasonably showed that duly established Euro 6 emission standards constituted a legal certainty for addressees of the Regulation. Therefore, the term 'circulation of vehicles' must be interpreted. The term can have different meanings, but one cannot forget that *circulation* points to the circulation of goods or products (such as vehicles) placed on the internal market, according to Article 28 TFEU. In this sense, any limitation or restriction could be viewed as infringing Article 35 TFEU (even based on health or environmental reasons). However, municipalities and cities retain the power to limit and restrict traffic according to their respective national

55 Ibid., para. 96.
56 Ibid., para. 97.
57 Ibid., para. 98.
58 Ibid., para. 106.
59 Ibid., para. 104.
60 Ibid., para. 107.
61 Ibid., para. 108.

laws, as well as vehicles that fall outside of Euro 6 emission standards, or to restrict vehicles based on general criteria such as fuel.

On the other hand, the AG is on point regarding broadening the acceptability of actions under Article 263 TFEU. A swifter procedure and more flexible criteria could save time and money. Furthermore, a swifter procedure would enable the EU Court to express its opinion on current affairs more promptly.[62]

4.1.3. Ville de Paris and Others – Court's Approach

In January 2022, the Court issued its ruling on the appealed case of *Ville de Paris v. Commission*.[63] The Court dismissed the judgment of the General Court on the grounds that municipalities were not directly concerned by the Act in question (Directive 2007/46), as is required by the fourth paragraph of Article 263 TFEU; therefore, actions initiated by municipalities were inadmissible.[64]

The Court came to this conclusion by interpreting the phrase 'circulation on the road'. According to the CJEU, this phrase includes registration, sale and entry into service.[65] However, the provision's reach stops there, and possible subsequent vehicle use is outside the scope of Article 4(3) of Directive 2007/46.[66]

The Court set aside the General Court's broad interpretation of the provision in question. It concluded that the court of first instance had purposely interpreted the provision as precluding municipalities from restricting the circulation of vehicles on the road to protect the environment.[67]

The CJEU took a different path in its judgment from those of the General Court and the AG. The conservative interpretation of the CJEU means that the General Court and AG Bobek both perceived the issues in question more progressively.[68] The CJEU's approach is not necessarily wrong, but one ponders whether it is correct, because the judgment preserves the current approach to the fourth paragraph of Article 263 TFEU. The Court had a unique opportunity to change this, and bring the EU judicial system closer to the people. The judgment also follows a long-standing approach that values the core freedoms of the EU; however, in the current day and age, one has to ponder whether the conservative values that the CJEU guards should not be enriched with environmental protection.

---

62 Cf. G. Winter, '*Plaumann* withering: standing before the EU General Court underway from distinctive to substantial concern' (Online First 27.04.2023), *European Journal of Legal Studies*, 2023 (15), pp. 86–126.

63 Judgment of the Court (Fifth Chamber) of 13 January 2022, in Joined Cases C-177/19 P to C-179/19 P, *Allemagne – Ville de Paris and Others v. Commission*, ECLI:EU:C:2022:10.

64 Ibid., para. 102.

65 Ibid., para. 83.

66 Ibid., para. 85.

67 Ibid., para. 89.

68 This can be seen in para. 91 of the judgment, in which Court points at free movement of goods.

In summary, the CJEU's judgment leaves a considerable gap between air quality legislation and type-approval legislation. According to the CJEU, if vehicles are duly type-approved, but based on false information provided during the type-approval procedure, or on comitology legislation containing more lenient limits than ordinary legislation, Member States and infra-state bodies cannot effectively restrict such vehicles. This poses a problem not only for municipalities, which cannot limit or restrict them without a political backlash, or infringing EU law, but also for Member States, because inadequate air quality under Directive 2008/50 will lead to the commencement of infringement proceedings under Article 258 TFEU.

4.2. ENVIRONMENTAL PROVISIONS

According to the recitals of Regulation No. 715/2007, one of its aims is air quality protection (and thus environmental protection), and so it can be inferred that the Regulation, or a specific provision thereof, could be an environmental regulation and, therefore, that Article 191 TFEU is applicable. The CJEU (somewhat surprisingly) inferred this conclusion in *Deutsche Umwelthilfe* case,[69] because the case mainly concerned access to justice in environmental matters.

In this case, the Court concluded that environmental associations[70] may judicially challenge duly approved EC type-approval certificates of the national approval authority, provided that the vehicles in question are using an illegal *defeat device*. The Court (based on case law relating to the judicial review of defeat devices) stated that Article 5(2) of Regulation No. 715/2007 was a provision of environmental law, and was directly applicable, and therefore fulfilled the meaning required by Article 9(3) of the Aarhus Convention.[71] The provision of the Aarhus Convention 'read in conjunction with Art. 47 of the [Charter of Fundamental Rights of the European Union], imposes on Member States an obligation to ensure effective judicial protection of the rights conferred by EU law, in particular the provisions of environmental law'.[72]

The judgment is significant because the Court directly interpreted the provision restricting defeat devices (Article 5(2) of Regulation No. 715/2007)

---

69 Judgment of the Court (Grand Chamber) of 8 November 2022, C-873/19, *Deutsche Umwelthilfe*, ECLI:EU:C:2022:857.

70 For general conditions, see V. Vomacka, 'To the Bitter End: The Limits to the CJEU's Interpretation of *Locus Standi* in Environmental Matters' in R. Simon and H. Mullerova (eds.), *Efficient Collective Redress Mechanisms in Visegrad 4 Countries: An Achievable Target?*, Praha: Institute of State and Law of the Czech Academy of Sciences, 2019, pp. 146–168.

71 Case C-873/19, supra, note 68, para. 58.

72 Ibid., para. 66.

as an environmental law provision. Until this decision, the Court only inferred environmental objectives of Regulation No. 715/2007 from recitals (for example, *CLCV and Others*,[73] *GSMB Invest*,[74] *Volkswagen*,[75] and *Porsche Inter Auto and Volkswagen*).[76]

It must be concluded that, even though type-approval legislation contains provisions for environmental protection (and air quality, through Regulation No. 715/2007), it does not contain any acknowledgements of Directive 2008/50 or ambient air quality.

However, the Court's interpretation effectively means that defeat-device provisions must be assessed under Article 191 TEFU. Thus, since the CJEU inferred environmental provisions in Regulation No. 715/2007, it can also be assumed that a few selected provisions (or some parts of them) in Regulation 2018/858 – especially Article 13(5) – could also be partially interpreted as environmental law provisions. This might pave the way for a proper application of environmental principles, such as the polluter-pays principle.[77]

4.3. EURO 7 AND THE NEW AMBIENT AIR QUALITY DIRECTIVE

The proposal[78] for a new Ambient Air Quality Directive (AQD) proclaims that air pollution is an issue, especially within urban agglomerations and cities, and that the proposal aims to curb it, together with Euro 7 regulation, which focuses on vehicles. In this sense, the proposed Directive and Euro 7 regulation should be complementary to one another. On the other hand, the proposed directive does not contain any new or unique power for Member States or municipalities plagued by poor air quality due to transport.

The AQD proposal contains, to a large extent, very similar provisions regarding traffic and transport to current AQD. Nevertheless, Part B of Annex VIII of the proposed directive contains a list of indicative abatement measures

73 Judgment of the Court (Second Chamber) of 17 December 2020, C-693/18, Preliminary ruling, *CLCV and Others (Dispositif d'invalidation sur moteur diesel)*, ECLI: EU:C:2020:1040.

74 Judgment of the Court (Grand Chamber) of 14 July 2022, C-128/20, *GSMB Invest GmbH & Co. KG v. Auto Krainer GesmbH*, ECLI:EU:C:2022:570.

75 Judgment of the Court (Grand Chamber) of 14 July 2022, C-134/20, *Volkswagen AG*, ECLI:EU:C:2022:571.

76 Judgment of the Court (Grand Chamber) of 14 July 2022, C-145/20, *Porsche Inter Auto GmbH & Co. KG, Volkswagen AG*, ECLI:EU:C:2022:572.

77 Sadeleer, N. de. Car emissions in the wake of the Dieselgate. In M. Peeters and M. Eliantonio et al. EU *Environmental Law Research Handbook*. Edgar Elgar Publishing, 2020. pp. 379–395, 17 p. 394.

78 Proposal for a directive of the European Parliament and of the Council on ambient air quality and cleaner air for Europe, COM/2022/542 final.

that can be considered for inclusion in air quality plans, to curb air pollution from vehicles. The list contains, *inter alia*:

- Reduction of emissions from vehicles through retrofitting with zero emissions powertrains and emission control equipment. The use of economic incentives to accelerate take-up shall be considered.
- Procurement by public authorities, in line with the handbook on environmental public procurement, of zero-emissions road vehicles fuels and combustion equipment to reduce emissions.
- Measures to limit transport emissions through traffic planning and management (including congestion pricing, differentiated parking fees or other economic incentives, and establishing urban vehicle-access restriction schemes, including low-emission zones).[79]

Compared to Directive 2008/50 and its Annex XV, the proposed directive's measures, in Annex VIII, are more prescriptive. However, they still leave the adoption of specific measures up to the Member States or infra-state bodies.

The proposed Euro 7 regulation is supposed to help air quality by, among other things, introducing stricter limit values for diesel cars, extending the in-service conformity period, and measuring particulate matter from brakes and tyres.[80]

According to the proposed Euro 7 regulation, emission standards should help to reduce air pollutants and achieve air quality, in accordance with the proposed Ambient Air Quality Directive. However, it is still too early to say whether the Euro 7 will bring any significant change at all.

5. CONCLUSION

The aim of this chapter can be divided into several sub-aims. The first aim was to ascertain whether the AQD contains instruments to regulate vehicles.

The chapter analysed several provisions (namely Articles 23, 24, and Annexes) of the AQD that are relevant to traffic and transport. It can be concluded that occurrences of traffic and vehicle provisions in the Directive are mostly incidental, without any direct legal instruments to be effectively used to lower air pollution from vehicles. However, this is to be expected, since the Directive represents a general legal instrument with specific aims to be achieved (for example, limit values of air pollutants in the air). Therefore, the

79 Ibid., Point 2, part B of Annex VIII.

80 European Commission, 'European vehicle emissions standards – Euro 7 for cars, vans, lorries and buses', https://ec.europa.eu/info/law/better-regulation/have-your-say/initiatives/12313-European-vehicle-emissions-standards-Euro-7-for-cars-vans-lorries-and-buses_en.

Directive leaves room for Member States to choose the most suitable forms of national instrument to regulate vehicles or traffic to improve air quality, such as low-emission zones, tolls or vehicle restrictions.

The second aim of the chapter was to ascertain to what extent infra-state bodies can regulate duly type-approved vehicles to protect air quality. To fulfil this aim, a short analysis of possible environmental provisions of Regulation 2018/858 and Regulation No. 715/2007, and relevant case law of the CJEU, was conducted.

The analysis showed that type-approval legislation protects (to some extent) the environment. However, the protection is not comprehensive, and air protection is to be inferred from the legislation. The CJEU has already inferred that some provisions are to be interpreted as environmental provisions (such as provisions on defeat devices, which can indirectly influence air quality in urban areas). The analysis also focused on the case law of the CJEU. The Court of Justice, in *Ville de Paris and Others*, ultimately limited and weakened the position of infra-state bodies in regulating and restricting duly type-approved vehicles, where approval was based on false information, or on comitology legislation containing more lenient limits than ordinary legislation.

It can be concluded from the analysis that infra-state bodies can strictly regulate vehicles that fall outside the scope of the legislation already in effect. Another possibility is to introduce measures not aimed at requirements defined in the legislation already in effect, such as implementation of residential parking, a ban on combustion engines, or the introduction of no-entry bans. However, due to their sensitive political nature, such measures are not easily accepted.

Furthermore, the chapter also compared specific air pollutants listed in individual pieces of legislation. There was some overlap between these (NO_X, CO and PM), and this finding could be used as a cornerstone for future, more synchronised, legislation on air quality and type-approval.

The end of the chapter briefly examined future legislation (the proposed new AQD and Euro 7 regulation). The proposed AQD contains a list of indicative measures that infra-state bodies can adopt. Nevertheless, it leaves it up to the discretionary power of Member States to adopt them. The Euro 7 does not bring any new or specific instruments that should work in synergy with AQD. However, it introduces measures aimed at newly type-approved vehicles that could help to tackle air pollution in urban areas.

THE ENERGY CHARTER TREATY AND ITS IMPLICATIONS FOR PREVENTING PLASTICS PRODUCTION

Stirring the Plastic Soup?

Endrius Cocciolo and Leonie Reins*

ABSTRACT

This chapter delves into the intricate relationship between the plastics industry and fossil fuels. Despite the climate crisis, the plastics sector continues to grow, which may increase demand for fossil fuels. At present, environmental issues are addressed within specific sectors, which masks the more general consequences

---

* This chapter is part of the research project "Climate change and plastic waste: legal challenges of the circular economy as a paradigm for the protection of planetary health and justice", with reference PID2020-115551RA-I00, funded by MCIN/AEI/10.13039/501100011033. Endrius Cocciolo has contributed to this chapter as a member of the Research Group Territory, Citizenship and Sustainability of the Universitat Rovira i Virgili, recognised as a consolidated research group with the support of the Research and Universities Department of the Generalitat de Catalunya (2021 SGR 00162).
This chapter is the result of the joint research of the two authors, who have contributed equally to its conceptualisation, writing and final revision. Endrius Cocciolo has contributed especially to the writing of sections 1, 2, 3 and 4, and Leonie Reins to sections 3.1, 3.2., 3.3 and 5. However, all sections have been discussed in depth and agreed upon by both authors.

of fossil fuel-based plastics for health, biodiversity and the climate. Against this backdrop, the study examines the global regulatory landscape, in particular the Energy Charter Treaty (ECT) and its support for fossil fuel investments, which contribute to ongoing plastic production. The limitations of the ECT are contrasted with the potential of the future United Nations Treaty on Plastic Pollution, which was designed to address the plastics life cycle comprehensively. Many uncertainties surround the future Plastics Treaty, and existing policies are geared towards waste management rather than the prevention of plastics production. Therefore, an innovative Earth system law approach is proposed as a response to the mounting evidence of plastics being a substantial threat to the planet. This approach aims to establish transnational regulations that are aligned with the objective of preserving planetary integrity.

1. INTRODUCTION

The latest climate report of the World Meteorological Organization presents compelling evidence for the proposition that global temperatures are highly likely to increase to unprecedented levels in the next five years.[1] These data on the climate emergency underscore the urgency of the socio-ecological transition, at the heart of which is the energy transition (or, rather, the energy transformation).[2] The primary obstacle to efforts to mitigate global warming is reliance on fossil fuels, of which plastic is a derivative. The production of plastic on a global scale has grown exponentially over the past few decades. The annual volume of production has reached approximately 400 million tonnes. That estimates show that a mere 12 per cent of total plastic output is incinerated, and that only 9 per cent is recycled, should be a matter of grave concern; the remainder is either deposited into landfills or released into the environment, including into marine ecosystems.[3] The destructive planetary consequences of human activity in the Anthropocene, especially through activity that involves synthetic substances that do not exist in nature, such as plastics, can only be mitigated through human intervention.

The relationship between climate change, fossil fuels and the plastics industry is a matter of concern for researchers, policymakers, civil society organisations and communities. Plastics are derived from fossil fuels, with oil, gas and coal

---

1 World Meteorological Organization (WMO), 'Global temperatures set to reach new records in next five years', press release, 17 May 2023, https://public.wmo.int/en/media/press-release/global-temperatures-set-reach-new-records-next-five-years.

2 J. Paterson, 'Energy law and Energy Transformation' in R. Fleming, et al. (eds.), *A Force of Energy: Essays in Energy Law in Honour of Professor Martha Roggenkamp*, University of Groningen Press, 2022, pp. 20 *et seq.*

3 United Nations Environment Programme (UNEP), *Report: Drowning in Plastics – Marine Litter and Plastic Waste Vital Graphics*, UNEP, 2021, https://www.unep.org/resources/report/drowning-plastics-marine-litter-and-plastic-waste-vital-graphics.

serving as raw materials for their production.[4] Plastic waste contributes to climate change[5] and biodiversity loss, impacts on health, and persists in the environment, creating other toxic products and affecting society.[6]

Policies and regulations play a crucial role in mitigating the impact of the plastics industry on climate change. The present authors argue that there should be a shift from treating plastics primarily as a problem for waste management law, to a legal approach that prevents their production and consumption, hence its entire lifecycle. Law-driven innovation should focus on the immediate phasing-out of the production of fossil fuel-based virgin plastic, as well as of the use of plastic waste for energy.[7] The plastics industry can achieve large short-term reductions in emissions by maximising the use of renewable electricity across its supply chain.[8] The environmental and climate risks of plastics cannot be addressed without binding legal provisions that establish targets, rules and methodologies that generate clear duties for the participants in the plastics supply chain, which is inordinately complex and opaque.[9] In a business-as-usual scenario, in which policies continue to foster plastic production, fossil fuel consumption in the sector will increase.[10] Worldwide plastic-related greenhouse gas emissions are projected to reach 1.34 gigatons annually, by 2030, and to increase to 2.8 gigatons per year by 2050.[11]

In order to address these problems, the United Nations Environment Programme (UNEP) recently unveiled a comprehensive suite of measures aimed at rectifying the inadequate functioning of the plastic-recycling system. Its ultimate objective is to reduce pollution from plastics by 80 per cent, by 2040. If political commitments are to be converted into legally binding objectives, the next step should be an international treaty. Such a treaty is currently being negotiated under

---

4 B. Bauman, 'How plastics contribute to climate change', *Yale Climate Connections*, 20 August 2019, https://yaleclimateconnections.org/2019/08/how-plastics-contribute-to-climate-change/.

5 Studies such as *Plastic and Climate: The Hidden Costs of a Plastic Planet* (2019), by the Center for International Environmental Law (CIEL), provide valuable insights into the relationship between plastics and climate change: https://www.ciel.org/wp-content/uploads/2019/05/Plastic-and-Climate-FINAL-2019.pdf.

6 M. Macleod et al., 'The global threat from plastic pollution', *Science*, (2021) 373, p. 61, https//doi.org/10.1126/science.abg5433.

7 T. Walker, 'Policies to Mitigate Climate Change by Addressing Single-Use Plastic Production and Waste Disposal', June 2021, https://ssrn.com/abstract=3857828.

8 M. Peltier, J. Fallurin and S. Hughes 'Clean Energy 101: Reducing Climate Pollution from the Plastics Industry', RMI, February 21, 2023, https://rmi.org/clean-energy-101-reducing-climate-pollution-from-the-plastics-industry/.

9 Ibid.

10 Bauman, supra, note 4.

11 M. Shen et al., '(Micro)plastic crisis: Un-ignorable contribution to global greenhouse gas emissions and climate change', *Journal of Cleaner Production*, (2020) 254, 120138, https://doi.org/10.1016/j.jclepro.2020.120138.

the auspices of the United Nations, and it is slated for approval in 2024. This treaty aims to prevent severe pollution from plastics and the use of fossil fuels.

The analysis presented here is organised as follows: section 2 explains the relationship between the plastics-producing petrochemical industry and fossil energy resources. The extant data indicates that, despite the climate emergency, the industries within the plastics sector are growing. This expansionary trend is poised to result in investments that would perpetuate global demand for fossil fuels. Those investments would extend beyond the conventional energy sector. Fossil fuels are linked to the plastics industry, and the tendency to address socio-ecological problems from a sectoral perspective obscures the complexity of this industrial cluster, as well as the consequences of fossil fuel-derived plastics for health, biodiversity and the climate. Section 3 will present the international regulatory framework, including attempts to improve it. To that end, section 3.1. will present a critical legal examination of the Energy Charter Treaty (ECT), and of the contentious and ultimately unsuccessful attempt to modernise it. The ECT endorses investments in fossil fuel initiatives, and thus contributes to the perpetuation of the plastics production cycle. The inadequacies of the ECT may be contrasted with the output of the ongoing negotiations on a United Nations Treaty on Plastic Pollution (section 3.2.). The Plastics Treaty marks a break with past practice, because it addresses the entire life cycle of plastics. However, lingering uncertainties remain about the model of the forthcoming treaty, the operational mechanisms by which its goals will be realised, and its interplay with the other international legal regimes that govern the intertwined planetary boundaries. Section 3.3 introduces some preliminary observations on the interactions between these instruments. Section 4 draws on evidence that indicates that plastics have emerged as a threat to planetary boundaries, and adumbrates an Earth system law approach aimed at establishing transnational regulations which are aligned with the imperative of safeguarding planetary integrity. Section 5 contains the authors' concluding remarks.

2. HOW THE PLASTIC INDUSTRY ENTRENCHES FOSSIL FUEL LOCK-IN

A voluminous body of climate change law has accumulated across the globe. At the same time, recent reports and studies have raised concerns about the role of 'other fossil-dependent industry sectors' in jeopardising the decarbonisation of economies, and in hindering efforts to preserve biodiversity and the environment. The petrochemical industry, which produces plastics, is one such sector. Plastics are produced from organic polymers sourced from fossil fuels. According to the Center for International Environmental Law (CIEL), '[p]lastics are materials formed from organic polymers – giant molecules made by linking together long chains of smaller molecules, called monomers. These molecules are products of a supply chain that almost always starts at a wellhead, oil rig, or coal mine'. The term 'plastic' covers a large variety of resins, synthetic fibres and additives, all of which have different properties. Despite the wide variety of plastic polymers, at present most plastics are produced from five such substances: polyethylene (PE), polypropylene (PP), polyvinyl chloride (PVC), polyethylene terephthalate (PET) and polystyrene (PS).[12] PE, PVC, PET and PS are based on ethylene, and PP is based on propylene.[13] Propylene is mainly a co-product in ethylene production, and ethylene is sourced from natural gas liquids (NGLs), or from naphtha, a petroleum product. In the US, 90 per cent of the plastics produced come from NGLs, because of the abundance of gas in that country. In China, Europe, South East Asia and Japan, plastics come primarily from petroleum.[14]

The dependency of the plastics sector on the hydrocarbon industry is due not only to the need for feedstock material, but also to the integration of the physical infrastructure and the technologies that are employed to produce plastics.[15] Petrochemical facilities are usually located close to places where petroleum oil and gas are extracted, because fossil fuel serves both as feedstock material and as process energy. Furthermore, those facilities are clustered. In petrochemical industries, process units operate at very high temperatures and pressures: for that reason, clusters are organised so that heat can be recovered from different processes through exchanger networks, water systems and on-site electricity generation. Reaction vessels, process units, heat exchangers, pipelines, valves, sensors and control systems are all integrated.[16] According to Bauer et al.:

> The petrochemical sector is not one or two defined processes but instead the agglomeration of many processes and material flows and hundreds of thousands of plastics and other chemical products. Production processes operate across a vast and complex network of facilities and processes, where a high level of physical integration drives efficiency gains and lower[s] production costs.[17]

Unlike energy and transportation, in which demand for fossil fuel is expected to drop because of decarbonisation strategies, the plastics sector is growing

---

12 CIEL, 'Fueling Plastics: Fossil, Plastics, and Petrochemical Feedstocks', 2017, https://www.ciel.org/wp-content/uploads/2017/09/Fueling-Plastics-Fossils-Plastics-Petrochemical-Feedstocks.pdf.

13 Ibid.

14 Ibid.

15 F. Bauer and G. Fontenit, 'Plastic dinosaurs – Digging deep into the accelerating carbon lock-in of plastics', *Energy Policy*, vol. 156, Sep. 2021, 112418, https://doi.org/10.1016/j.enpol.2021.112418.

16 F. Bauer et al., 'Plastics and climate change – Breaking carbon lock-ins through three mitigation pathways', *One Earth*, (2022) (5–4), pp. 361–376, https://doi.org/10.1016/j.oneear.2022.03.007.

17 Ibid., pp. 363–365.

consistently. For example, '[g]lobal plastic resin production has increased from about 1.7Mt in 1950 to 368 Mt in 2019, with an average annual growth rate of about 3.5% since 2011'.[18] Plastics have created new consumer habits and cultures, as exemplified by the widespread use of single-use packaging, and the popularity of online shopping, takeaway food and disposable items. These cultures are more mature in wealthier regions, as is evident from statistics on annual per capita consumption. In 2015, it was estimated that the average resident of the NAFTA and Western European regions consumed 140 kilogrammes of plastics. The corresponding figure for Japan was 108 kilogrammes. At the same time, the average person in Asia consumed 36 kilogrammes of plastics, and the average for the Middle East and Africa was as low as 16 kilogrammes. As populations grow, and as regions become wealthier, plastic consumption is expected to increase more rapidly. For instance, '[a]ssuming annual growth levels of 2% or 4% would lead to global plastic production levels of 680 or 1240 Mt in 2050'.[19] According to the CIEL, if current trends in oil consumption and plastic production persist, 'the consumption of oil by the entire plastics sector will account for 20% of the total consumption by 2050'.[20]

Plastics have become a backup industry for prominent actors in oil, gas and transportation, in this period of intensive climate action.[21] Recent studies have shown that the giants of the hydrocarbon industry are making large investments into the production of plastics and other chemicals.[22] Between 2010 and 2019, 221 billion euros were applied to that end, in the US alone,[23] and the chemical industry is projected to spend $164 billion on 264 new plastics facilities or other expansion projects across the globe, by the end of 2023.[24]

Although Europe has traditionally been an important region for plastics production, it attracts little investment at present. Bucking this trend, the chemical company INEOS recently announced plans to build a propane dehydrogenation plant for propylene production in Antwerp. The project is expected to produce up to 750,000 tonnes of propylene.[25] One of the most

---

18 Ibid., pp. 362–363.

19 Ibid.

20 CIEL, 'Fueling Plastics', supra, note 12.

21 Africa Oil+Gas Report, 'Fossil Fuel-based Production Growth of Polyethylene is Forecast to Continue Until the Early 2040s While Focus Increases on Reducing Plastic Waste', 28 February 2022, https://africaoilgasreport.com/2022/02/in-the-news/fossil-fuel-based-production-growth-of-polyethylene-is-forecast-to-continue-until-the-early-2040s-while-focus-increases-on-reducing-plastic-waste/.

22 F. Bauer and T.D. Nielsen, 'Oil companies are ploughing money into fossil-fuelled plastics production at a record rate – new research', *The Conversation*, 2 November 2021, https://theconversation.com/oil-companies-are-ploughing-money-into-fossil-fuelled-plastics-production-at-a-record-rate-new-research-169690.

23 Bauer et al., supra, note 16, p. 367.

24 CIEL, '*Plastic and Climate: The Hidden Costs of a Plastic Planet*', supra, note 5.

25 CIEL, 'Fueling Plastics', supra, note 12.

significant plastics expansion projects in the US Gulf Region is a joint venture between ExxonMobil and Saudi Basic Industries Corporation (SABIC): $20 billion will be spent on the construction of 11 chemical, refining, lubricant and liquefied natural gas (LNG) projects. Moreover, a $20 billion ethane cracker will be built in Texas.[26]

The SADARA project in Saudi Arabia is another significant investment that evinces the growing involvement of oil and gas companies (and oil-exporting countries) in the plastics industry. This project is a joint venture between the state-owned oil company Saudi Aramco, which is contributing $4.39 billion to it, and the US-based Dow Chemical Company, which is contributing $2.37 billion. The complex will include 26 manufacturing units, a mixed-feed steam cracker, and an aromatics plant. The project is based in Jubail Industrial City II. The facility is expected to produce 1.5 million tonnes of ethylene and 400,000 tonnes of propylene per annum, which will provide plastics for use in the energy, transportation, construction, electrical and electronic sectors. Interestingly, beyond Dow and Aramco, the project has also attracted $1.3 billion from the Saudi Public Investment Fund, $220 million from the Islamic Development Bank (in the form of debt), $169 million in public funds from the development banks of Canada and Germany, and $5 billion in direct financing from the Export–Import Bank of the US.[27] These investments are likely to lock in global demand for fossil fuels beyond the energy sector.

3. THE ENERGY CHARTER TREATY AND THE UN PLASTICS TREATY ROAD MAP

The United Nations Environment Assembly recently adopted the Resolution 'End plastic pollution: Towards an international legally binding instrument', in Nairobi. Before that Resolution, transnational regulation on plastics was typically fragmented and tangential. The 2022 *Global Plastics Outlook*[28] report, by the Organisation for Economic Co-operation and Development (OECD), emphasises that, before plastics became a prominent item on the political agenda, a range of international agreements had established mandatory obligations and non-binding guidance for their management, and the prevention of pollution. There are notable gaps in this mosaic of agreements. There is no overarching international governance framework that addresses the multifaceted challenges

---

26 Ibid.

27 J. Skovgaard, et al., 'Finance for Fossils – the Role of Public Financing in Expanding Petrochemicals', June 2022, http://dx.doi.org/10.2139/ssrn.4141958.

28 OECD, *Global Plastics Outlook: Economic Drivers, Environmental Impacts and Policy Options*, OECD, 2022, pp. 142–143, https://read.oecd-ilibrary.org/environment/global-plastics-outlook_e01d60f3-en#page1.

of the various stages of the plastics life cycle comprehensively. The table below[29] provides an overview of the international legal instruments and their provisions on plastics. These provisions are categorised into four distinct domains, namely pollution, biodiversity, chemicals and the waste trade.

Table 1. Fragmentation of global agreements on plastics

Binding agreements		
Domain	**Agreement**	**Objective**
Pollution	United Nations Convention on the Law of the Seas (UNCLOS)	Establishes the legal foundation for human activities, encompassing a broad mandate to implement all required measures for the prevention, reduction, and control of plastic pollution. UNCLOS was enacted in 1994.
	The Convention on the Prevention of Marine Pollution by Dumping of Wastes and Other Matter (London Convention) and its Protocol (the London Protocol)	The London Convention prohibits the direct disposal or discharge of plastic waste into the ocean. The London Convention came into force in 1972 and its Protocol was enacted in 1996
	Annex V of the International Convention for the Prevention of Pollution from Ships (MARPOL)	MARPOL stands as the singular global international treaty dedicated to addressing maritime debris. Annex V specifically prohibits ships from dumping plastic waste into the ocean, with the Annex becoming effective in 1988.
Biodiversity	The Convention on Biological Diversity (CBD)	Alchi Biodiversity Target 8 set a goal to diminish plastic pollution to levels that do not harm ecosystem function by the year 2020. The 2022 Kunming-Montreal Global Biodiversity Framework includes Target 7, which seeks to eliminate the discharge of plastic waste, emphasising a stronger stance on global efforts to combat plastic pollution.
	The United Nations Fish Stocks Agreement	The agreement mandates that states must work to minimise (plastic) pollution, waste, discards, and catches caused by ghost fishing gear.
Chemicals	The Stockholm Convention on Persistent Organic Pollutants (Stockholm Convention)	The Stockholm Convention oversees the production, utilization, and disposal of additives present in plastics identified as persistent organic pollutants. This regulatory framework came into effect in 2004

(continued)

29 Table 1 is based on OECD, *Global Plastics Outlook: Economic Drivers, Environmental Impacts and Policy Option*, 2022, https://read.oecd-ilibrary.org/environment/global-plastics-outlook_e01d60f3-en#page3.

Table 1 *continued*

Waste trade	The Basel Convention on the Control of Transboundary Movements of Hazardous Wastes and their Disposal (Basel Convention)	The Basel Convention establishes requisites and restrictions for the transboundary movement of hazardous and other (plastic) wastes. It came into force in 1992, and in 2020, amendments specifically addressing the trade of plastic waste were introduced
	Non-binding agreements	
Domain	**Agreement**	**Objective**
Pollution	FAO Code of Conduct for Responsible Fisheries	Adopted in 1995, the Code establishes legal principles for responsible fishing, encompassing measures to address issues such as ghost fishing gear.
	Global Programme of Action for the Protection of the Marine Environment form Land-based Activities	The GPA serves as an intergovernmental forum providing guidelines on addressing land-based sources of marine (plastic) pollution.
	Global Partnership on Marine Litter (GPML)	The GPML serves as a collaborative platform for sharing best practices and fostering cooperation on instruments designed to tackle marine plastic pollution. This initiative was inaugurated at the UN Conference Rio+20
	Clean Seas Pact	Within the framework of the Clean Seas Pact, nations committed to diminishing pollution originating from single-use plastics, safeguarding their national waters, and promoting recycling efforts. This pact gained endorsement in 2017.
	Honolulu Strategy	The Honolulu Strategy establishes a comprehensive global framework, suggesting strategies and potential actions to mitigate the quantity and repercussions of plastic litter. Notably, the strategy refrains from prescribing specific targets or actions
Waste trade	The Plastic Waste Partnership (PWP) of the Basel Convention	An initiative aimed at fostering environmentally sound management of waste trade, the PWP was inaugurated in 2019.

Source: OECDE, *Global Plastics Outlook: Economic Drivers, Environmental Impacts and Policy Option*, 2022.

Scholars of law, and in the field of plastics, have conducted thorough examinations of the deficiencies of the existing regulatory frameworks. However, as Johnson et al.[30] demonstrated convincingly, due mainly to the catastrophic repercussions

30 H. Johnson et al., 'Conceptualizing the Transnational Regulation of Plastics: Moving Towards a Preventative and Just Agenda for Plastics', *Transnational Environmental Law*, (2022) 11(2), pp. 325–355, https://doi.org/10.1017/S2047102521000261.

of plastics for marine ecosystems, most doctrinal proposals for shaping novel legal mechanisms tend to concentrate on the reduction of pollution. It is imperative that other critical problems be acknowledged too. Firstly, no international or transnational instrument addresses plastics comprehensively within the context of justice and human rights.[31] Secondly, international plastics law chiefly concerns pollution-related issues, which has resulted in waste management regulation being prioritised, often at the expense of the proactive prevention of production. Target 12.5 of UN Sustainable Development Goal (SDG) 12 (sustainable consumption and production) should be relevant to the prevention of plastics production. However, the indicator for measuring progress 'is wholly focused on national recycling rates and the weight (tonnes) of materials recycled'.[32] Similarly, the abstract metric definition of Target 12.2, which is directed at the sustainable management and efficient use of natural resources, 'could be met without any prevention at all'.[33] Therefore, all analyses indicate that SDG 12 is 'overly focused on end-of-pipe solutions'.[34]

The legal framework should promote the phasing-out of plastics, as opposed to reinforcing the established patterns of plastics production and consumption that are governed by international economic law.[35] Against this backdrop, this contribution's analysis focuses on a particularly contentious multilateral investment law instrument – the ECT. Its provisions extend protection to investments in fossil fuels, thereby fostering the production of plastics.

3.1. THE ENERGY CHARTER TREATY, FOSSIL FUELS, AND PLANS FOR MODERNISATION

The ECT was signed in Lisbon on 17 December 1994, and entered into force in 1998.[36] Its scope is wide,[37] and its purpose is to promote 'long-term cooperation in the energy field, based on complementarities and mutual benefits, in accordance with the objectives and principles of the Charter'.[38] As

---

31 Ibid.

32 Ibid.

33 Ibid.

34 Ibid.

35 Ibid.

36 Energy Charter Secretariat, *The Energy Charter Treaty – A Reader's Guide*, Energy Charter Secretariat, 2002, https://is.muni.cz/el/1422/jaro2017/MVV2368K/um/ECT_Guide_ENG.pdf (hereinafter 'ECT Reader's Guide'). Energy Charter Treaty, 16 April 1998 (2080 UNTS 95), OXIO 221.

37 See Art. 2 ECT, as well as *Cem Cengiz Uzan v. Republic of Turkey*, SCC Case No. V 2014/023, Award on Respondent Bifurcated Preliminary Objection, 20 April 2016, 151–152.

38 *Eiser Infrastructure Limited and Energía Solar Luxembourg S.à r.l. v. Kingdom of Spain*, ICSID Case No. ARB/13/36, Award, 4 May 2017, 378–379.

an instrument of international economic law, the ECT has fossil resources in its DNA. It has been said to be a liberalising measure[39] whose content was shaped chiefly by geopolitical concerns.[40] It originates from a time when few objectives were thought to be sufficiently important to override the imperative to invest, and it has been subjected to intensive criticism. For example, the environmental assessments described in Article 19 are unlikely to be Paris-proof, and the environment and sustainability seldom feature in the proportionality analyses of the arbiters who are tasked with applying the Charter.[41] A modernisation effort that began in 2009 culminated in a political declaration about a new treaty, which resulted in the adoption of the political declaration of an International Energy Charter, on 20 May 2015. However, this effort has not proven to be sufficient, and several states have threatened to withdraw from the Treaty; some have even made good on their threats.[42] A fresh attempt was launched in 2015, and it produced an Agreement in Principle, in June 2022. That Agreement will enter into force 90 days after three-quarters of the contracting parties ratify it. However, even after the Agreement in Principle, several EU Member States withdrew or expressed their intention to withdraw from the ECT.[43] This decision generated much pressure across the Union, and that pressure eventually prompted the European Commission to announce and orchestrate the collective withdrawal of the Union from the system, in July 2023.[44] The following paragraphs provide an overview of the proposed amendments pertaining to fossil fuels.

The ECT covers all energy sources, including renewables and fossils, as well as an unusually wide range of activities, from exploration and extraction to marketing and sales.[45] The list of 'energy materials and products' to which its provisions are relevant includes nuclear energy, coal, natural gas, petroleum, petroleum products, electrical energy, fuel wood, and wood charcoal.[46] The ECT

39 M. Magnarelli, A. Monti and M. Fermeglia, 'Expert Roundtable: The Energy Charter Treaty at a Crossroads', *Kluwer Arbitration Blog*, 18 November 2022, http://arbitrationblog.kluwerarbitration.com/2022/11/18/expert-roundtable-the-energy-charter-treaty-at-a-crossroads/.

40 A. Belyi, 'The Energy Charter process in the face of uncertainties', *Journal of World Energy Law and Business*, (2021) 14(5), pp. 363–375, https://doi.org/10.1093/jwelb/jwab032.

41 L. Reins, 'Article 2: Purpose of the Treaty' in R. Leal-Arcas (ed.), *Commentary on the Energy Charter Treaty*, Edward Elgar Publishing, 2018, pp. 49–58.

42 European Parliament resolution of 24 November 2022 on the outcome of the modernisation of the Energy Charter Treaty (2022/2934(RSP)), OJ C 167, 11.5.2023, pp. 68–73., https://oeil.secure.europarl.europa.eu/oeil/popups/ficheprocedure.do?lang=enandreference=2022/2934(RSP).

43 Ibid.

44 European Commission, 'Proposal for a Council Decision on the withdrawal of the Union from the Energy Charter Treaty', Brussels, 07.07.2023, COM(2023) 447 final, 2023/0273.

45 *Electrabel S.A. v. Republic of Hungary*, ICSID Case No. ARB/07/19, Decision on Jurisdiction, Applicable Law and Liability, 30 November 2012, para. 5.50.

46 Annex EM I, based on the Harmonised System of the World Customs Organization and the Combined Nomenclature of the European Communities.

does not, however, account for new trends in carbon-neutral energy, energy efficiency and digitalisation.[47] The Agreement in Principle covers sustainable fuels, such as hydrogen, anhydrous ammonia, biomass, biogas and synthetic fuels. Brauch has argued that these additions do not improve sustainability, but instead merely serve to constrain the ability of states to legislate on the matter.[48] It has also been argued that it would have been better for the ECT to have included interpretative guidance for arbitral tribunals, and for a distinction to have been drawn between investments into the energy transition and investments into fossil fuels.[49]

The modernised list of materials and products is to be reviewed at least once every five years. At present, fossil fuel investments are not excluded from it. This proposition is subject to one qualification: the contracting parties can derogate from their obligation to protect those investments, by using the Annex NI mechanism. If that mechanism is employed, fossil fuel investments can be phased out after 10 years, which is an improvement on the cooling-off period under the current version of the ECT, which is 20 years. This flexibility mechanism is also to be reviewed every five years. Only the EU and the UK are expected to avail themselves of it. Even there, fossil fuel investments will be protected into the 2030s.[50] The decision to retain investment protection for fossil fuels has been called unscientific, and has been described as 'climate madness'.[51]

Article 10(4) of the modernisation package establishes climate change mitigation as a legitimate objective that the contracting states may pursue. Article 19 reaffirms the validity of the international agreements to which the contracting states are party. It also describes various requirements for environmental impact assessments, which may now account for a wider range of policy desiderata. Thus, the contracting parties are to consider the effect of energy investment projects on human health, the land, the soil, the air, the climate and water, as well as on cultural heritage and the need to protect natural landscapes. Moreover, Article 19 requires impact assessments to be accompanied with public participation processes. However, the commitment in question is vague, and no reference is made to the Aarhus Convention. Perhaps more critically, fossil fuel subsidies are not prohibited under the Agreement in Principle – Article 17 only

---

47 O. Quirico, *Investment Governance between the Energy Charter Treaty and the European Union: Resolving Regulatory Conflicts*, Brill Nijhoff, 2021, pp. 75 *et seq.*

48 M.D. Brauch, 'The Agreement in Principle on ECT "Modernization": A Botched Reform Attempt that Undermines Climate Action', *Kluwer Arbitration Blog*, 17 October 2022, http://arbitrationblog.kluwerarbitration.com/2022/10/17/the-agreement-in-principle-on-ect-modernization-a-botched-reform-attempt-that-undermines-climate-action/.

49 Magnarelli et al., supra, note 38.

50 Brauch, supra, note 47.

51 T. Fisher, 'The Modernised Energy Charter Treaty: The New Text', *Kluwer Arbitration Blog*, 15 October 2022, http://arbitrationblog.kluwerarbitration.com/2022/10/15/the-modernised-energy-charter-treaty-the-new-text/.

requires them to be non-arbitrary.[52] Finally, the Agreement in Principle contains a new provision on the energy transition, which will appear after the current Article 19, if and when the treaty is ratified. This provision is neither ambitious nor especially novel: for the most part, it refers to the Paris Agreement[53] and the United Nations Framework Convention on Climate Change (UNFCCC).[54] Beyond that, its content is vague, and the obligations that it creates are couched in highly abstract terms.

Conceptually, the ECT is underlain by a dilemma: at the present juncture, it is obvious that investment into sustainable development must be accelerated; however, international investment law and the treaties that comprise it are liable to obstruct progress towards sustainable development.[55] Environmental issues only began to permeate that domain of law very recently,[56] and only because they were inserted into international investment agreements in response to societal concerns.[57] In this regard, the ECT is wholly conventional. Like other treaties of its kind, it relies on investor–state dispute settlement for the adjudication of disagreements between governments and private entities. That mechanism is of doubtful legitimacy, due to the use of privately appointed arbitrators,[58] and because it can be misused to halt the energy transition. The Charter has served as a basis for at least 46 challenges to renewable energy incentives[59] and coal phase-outs.[60] Presumably, a more institutionalised form of investor–state dispute settlement would accommodate environmental objectives more easily than the present version of the mechanism. In investor–state dispute settlement, pro-environmental concerns can function both as a sword (when investors complain about breaches of environmental commitments) and as a shield (when states use the environment to justify interferences or takings).[61] That said, although the legal importance of this proposition is self-evident, the practical influence

52 Brauch, supra, note 47.

53 Paris Agreement to the United Nations Framework Convention on Climate Change, 12 December 2015, T.I.A.S. No. 16-1104.

54 Ibid.

55 M.C. Cordonier Segger, 'Innovative Legal Solutions for Investment Law and Sustainable Development Challenges' in Y. Levashova, T. Lambooy and I. Dekker (eds.), *Bridging the Gap between International Investment Law and the Environment*, Eleven International Publishing, 2015.

56 Ibid.

57 Ibid.

58 C. Baltag and Y. Dautaj, 'Investors, States, and Arbitrators in the Crosshairs of International Investment Law and Environmental Protection', *Brill Research Perspectives in International Investment Law and Arbitration* (2020) 3(1), 1–77.

59 M. Fermeglia, 'Cashing-In on the Energy Transition? Assessing Damage Evaluation Practices in Renewable Energy Investment Disputes', *Journal of World Investment and Trade* (2022) 23, pp. 982–1019, https://doi.org/10.1163%2F22119000-12340276.

60 Ibid.

61 ibid.

of the ECT may be doubted: it was recently shown that legal protections have no demonstrable impact on foreign investment in, among other things, renewable energy.[62] On the whole, it appears that the changes to the ECT, regardless of whether they are considered in isolation or in their totality, are cosmetic, and further entrench fossil fuel lock-in.

3.2. THE UN TREATY ON PLASTIC POLLUTION

After more than a decade of policymaking efforts,[63] on 2 March 2022 the UNEA adopted a resolution that initiated an international lawmaking process intended to combat pollution from plastics, including marine plastic pollution. That process is expected to bear fruit by 2024.[64] A zero draft of the instrument's text was published in September 2023.[65] This historical mandate to negotiate a UN Plastics Treaty has been hailed as 'the beginning of the end of the scourge of plastic pollution',[66] and as the 'Paris of the plastic debate'.[67] The Resolution breaks new ground in three ways: first, it reflects a full-life-cycle approach to the problem. Second, it contains a set of basic objectives that should be incorporated into the future treaty. Those objectives include sustainable production and consumption, waste management, periodical assessments, and the conduct of research on plastics pollution. Third, the Resolution calls for international cooperation, and hints at synergies between the proposed convention and other international law instruments.[68] That said, the Resolution has not been spared criticism, especially in light of the vagueness of some of the principles being mooted, such as the full-life-cycle approach, and common but differentiated responsibility.[69] These issues have been left to the Intergovernmental Negotiating

62 L. Mehranvar and S. Sasmal, 'The Role of Investment Treaties and Investor–State Dispute Settlement (ISDS) in Renewable Energy Investments', *Columbia Center on Sustainable Investment (CCSI)*, December 2022, https://scholarship.law.columbia.edu/cgi/viewcontent.cgi?article=1004andcontext=sustainable_investment; M. Aydos et al., 'Scaling Investment in Renewable Energy Generation to Achieve Sustainable Development Goals 7 (Affordable and Clean Energy) and 13 (Climate Action) and the Paris Agreement: Roadblocks and Drivers', *Columbia Center on Sustainable Investment*, December 2022, https://dx.doi.org/10.2139/ssrn.4309067.

63 See G. Nagtzaam, 'Crafting a Global Plastics Treaty' in G. Nagtzaam, G. van Calster, S. Kourabas and E. Karateva (eds.), *Global Plastic Pollution and its Regulation*, Edward Elgar Publishing, 2023, for an overview of the historical negotiation context.

64 Resolution adopted by the United Nations Environment Assembly on 2 March 2022, UNEP/EA.5/Res.14.

65 Zero draft text of the international legally binding instrument on plastic pollution, including in the marine environment, UNEP/PP/INC.3/4.

66 Nagtzaam, supra, note 61, p. 304.

67 Ibid.

68 S. Wang, 'International Law-Making Process of Combating Plastic Pollution: Status Quo, Debates and Prospects', *Marine Policy*, (2023) 147, 105376.

69 Ibid.

Committee. The same is true of other matters, such as the definition of 'plastics', the treatment of microplastics, the bindingness of the various obligations that the treaty is expected to contain, and coordination with the extant international law on chemicals and the recycling of plastics.[70] The parts of the zero draft that cover definitions, principles and the scope of the instrument remain blank.

It has been emphasised that the Plastics Treaty must be merged effectively with the other treaties on environmental matters, which are fairly voluminous. Although those treaties do not target plastics directly, their provisions do intersect with those of the prospective instrument, which is a matter that the Intergovernmental Negotiating Committee will have to consider.[71] The piecemeal approach to plastics that has predominated historically is in evidence in the Convention on the Prevention of Marine Pollution by Dumping of Wastes and Other Matter (the London Convention) and the International Convention for the Prevention of Pollution from Ships (MARPOL), which only regulate pollution from vessels. Another marine convention that may overlap with the proposed treaty is the United Nations Convention on the Law of the Sea (UNCLOS). The danger is particularly pronounced in the context of Articles 194 and 207 of UNCLOS.[72] Several other (non-binding) international initiatives[73] also concern plastics. For example, some have inquired whether plastic may be a form of 'hazardous waste' under the Basel Convention on Hazardous Waste of 1992, or whether it may be classified as a persistent organic pollutant under the Stockholm Convention on Persistent Organic Pollutants of 2004.[74]

It is evident from the foregoing that the interactions between various legal regimes will be critical to the success of the future Plastics Treaty. That treaty will have to possess a wide range of jurisprudential virtues, including cohesion and effectiveness; it will also have to be unusually wide in its scope – it must cover land, air and sea.[75] It has been argued that it should contain binding, measurable and time-bound global reduction targets,[76] as well as a mixture of binding and voluntary provisions.[77] Whether the framework approach that was adopted in the UN Convention on Biological Diversity, the Montreal Protocol and the UN Framework Convention on Climate Change (UNFCCC) could serve as a model is the subject of a heated debate. According to some, these agreements provide tools that are sufficiently flexible. However, it has also been argued that 'a different

70 Nagtzaam, supra, note 61.
71 Ibid.
72 Ibid., also for a detailed analysis of how these international instruments address plastic pollution.
73 Ibid.
74 Ibid.
75 Ibid.
76 Ibid.
77 Ibid.

type of Treaty',[78] which focuses on 'non-harmful solutions',[79] is needed. The 1987 Montreal Protocol on Substances that Deplete the Ozone Layer is a viable model, because of its commitment to phasing-out the substances that are listed in its Annex A, which is accompanied with specific regulations aimed at the gradual prohibition of their use, and because of its sensitivity to the needs of developing nations. Both ozone-depleting chemicals and plastics are synthetic materials that persist when they are released into the environment. Furthermore, the Montreal Protocol conveys a clear message to state and non-state actors, and urges them to revise policies and products. At the same time, its model is such that it allows for an adaptation period in which alternative materials or operational methods can be explored. However, according to Kirk, the Montreal Protocol approach may have drawbacks. Some states might oppose stringent standards, advocating an approach that is instead grounded in the principle of common but differentiated responsibility. This principle assigns varying obligations to parties on the basis of their level of development and their capabilities.[80] The associated risk is that a treaty that combines progressive bans on plastics with waste management could inadvertently prioritise the latter. Such prioritisation might entail less disruption to existing systems of plastic production and consumption, potentially undermining efforts to address the root causes of the problem.[81]

Kirk has suggested the inclusion of a mechanism that would make the removal of plastics from the ocean a key milestone. The funds and techniques that are employed to combat oil pollution, such as those that feature in the International Convention on the Establishment of an International Fund for Compensation for Oil Pollution Damage (Fund Convention), supply a salient analogy.[82] In addition, Kirk has recommended guidance that would ensure progress 'toward[s] new ways of organizing the production and distribution of goods'.[83] UNEP Resolution 5/14 refers to the principles of the 1992 Rio Declaration, but does not elaborate on them,[84] which is likely to precipitate an animated debate during the negotiations, especially in the context of the principle of common but differentiated responsibility.[85] In the zero draft, the Rio Declaration is mentioned in the notes of the secretariat, and in the chair's explanatory note, but not in the main text.

[78] E. Kirk, 'The Montreal Protocol or the Paris Agreement as a Model for a Plastics Treaty?', *American Journal of International Law*, 2020 (114), p. 212, https://doi.org/10.1017/aju.2020.39.

[79] Ibid.

[80] Ibid.

[81] Johnson et al., supra, note 29.

[82] International Convention on the Establishment of an International Fund for Compensation for Oil Pollution Damage (Fund Convention), 18 December 1971, 1110 UNTS 57.

[83] Kirk, supra, note 76, p. 212.

[84] Wang, supra, note 66.

[85] Ibid.

The content of the new Treaty is far from clear. The first round of treaty negotiations has been marred by disagreements about procedure and timetables, and by poor organisation.[86] So far, the negotiations have not turned to the substance of the treaty, or to its interaction with other regimes. During the second meeting of the Intergovernmental Negotiating Committee (INC-2), which took place in May and June of 2023, in Paris, the delegates agreed that they should proceed from a zero draft. That zero draft was published in September 2023, and describes differences in opinion on various matters, including the set of problematic materials and products, the notion of circularity, and implementation techniques.[87] The text includes alternative formulations of each prospective provision: therefore, how effective the regime will be remains to be seen. The differences between the formulations of the objectives are already pronounced. The first formulation states clearly that the objective of the instrument is 'to end plastic pollution', and to protect human health and the environment. The second option emphasises the protection of human health and the environment *from* plastics, but does not explicitly state, in all its suboptions, that plastic pollution should be ended.

3.3. PRELIMINARY OBSERVATIONS ON REGIME INTERACTION

The UN Plastics Treaty and the ECT are parts of different international (sectoral) regimes. They do not refer to each other, and the interactions between them are not obvious. Whereas 'regime complexities'[88] and the fragmentation of international law are inevitable in a globalised world,[89] 'problem-shifting'[90] is also a live issue in the context of plastics. As shown in the introduction and in section 2, plastics and fossil fuels are linked in reality. But the law as it currently stands is blind to this link. Here, we analyse the interplay between the ECT and the Plastics Treaty by drawing on Piselli and van Asselt's[91] work on planetary boundaries and regime interaction. Dunoff defined regime interaction as 'a more systematic, dynamic and forward-looking perspective on how different international legal

86 Ibid.

87 International Institute for Sustainable Development (IISD), 'Earth Negotiations Bulletin', 5 June 2023, (36–12), https://enb.iisd.org/sites/default/files/2023-06/enb3612e.pdf.

88 K. Raustiala and D.G. Victor, 'The Regime Complex for Plant Genetic Resources', *International Organization*, (2004) 58, pp. 277 *et seq.*, https://doi.org/10.1017/S0020818304582036.

89 D. Piselli and H. van Hasselt, 'Planetary boundaries and regime interaction in international law' in D. French and L.J. Kotzé, *Research Handbook on Law, Governance and Planetary Boundaries*, Edward Elgar Publishing, 2021, pp. 125 *et seq.*

90 R.E. Kim and H. van Asselt, 'Global governance: Problem shifting in the Anthropocene and the limits of international law' in E. Morgera and K. Kulovesi, *Research Handbook on International Law and Natural Resources*, Edward Elgar Publishing, 2016, https://www.elgaronline.com/display/edcoll/9781783478323/9781783478323.00039.xml.

91 Piselli and van Hasselt, supra, note 87.

regimes relate to each other'.[92] He focused on relational interactions, as opposed to transactional ones, and distinguished between operational interactions – that is, practical arrangements; regulatory interactions – that is, exchanges between different bodies that produce regulatory guidance; and conceptual interactions, which have the transfer of social knowledge across regimes as their purpose.[93] The concept of regime interaction is relevant to lawmaking, the implementation of legal measures, and dispute settlement.[94] It entails transcending the constraints of black-letter analysis, and the identification of solutions to the problem of conflicting norms.[95] Understanding regime interaction can thus be a starting point in the development of 'mutually supportive regimes'.[96] Since the negotiations are still under way, and the zero draft of the Plastic Treaty remains highly general and contingent, it is not possible to analyse regime interaction in detail. This section instead presents some preliminary observations on the interaction between the ECT and the Plastics Treaty Resolution (and the zero draft).

It is evident from the preceding section that there are numerous conflicts between the norms of the ECT and those of the Plastics Treaty Resolution. Moreover, the operational and regulatory interactions between the two are limited. These interactions are highly important, but lack formal legal recognition. The UNFCCC is intended to fulfil a 'linking role' in both regimes. In the Plastics Treaty, it is referred to as a model. The Resolution reaffirms the Convention, as well as many other instruments. The zero draft does not refer to it. The Preamble to the ECT refers to the UNFCCC, and recognises the urgency of climate change issues. The Agreement in Principle contains more extensive references to the UNFCCC, the Paris Agreement and the International Labour Organisation (ILO) conventions, all of which it 'reaffirms'. The Preamble also recognises the urgency of environmental concerns. The ECT is thus not divorced from the international agenda,[97] or blind to the Paris targets. However, it also does not make those targets binding on its signatories. In fact, Article 18 confirms the sovereignty of states over the environment,[98] and

---

92 J.L. Dunoff, 'How to Avoid Regime Collisions' in A. Fischer-Lescano et al. (eds.), *Contested Regime Collisions: Norm Fragmentation in World Society*, Cambridge University Press, 2016, https://www.cambridge.org/core/books/contested-regime-collisions/how-to-avoid-regime-collisions/0BF34359CA7E1F7AEE0F20A4F185777C; see also Piselli and van Hasselt, supra, note 87.

93 Dunoff, supra, note 90.

94 M.A. Young, 'Regime Interaction in Creating, Implementing and Enforcing International Law' in M.A. Young (ed.), *Regime Interaction in International Law: Facing Fragmentation*, Cambridge University Press 2012, p. 85, https://www.cambridge.org/core/books/regime-interaction-in-international-law/regime-interaction-in-creating-implementing-and-enforcing-international-law/8F958E230DD068D4E6CE9F1141B9D65B.

95 Piselli and van Hasselt, supra, note 87.

96 Ibid., p. 142.

97 A. Morelli, 'Preamble' in R. Leal-Arcas, supra, note 40, pp. 6–12, https://www.e-elgar.com/shop/gbp/commentary-on-the-energy-charter-treaty-9781788117487.html.

98 T. Waelde and A. Kolo, 'Environmental Regulation, Investment Protection and "Regulatory Taking" in International Law', *The International and Comparative Law Quarterly*, (2001) 50(4), pp. 811–848.

reserves for them the right to regulate energy exploration and development on their territories (Art 18 (3)).[99] Both regimes also mention sustainable development and the Rio Declaration. The vagueness of the notion of 'sustainable development' has been said to be a diplomatic stratagem, in that the ambiguity of the principle can be harnessed to promote agreements on economic, social and environmental issues.[100] However, this ambiguity has also prevented the emergence of firm global commitments to social equity and ecological sustainability.[101] The informality of the concept also perpetuates the same hierarchy of international relations that produced the present state of affairs.[102] On the whole, the role of sustainable development in the ECT is such that the probability of it producing significant change, in practice, is highly remote.[103] The same is true of the Plastics Treaty. The concept of sustainable development is mentioned explicitly in the Resolution, which also emphasises the role of sustainability in the governance of plastics. The Resolution thus refers to 'sustainable alternatives and technologies available to address the full cycle of plastics', the 'importance of promoting sustainable design of products and materials' for reuse and recycling, and research on the development of 'sustainable, affordable, innovative and cost-efficient approaches'. However, no mention is made of the proposition that plastic production should be prevented.

4. EARTH SYSTEM LAW FOR THE TRANSNATIONAL REGULATION OF PLASTICS

The production, utilisation and disposal of plastics have become so pervasive that they are now recognised as a geological indicator of the Anthropocene.[104] Plastics have recently garnered scientific attention as a potential threat to the

---

99 Hunter, T. "Article 18 Sovereignty over Natural Resources." In Commentary on the Energy Charter Treaty, edited by Leal-Arcas, R., 259–68. Cheltenham: Edward Elgar Publishing, 2018.

100 Vinuales, Jorge E., The Rise and Fall of Sustainable Development (13 January, 2013). Available at SSRN: https://ssrn.com/abstract=2200083 or http://dx.doi.org/10.2139/ssrn.2200083.

101 A. Cardesa-Salzmann and E. Cocciolo, 'Global Governance, Sustainability and the Earth System: Critical Reflections on the Role of Global Law', *Transnational Environmental Law*, (2019) (8–3), pp. 437–461, https://doi.org/10.1017/S2047102519000098.

102 M. Koskenniemi, 'Empire and International Law: The Real Spanish Contribution', *University of Toronto Law Journal*, 2011, (61–1), pp. 1–36; K. Miles, 'International Investments Law: Origins, Imperialism and the Conceptualizing the Environment', *Colorado Journal of International Environmental Law and Policy*, 2010 (21), pp. 1–48, https://www.cisdl.org/wp-content/uploads/2018/05/CJ-Vol.21.1-2010.pdf.

103 N. Bernasconi-Osterwalder and M.D. Brauch, 'Redesigning the Energy Charter Treaty to Advance the Low-Carbon Transition', *Transnational Dispute Management*, February 2019, p. 3, https://www.transnational-dispute-management.com/article.asp?key=2632.

104 P. Villarrubia-Gómez, S.E. Cornell and J. Fabres, 'Marine plastic pollution as a planetary boundary threat – The drifting piece in the sustainability puzzle', *Marine Policy*, (2018) (96), p. 213, https://doi.org/10.1016/j.marpol.2017.11.035.

planetary boundaries. Planetary boundaries define the 'safe operating space' for humanity, on the basis of the intrinsic biophysical processes that regulate the stability of the Earth system.[105] Studies have lately pointed out that human activity has caused at least six of these nine planetary boundaries to be exceeded, namely climate change, loss of biosphere integrity, land use, biogeochemical cycles, freshwater change and other 'novel entities' (NE).[106] The NE concept refers to chemical pollution. It is defined as 'new substances, new forms of existing substances and modified life forms', including 'chemicals and other new types of engineered materials or organisms not previously known to the Earth system as well as naturally occurring elements'.[107] Plastic pollution is regarded as a significant issue within the broader context of the NE planetary boundary.[108] Extensive research has shown that chemicals, including plastics, possess the defining attributes of NE, which means that they merit attention and concern.[109]

Against the planetary boundaries framework, Earth system governance (ESG) has emerged. ESG, a social science, is not about 'governing the Earth, or the management of the entire process of planetary evolution. Instead, ESG is about the human impact on planetary systems. It is about the societal steering of human activities with regard to the long-term stability of geobiophysical systems'.[110] Nevertheless, as Collins has argued, 'even if the planetary boundary framework is scientifically valid, ethically viable and political persuasive, it is not – as lawyers would say – "self-executing"'.[111] Thus, it is pertinent that Earth system law (ESL), the legal dimension of ESG, is being developed. ESL provides a

---

105 J. Rockström et al., 'Planetary Boundaries: Exploring the Safe Operating Space for Humanity', *Ecology and Society*, 2009 (14–2:32), https://www.ecologyandsociety.org/vol14/iss2/art32/; L. Persson et al., 'Outside the Safe Operating Space of the Planetary Boundary for Novel Entities', *Environmental Science and Technology*, 2022, (56–3), pp. 1510–1521, https://doi.org/10.1021/acs.est.1c04158. K. Richardson et al., 'Earth beyond six of nine planetary boundaries', *Science Advances*, (2023) 9(37), https://doi.org/10.1126/sciadv.adh2458.

106 Persson et al., supra, note 101.

107 W. Steffen et al., 'Planetary boundaries: Guiding human development on a changing planet', *Science* (2015), 347 (6223), 1259855–1259855, https://doi.org/10.1126/science.1259855.

108 M. MacLeod et al., 'Identifying chemicals that are planetary boundary threats', *Environmental Science and Technology*, (2014), 48(19), 11057–11063; H. Arp et al., 'Weathering Plastics as a Planetary Boundary Threat: Exposure, Fate, and Hazards', *Environmental Science and Technology*, (2021), 22(11), 7246–7255.

109 Persson et al., supra, note 101.

110 F. Biermann, 'The Anthropocene: A governance perspective', *The Anthropocene Review*, (2014) 1(1), p. 57. See also F. Biermann, '"Earth system governance" as a crosscutting theme of global change research', *Global Environmental Change*, (2007) 17(3–4), 326–337, https://doi.org/10.1016/j.gloenvcha.2006.11.010; F. Biermann et al., 'Navigating the Anthropocene: Improving Earth System Governance', *Science*, (2012), 335, issue no. 6074, https://doi.org/10.1126/science.1217255; F. Biermann, 'The future of "environmental" policy in the Anthropocene: time for a paradigm shift', *Environmental Politics* (2021) 30, nos. 1–2, pp. 61–80, https://doi.org/10.1080/09644016.2020.1846958.

111 L. Collins, 'Science, law and planetary uncertainty' in D. French and L. Kotzé, supra, note 87, p. 93.

holistic analytical lens, normative perspectives, a new paradigm for lawmaking,[112] and operations, such as implementation and enforcement, that may enable the problems of mainstream international legal regimes to be overcome.[113] In fact, the emergence of a global *polis*,[114] and the ecological transformation that it has entailed, call for new regulatory thinking.[115] ESL has been developed to improve the connectivity[116] between different branches of law and science.[117] It is intended to generate means of assessing legal orders by reference to the needs of Earth as a system, and to identify measures that would enable socio-ecological processes to continue reproducing. In this sense, it coheres with global law,[118] and with the transformative law episteme.[119] ESL can also complement Dunnoff's regime interaction. All of these concepts are necessary to plug the 'Anthropocene gap';[120] that is, to address the uncertainties and interdependencies of our day at the structural level, a task to which Holocene law has proven unequal.[121] If it reaches maturity, the ESL project would yield laws that provide for 'governance by and for all living beings'.[122]

ESL can facilitate the integration of concepts such as the planetary boundaries. As Kim and Kotzé have noted, the planetary boundaries framework points to important reasons for addressing the misfit between the complexity of

---

112 G. Frisso and E. Kirk, 'Changing role of law-making in responding to planetary boundaries' in D. French and L. Kotzé, supra, note 87, pp. 147–166.

113 Piselli and van Hasselt, supra, note 87; H. Schellnhuber et al., *Earth System Analysis for Sustainability*, MIT Press, 2004; C. Hamilton, 'The Anthropocene as rupture', *The Anthropocene Review*, (2016) (3:2), https://doi.org/10.1177/2053019616634741.

114 J. Jaria Manzano, *La Constitución del Antropoceno*, Tirant lo Blanch/Tirant Humanidades, 2020.

115 L.J. Kotzé and R.E. Kim, 'Earth system law: The juridical dimensions of earth system governance', *Earth System Governance* (2019) 1, 100003, https://doi.org/10.1016/j.esg.2019.100003.

116 This contribution transfers the notion of 'connectivity', which was elaborated by Paul Kjaer in relation to global law, to ESL. According to Kjaer, from an inter-systemic perspective, connectivity norms function so as to increase the probability of transfers of condensed social component *(Sinnkomponente)*, as scientific knowledge, from a legally structured context to another context, positioned within world society: P.F. Kjaer, 'Constitutionalizing Connectivity: The Constitutional Grid of World Society', *Journal of Law and Society*, 2018 (45), S114–S134, https://doi.org/10.1111/jols.12106.

117 L.J. Kotzé et al., 'Earth system law: Exploring new frontiers in legal science', *Earth System Governance* (2022) 11, 100126, https://doi.org/10.1016/j.esg.2021.100126.

118 Cardesa-Salzmann and Cocciolo, supra, note 97.

119 P.F. Kjaer, 'What is transformative law?', *European Law Open*, (2022) (4–1), pp. 760–780, https://doi.org/10.1017/elo.2023.1.

120 V. Galaz, *Global Environmental Governance, Technology and Politics*, Edward Elgar Publishing, 2014.

121 Kotzé et al., supra, note 113; Kotzé and Kim, supra, note 111; L.J. Kotzé, 'Earth System Law for the Anthropocene', *Sustainability* (2019) 11(23), https://doi.org/10.3390/su11236796; L. Du Toit and L.J. Kotzé, 'Reimagining international environmental law for the Anthropocene: An earth system law perspective', *Earth System Governance* 2022 (11), 100132, https://doi.org/10.1016/j.esg.2022.100132.

122 Kotzé and Kim, supra, note 111, pp. 6–7.

the Earth, as a system, and the fragmentation of the extant regulatory systems.[123] Furthermore, the Anthropocene calls for planetary integrity to be elevated to the status of a legal principle.[124] Human hierarchies sustained by the global neo-liberal legal order must assume responsibility for the global climate crisis.[125] ESL can be instrumental to that end, because, as Lenton has observed, it is capable of precipitating transformation 'across coupled social-technological-ecological systems'.[126]

The application of the ESL paradigm to the *problématique* of this chapter reveals the existence of a research agenda that can address the complex regulatory interdependencies of the fossil chemical industry and plastic pollution, and their impacts on the planetary boundaries. This agenda is important because the ECT prevents the environmental impacts of energy investments from being taken seriously. In essence, the ECT aims to serve as a stable legal framework for liberalisation and competition in the energy trade. At the same time, SDG 12, which should guide political and regulatory action on sustainable consumption and production patterns, at all levels of government, has been articulated into targets and indicators shaped by the neo-liberal business interests that are embedded in the concept of sustainable development.[127]

5. CONCLUSIONS

In this contribution, we explained the relationship between the plastics-producing petrochemical industry and fossil energy resources. There is a link between the growth of the plastics industry and fossil fuel investments. The underlying international regulatory regimes do not account for this reality. They are fragmented and tend to shift problems from one legal regime to another. Despite the efforts to modernise it, the ECT entrenches the fossil fuel lock-in, and thus contributes indirectly to plastic pollution. The UN Resolution promotes a life-cycle approach to plastics, and aims to change the current

123 R. Kim and L.J. Kotzé, 'Governing the complexity of planetary boundaries: a state-of-the-art analysis of social science scholarship' in D. French and L. Kotzé, supra, note 87, pp. 54 *et seq.*

124 L.J. Kotzé et al., supra, note 113.

125 A. Grear, 'Deconstructing *Anthropos*: A Critical Legal Reflection on "Anthropocentric" Law and Anthropocene "Humanity"', *Law Critique*, (2015) 26, p. 227, https://doi.org/10.1007/s10978-015-9161-0.

126 T.M. Lenton et al., 'Operationalising positive tipping points towards global sustainability', *Global Sustainability*, (2022) (5–1), pp. 1–16, https://doi.org/10.1017/sus.2021.30.

127 L.J. Kotzé et al., 'Planetary Integrity' in F. Biermann, T. Hickmann, and C.-A. Sénit (eds.), *The Political Impact of the Sustainable Development Goals: Transforming Governance Through Global Goals?*, Cambridge University Press, 2022, p. 145, https://do.org10.1017/9781009082945.007.

international regulatory framework, which focuses on waste management. It is too early to say whether the new regime will prove effective. We argued that, in the course of the negotiations of a UN Plastics Treaty, attention should be paid to regime interaction between both regimes of plastics and energy investments, so that problem-shifting can be avoided. Finally, we concluded that adopting an Earth system perspective to the regulation of plastics could facilitate a new type of lawmaking, and a new approach to regime interaction that would prioritise planetary integrity and the creation and maintenance of a safe and just operating space for humanity.

POWER PURCHASE AGREEMENTS AFFECTED BY UNEXPECTED CIRCUMSTANCES

A Contract Law Issue with Climate Consequences

Gonzalo Vial FOURCADE

ABSTRACT

Climate change is a multidimensional dilemma involving challenges in diverse areas. This chapter identifies a problem in the intersection between the climate crisis and the law of contracts. In particular, it observes that, in disputes involving power purchase agreements, the traditional understanding of how doctrines of contracts affected by unexpected circumstances should be applied can negatively impact on efforts to tackle the climate crisis. This finding is illustrated by the description of a real case that took place within the Chilean electricity system. As a solution to this concern, it is posited that climate principles should be incorporated into the regulatory frameworks of electricity systems, in such a way as to ensure that the parties to power purchase agreements would understand, in advance, that climate values will be incorporated to their contracts.

1. INTRODUCTION: A PROBLEM IN THE INTERSECTION BETWEEN CLIMATE CHANGE AND CONTRACT LAW

Climate change is commonly characterised as a phenomenon that involves long-lasting modifications to the temperatures and weather patterns of our planet.[1] But despite having a scientific description, the issue is much more than a mere technical concern. It is a multidimensional challenge: a global problem,[2] a local distress,[3] a political issue,[4] a social dilemma,[5] a philosophical question,[6] and an economic challenge,[7] among many other things.

In the legal arena, the challenges posed by the climate crisis have usually been dealt with by international public law and international environmental law.[8] However, the scale of the problem demands more hands.[9] Therefore, calls have been made to address the issue under the lens of other legal fields, such as human rights law or constitutional law.[10]

This chapter brings contract law into the discussion, and specifically the contracts known as power purchase agreements. These agreements have been defined in different ways,[11] but in general terms they can be described as contracts

---

1 For instance, the Glossary of Annex II of the Synthesis Report, produced in the context of the Fifth Assessment Report of the Intergovernmental Panel on Climate Change (IPCC), states the following: 'Climate change refers to a change in the state of the climate that can be identified (e.g., by using statistical tests) by changes in the mean and/or the variability of its properties and that persists for an extended period, typically decades or longer': Intergovernmental Panel on Climate Change, *Climate Change 2014: Synthesis Report*, IPCC, 2015, Annex II, p. 120.

2 See D. Bondi, 'Foreword' in C. Carlarne, K. Gray and R. Tarasofsky (eds.), *The Oxford Handbook of International Climate Change Law*, Oxford University Press, 2016, p. vi; D. Bodansky, J. Brunnée and L. Rajamani, *International Climate Change Law*, Oxford University Press, 2017, p. 3.

3 Ibid.

4 See D. Jamieson, 'The Moral and Political Challenges of Climate Change' in S. Moser and L. Dilling (eds.), *Creating a Climate for Change: Communicating Climate Change and Facilitating Social Change*, Cambridge University Press, 2007, p. 475.

5 Ibid.

6 Ibid.

7 F. Aguayo, 'El cambio climático como problema global: herramientas jurídicas para conciliar ambición y eficacia y el rol del Acuerdo de París', *Desafíos*, (2022) 34, pp. 1, 5.

8 Bodansky, Brunnée and Rajamani, supra, note 2, p. 11.

9 K. Bouwer, 'The Unsexy Future of Climate Change Litigation', *Journal of Environmental Law*, (2018) 30, pp. 483, 485.

10 See, e.g. B. Sánchez, 'Retos del Derecho Constitucional a la Luz del Cambio Climático' in A. Pérez Mira et al. (eds.), *Setenta Años de Constitución Italiana y Cuarenta Años de Constitución Española*, EUCONS, 2020, p. 367; I. Linazasoro, 'La buena administración como regla de adaptabilidad ante el cambio climático', *Revista de Derecho Ambiental*, (2020), p. 145; J. Fraser and L. Henderson, 'The Human Rights Turn in Climate Change Litigation and Responsibilities of Legal Professionals', *Netherlands Quarterly of Human Rights*, (2022) 40, p. 3.

11 See, e.g. J. Tippett, 'Development: Energy off-take and power purchase agreements' in A. Fong and J. Tippett (eds.), *Project Development in the Solar Industry*, CRC Press/Taylor &

that involve the sale of electrical energy to a buyer, for which – the electrical energy – a seller is responsible.[12] They are key to the sustainable development of energy matrices,[13] and thus to the efforts to tackle the climate crisis.[14]

Sometimes, during the performance of these contracts, situations can arise that severely affect the relationship originally configured by the parties. In such cases, is not unusual for the affected parties to file a request for the review or termination of their power purchase agreements, before a tribunal,[15] on the grounds of the available doctrines regarding contracts affected by unexpected circumstances, like the *'théorie de l'imprévision'*.[16]

In this regard, this chapter submits that the traditional application of these doctrines, in the context of disputes involving power purchase agreements, can lead to results that are prejudicial to the global efforts to tackle the climate crisis. Also, the work proposes a path that should be explored in order to solve the concern described.

In sum, this chapter aims to make a contribution by: (a) defining the problem referred to; and (b) proposing a possible solution for this concern. For that purpose, the work is structured under six different sections. After this introduction (section 1), it explains the legal discussion regarding contracts affected by unexpected circumstances (section 2). Thereafter, it describes the

---

Francis, 2013, p. 75; J. Vimpari, 'Financing Energy Transitions with Real Estate Wealth', *Energies*, 2020 (13), p. 4289.

12 Ibid. This broad and general definition is adopted because power purchase agreements are not a standardised type of contract around the globe, and can take different forms in different places. In this regard, see G. Vial, 'Power purchase agreements affected by unexpected circumstances: lessons from real litigation', *Journal of World Energy Law and Business*, (2023) 16, pp. 2–5.

13 For instance, by helping renewable energy producers to develop their projects, or by allowing companies to reach their green consumption goals. See, e.g. L. Mendicino et al., 'Corporate power purchase agreement: Formulation of the related levelized cost of energy and its application to a real-life case study', *Applied Energy*, (2019) 253, p. 113577; Y. Ghiassi-Farrokhfal, W. Ketter and J. Collins, 'Making green power purchase agreements more predictable and reliable for companies', *Decision Support Systems*, (2021) 144, p. 113514.

14 Indeed, addressing climate change requires a speedy energy transition, in which decarbonisation is crucial. See IPCC, 'Summary for Policy Makers' in *Special Report: Global Warming of 1.5°C*, IPCC, 2018, pp. 14–15; V. Smil, 'What we need to know about the pace of decarbonization', *Substantia*, (2019) 3, pp. 69, 72.

15 In this contribution, the term 'tribunal' refers to any organ or person in charge of deciding on controversies that are judicially relevant, like an ordinary court of justice or an arbitrator, without considering other situations that could be relevant, in some legal systems, for such a definition, such as whether the entity in question is part of a constitutionally established justice system. This use of the term follows the traditional scholarly definition that has been given for the word tribunal, in the Chilean legal system. See A. Bordalí, 'Organización Judicial en el Derecho Chileno: un Poder Fragmentado', *Revista Chilena de Derecho*, (2009) 36, p. 215.

16 See, e.g. F. Bahamóndez, 'Fallo Gasatacama: El Cambio de circunstancias en los contratos. *Quo vadis?*' in A. Fermandois and R. Delaveau (eds.), *Sentencias Destacadas 2008*, Libertad y Desarrollo, 2009, p. 351; K. Conrads and C. Berner, 'Una Mirada Contemporánea a la Revisión del Contrato de Suministro Eléctrico ante Eventos Imprevistos', *Revista Chilena de Derecho Privado*, (2020) 34, p. 9.

ways in which this legal topic, which is traditionally a matter of contract law, relates to the phenomenon of climate change (section 3). Later, the chapter focuses on power purchase agreements. In particular, it describes a situation that took place within the Chilean electricity system, and which illustrates that, when such contracts are affected by unexpected circumstances, the traditional application of the relevant contract law doctrines can negatively impact on the efforts to tackle the climate crisis (section 4). The following section proposes a possible solution for this problem (section 5). Finally, the chapter presents its conclusions (section 6).

2. THE LEGAL DISCUSSION ON CONTRACTS AFFECTED BY UNEXPECTED CIRCUMSTANCES

The discussion on contracts affected by unexpected circumstances refers to the legal system's reaction when the performance of a contract becomes impossible, excessively onerous or meaningless, due to unexpected events that arose after its conclusion.[17] An unexpected circumstance can involve a new event, but also 'a failure of an existing circumstance to persist or recurring circumstances to occur'.[18]

There are countless examples of events with the potential to affect the fulfilment of an agreement, as they can take almost any form. These changes can be technical, commercial or environmental, to name just a few.[19] For instance, cases involving unexpected circumstances have included the devaluation of currencies, financial crises, hurricanes, droughts, and the cancelation of licences, among other things.[20]

Judicial decisions in this regard usually balance what was freely agreed by the parties, on the one hand, and the justice behind adapting the agreement to a new scenario, on the other.[21] Therefore, the problem generally involves the interplay of two traditional legal principles: *pacta sunt servanda* and *clausula*

[17] The description regarding the effect of the event on the performance of a contract must be understood broadly; that is to say, encompassing the different hypotheses that the doctrines on contracts affected by unexpected circumstances, from different jurisdictions, usually consider. This is because this contribution is referring to the problem of unforeseen events, so far, in a generic manner, and not using the exact terminology that a specific jurisdiction or set or norms could employ to address that matter.

[18] M. Eisenberg, *Foundational Principles of Contract Law*, Oxford University Press, 2018, p. 626.

[19] K. Berger and D. Behn, '*Force Majeure* and Hardship in the Age of Corona: A Historical and Comparative Study', *McGill Journal of Dispute Resolution*, (2020) 6, pp. 76, 82.

[20] Ibid., pp. 82–83.

[21] See, e.g. *Taylor v. Caldwell* [1863] EWHC J1 (QB), (1863) 122 ER 309; *Davis Contractors Ltd v. Fareham Urban District Council* [1956] UKHL 3, (1956) AC 696; *Sentencia del Tribunal Supremo Español* STS 2823/2014.

rebus sic stantibus.[22] The first of these refers to the stability of contractual relations, and provides that commitments assumed must be observed, which is a fundamental principle of most national contract laws. The other principle allows a more flexible approach to situations of changes of circumstances, by assuming that the proper fulfilment of a contract is subject to the continuity of the context that was present when it was concluded.[23] The dilemma is the following: a contract 'binds the parties and is intended to remain binding even if the circumstances change',[24] but 'some occurrences that go beyond the reasonable expectations of the parties may raise serious doubts as to the binding nature of contracts'.[25]

There is no single solution to address this legal situation. Jurisdictions around the world deal with contracts affected by changes of circumstances in different ways.[26] They usually resort to different doctrines, which have specific requirements and particular effects, in the event of being applied.[27] Another variable element when dealing with this matter is that some jurisdictions are more inclined than others to review or terminate a contract due to alterations of the scenario projected when it was concluded.[28] In other words, even if similar doctrines are available in two different places, the tribunals of one of them could be more (or less) accustomed to applying them than those of the other.

In fact, the diversity of approaches even extends to what is understood by a doctrine that bears the same name, in different locations. As explained by Berger and Behn, quoting Puelinckx, '[f]rustration is not the equivalent of force majeure or Unmöglichkeit [impossibility] nor is force majeure Unmöglichkeit; even force majeure under Belgian law is not force majeure under French law'.[29]

Despite the differences between jurisdictions when dealing with contracts affected by unexpected circumstances, it is possible to identify two dimensions that most approaches have in common.[30] The first is that the need to analyse whether to apply a doctrine is triggered by the occurrence of an event that affects

22 Berger and Behn, supra, note 19, pp. 84–86.

23 Ibid.

24 E. Hondius and C. Grigoleit, 'Introduction: An Approach to the Issues and Doctrines Relating to Unexpected Circumstances' in E. Hondius and C. Grigoleit (eds.), *Unexpected Circumstances in European Contract Law*, Cambridge University Press, 2011, p. 3.

25 Ibid.

26 See ibid., p. 14; Berger and Behn, supra, note 19, p. 81.

27 See, e.g. Hondius and Grigoleit, supra, note 24; J. Castiñeira, 'The Unexpected Change of Circumstances Under American and Spanish Contract Law: Different Concepts, Different Methodology, Similar Outcomes', *European Review of Private Law*, (2017) 29, p. 909.

28 Hondius and Grigoleit, supra, note 24, p. 14.

29 Berger and Behn, supra, note 19, p. 97, quoting A. Puelinckx, 'Frustration, Hardship, Force Majeure, Imprevisión, Wegfall der French, German and Japanese Law', *Journal of International Arbitration*, (1986) 3, pp. 47 *et seq*.

30 This refers to 'most' instead of 'all' approaches, because the different ways in which jurisdictions deal with unexpected circumstances prevent it from being stated that everything explained in

the performance of a contract in a significant way, making it impossible, more onerous or meaningless.[31] In this regard, it must be noted that the effect that the situation triggering the analysis has on the fulfilment of the agreement is of critical importance. By way of example, an event that made it impossible to fulfil a contract governed by Spanish law could support a claim based on the doctrine of *force majeure*, but not on the *rebus sic stantibus* clause – both of which are available under Spanish law – since the latter operates, in Spain, in cases of excessive onerousness, and not of impossibility of performance.[32]

The second dimension that most approaches regarding unexpected circumstances share is the need for certain requirements to be present in order to apply the pertinent doctrines. In particular, their application usually requires the occurrence of an unforeseeable event, the lack of responsibility of the debtor for such an event, and that the risks from that circumstance were not allocated to the debtor.[33]

In sum, the legal discussion regarding changes of circumstances takes place when an unexpected event makes the performance of a contract impossible, excessively onerous, or meaningless. This matter is usually addressed by legal doctrines, whose availability depends on two factors: first, the jurisdiction

---

the following paragraphs applies to all jurisdictions. However, it applies to most of them, or at least to a relevant part of the jurisdictions that have traditionally been considered as influential for comparative analysis. As an example of a minor difference between jurisdictions, some authors suggest that, in the United States, reasonable foreseeability of the event that triggers the need of an analysis is significant, but not decisive, in deciding whether a doctrine of unexpected circumstances applies to a specific case. Similar statements have been made in relation to the contract laws of England and Wales. In contrast, in other jurisdictions, the impossibility of foreseeing the same event would be a decisive issue in the analysis of whether or not to apply a particular doctrine regarding unexpected circumstances: see Eisenberg, supra, note 18; Berger and Behn, supra, note 19; E. Peel, *Treitel on The Law of Contract*, 15th ed., Sweet & Maxwell/Thomson Reuters, 2020; E. McKendrick, *Contract Law*, 14th ed., Macmillan International, 2021.

31 See, e.g. Hondius and Grigoleit, supra, note 24; Castiñeira, supra, note 27; Berger and Behn, supra, note 19.

32 Castiñeira, supra, note 27, p. 913; B. Gregoraci, 'El impacto del COVID-19 en el Derecho de contratos español', *Anuario de Derecho Civil*, (2020), pp. 455, 467; C. Diez and I. González, 'Los principios de UNIDROIT sobre los contratos comerciales internacionales y los efectos derivados del Covid-19 sobre las relaciones contractuales: una perspectiva desde el Derecho español', *Cuadernos de Derecho Transnacional*, (2021), p. 180, 192.

33 See, e.g. M. Cenini, B. Luppi and F. Parisi, 'Law and Economics: the Comparative Law and Economics of Frustration in Contracts' in E. Hondius and C. Grigoleit (eds.), supra, note 24, p. 33; Eisenberg, supra, note 18, pp. 625–663; Castiñeira, supra, note 27; Berger and Behn, supra, note 19. The reference to the requirements usually common among doctrines in different jurisdictions must be understood broadly: that is to say, encompassing the different requisites that doctrines on contracts affected by unexpected circumstances usually consider. This is because this contribution is referring to these requisites in a generic manner, and not using the exact terminology that a specific jurisdiction or set or norms could employ to refer to them. For instance, under English law there has been some discussion on whether foreseeability is always a factor that will lead to the exclusion of the doctrine of frustration. In this regard, see, e.g. McKendrick, supra, note 30, p. 300.

or norms that govern the affected contract, which determines the available doctrines;[34] and, second, the way in which the event in question affects the performance of the contract, which could determine the specific doctrine to be applied, among those available in a particular jurisdiction.

3. THE RELATIONSHIP BETWEEN CLIMATE CHANGE AND CONTRACTS AFFECTED BY UNEXPECTED CIRCUMSTANCES

The relationship between the phenomenon of climate change and the issue of contracts affected by unexpected circumstances can be described as bidirectional: they mutually impact on each other.

On the one hand, situations related to the climate crisis can affect the performance of a contract, and trigger the need to analyse whether a particular doctrine of unexpected changes should be applied.[35] This is a scenario of the climate affecting contracts. On the other hand, the usual understanding of how doctrines of unexpected changes should be applied can have an impact, either positive or negative, on the efforts to tackle climate change.[36] This is a case of contractual structures affecting the climate crisis.

It must be noted, however, that is possible to have both types of interaction simultaneously. This will occur where a situation related to climate change triggers an analysis of the application of a doctrine of unexpected changes, and in which the decision regarding its application could impact on the efforts to maintain a healthy climate.

The two different ways in which climate change and contracts affected by unexpected circumstances interact, mutually impacting each other, are expanded on below.

3.1. CLIMATE AFFECTING CONTRACTS: FROM IMPACTS TO CONTRACTUAL RISKS

It is common to hear statements about the impacts of the climate crisis. An impact is 'the force of impression of one thing on another: a significant or major

[34] This refers to norms agreed by the parties, because it might be possible for them to agree that the contract will be governed by norms or instruments different from those of a specific jurisdiction, e.g. the UNIDROIT Principles of International Commercial Contracts.

[35] This is the case, for instance, of a natural disaster, like a flood or a hurricane, that occurs as an effect of climate change.

[36] These cases are independent of the nature of the event that triggers the need for an analysis of the application of the pertinent doctrines.

effect'.[37] Accordingly, when mention is made of the impacts of climate change, it is natural to think about the relevant consequences that derive from said phenomenon.

Such consequences have been categorised in different ways in the academic literature. In this regard, it is common to distinguish between the physical changes to the climate system itself, and the ways in which those changes affect human and natural systems. The first group of impacts includes an increase in the average global temperature; changes in the amounts, forms and patterns of precipitation; a rise in the sea level; the acidification of the oceans; and more extreme weather events.[38] The second group of consequences encompasses the most varied effects. For instance, climate alterations have affected human health, food security, water availability, and several types of ecosystems.[39] Even geopolitical consequences, like migrations due to changing climate conditions, have been attributed to the crisis.[40] As noted by Richardson, Steffen and Liverman, the issue of climate change would be 'of purely academic interest but for the fact that these changes in climate conditions influence the conditions for all life on earth'.[41]

In this context of profound changes, it is not only reasonable, but correct, to assume that the impacts of climate change imply various risks.[42] This concept has been defined in different ways,[43] and has been considered as something that can either be positive or negative.[44] In other words, '[r]isks means different things to different people'.[45] However, the concept has evolved to become commonly understood as something negative,[46] which entails the possibility of a loss, an injury or a hazard.[47] In this downside scenario, risk can be defined as

37 https://www.merriam-webster.com/dictionary/impact. As a noun, 'impact' can also refer to strikes between bodies. As a verb, it can imply to fix something firmly, or, more commonly, to strike forcefully or impinge on something.

38 K. Richardson, W. Steffen and D. Liverman, *Climate Change: Global Risks, Challenges and Decisions*, Cambridge University Press, 2011, p. 117; A. Dessler, *Introduction to Modern Climate Change*, Cambridge University Press, 2012, pp. 139–143.

39 IPCC, 'Summary for Policy Makers' in *Climate Change 2022: Impacts, Adaptation and Vulnerability*, IPCC, 2022, pp. 9–11.

40 Richardson, Steffen and Liverman, supra note 38, p. 123.

41 Ibid., p. 101.

42 See, e.g. W. Adger, I. Brown and S. Surminski, 'Advances in Risk Assessment for Climate Change Adaptation Policy', *Philosophical Transactions*, 2018, p. 1.

43 C. Althaus, 'A Disciplinary Perspective on the Epistemological Status of Risk', *Risk Analysis*, (2005) 25, pp. 567, 568.

44 T. Aven, 'The Risk Concept – Historical and Recent development trends', *Reliability Engineering and System Safety*, 2012, pp. 33, 35.

45 H. Haapio and G. Siedel, *A Short Guide to Contract Risk*, Routledge/Taylor and Francis Group, 2013, p. 17.

46 Aven, 'The Risk Concept', supra, note 44, p. 36.

47 See https://www.merriam-webster.com/dictionary/risk.

the chance of experiencing an adverse effect from an activity or exposure,[48] or as 'the possibility that something unpleasant or unwelcome will happen, leading to unfavourable outcomes'.[49] Specifically in the context of climate change, the Intergovernmental Panel on Climate Change (IPCC) has defined risk as 'the potential for adverse consequences for human or ecological systems, recognising the diversity of values and objectives associated with such systems'.[50]

Sometimes variations regarding the definition of risk are related to the discipline or area that is working with the concept, as different specialities have diverse descriptions for such a notion.[51] As explained by Althaus, the concept of risk 'can act as a mirror, reflecting the preoccupations, strengths, and weaknesses of each discipline as they grapple with uncertainty'.[52] Thus, unsurprisingly, all disciplines have to explain how risk is understood in their own particular context.[53] In contract law literature, the notion of risk has been used to refer to deviations from what was projected, with either positive or negative results. But when it comes to contracts affected by unexpected circumstances – the legal topic of this chapter – one of the parties is affected by the negative outcome of an event that took place, or did not take place, after the contract was concluded.

That said, and in a context of multiple and varied climate impacts (as explained before), it is necessary to find a way to categorise such hazards in terms that are suitable to explain how they might interact with the legal issue of contracts affected by unexpected circumstances. Among the different classifications that have been made about climate change risks,[54] one is especially useful to portray the different hazards that derive from the climate crisis, and which have the potential to affect the performance of a contract. Furthermore, this classification has been used in legal scholarship and financial literature, to identify how certain activities can be affected by the climate crisis.[55] In particular,

48 K. Foster, D. Bernstein and P. Huber, 'A Scientific Perspective' in K. Foster, D. Bernstein and P. Huber (eds.), *Phantom Risk: Scientific Inference and The Law*, MIT Press, 1999, pp. 1, 2.

49 Haapio and Siedel, supra, note 45, p. 18.

50 IPCC, 'Summary for Policy Makers', supra, note 39, p. 5.

51 See Althaus, supra, note 43, p. 567.

52 Ibid.

53 Aven, 'The Risk Concept', supra, note 44, p. 34.

54 Climate change risks can be classified in ways other than physical and transitional risks. For instance, it is possible to argue that there are direct and indirect risks flowing from such phenomena, as well as individual and systemic ones. See, e.g. M. Skancke et al., *Climate risk and the Norwegian economy*, Official Norwegian Reports NOU, 2018: 17 Summary, Commission appointed by Royal Decree on 6 October 2017 to assess climate-related risk factors and their significance for the Norwegian economy, p. 21. The original report is in Norwegian, and was delivered to the Ministry of Finance on 12 December 2018; IPCC, 'Summary for Policy Makers', supra, note 39, p. 8; D. King et al., *Climate Change: A Risk Assessment*, Centre for Science and Policy, University of Cambridge, 2015, p. 9.

55 See, e.g. T. Aven, 'Climate Change Risk – what it is and how should it be Expressed?', *Journal of Risk Research*, (2020) 23, pp. 1387, 1391; S. Díaz et al., 'La gestión de riesgos asociados

reference is made to the categorisation according to which the risks flowing from climate change can be divided into two main categories, namely 'physical' and 'transitional'.[56] Physical risks are those derived from the intensification of extreme weather events, like wildfires and hurricanes (acute events), and from the long-term impacts of changes in climate characteristics, like rising sea levels or the increased regularity of heatwaves (chronic events).[57] Transitional risks refer to those flowing from the evolution towards a lower-carbon economy, and have been subdivided into different categories (which can differ among authors), such as technological, policy, legal, market and reputational hazards.[58] Some authors add, to the foregoing classification, a third category, which has been labelled as 'liability risks'.[59] These relate to the possibility of facing litigation for contributing to, or not adapting to, the climate crisis,[60] and are usually attributed to governments and corporations.[61]

A first route to interaction between climate change and contracts affected by unexpected circumstances occurs when a situation related to the climate crisis, whether a physical or transitional risk, triggers the need to analyse whether a specific doctrine related to a particular legal topic, like frustration or impracticability, should be applied.[62] In other words, an event related to climate change affects the performance of a contract, making it impossible, more onerous, or meaningless. For instance, a power purchase agreement that was projected to be fulfilled for decades, through the generation of hydraulic energy, could become excessively onerous to perform, or even impossible, due to a drought flowing from the climate crisis. Situations like this will likely lead to an analysis regarding the pertinence of applying certain doctrines of unexpected circumstances.[63]

al cambio climático (Report)', Management Solutions, 2020; B. Preston, 'Climate Conscious Lawyering' *Australian Law Journal*, (2021) 95, pp. 51, 53.

56 Ibid.

57 Ibid.

58 Ibid.; A. Farmer, M. Foote and J. Morawetz, 'COVID-19 Offers Force Majeure Lessons for Climate Planning', *Law 360*, July 2020. Physical and transitional risks are closely linked, especially in the long term. Indeed, 'a rapid transition reduces physical risk in the long term but increases the transition risk in the short term. On the other hand, a business-as-usual scenario may not generate transition risk, but will increase physical damage in the future due to more profound climate change': M. Ferrazzi, F. Kalantzis and S. Zwart, *Assessing climate change risks at the country level: the EIB scoring model*, European Investment Bank Economics Department, Working Paper, 2021, p. 4.

59 See Preston, supra, note 55; N. Brook and Z. Sedilekova, *Horizon Scanning: Climate change risks – the future of law as we know it?*, The Law Society, 2021, p. 5.

60 Preston, supra, note 55.

61 See, e.g. Brook and Sedilekova, supra, note 59.

62 See, e.g. M. Dellinger, 'Acts of God or Acts of Man? Rethinking Contractual Impracticability in Times of Climate Change', *Natural Resources and Environment*, (2016) 30, p. 31.

63 Regarding power purchase agreements affected by unexpected circumstances, see Bahamóndez, supra, note 16; Conrads and Berner, supra, note 16.

Regarding the foregoing, it must be noted that climate change will rarely present itself in a straightforward way. Instead, it will be camouflaged in a range of different experiences, like a drought, a flood, or even a policy. Also, on occasion, an event related to the climate crisis will be only one of many others affecting the fulfilment of a contract. Thus, sometimes it will be challenging to establish a clear relationship between the phenomenon and the situation impacting on an agreement. However, the difficulty of identifying and isolating the specific event that affected the performance of a contract is a common challenge in disputes regarding unexpected circumstances, and not a problem that appears only when the contractual scenario has been altered by an event related to the climate crisis.

In sum, a first type of interaction between climate change and contracts affected by unexpected circumstances occurs when an event related to the climate crisis, whether a physical or transitional risk, affects the performance of an agreement, and triggers the need to analyse whether a doctrine of unexpected changes should be applied.

3.2. CONTRACTS AFFECTING CLIMATE: THE POSSIBILITY OF UNDESIRED OUTCOMES

A second route to interaction between climate change and contracts affected by unexpected circumstances occurs when the traditional application of the pertinent doctrines impacts on efforts to tackle the climate crisis, either in a positive or negative way. In this case, it is irrelevant whether the event *itself* that affected the performance of a contract was related to climate change. What matters here is the outcome derived from the doctrinal rules on how contract law should be applied.

This type of interaction is developed on in the next section of this chapter, through the description of a situation that took place within the Chilean electricity market.

4. POWER PURCHASE AGREEMENTS AFFECTED BY UNEXPECTED CIRCUMSTANCES: ILLUSTRATING UNDESIRED OUTCOMES FROM CONTRACT LAW RULES

When the performance of a contract is affected by events arising after its conclusion, the consequences will usually depend on the contract law rules governing that agreement. This section shows that, in the context of power purchase agreements affected by unexpected circumstances, those rules can have negative impacts on the efforts to maintain a healthy climate. In particular, it describes a situation that took place within the boundaries of what is currently known as the National Electric System of Chile: the grid that serves almost 98 per cent of the country's population.[64]

In Chile, the energy industry, and thus the way in which the aforementioned system works, is divided into three main tasks: generation, transmission and distribution.[65] Generation is the only one of these open to competition, while the other two are considered monopolies, and thus are strictly regulated.[66] In this context, generation companies can enter into power purchase agreements with two kind of clients: free clients, whose connected power *(potencia conectada)* is more than 5,000 kilowatts; and distribution companies, which are entities in charge of delivering electricity to regulated clients – that is, consumers whose connected power is equal to or less than 5,000 kilowatts.[67]

At the beginning of the century, the generation firm Gas Atacama Generación S.A. entered into power purchase agreements, committing to the delivery of electricity, with several distribution companies related to the Emel corporation.[68] The firm expected to fulfil those contracts by generating electricity with natural gas,[69] which was a common resource for the production of electricity in Chile, at that time.[70] The gas was mainly delivered from Argentina, and its availability seemed secure, because it was guaranteed under international agreements, and also related to massive investments.[71]

---

64 Generadoras de Chile, 'Generación Eléctrica en Chile', http://generadoras.cl/generacion-electrica-en-chile; Coordinador Eléctrico Nacional, 'Sistema Eléctrico Nacional', https://www.coordinador.cl/sistema-electrico/.

65 R. Castillo, 'Los contratos de suministro de energía eléctrica: naturaleza y problemas en cláusulas arbitrales', *Revista de Derecho Administrativo Económico*, 2017 (24), pp. 69, 71.

66 See Decree with Force of Law N° 4 of 1982, which fixes, consolidates, coordinates and systematises Decree with Force of Law N° 1 of 1982, General Law of Electrical Services in the Matter of Electrical Energy; National Energy Commission of Chile, 'La Regulación del Segmento Transmisión en Chile', Work Document, Chilean Government, 2005, p. 7; Castillo, supra, note 65; J. Valdés, 'El rol del nuevo Coordinador Eléctrico Nacional en su misión de monitorear las condiciones de competencia en el mercado eléctrico', *Revista de Derecho Administrativo Económico*, (2018) 26, pp. 95, 104.

67 Decree with Force of Law N° 4 of 1982, supra, note 66; Comisión Nacional de Energía, 'Tarificación', https://www.cne.cl/tarificacion/electrica/; National Energy Commission of Chile, supra, note 66, p. 6; Castillo, supra, note 65, pp. 69–70; M. Martínez, 'Naturaleza Jurídica del Contrato de Suministro de Energía Eléctrica Celebrado entre Empresas Generadoras y Clientes Libres', LLM thesis, Universidad de Concepción, 2018, pp. 74–92; Conrads and Berner, supra, note 16, p. 12.

68 Bahamóndez, supra, note 16, pp. 351, 352, 367 and 378.

69 Bahamóndez, supra, note 16, pp. 367 and 378.

70 G. Vial, 'Application of the Essential Facilities Doctrine to Liquefied Natural Gas Regasification Terminals: An Analysis through a Chilean Case', *Environmental Claims Journal*, 2016, p. 261.

71 C. Huneeus, 'Argentina y Chile: el conflicto del gas, factores de política interna Argentina', *Estudios Internacionales, Instituto de Estudios Internacionales de la Universidad de Chile*, 2007, pp. 179, 181; Bahamóndez, supra, note 16; Vial, 'Application of the Essential Facilities Doctrine', supra, note 70.

However, Argentina started to curtail the deliveries of natural gas.[72] Suddenly, it was no longer possible for Gas Atacama Generación S.A. to fulfil its contractual commitments using such a resource. Thus, in order to comply with the commitments assumed under the aforementioned power purchase agreements, the firm had to buy electricity from other producers (to be delivered to the distribution companies), and to generate it by other means (instead of using natural gas).[73] The problem was that those alternatives were much more expensive than producing electricity with natural gas, and so resulted in huge losses for the firm.[74]

Due to the new and unexpected scenario brought about by the gas crisis, Gas Atacama Generación S.A. requested, before a tribunal, the termination or modification of the aforementioned power purchase agreements. In its efforts to convince the arbitrator, the firm resorted to different doctrines relating to contracts affected by unexpected circumstances, namely *ausencia de culpa*, whose literal translation is *absence of guilt* (but refers more to the idea of absence of fault or negligence); *théorie de l'imprévision*; and *caso fortuito o fuerza mayor*, commonly known as *force majeure*.[75] But their claims were rejected. The tribunal considered that, according to the rules of the aforementioned doctrines of unexpected changes, they did not apply to the firm's situation. In other words, the prerequisites that were necessary for their application were not present in the case.[76] It has been stated that this decision by the arbitrator was legally correct, according to Chilean laws.[77]

However, the decision had negative impacts on efforts to tackle the climate crisis. Indeed, as the claimant was forced to comply with the power purchase agreements in their original terms, they were obliged, as mentioned above, to buy energy from other producers, and to generate it by means other than natural gas. And those two alternatives both implied the use of diesel: a resource with a bigger carbon footprint than natural gas.[78] In other words, the decision by the

72 More specifically, it started in 2004. It has been stated that its peak occurred in 2006. See Conrads and Berner, supra, note 16, p. 15.

73 Minería Chilena, 'Los Errores tras la Crisis de GasAtacama', Newsletter, 2007, https://www.mch.cl/2007/06/11/los-errores-tras-la-crisis-de-gasatacama/#.

74 Ibid.

75 Bahamóndez, supra, note 16, p. 363; Conrads and Berner, supra, note 16, p. 39.

76 Notwithstanding the scholarly debate regarding the possibility of applying the *théorie de l'imprévision* in the Chilean legal system. See Bahamóndez, supra, note 16, in which a detailed analysis of the arbitrator's decision appears from p. 370 onwards.

77 Ibid., p. 351.

78 This coincides with the content of a report by relevant consultants in the Chilean energy market, in which it was explained that one of the effects of the Argentine gas crisis was that units thought to operate with natural gas had to start using diesel, leading to a bigger carbon footprint in some industries: Consultora Más Energía Limitada, 'Informe Final Estudio: Diagnóstico y Perspectivas para la Operación de los Terminales de GNL en Chile', 2015, https://www.cne.cl/estudios/hidrocarburo/.

tribunal resulted in negative impacts for the climate, because it promoted more extensive use of diesel for electricity generation.[79]

The foregoing illustrates that, in the context of power purchase agreements affected by unexpected circumstances, the traditional understanding of how the relevant contract law doctrines should be applied can have negative effects on efforts to maintain a healthy climate. This is an undesired outcome from the apparently correct application of contract law rules. Accordingly, the next section explores a possible solution to this problem. In this regard, it must be noted that the possibility of the application of contract law rules impacting on the climate is not limited to cases involving power purchase agreements. However, as this chapter focuses on such contracts, the proposal to address this problem, developed below, is given within the context of those agreements (notwithstanding the possibility of having a broader application).

5. A POSSIBLE WAY FORWARD TO ADDRESS THE PROBLEM

The previous section identified the following problem: in the context of power purchase agreements affected by unexpected circumstances, the traditional understanding of how the pertinent doctrines should be applied can have negative impacts on the climate crisis.[80] This section proposes a path towards addressing this concern.

In this regard, some might argue that it is enough to disregard the rules for contracts affected by unexpected circumstances, and to impose a vision that favours climate efforts. However, it is hard to suggest that a contractual problem should be addressed simply by ignoring contract law itself. That not only overlooks the value of this legal field, but also forgets that contracts can provide critical tools in the fight against climate change.[81] Therefore, a proper solution must respect the way in which contract law deals with agreements affected by unexpected circumstances.

---

79 According to the rules in force at that time in the Chilean electricity system, if the arbitrator had accepted the claims of Gas Atacama, it is possible that the same scenario of intensive diesel-buying would have been reached, only with a different distribution of the new costs involved. However, the actual outcome can be considered as more climate-harmful than the alternative one. This, because by securing to the buyers access to energy at certain prices notwithstanding the means used for its production, it closed climate-healthier possibilities that perhaps would have been considered in a different scenario, by the parties itself or even by the regulator.

80 See section 4 above.

81 For instance, a power purchase agreement can reduce the risk in a clean energy project, and make it more attractive for developers: see Mendicino et al., supra, note 13.

In this regard, it must be noted that, despite different jurisdictions having diverse solutions for the aforementioned matter, they all tend to recognise that the parties have the possibility to freely allocate contractual risks.[82] Therefore, if a specific distribution of hazards is agreed, and there is no legal prohibition in that regard, a contract can generally be performed and interpreted in the manner established by the parties, even if unexpected events arise; in other words, favourable climate consequences can be freely incorporated within contractual relationships.

But the foregoing proposal presents an obvious problem, namely that the parties are not always going to reach agreements that favour climate efforts. Thus, it is necessary to find a solution that, while recognising and protecting freedom of contract, channels it in a way that does not jeopardise the future of the planet.

In this regard, it is posited that a possibility is to incorporate climate principles within the regulations of power systems; that is to say, the environment in which power purchase agreements take place. Those principles could be understood as part of the aforementioned contracts, and the parties would be aware in advance of that fact. This might allow disputes involving power purchase agreements to be interpreted according to climate needs, without ignoring the intentions of the parties that subscribed to them, as the risks involved in the application of climate values would have been accepted by the parties when entering into the contract.

A solution of this kind would probably be naive and impractical for contracts in general. It is unfeasible to assume that any contract, such as a lease or a loan, could be interpreted under climatic principles that might be incorporated within the legal framework sheltering it. Nevertheless, such a solution could be an alternative in the case of power purchase agreements. Indeed, such contracts usually take place within a certain regulatory context, and spaces of individual freedom and mandatory regulations can coexist within them.[83] Moreover, there is nothing new in using the principles of an electricity system to interpret power purchase agreements. For instance, the tribunal did that in the case of *Gas Atacama Generación S.A.*, mentioned in the previous section.[84]

In sum, a possible way to address the problem identified in the previous section would be to incorporate climate principles within the regulatory context that usually encompasses power purchase agreements.

---

82 See, e.g. Berger and Behn, supra, note 19; Peel, supra, note 30.

83 See Castillo, supra, note 65 p. 69; Mendicino et al., supra, note 13; M. Bruck and P. Sandborn, 'Pricing bundled renewable energy credits using a modified LCOE for power purchase agreements', *Renewable Energy*, (2021) 170, p. 224.

84 See Bahamóndez, supra, note 16.

6. CONCLUSION

Climate change is a multidimensional problem. As such, it is not surprising that it extends into legal fields that are not traditionally associated with the phenomenon, like the law of contracts. In this context, this chapter raises a climate concern relating to the legal dilemma of contracts affected by unexpected circumstances, discussion of which refers to how a legal system reacts when the performance of a contract becomes impossible, excessively onerous or meaningless, due to unexpected events that arose after its conclusion.

In particularly, the chapter notes that, in cases of power purchase agreements affected by unexpected circumstances, the traditional understanding of how the pertinent contract law doctrines should be applied can have negative impacts on efforts to maintain a healthy climate. As a solution for this concern, it suggests the incorporation of climate principles within the regulatory context in which power purchase agreements are inserted, in such a way that the parties can understand and accept, in advance, that climate values will be incorporated into those contracts.

SUSTAINABILITY OF GREEN ENERGY PRODUCTION

A Comparative Perspective between Brazil and the United Kingdom

Lissia Queiroz de Menezes and Tilak Ginige

ABSTRACT

The global effort to reduce carbon emissions and decelerate climate change must include the generation of green energy. The key to building a sustainable future is using renewable energy sources, mainly hydrogen. This chapter offers a comparative viewpoint on the hydrogen frameworks in Brazil and the United Kingdom. Additionally, it explores hydrogen's function in the new green industrial revolution, and how it might help develop the world's sustainable goals, considering the different social, economic, and political perspectives.

1. INTRODUCTION

Earth's temperature has increased significantly since the beginning of the Industrial Revolution, as evidenced by the Intergovernmental Panel on Climate Change (IPCC),[1] and the implication is that human activity is having an enormous

[1] Intergovernmental Panel on Climate Change (IPCC), *Climate Change 2022: Impacts, Adaptation and Vulnerability*, Cambridge University Press, 2022, available at https://www.ipcc.ch/report/ar6/wg2/.

impact on the natural world. Moreover, it is questionable whether this climate change crisis is substantially influencing industry and business to achieve a faster transition towards an ecologically sustainable economic system, since investments in non-renewable sources of energy are not increasing exponentially,[2] which is the opposite to what would be expected in a world where a green paradigm shift has taken place.[3]

Furthermore, it is argued that the necessary green paradigm shift will differ, depending on the country, market and industry. Moreover, a global problem such as climate change has specific local consequences, so it is essential to conduct a comparative analysis to observe the impact of these changes and solutions, when building a sustainable future.[4] This chapter will discuss the legal intersection between two different judicial systems (Brazil and the United Kingdom (UK)) that are functioning under international climate change laws, and are attempting to put in place nation-specific regulations to support the development of a Green Industrial Revolution.

It is important to note that the effects of climate change in Brazil and other less economically developed countries[5] are exacerbated by problems such as hunger and lack of adequate housing, which are ongoing and severe social problems.[6] Thus, these realities push climate issues into the background, rather than being integrated into these countries' sustainable economic solutions. Furthermore, it is predicted that climate change will likely trigger further social changes that increase the vulnerability of women and minorities during extreme weather events.[7] Accordingly, this is the ideal time for sustainable economic and social growth for underdeveloped and developing countries with significant natural resources for renewable energy.

It is still challenging to imagine an effective and immediate solution, especially given the widespread use of fossil fuels, and the high carbon and methane emissions into the atmosphere. Nevertheless, numerous proposals exist, in various spheres,

---

2 International Renewable Energy Agency (IRENA), 'Investments in Renewables Reached Record High, But Need Massive Increase and More Equitable Distribution', 22 February 2023, https://www.irena.org/News/pressreleases/2023/Feb/Investments-in-Renewables-Reached-Record-High-But-Need-Massive-Increase-More-Equitable-Distribution.

3 A. Kolk and R. van Tulder. 'International business, corporate social responsibility and sustainable development', *International Business Review* 19(2) (April 2010), pp. 119–25, doi:10.1016/j.ibusrev.2009.12.003.

4 Intergovernmental Panel on Climate Change (IPCC), 'Climate change widespread, rapid, and intensifying – IPCC', 9 August 2021, https://www.ipcc.ch/2021/08/09/ar6-wg1-20210809-pr/.

5 N. Singh Khadka, 'Climate change: Low-income countries "can't keep up" with impacts', *BBC News*, 8 August 2021, https://www.bbc.co.uk/news/world-58080083.

6 The World Bank, 'Brazil Overview: Development news, research, data', 14 April 2023, https://www.worldbank.org/en/country/brazil/overview.

7 K. Robin van Daalen et al., 'Extreme events and gender-based violence: a mixed-methods systematic review', *The Lancet Planetary Health* 6(6) (June 2022), e504–23. doi:10.1016/S2542–5196(22)00088-2.

for building a more sustainable society for the planet.[8] Moreover, especially at the current time of war in Ukraine, the world, mainly Europe, is seeking to develop alternative energy sources and technologies aimed at sustainability. In this context, there is the rise of hydrogen as a viable energy source.[9]

Hydrogen is the most abundant element on the planet, and can be obtained in its pure form through several processes. When hydrogen is obtained from renewable sources, such as solar and wind, this is 'green' hydrogen, free of carbon emissions, and an appropriate energy source in the context of climate change.[10] It is noteworthy that the search for new energy sources and green hydrogen is part of a larger scenario of a possible new Green Industrial Revolution,[11] as labelled by scholars and political leaders, especially in the UK.[12]

It is undeniable that, since the first Industrial Revolution,[13] there has been a significant increase in the amount of carbon in the atmosphere,[14] given that the capitalist market's model of production and structuring was based on unbridled consumption, and the incessant pursuit of purposeless profit. Today the UK, once at the forefront of the Industrial Revolution, is designing one of the most ambitious energy transition plans, which, like that of the European Union (EU), includes hydrogen as a priority fuel. To this end, Europeans, for example, seek partnerships and investments in other countries, generally underdeveloped or emergent economies with excellent potential for renewable energies.

Brazil, a country of great natural wealth, currently has a robust renewable energy matrix, and one of the world's greatest potentials for producing green hydrogen on a large scale, and at competitive prices. Thus, the Brazilian market is preparing to receive significant investments from companies and governments worldwide.[15] However, it must be remembered that Brazil, like other countries

---

8 International Energy Agency (IEA), 'Global Methane Tracker 2022: Strategies to reduce emissions from fossil fuel operations', https://www.iea.org/reports/global-methane-tracker-2022/strategies-to-reduce-emissions-from-fossil-fuel-operations.

9 S. van Renssen, 'The hydrogen solution?', *Nature Climate Change* 10, 799–801 (2020), https://doi.org/10.1038/s41558-020-0891-0.

10 U. Weichenhain and C. Schmitt, 'Green Hydrogen: A Key Building Block of Climate Neutrality', *Roland Berger*, https://www.rolandberger.com/en/Insights/Publications/Green-H2-investments-Enabling-clean-energy-and-industry.html.

11 D. Castelvecchi, 'How the hydrogen revolution can help save the planet – and how it can't', *Nature*, 16 November 2022, https://doi.org/10.1038/d41586-022-03699-0.

12 F. Harvey, 'The key areas of Boris Johnson's "green industrial revolution"', *The Guardian*, 17 November 2020, https://www.theguardian.com/environment/2020/nov/17/the-key-areas-of-boris-johnsons-green-industrial-revolution.

13 The Editors of Encyclopaedia Britannica, 'Industrial Revolution', *Encyclopedia Britannica*, 15 November 2023, https://www.britannica.com/event/Industrial-Revolution.

14 H. McGregor et al., 'The Industrial Revolution kick-started global warming much earlier than we realised', *The Conversation*, 24 August 2016, https://theconversation.com/the-industrial-revolution-kick-started-global-warming-much-earlier-than-we-realised-64301.

15 McKinsey & Company, 'Green Hydrogen: an opportunity to create sustainable wealth in Brazil and the world', 25 November 2021, https://www.mckinsey.com/br/en/our-insights/

in Latin America, Africa and South Asia, faces a challenging social and economic context that imposes the application of public policies and legislation that encourage sustainable progress.

Comparing the different perspectives between countries, according to their economic and social progress, the question arises about the role of the law in directing, even in such diverse contexts, this Green Industrial Revolution that will enable us to reconcile economic development and the preservation of nature. The main point of this chapter will be to investigate, from a comparative legal perspective, the Brazilian and British legislation, and to verify whether the production and exportation of green hydrogen can be effectively sustainable. In addition, possible legal alternatives that would allow the rise of the Green Industrial Revolution, around the production of green hydrogen, will be demonstrated.

The analysis will start with a technical and commercial overview of green hydrogen, considering the opportunities and challenges of its production and exportation. The UK's situation, policies and legislation around decarbonisation and encouraging hydrogen production, to develop a new Green Industrial Revolution, will then be examined. Next, the Brazilian case – its environmental protection system and energy policy in general, including policies and legislation around renewable energies and hydrogen – will be analysed. To go deeper, hydrogen production in the Pecém Port, in the Brazilian state of Ceará, will be treated as a case study, detailing the project's potential, peculiarities and possible impacts. The analysis will then move on to the comparative approach between Brazil and the UK, observing the key points and possible gaps within the global context of the reality of each jurisdiction. Finally, after considering both approaches, conclusive provisions on green hydrogen will be formulated.

2. GREEN HYDROGEN

Hydrogen is called the 'fuel of the future', as it represents a significant change from the energy matrix widely used today, which arose from an industrial and market structure based primarily on highly polluting fossil fuels. This new development is not just about creating a new fuel, or alternative energy source, but the development of a new hydrogen-based economy which has the potential to replace fossil fuels and change the current mode of production.[16]

---

hidrogenio-verde-uma-oportunidade-de-geracao-de-riqueza-com-sustentabilidade-para-o-brasil-e-o-mundo.

16 P. Ekins, *Hydrogen Energy: Economic and Social Challenges*, Routledge, 2010, p. 9.

The significant difference between hydrogen and fossil fuels is precisely because it is abundant, and produces H2O when burnt.[17] Technology has been improving over the years, and hydrogen can be grey, blue, pink, green, or many other 'colours',[18] depending on how it is manufactured. Although there are many methods of producing hydrogen, there is no universal agreement on the requirements for hydrogen: for instance, there is no set carbon-intensity cap for low-carbon and renewable hydrogen.[19]

Green hydrogen is described as hydrogen created using the electrolysis process, which separates water into hydrogen and oxygen, using renewable electricity. As a result, there are very little or no carbon emissions. The definition of 'renewable energy', the parameters of the carbon accounting system, the emission thresholds at which hydrogen is considered green, and the feedstocks and production technologies employed, vary greatly among emerging green hydrogen initiatives and policies. The aim to expedite the usage of green hydrogen is being undermined by this lack of standardisation.[20]

Green hydrogen is essential for decarbonising industries that are difficult to electrify, such as those that make basic chemicals or primary steel.[21] There is the potential for a billion-dollar market internationally, with exports. There is also the possibility of an internal market, using hydrogen for the steel, fertiliser, refinery and transport industries. Europe, for example, needs green hydrogen to achieve its decarbonisation targets, which is an excellent opportunity to develop this market. There are still several challenges for hydrogen, mainly green hydrogen, including the price of production and the difficulty of transportation.[22] However, according to some research, green hydrogen will cost between US$1.5 and $5 per kilogram by 2050, with some nations with good renewable resource availability anticipating costs as low as US$1 per kilogram.[23]

---

17 J. Rifkin, *The Hydrogen Economy*, Penguin Group, 2003, p. 8.

18 The Energy Industry use colour codes to distinguish the types of hydrogen, considering the energy source and production method.

19 N. Boussidan, 'Everything you need to know about hydrogen in the clean energy transition', *World Economic Forum*, 12 January 2023, https://www.weforum.org/agenda/2023/01/hydrogen-clean-energy-transition-2023/.

20 Green Hydrogen Organisation, 'What is Green Hydrogen', https://gh2.org/what-green-hydrogen.

21 IRENA, *Renewable energy targets in 2022: A guide to design*, IRENA, 2022, https://mc-cd8320d4-36a1-40ac-83cc-3389-cdn-endpoint.azureedge.net/-/media/Files/IRENA/Agency/Publication/2022/Nov/IRENA_RE_targets_2022.pdf?rev=f39ae339801e4853a2a0ebdb4d167f83.

22 P. Day, 'Hydrogen as a backup for renewables remains a distant proposition', *Thomson Reuters*, https://www.reuters.com/business/energy/hydrogen-backup-renewables-remains-distant-proposition-2023-02-01/.

23 World Energy Council, *Working Paper: Hydrogen Demand and Cost Dynamics*, September 2021, https://www.worldenergy.org/assets/downloads/Working_Paper_-_Hydrogen_Demand_And_Cost_Dynamics_-_September_2021.pdf?v=1658324860.

The lack of specific legislation and a uniform standard for characterising green hydrogen is a critical point. The EU has begun the development of hydrogen legislation,[24] initiating policies to implement a possible energy transition on the European Trade bloc. The essential components characterising green hydrogen and its derivatives, such as green ammonia or green methanol, to be generated in, or imported to, the EU in the coming years, are contained in two delegated Acts on renewable fuels of non-biological origin (RFNBOs).[25] The European Commission approved the delegated Acts in February 2023, that came into force in July 2023.[26] There has already been criticism of the new legislation, considered by some to be just another form of greenwashing, mainly due to the supposed political and market influence to authorise loopholes in the law, to continue to allow, and even encourage, the use of fossil fuels, primarily due to the additionality rule imposed on hydrogen production.

It is possible to notice a particular predilection for using terms such as 'renewable hydrogen', or even 'low-carbon hydrogen', in official guidelines and policies. By moving away from the technical term 'green hydrogen', there seems to be an attempt to distance ourselves from the idea of zero-carbon hydrogen, or hydrogen from genuinely renewable energy sources, such as solar and wind. Suppose that, in the future, proper standardisation is not taken seriously. In that case, there will be considerable gaps that would allow, or even encourage, the production of hydrogen with high carbon emissions, from fossil energy sources, such as grey or blue hydrogen. Also, there is still discussion around 'pink' hydrogen, which uses nuclear energy, and which, despite having low carbon emissions, is not technically considered renewable, and brings high risks of pollution to the environment.

3. UK POLICIES AND REGULATIONS, AND THE AIM OF A NEW GREEN INDUSTRIAL REVOLUTION

To expedite decarbonisation across seven economic pillars – power, fuel supply (including hydrogen), industry, heat and buildings, transport, natural resources,

---

24 European Commission, *Delegated regulation on Union methodology for RFNBOs*, 7 February 2023, https://energy.ec.europa.eu/delegated-regulation-union-methodology-rfnbos_en; European Commission, *Delegated regulation for a minimum threshold for GHG savings of recycled carbon fuels and annex*, 7 February 2023, https://energy.ec.europa.eu/delegated-regulation-minimum-threshold-ghg-savings-recycled-carbon-fuels-and-annex_en.

25 Green Hydrogen Standard, 'GH2 statement on new EU rules defining green hydrogen', 13 February 2023, https://www.greenhydrogenstandard.org/news/gh2-statement-new-eu-rules-defining-green-hydrogen.

26 European Commission, *Renewable hydrogen production: new rules formally adopted*, 20 June 2023, https://energy.ec.europa.eu/news/renewable-hydrogen-production-new-rules-formally-adopted-2023-06-20_en.

and waste – and to expedite greenhouse gas removal, the UK has developed the Net Zero Strategy. The strategy identifies vital quantitative targets for actions throughout the various strands that make up the path to net zero.[27] A strategy paper, titled 'UK hydrogen strategy', was presented to Parliament, by the Department for Business, Energy & Industrial Strategy, in August 2021.[28] The strategy aims to create a thriving low-carbon hydrogen industry in the UK. The approach is a complete package, establishing a hydrogen economic model to promote the production and use of low-carbon hydrogen, designed to work for both 'green' and 'blue' hydrogen.[29]

There is, currently, in the global geopolitical context, and in the context of global warming, much interest in green hydrogen as a viable source of ecological energy production. The UK, which aims to increase the use of hydrogen in the coming decades, has begun to focus its attention on green hydrogen. Today, most hydrogen produced and used in the UK, and globally, is blue hydrogen, from fossil fuels, with no carbon capture; only a tiny fraction can be called low-carbon hydrogen. For hydrogen to play a part in the journey to net zero, all current and future production must be of low-carbon hydrogen.

It is curious that, in the UK, the term 'Green Industrial Revolution' is used to describe the package of investments in solutions for the environment, and the production of energy from renewable and less polluting sources.[30] It is an interesting term that could even be applied, analogically, worldwide. But the question is, is it really a new Industrial Revolution? The UK, having been a pioneer of the first Industrial Revolution, now presents itself as being at the forefront of a paradigm shift, through the most ambitious plan for energy transition in the world.[31] However, we cannot, and should not, repeat past mistakes in order to create a better future. Perhaps this is the time to anticipate the future instead of just solving existing problems. We now have the tools, knowledge, opportunity and possibility to build a better and more sustainable future for all. What can we do differently this time around?

The UK's strategy for this Green Industrial Revolution has some key points. It supports the UK's top-tier vehicle manufacturing facilities, to quicken the switch to electric vehicles, and improve the nation's infrastructure to accommodate them, including a ten-year-earlier prohibition on selling new petrol and diesel

---

27 *Renewable energy targets in 2022: A guide to design*, supra, note 20.

28 UK Government, Department for Energy Security & Net Zero, *UK hydrogen strategy*, Cm 475, August 2021, https://www.gov.uk/government/publications/uk-hydrogen-strategy/uk-hydrogen-strategy-accessible-html-version#chapter-3-realising-economic-benefits-for-the-uk.

29 Green Hydrogen Organisation, 'United Kingdom', https://gh2.org/countries/united-kingdom.

30 UK Government, *The Ten Point Plan for a Green Industrial Revolution*, November 2020, https://assets.publishing.service.gov.uk/government/uploads/system/uploads/attachment_data/file/936567/10_POINT_PLAN_BOOKLET.pdf.

31 Green Hydrogen Organisation, supra, note 28.

cars and vans, starting in 2030. Another topic is promoting walking and cycling as more appealing forms of mobility, and funding future zero-emission public transport.[32] The interesting point is that, in the UK plans, the goal, by 2030, is to make homes, schools and hospitals greener, warmer and more energy-efficient. By 2028, the objectives are for 600,000 heat pumps to be installed annually, the use of fossil fuels for heating to be phased out, and for the support offered to those who switch to low-carbon heat via heat pumps to be specified. These are specifically relevant to the energy market. But it remains to be seen how these changes will be made, and what concrete actions will be taken for this gradual transition, which seems complex.[33]

The UK has a conflicted political scene, as reflected, amongst other things, by the numerous recent changes of prime minister. In general, the Conservatives in charge believe in minimal state intervention, and so provide insufficient economic and legal incentives for the uptake of alternative energy systems. However, this economic approach is causing financial losses and increasing inflation, raising questions about how beneficial this overly liberal agenda really is. In this regard, the influence of more progressive politicians has led the UK to seek inspiration in policies such as those of the US, which intends to support the net-zero industry and the development of green technology through billions of dollars in subsidies, including loans and tax exemptions.[34] This raises the issue of how building a greener and more sustainable future is more than just an environmental, scientific or legal discussion. The political and economic scenario influences the achievement and development of the energy transition, and the construction of a green economy.

Like many other nations, the UK needs a more precise legislative framework for hydrogen initiatives in various industries. Although the government expects to see several significant paradigm shifts and milestones in the production and use of hydrogen throughout the 2020s, the UK Hydrogen Strategy estimates that a first network regulatory framework will not be in place until at least 2025. Until then, networks are intended to be offered through current frameworks. It is suggested that many gaps and uncertainties must be filled before the hydrogen economy can take off.[35] Currently, as hydrogen falls under the

---

32 UK Government, *The Ten Point Plan for a Green Industrial Revolution*, supra, note 29.

33 Energy Saving Trust, 'Ten Point Plan: what progress has been made in the first year?', 19 November 2021, https://energysavingtrust.org.uk/ten-point-plan-what-progress-has-been-made-in-the-first-year/.

34 T. Helm, 'Labour planning £8bn Biden-style green energy revolution', *The Guardian*, 12 March 2023, https://www.theguardian.com/environment/2023/mar/12/labour-planning-8bn-green-revolution-for-uk-industry-in-deprived-regions.

35 D. Majumber-Russell, C. Rihoy and K. Mitchell, 'Hydrogen Law, Regulations & Strategy in the United Kingdom', *CMS*, https://cms.law/en/int/expert-guides/cms-expert-guide-to-hydrogen/united-kingdom.

definition of 'gas' in the Gas Act 1986,[36] it is governed as a component of the gas network, and requires a licence based on the Gas Act to operate. Additionally, there is a legal system and structure, related mainly to operation and security, that can be applied to both hydrogen and pipelines for gas.[37]

Nevertheless, hydrogen has its peculiarities, mainly because it is a volatile element, and requires specific infrastructure for its transport and production.[38] Section 48 of the Gas Act, for example, simply extends the interpretation of the law to contemplate hydrogen, which is prejudicial for the legislation's practical application in this new market. It is relevant to consider that the UK's energy framework underwent an extensive update in October 2023 thanks to the Energy Act,[39] which also addressed the financing of hydrogen gas pipeline projects and provided subsidies for carbon emission reduction. However, hydrogen still lacks detailed and specific laws that reflect its technical challenges for the British strategy. In addition, implementing hydrogen production and commercialisation projects requires advanced and complex environmental studies, which will have impacts that are still partly unknown,[40] and will need supplementary legislation with more useful information.[41] Therefore, to apply the principles of precaution and prevention effectively, the market and production of green hydrogen need specific legal definitions, especially since the United Kingdom aims to foster a truly green and sustainable industrial revolution. This would help to avoid ambiguity and confusion in the regulation and governance of this emerging sector.

Despite having a bold strategy for hydrogen, in terms of targets, the UK, like other European countries, often uses an approach focusing on low-carbon hydrogen, and not necessarily using the term 'green hydrogen'.[42] There seems to be a contradiction here, since while the ambition is to reach one of the highest levels of decarbonisation in the world, there is insufficient focus on the most technically efficient energy source, i.e. green hydrogen produced from renewable sources. When legislators use terms such as 'sustainable hydrogen' or

---

36 Section 48, Gas Act 1986 (c. 44).

37 J. Cowlan and L. White, 'UK hydrogen safety law: the developing framework', *Pinsent Masons*, 28 February 2023, https://www.pinsentmasons.com/out-law/guides/uk-hydrogen-safety-law#:~:text=Hydrogen%20falls%20in%20the%20definition,licence%20under%20the%20Gas%20Act.

38 A.I. Osman, N. Mehta, A.M. Elgarahy et al. 'Hydrogen production, storage, utilisation and environmental impacts: a review', *Environmental Chemistry Letters*, 20, 153–188 (2022), https://doi.org/10.1007/s10311-021-01322-8.

39 Energy Act 2023 (c. 52).

40 See note 38.

41 Norton Rose Fulbrght, 'UK Energy Act 2023: Summary of the provisions relating to hydrogen', December 2023, https://www.nortonrosefulbright.com/en/knowledge/publications/8d5111de/summary-of-energy-act-2023-provisions-relating-to-hydrogen.

42 UK Government, 'Guidance: UK Low Carbon Hydrogen Standard: emissions reporting and sustainability criteria', 8 April 2022, https://www.gov.uk/government/publications/uk-low-carbon-hydrogen-standard-emissions-reporting-and-sustainability-criteria.

'low-carbon hydrogen', it leads to the conclusion that, ultimately, blue, grey and pink hydrogen, for example, will still be produced. Accordingly, investments in fossil fuels and nuclear energy will continue to be appealing. Given the potential political power of traditional markets, which perceive the development of green hydrogen as a danger to their financial returns, there is controversy about the legal uncertainty, and how much of it is purposeful.[43]

In the past, the significant changes and advances of the Industrial Revolution brought an idea of a better and promising future for humanity.[44] But these same changes, seen today as the origin of the mode of production, are a prospectus for a possibly devastating future if we continue to use the same energy base structure. In general, there is a global scenario in which developed countries are trying to reduce their dependence on fossil fuels, and hydrogen has emerged as an alternative energy source. Thus, hydrogen, mainly green hydrogen, currently appears the most promising alternative to fossil fuels, considering the goal of net-zero carbon emissions. It should be borne in mind that these countries (predominantly European) intend to solve the problem of dependence on fossil fuels, whether for economic or environmental reasons. However, at a global and European level, there is a trend towards the development of projects and partnerships for the production and distribution of green hydrogen in other countries, such as Brazil, which, despite its enormous energy potential, still faces incredible difficulties and inequalities, for example at a social and economic level.[45]

The 2023 IRENA Report on investment and global financing of renewable energies corroborates this idea.[46] This report stresses the need for public funding to play a significant role, beyond minimising investment risks. It emphasises how loans to less economically developed countries wishing to deploy renewables must be modified. The research recommends deeper international cooperation, including a significant increase in financial flows from the Global North to the Global South, in recognition of the limited public finances available in developing countries.[47]

---

43 Global Witness, 'Press Release: EU green hydrogen plans "a gold standard for greenwashing" which would burn more fossil fuels', 13 February 2023, https://www.globalwitness.org/en/press-releases/eu-green-hydrogen-plans-a-gold-standard-for-greenwashing-which-would-burn-more-fossil-fuels/.

44 F. Wilkinson, 'Industrial Revolution and Technology', *National Geographic*, https://education.nationalgeographic.org/resource/industrial-revolution-and-technology/.

45 IEA, *Global Hydrogen Review 2022*, September 2022, https://www.iea.org/reports/global-hydrogen-review-2022; IEA, *The Future of Hydrogen*, June 2019, https://www.iea.org/reports/the-future-of-hydrogen.

46 IRENA, 'Press Release: Investments in Renewables Reached Record High, But Need Massive Increase and More Equitable Distribution', 22 February 2023, https://www.irena.org/News/pressreleases/2023/Feb/Investments-in-Renewables-Reached-Record-High-But-Need-Massive-Increase-More-Equitable-Distribution.

47 Ibid.

Since nation states may have to partner with economically and socially less developed countries, which often need to be prepared or adequately regulated to obtain the best benefits from external capital, what will be the social and environmental impacts of this new context/dimension/development? And, in this context, how can innovative projects like green hydrogen/alternative energy projects be implemented?

From the sociological perspective, laws can be seen as a social fact arising from events/situations that have had an impact or value in society, and require state regulation, especially regarding conflict resolution. This can be observed about new technologies, for example, because, in general, technology comes before legislation. Thus, when analysing legislation, it is always important to interpret the laws according to the national historical and social context. To design a market and industry model that allows us to envision a real/actual sustainable future, in a more integrated world concerned with preserving the natural environment, the key is to redefine the intersection between the environment and society through a joint effort between different areas of science, including sociology, economics, law and technology. The moment is exciting but, at the same time, challenging.

Figure 1. The Interplay of Law, Science, Economy, and Sociology in Addressing Sustainable Future

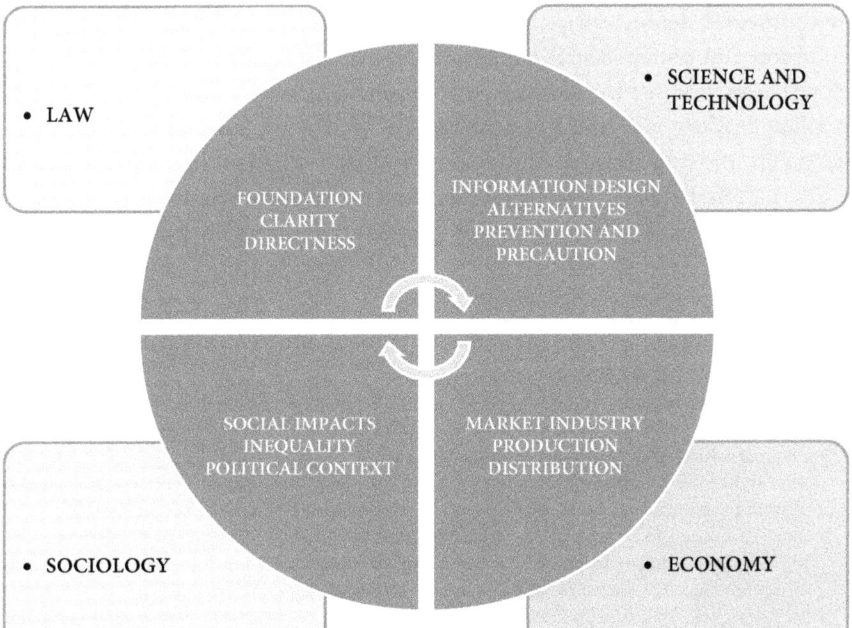

Source: Produced by the authors.

One possible way to approach hydrogen policy is to establish a legal framework based on scientific and technological evidence, and which offers design choices that prioritise prevention of, and precautions against, environmental damage. Such a policy would also examine the economic dimensions of hydrogen, such as its market, industry, production and distribution, and evaluate their social implications, in particular how they affect inequality and power relations in the political context.

4. BRAZILIAN LEGISLATION AND POLICIES

The Brazilian territory has excellent climatic conditions for energy production through sun, wind, water and biomass,[48] and Northeast Brazil has great potential for producing green hydrogen, and is a privileged geographic location for substantial hydrogen exportation, especially to the European continent.[49]

Protection of the environment is a constitutionally enshrined value in Brazilian legislation, in Article 225 of the Constitution.[50] From this constitutional base, a whole legal system was built for environmental protection, based on dividing competencies between the federal entities. Depending on the matter to be dealt with, there may sometimes be a joint or even concurrent attribution. In addition, it should not be forgotten that the Brazilian economic order is based on the environmental defence principle. In recent years, mainly due to a disastrous environmental policy, Brazil has faced a sad statistic: the unbridled growth of deforestation, and an increase in environmental crimes.[51] Especially at present, Brazilian leaders face the great challenge of leaving behind this dark past, and finally moving towards the goals set at the international level, especially in international treaties and agreements to which the country is a signatory, such as the Paris Agreement.[52] The question, therefore, is how to guarantee

48 C. Chantre et al., 'Hydrogen economy development in Brazil: An analysis of stakeholders' perception', *Sustainable Production and Consumption* (2022) 34, pp. 26–41, https://doi.org/10.1016/j.spc.2022.08.028.

49 McKinsey & Company, 'The green hidden gem – Brazil's opportunity to become a sustainability powerhouse', 4 November 2022, https://www.mckinsey.com/br/en/our-insights/all-insights/the-green-hidden-gem-brazils-opportunity-to-become-a-sustainability-powerhouse; FGV, 'Researchers reveal opportunities to use green hydrogen in Brazil', 17 February 2023, https://portal.fgv.br/en/news/researchers-reveal-opportunities-use-green-hydrogen-brazil.

50 Brazil, Constituição Federal, https://www.planalto.gov.br/ccivil_03/constituicao/constituicao.htm.

51 M. Rodrigues, 'Bolsonaro's troubled legacy for science, health and the environment', *Nature*, 27 September 2022, https://www.nature.com/articles/d41586-022-03038-3.

52 M. Rodrigues, 'Will Brazil's President Lula keep his climate promises?', *Nature*, 6 January 2023, https://www.nature.com/articles/d41586-023-00011-6; K. Baragwanath, 'The New Lula Government Faces Significant Challenges on the Road to Zero-Deforestation', *Australian Institute of International Affairs*, 8 March 2023, https://www.internationalaffairs.org.au/australianoutlook/the-new-lula-government-faces-significant-challenges-on-the-road-to-zero-deforestation/.

the cooperation of federal entities, to promote environmental protection and economic growth based on sustainable development. This reveals the urgency of a cross-cutting environmental agenda integrating various government sectors.

Within the theme of the distribution of legislative competencies in Brazil, and its influence on the hydrogen issue, the attributions for enacting laws on certain subjects is crucial. For the energy issue, for example, the Federal Union has exclusive competence. Therefore, as a rule, the directive at the national level authorises and directs legislation throughout the rest of the territory. However, one cannot forget that, to develop the hydrogen economy and other strategies around renewable energies, a complex legislative framework is necessary, including direct rules for regulating the producer market and the exportations, and indirect strategies aimed at costs and the production-consumption chain, such as taxes and fiscal incentives. This is perhaps Brazil's most significant challenge in the renewal energy sphere: defining the limits of each government entity in regulating green hydrogen.

Another critical point concerns integrating all sectors of the economy and society towards the common goal of the energy transition. Brazil already has numerous pieces of legislation focusing on renewable energy, technology and innovation, such as InovarAuto,[53] RenovaBio,[54] Rota 2030,[55] and others. The National Biofuels Policy (RenovaBio),[56] which is based on the use of biofuels and the environmental effectiveness of biofuel production, sets as its aim decarbonisation, focusing in particular on the transportation sector. The National Energy Policy Council (ministerial board) annually approves the goals for the following ten years.[57] In addition, two legislative proposals (PLS 725/22 and PLS 1878/22) intend to regulate the production and use of green hydrogen for energy.[58] The Brazilian government launched the Guidelines for the National Hydrogen Program (PNH2) in August 2021, and related actions are being developed and coordinated by the Ministry of Mines and Energy (MME). The PNH2[59] comprehends six priority axes: reinforcement

---

53 Brazil, Inovar-Auto, Ministério da Economia, https://www.gov.br/produtividade-e-comercio-exterior/pt-br/assuntos/competitividade-industrial/setor-automotivo/inovar-auto.

54 Brazil, Lei 13.256/2017, https://www.planalto.gov.br/ccivil_03/_ato2015–2018/2017/lei/l13576.htm.

55 Brazil, Rota 2030, https://www.rota2030.com.br/.

56 Brazil, 'RenovaBio', Ministério de Minas e Energia, https://www.gov.br/mme/pt-br/assuntos/secretarias/petroleo-gas-natural-e-biocombustiveis/renovabio-1#:~:text=O%20RenovaBio&text=Dita%20pol%C3%ADtica%20de%20Estado%20leva,e%20a%20previsibilidade%20do%20mercado.

57 IRENA, *Renewable energy targets in* 2022, supra, note 20.

58 N. Machado, '"PIB do hidrogênio verde" se articula por política industrial', EPBR, 16 March 2023, https://epbr.com.br/pib-do-hidrogenio-verde-se-articula-por-politica-industrial/.

59 Brazil, 'Despacho nº 63 do Presidente da República', Imprensa Nacional, https://in.gov.br/en/web/dou/-/despacho-do-presidente-da-republica-419972141.

of R&DI (Research, Development and Innovation) and technological bases;[60] capacity-building and human capital formation; energy planning; legal and regulatory framework; market development and competitiveness; and international partnership and cooperation.[61]

What can be observed is that, most of the time, legislation and public policies in Brazil establish criteria and goals, but do not detail the means to achieve these objectives. For example, PNH2, initiated by the MME, is under pressure, from stakeholders in the energy and low-carbon hydrogen sectors, to clarify its goals and objectives. The general worry is that Brazil may fall behind other nations in the competition for investments to produce green hydrogen, because of a lax approach to goal-setting, and a lack of attention to low-carbon hydrogen, particularly green hydrogen[62] Furthermore, the Brazilian strategy for developing low-carbon hydrogen does not establish targets for producing and using hydrogen that will influence end-users. Therefore, Brazilian policy will significantly influence the dynamics of the energy market without direct practical effects on the population at first.[63]

Although there is legislation in Brazil that contemplates the production chain in general, it is still necessary to regulate the production, distribution, transport, consumption and quality of different sources of hydrogen for different uses, as well as to define the certification criteria, especially for green hydrogen.[64] Subsidies, exemptions, and other regulatory incentives, could be the key to encouraging the green hydrogen market in Brazil. Energy sector entities support a tax reform that streamlines the tariff, increases its efficiency, lowers the cost of compliance for productive operations, and ensures that the money made from concessions is used to lower fees and energy transport rates.[65] With its renewable energy potential, the focus on green hydrogen is, in addition to being sustainable, an intelligent initiative for Brazil to develop its market, which is why a political and legal strategy for developing that market is so important. If Brazil is not quick to legislate, it will squander one of the most significant economic and environmental opportunities ever to present itself to a nation-state in the twenty-first century.

---

60 Brazil, '2031 – Ten-years energy expansion plan', Ministério de Minas e Energia, https://www.gov.br/mme/pt-br/assuntos/secretarias/sntep/publicacoes/plano-decenal-de-expansao-de-energia/pde-2031/english-version/relatorio_pde2031_cap12_eus.pdf.

61 Green Hydrogen Organisation, 'Brazil', https://gh2.org/countries/brazil.

62 G. Chiappini, 'Hidrogênio verde: Brasil corre ou perde o bonde', *EPBR*, 13 January 2023, https://epbr.com.br/plano-para-o-hidrogenio-verde-brasil-corre-ou-perde-o-bonde/.

63 Green Hydrogen Organisation, 'Brazil', supra, note 59.

64 Legislação e Mercados, 'Regulação do hidrogênio entra em pauta no Brasil', 26 April 2022, https://legislacaoemercados.capitalaberto.com.br/regulacao-do-hidrogenio-verde-entra-em-pauta-no-brasil/.

65 R. Hessel, 'Estudo inédito aponta caminho do sucesso da política energética do novo governo', *Correio Braziliense*, 30 January 2023, https://www.correiobraziliense.com.br/

Brazil's first green hydrogen production occurred in January 2023, at the Pecém Port Complex, in partnership with the private sector.[66] The Port Complex of Pecém is attempting to promote a solution to the climate crisis via its green hydrogen hub project, which will act as one of the country's main green hydrogen sites. Ultimately, this complex aims to become a complete site, with hydrogen production, storage and global exportation.[67]

Pecém is located about 60 kilometres from the capital of the state of Ceará, Fortaleza. About 20 years ago, after surveys by the Brazilian Navy, the project to build the port terminal began, as the state had a need for a new port that could receive larger ships.[68] From a legal and legislative point of view, the complex was conceived as an area destined not only for the construction of the port, but also for an entire industrial and logistical centre around it. Thus, specific areas are intended for certain types of industries, such as refineries. Due to its privileged geographic location, and other factors, the Pecém Complex has significant potential for growth and economic development, especially for projects related to energy production from renewable sources, such as wind and solar power. Consequently, this growth potential attracted foreign investors, especially European ones. In 2018, the Port of Rotterdam became a shareholder in the company that manages the Pecém Complex. In addition, numerous foreign companies have already established themselves, or have already expressed formal interest in installing themselves, in Pecém. However, it must be said that, since the project's conception, there have always been debates involving urban planning, the environment, sustainability, and the complex's relationship with the surrounding communities, including fishermen and indigenous colonies, for example, in addition to an entirely undeveloped area around the project.[69]

The significant advances made by the Port of Rotterdam, in the development of, and investment in, technology for the production and export of hydrogen, is well known. Thus, from the partnership with Rotterdam, the opportunity arises for Pecém to attract further projects in this direction, considering that there is already renewable energy potential in general. Partnerships with other countries and investors, related to renewable energy sources, such as offshore wind energy production, would be a positive way forward to support the

economia/2023/01/5069837-estudo-inedito-aponta-caminho-do-sucesso-da-politica-energetica-do-novo-governo.html.

66 I. Campos, 'Primeira molécula de Hidrogênio Verde produzida no Brasil é lançada no Ceará', Governo do Estado do Ceará, 19 January 2023, https://www.casacivil.ce.gov.br/2023/01/19/primeira-molecula-de-hidrogenio-verde-produzida-no-brasil-e-lancada-no-ceara/.

67 Complexo Industrial e Portuário do Pecém, 'Hub de Hidrogênio Verde do Complexo do Pecém', https://www.complexodopecem.com.br/hubh2v/.

68 N. Hakirevic Prevljak, 'Brazil's Pecém Port could get green hydrogen export hub', *Offshore Energy*, https://www.offshore-energy.biz/brazils-pecem-port-could-get-green-hydrogen-export-hub/.

69 F. Bruna Santiago Viana Cavalcante, 'Pecém: Do Local ao Global', *Geosaberes: Revista de Estudos Geoeducacionais*, (2019) 10(21), pp. 1–16, doi:10.26895/geosaberes.v10i21.723.

economic development of the nascent Brazilian green hydrogen industry, and the move to promote an environmentally sustainable energy source.

The development of this project generates a variety of complexities and uncertainties concerning the application of environmentally sustainable policies and legislation in Brazil, alongside economic and societal impacts. The Pecém Complex project is promising, but at the same time challenging. The project is very distinctive for many reasons, like the design of the industrial and port complex; the existence, in such a large area, of communities with more potential to suffer from the impacts of such significant economic development projects (fishermen and indigenous colonies); the influence of the European example, through the investment of the Port of Rotterdam and other partners; and the complexity of the Brazilian reality, especially in legal and environmental terms. For example, the thermoelectric plants, two conveyor belts, and the production of cement and steel may all contaminate soil, water resources and the atmosphere, and pose potential risks to nearby populations' health and living conditions,[70] not to mention the impact on marine life and the surrounding environment, typical of port and maritime activities.[71]

A project like Pecém, involving renewable energy sources and carbon emission reduction, is obviously auspicious. But such a project will have different impacts, consequences and results when implemented in different social, economic and environmental realities. That is why the idea of sustainable development around these projects is so essential, mainly because the impact must be considered according to society and the surrounding environment.

5. CONCLUSION

As the number of hydrogen projects and policies worldwide increases quickly, hydrogen is experiencing unparalleled political and commercial impetus. A report by the International Energy Agency provided an analysis of the present hydrogen market and recommendations for its future development.[72] According to the report, it is necessary to scale up technologies and reduce costs, to enable the widespread use of hydrogen. Along with the expansion of the industries targeted, the number of nations with laws that actively encourage investment in hydrogen technology is rising. Nine countries have adopted hydrogen

70 N. Santos-Junior et al., 'Cumulative Environmental Vulnerability Assessment in the Area of Influence of the Pecém Port Industrial Complex (Ceará, Brazil): A Spatial Analysis', *International Journal of Environmental Research and Public Health*, (2021) 18(5), doi:10.3390/ijerph18052404.

71 N. Mueller, M. Westerby and M. Nieuwenhuijsen, 'Health impact assessments of shipping and port-sourced air pollution on a global scale: A scoping literature review', *Environmental Research*, (2023) 216 (Pt. 1): 114460, doi:10.1016/j.envres.2022.114460.

72 IEA, *The Future of Hydrogen*, supra, note 43.

strategies in the past year, with about 50 targets,[73] requirements and policy incentives that directly support the development of hydrogen, the bulk of which are geared towards hydrogen transportation.[74]

With an emphasis on industries where hydrogen can help decarbonise and reduce dependence on fossil fuels, such as heavy industries, heavy-duty road transport, and shipping, such legislative action should be supplemented by novel hydrogen uses in innovation and demonstration activities.[75] This can be seen in both the Brazilian and the UK legislation. Sectors such as transport, for example, lead the legal incentive strategy for developing the hydrogen industry. There is a tendency now to develop more abstract goals, supported by legislation, that do not necessarily regulate the production and exportation of hydrogen, but are related to sustainability goals and the use of renewable energy. The UK has more audacious goals in comparison to Brazil, and intends to reduce carbon emissions in a shorter time, using hydrogen as an essential asset. In addition, the UK presents a theoretically broader strategy, based not only on the energy transition, but also on the idea of a new Green Industrial Revolution, which the present authors believe will necessitate the idea of ecological sustainability being used to interpret relevant legislation. Thus, there would be a paradigm shift that can lead to a more solid foundation for environmental protection, since the idea of a green economy must be the primary agenda.

Given the extent and natural potential of its territory and geographic location, Brazil already has a resource and technical advantage regarding renewable energy, which has attracted the attention of investors worldwide, as seen in the case of the Pecém Port. Brazil already has a strong foundation, in terms of renewable energy legislation, but has no clear goals or policies to deal specifically with hydrogen, or to place it at the centre of its economic growth.

The UK and Brazil have vastly different political, economic and social contexts, which shape their legal systems and their implementation and application of laws. This is especially relevant for the emerging hydrogen production and transportation field, which is a critical component of the global energy transition.[76] As this field is still evolving, with limited practical experience, no one-size-fits-all model for regulating hydrogen activities can be replicated or adapted. Therefore, each jurisdiction must develop a regulatory framework that suits its specific circumstances and objectives.[77]

---

73 Ibid.

74 IEA, 'Hydrogen', September 2022, https://www.iea.org/reports/hydrogen.

75 IEA, *Global Hydrogen Review 2022*, supra, note 42.

76 D. Majumber-Russell and M. Hassam, 'CMS Expert Guide to hydrogen energy law and regulation-Facing the Future of Hydrogen', *CMS*, https://cms.law/en/int/expert-guides/cms-expert-guide-to-hydrogen.

77 ReedSmith, 'Hydrogen regulations by jurisdiction and changing transmission systems', 27 June 2022, https://www.reedsmith.com/en/perspectives/energy-transition/2022/06/hydrogen-regulations-by-jurisdiction-and-changing-transmission-systems.

New horizons are opening in this area, as seen in the US government's new greenhouse gas emissions reduction strategy, which has been praised for the vast financial investment committed by the Federal State concerning the green economy and hydrogen, with billions of dollars in incentives, subsidies and tax breaks.[78] This strategy recognises the versatility and potential of hydrogen as a clean energy carrier that can be produced from various sources, including fossil fuels, with carbon capture; renewable energy; and nuclear energy.[79] By supporting the development and deployment of hydrogen technologies, the US hopes to achieve multiple benefits, such as reducing its dependence on fossil fuels, enhancing its energy security and resilience, creating new jobs and industries, and improving its air quality and public health. Moreover, this strategy could serve as a model for other countries that are serious about promoting renewable energy and carbon reduction, which would lead to a cleaner atmosphere, as an indirect result of this regulatory approach, which encourages the consumption of good and services, and reduces costs for the industrial chain.

Brazil may need help adopting such a strategy, as the country urgently needs a comprehensive tax reform to facilitate the transition to a low-carbon economy. However, Brazil has a unique opportunity to become a leader in the new Green Industrial Revolution, driven by the global need to transition to a low-carbon economy and mitigate climate change. Brazil can also gain knowledge from other nations' successes in implementing policies and plans to encourage green growth and innovation, like China and India, which have made significant investments in hydrogen technologies, and raised the productivity of their agricultural sectors, through the Green Revolution.[80] As a result, Brazil could establish itself as a pioneer in the new Green Industrial Revolution, and profit from a cleaner, greener future, on an economic, social and environmental level, by utilising its natural potential and participating in international cooperation and learning.

---

78 J. Calma, 'The US wants to become a hydrogen production powerhouse', *The Verge*, 23 September 2022, https://www.theverge.com/2022/9/23/23368339/hydrogen-clean-energy-biden-administration-strategy.

79 The White House, 'Fact Sheet: President Biden Sets 2030 Greenhouse Gas Pollution Reduction Target Aimed at Creating Good-Paying Union Jobs and Securing U.S. Leadership on Clean Energy Technologies', 22 April 2021, https://www.whitehouse.gov/briefing-room/statements-releases/2021/04/22/fact-sheet-president-biden-sets-2030-greenhouse-gas-pollution-reduction-target-aimed-at-creating-good-paying-union-jobs-and-securing-u-s-leadership-on-clean-energy-technologies/.

80 L. Cabral, 'Green Revolutions in Brazil, China and India: epic narratives of the past and today's South–South technology transfers', *Institute of Development Studies*, 15 October 2019, https://www.ids.ac.uk/projects/green-revolutions-in-brazil-china-and-india-epic-narratives-of-the-past-and-todays-south-south-technology-transfers/.

FIXING THE CIRCULAR ECONOMY

A Limited Right to Repair Faces Core Constraints from Voluntary Approaches and Private Law

Alba Nogueira López*

ABSTRACT

The Right to Repair and Ecodesign proposals of the European Union (EU) are two relevant pieces of legislation to promote an ambitious circular economy.

* Funding: Agencia Estatal de Investigación, Economía circular local (ECIL): políticas públicas, herramientas jurídicas y buenas prácticas en la gestión circular de los residuos municipales (TED2021-129734B-I00). Xunta de Galicia, Axudas para a consolidación e estruturación de unidades de investigación competitivas (ED431B 2023/45).

Analysing these proposals for limitations arising from time delays, decision-making procedures, and intersections with other sectors of the legal system, might help to understand whether a new sustainable product policy is about to be born. The right to repair is also a good issue for exploring whether EU environmental law is at a turning point, and mandatory instruments of public environmental law are no longer the preferred means of implementing environmental policies, because private law approaches and voluntary/information tools are taking the lead.

1. INTRODUCTION

The second Circular Economy Action Plan, known as CEAP 2020,[1] recognised the right to repair (R2R) as a leading tool for sustainable transition and consumer empowerment. Durability and reparability were also identified as relevant criteria for a sustainable product legislation initiative. However, progress towards the right to repair seems to be facing serious obstacles. The legislative initiative to regulate the right to repair was blocked for a long time, and after three years, progress on R2R and eco-design proposals has been significantly limited.

Additionally, legal intersections with other branches of private law, and prevailing sectors of the European economic order, can hinder the aim of giving longer life to products and providing repair options. Market rules that are immune to sustainability criteria restrict efforts, and undermine expectations, about any ambitious push for the right to repair.[2]

This chapter examines the Proposal for a Directive on common rules to promote the repair of goods (hereinafter Right to Repair proposal), along with the Proposal for a Regulation establishing a framework for setting ecodesign requirements for sustainable products and repealing Directive 2009/125/EC (hereinafter Ecodesign proposal). The analysis includes the scope of the provisions, and their coherence with legislation on competition, consumer law, intellectual property and commercial law. Is European law working for sustainable, longer-lasting products, or are there shortcomings in the proposals and competing private law provisions or interests that could obstruct R2R and

---

1 COM(2020) 98 final, 'A new Circular Economy Action Plan For a cleaner and more competitive Europe', https://eur-lex.europa.eu/resource.html?uri=cellar:9903b325-6388-11ea-b735-01aa75ed71a1.0017.02/DOC_1&format=PDF (hereinafter 'CEAP').

2 A. Nogueira, 'Are Soft Legal Measures in Circular Economy Action Plans Enough to Permeate EU Strong Economic Core Regulations Bringing Systemic Sustainable Change?', *Circular Economy and Sustainability*, (2022) 3, pp. 1545–1568, https://doi.org/10.1007/s43615-022-00227-0.

product-life-extension measures? This contribution assesses how such legal provisions could limit product durability, reparability as a first option, access to spare parts, and product reuse and refurbishment, thereby promoting increasingly unsustainable consumption patterns for products and resources.

The aim is to assess the momentum of, and obstacles to, the circular economy, by studying limitations arising from time delays, decision-making procedures and intersections with other sectors of the legal system. The right to repair might also be a good issue to explore whether the EU is at a turning point, and mandatory instruments of public environmental law are no longer the preferred means of implementing environmental policies, because private law approaches and voluntary/information tools are taking the lead.

2. METHODOLOGY

Within a legal framework, the texts implementing the circular economy (CE) were examined in detail to: (1) assess the extent of the right to repair, the scope of the regulations, and their consistency with more stringent regulations of Member States; (2) determine the presence and type of durability or repair provisions; (3) understand whether the relevant measures ensure a clear, directly applicable right to repair, or depend on further legal developments or self-regulation that would delay or dilute their entry into force; (4) discern the mandatory/voluntary nature of the proposed measures; and (5) assess how other core economic legislation (competition law, Services Directive, consumer law, intellectual property law) obstruct R2R, and evaluate the level of ambition for implementing the CE in the European Union (EU).

The grey literature relevant to the proposed measures (negotiating position of the Council, EU Parliament amendments, monitoring reports, evaluation documents, working papers, official websites, etc.) was also carefully scrutinised, to assess the scope and the degree of compliance with timelines. Studying measures from their draft stages on their way to approval and assessment documents helps identify contentious issues, competing interests, shortcomings and coherence with political claims regarding transformative ambition. Academic literature from economic, political and sociological perspectives has also addressed the shortcomings of the EU's CE strategy. There are legal studies describing obstacles to the right to repair, but there is no complete review of the various intersections with other areas of law that must be addressed to push for durable and reparable products. Legal research methodology was used to study legal texts, academic literature, jurisprudence, and documents produced by the EU, its Member States, and stakeholders, to determine the deficiencies and efficacy issues linked to CE instruments and measures. This chapter will try to assess the scope and shortcomings of the right to repair, and ways to fix the shortcomings.

3. A LONG SLOW PATH TO THE RIGHT TO REPAIR PROPOSAL WITH VETO POWER FOR THE REGULATORY SCRUTINY BOARD

The right to repair was probably the most publicised measure of CEAP 2020. It specified feasible and affordable repair for all types of products, not just electrical and electronic ones, as a key feature. This, combined with new Ecodesign Regulation, would result in longer-lasting, sustainable products, and pave the way for circularity. Eco-design plays a central role in the plan, as it would facilitate reparability, dismantling, and standardisation of components. Information is also a crucial component, for accessing repair instructions and knowing about the availability of spare parts, repair services or degree of reparability (reparability scores). Another key issue to be addressed is access to repair services (either authorised or independent repair shops) and, in the case of ICT and electronics, to upgrading services. The plan also contemplates establishing appropriate regulatory time frames for compulsory availability of spare parts, product durability, and repair itself.

On the consumption side, making repair affordable constitutes a relevant policy issue that also affects taxation decisions. Proximity to repair shops is also a key feature for making repair easily and quickly available. Finally, the legal scope and conditions of product guarantees, and regulation of the choice of remedies for consumers, clearly influences repair decisions.

The European Parliament adopted a first plenary resolution on 25 November 2020, with very strong parliamentary support, to push for 'making repairs more attractive, systematic and cost-effective' by extending warranties, providing guarantees for replaced parts, and improving access to repair and maintenance information. It also insisted on increasing support for second-hand markets, and tackling practices that shorten the useful lives of products. This included access to information on product operation and disassembly, software that conditions operability, and diagnostic software. Availability of spare parts over a long period of time (particularly for consumer goods, such as white goods), along with the standardisation of these parts, and the tools needed for repairs, were also central issues. Additionally, taxation would need to be introduced to encourage repair. The resolution also mentioned removing competition barriers that block independent repairers from accessing information and spare parts. This plenary resolution was followed by two other resolutions, one of them concerning only the right to repair, which also had broad support.[3]

---

3 European Parliament, 'Resolution of 25 November 2020 Towards a More Sustainable Single Market for Business and Consumers', 2020/2021(INI), https://eur-lex.europa.eu/legal-content/EN/TXT/PDF/?uri=CELEX:52020IP0318; European Parliament, 'Resolution of

However promising this support might seem, the fact is that the Right to Repair proposal[4] did not see light until March 2023, long past the 2021 time limit established in the Annex to the CEAP 2020.[5] The two sets of initiatives announced in 2022, to 'make sustainable products the norm'[6] (March), and to put 'an end to wasteful packaging, boosting reuse and recycling' (November),[7] made no mention of the expected R2R regulation.

Although allegedly a milestone for Green Deal measures, the legislation faced a lengthy blockage, in the form of the Regulatory Scrutiny Board (RSB).[8] The Directive proposal explained the key role of the RSB in the proposal outcomes and the delay: 'The Commission's Regulatory Scrutiny Board first issued a negative opinion on 30 September 2022. After the initial draft underwent a significant revision, the RSB provided a positive opinion, with further comments, on 24 January 2023' (COM(2023) 155 final, 6). Both RSB opinions addressed the proposal's supposed lack of explanation of different regulatory choices, and demanded 'quantitative estimates', 'cost and benefits', 'results of cost benefit analysis' and a clearer 'methodological approach to estimate consumer savings', for many proposed actions. However, the RSB opinions contained no environmentally driven considerations (SWD (2023), 59 final, Annex I, 76–82).

Eller and Kampourakis[9] describe the RSB as 'a central gatekeeper in the European legislative process', because 'if an impact assessment does not satisfy the RSB twice, this brings the proposal to a halt. In such cases, only a decision by the College of Commissioners can overcome the blockage and take the proposal further.' Considering that about one-third of RSB opinions are negative, it is clear that non-elected actors, outside EU institutional power distribution, play a major role in legislative procedure. The current RSB members come from business/trade-oriented professional backgrounds,

---

10 February 2021 on the New Circular Economy Action Plan', 2020/2077(INI), https://www.europarl.europa.eu/doceo/document/TA-9-2021-0040_EN.html; European Parliament, 'Resolution of 7 April 2022 on the Right to Repair', 2022/2515(RSP), https://www.europarl.europa.eu/doceo/document/TA-9-2022-0126_EN.html.

4 Proposal for a Directive on common rules promoting the repair of goods (COM(2023) 155 final).

5 COM(2020) 98 final, Annex.

6 European Commission, Green Deal: New proposals to make sustainable products the norm and boost Europe's resource independence, press release 30.3.2022, https://ec.europa.eu/commission/presscorner/detail/en/ip_22_2013.

7 European Commission, European Green Deal: Putting an end to wasteful packaging, boosting reuse and recycling, press release 30.11.2022, https://ec.europa.eu/commission/presscorner/detail/en/ip_22_7155.

8 https://twitter.com/anna_cavazzini/status/1581931568662081537?s=20.

9 Eller, Klaas Hendrik; Kampourakis, Ioannis: Quantifying 'Better Regulation': The EU Regulatory Scrutiny Board and the Sustainable Corporate Governance Initiative, VerfBlog, 2022/2/21, https://verfassungsblog.de/quantifying-better-regulation/, DOI: 10.17176/20220222-001231-0.

with no non-industry environmental experts among them,[10] according to a maladministration complaint filed with the European Ombudsman, in March 2023, by the Corporate Europe Observatory.[11] The complaint also points out the lack of transparency that would violate access rights, as provided by Case *ClientEarth v. EU Commission*,[12] and a consistent track record of one-sided meetings with lobbies supportive of a better regulation agenda.

Finally, the proposal that emerged in March 2023 was quite diluted, as will be examined further on in this chapter, and many of its provisions were delayed through delegated acts, signalling a long road ahead for a strong R2R. The European Environment Bureau (a group of environmental non-governmental organisations) has observed that, for eco-design regulation, 'the slow pace of decision-making processes without clear deadlines is not really addressed. As all future measures will be set through future legal acts, it may take decades to set rules on products if the decision-making process continues to require more than 3 years per product'.[13] Considering that the R2R Directive proposal refers only to products that have, or will have, eco-design regulations, and that it also provides for several delegated acts that the Commission would have to adopt for R2R, it seems there is still a long way to go to ensure a fully fledged right to repair. The delays in reaching a proposal might also hamper the possibility of the Directive being passed before the next European Parliament elections, in June 2024.

4. HOW COMPREHENSIVE IS THE LEGAL APPROACH TO SUSTAINABLE PRODUCTS AND CONSUMPTION? THE SCOPE OF THE RIGHT TO REPAIR PROPOSAL AND THE FULL HARMONISATION APPROACH

The explanatory memorandum of the Directive proposal (COM(2023) 155 final, 2) refers to 'three initiatives that are complementary and generate synergies by establishing a comprehensive approach towards the common objective of sustainable consumption'. The R2R initiative would be one of the three pillars of Green Deal sustainable consumption: (1) on the *supply side*, Ecodesign for Sustainable Product Regulation (COM(2022) 142 final); (2) on the *demand side*,

10 https://commission.europa.eu/law/law-making-process/regulatory-scrutiny-board/members-regulatory-scrutiny-board_en.

11 https://www.ombudsman.europa.eu/en/opening-summary/en/168093.

12 Case C-57/16P, *ClientEarth v. EU Commission* (ECLI:EU:C:2018:660).

13 European Environmental Bureau (EEB), *Unpacking the Circular Economy Package*, EEB Briefing April 2022, https://eeb.org/wp-content/uploads/2022/04/CE-Briefing-April-4-2022.pdf, p. 4.

the Proposal for a Directive on empowering consumers (COM(2022) 143 final); and (3) to fill the gap focusing on the *use phase of goods*, the proposal deals with the right to repair, and amendment to the Sale of Goods Directive (Directive (EU) 2019/771) on the choice of remedies between repair or replacement. These three initiatives pursue 'the Green Deal objective of sustainable consumption in a comprehensive manner' (COM(2023) 155 final, 2).

The R2R measures contained in these initiatives must be analysed, to assess their comprehensiveness and scope, the type of regulatory approach chosen, and potential loopholes. How these issues are addressed in new and current EU regulatory proposals on eco-design, R2R and amendments to the Sale of Goods Directives shows the degree of ambition for longer-lasting goods, and sustainable policies. The extent to which related key policies remain untouched must also be considered.

In any case, the facts that R2R provisions are scattered among three legal texts, and that the provisions of the R2R proposal depend on the scope of each set of eco-design regulations, does not seem to favour the development of regulation with predictable and uniform content that would result in a universal, directly applicable obligation to repair.

Although Article 1 of the Directive proposal makes no exclusion concerning the scope of products, several provisions in the text limit its obligations to goods 'for which and to the extent that' reparability requirements are provided for in the EU legal Acts listed in Annex II (Art. 5). For now, this includes products subject to, 'but not limited' to, eco-design regulations, as any other requirement in future developments 'in any other field of Union law' would be covered (Recital 6 of the proposal): 'This limitation of the obligation to repair ensures that only those goods which are reparable by design are subject to that obligation' (Recital 16 of the proposal). In fact, in the future, the Commission could delegate acts that add new product groups to Annex II when new reparability requirements are adopted (Recital 17 of the proposal). Eco-design regulations and the right to repair are intertwined, but obligations for each type of product will actually be defined (to varying degrees) through future delegated acts of the Commission.

The lack of clarity concerning the scope of the proposal was one of the issues mentioned in the first negative opinion of the RSB ('the report is not clear on the preferred option regarding obligations to repair, i.e., all product scope vs ecodesign product scope', SWD (2023), 59 final, 80, 76). Then, in the January opinion, the RSB again asked for clarity regarding the legal enforceability of the right to repair and the scope of goods categories (SWD (2023), 59 final, 81). The Commission responded that the obligation 'is relevant for goods that are subject to reparability requirements under Union law'. That policy option was chosen after a proportionality test and an exclusively economic assessment. The Commission discarded an obligation to repair all goods, alleging that it would cause 'significant adjustment costs for business as well as significant losses in turnover and GVA'. Such a broad reparability option would also bring 'uncertainty as to when the obligation applies given that many products would remain unregulated and could be irreparable by design' (SWD (2023), 59 final, 71). To get the whole picture of the implications of that policy choice, the impact assessment reports confirmed that an obligation to repair all goods would '[have] higher benefits for the environment and the repair sector', and that 'consumers [would] not need to wait for the obligation to repair to become operational progressively for different product groups', presumably 'over the next decade' (SWD (2023), 59 final, 64). Ultimately, a delayed, limited, business-friendly right to repair was preferred over a comprehensive, directly applicable R2R.

The current proposal fails to provide a 'universal' or 'mainstream' right to repair, because it affects only an 'extremely limited set of products'.[14] Furthermore, reparability obligations can vary, because individual eco-design regulations can establish different reparability requirements ('for which *and to the extent*', Art. 5 of the proposal).

The Directive follows a full harmonisation approach (Art. 3), whereby Member States cannot maintain or introduce, in their national laws, provisions that diverge from those laid down in the Directive text. This harms the possibility of more ambitious national policies. The full harmonisation approach is consistent with the legal basis claimed by the proposal – Article 114 of the Treaty on the Functioning of the European Union (TFEU), on measures to ensure the establishment and functioning of the internal market – but could affect national measures already in force, such as France's repair rules. The explanatory memorandum accompanying the proposal argues that 'diverging mandatory national rules' might create obstacles to the internal market, discourage repairers from offering their services in more than one Member State, and limit cross-border movement of spare parts and repair equipment (COM(2023) 155 final, 2–3). The provisions subject to full harmonisation are modifications to the legal guarantees of the Sale of Goods Directive, and 'the standardised European Repair Information Form and obligation to repair, which have an internal market dimension'. Other provisions fall outside the full harmonisation mandate, so 'where a solution at national level is equally effective, in particular the repair platform, this is the preferred choice' (COM(2023) 155 final, 5). Recital 5 of the proposal states that the Directive 'should not affect the freedom of Member States to regulate aspects of contracts for the provision of repair services other than those harmonised in Union law'.

Views on the full harmonisation option differ. The European Law Institute asked for the proposal to open 'clauses or even regulatory sandboxes … in order

---

14 Right to Repair Europe Coalition (2023), 'Not yet accessible, affordable nor mainstream: campaigners tighten the screw on new EU Right to Repair proposal', 22.03.2023, https://repair.eu/news/not-yet-accessible-affordable-nor-mainstream-campaigners-tighten-the-screw-on-new-eu-right-to-repair-proposal/.

to allow Member States to introduce more sustainable measures'; it was looking for flexibility to enhance 'environmental added value'.[15] The technological industries association Orgalim fully supported the proposed maximum level of harmonisation, and added that:

> we are very concerned about different national initiatives adopted by various Member States to promote the repair of goods; for example, related to the repair score of products (e.g. in France, Belgium and Austria), because they fragment the internal market and do not offer credibility to consumers when the same product can have different scoring with different methodologies in the various Member States.[16]

The latter position is consistent with industry and business association positions on other recent environmental proposals, where full harmonisation has been used as a regulatory option to stop more stringent national schemes (for example, corporate sustainability due diligence).[17]

5. RIGHT TO REPAIR OR INFORMATION ABOUT REPAIRERS?

The decision to tackle the right to repair through three legal initiatives – the Ecodesign proposal and the R2R proposal, which also amends the Sale of Goods Directive (SGD) – means that producer and seller reparability obligations and consumer rights will be located in different legal texts. Also, the obligations arising from Article 5 of the Right to Repair proposal will depend on the scope of future eco-design regulations for each category of goods, passed down

---

15 European Law Institute (ELI), *European Commission's Proposal for a Directive on Common Rules Promoting the Repair of Goods (COM(2023) 155 final): Feedback of the European Law Institute*, ELI, 2023, https://www.europeanlawinstitute.eu/fileadmin/user_upload/p_eli/Publications/ELI_Feedback_Right_to_Repair.pdf. Also available as S. Augenhofer, 'EC's Public Consultation on Sustainable Consumption of Goods – Promoting Repair and Reuse, Response of the European Law Institute' (3 April 2022), http://dx.doi.org/10.2139/ssrn.4318524.

16 Orgalim, *Green Transition: Orgalim position and recommendations on the proposal for a Directive laying down common rules promoting the repair of goods*, Orgalim, 2023, https://orgalim.eu/position-papers/green-transition-orgalim-position-and-recommendations-proposal-directive-laying, p. 2.

17 European Round Table for Industry (ERT), Joint Statement: Ensuring harmonisation & consistency across due diligence frameworks, 16.12.2021, https://ert.eu/documents/joint-statement-ensuring-harmonisation-consistency-across-due-diligence-frameworks/; CLEPA (European Association of Automotive Suppliers), Joint statement of the business community: more harmonisation and realism are needed in the EU due diligence proposal (CS3D) 19.01.2023 https://clepa.eu/mediaroom/joint-statement-due-diligence-proposal/.

through delegated acts that will not be ready earlier than 2027–30.[18] In fact, the R2R proposal directly enacts two main issues: it gives slight priority to repair remedies within the legal guarantee (amendment of the SGD), and makes a set of information tools available to consumers about repairer availability, prices and conditions:

> On the basis of a multi-criteria and cost-benefit analysis as well as a qualitative assessment of the proportionality of the various options considered, a combination of six preferred policy options was proposed to address the problems:
>
> - prioritising repair whenever it is cheaper than replacement within the legal guarantee framework.
> - an online platform at national level, matchmaking consumers with repairers and promoting refurbished goods.
> - an obligation on repairers to issue upon request a quote on price and conditions for repair in a standardised form (European Repair Information Form).
> - an obligation on producers of goods to which reparability requirements under Union law apply to repair outside the legal guarantee against a price.
> - an obligation on producers to inform on their applicable obligation to repair.
> - a voluntary EU easy repair standard (European Standard for repair services).
>
> The preferred options package increases the repair of goods purchased by consumers both within and outside the legal guarantee by tackling several of the identified drivers of premature disposal of these goods (COM(2023)155 final, 7).

Those provisions must be transposed and applied by Member States, with infringements punished, 24 months after the Directive enters into force (Art. 17; Art. 11). They are expected to reach their full potential after the first two years of application of the measures (SWD (2023, 59 final, 71). Thus, if the proposal actually sees light in late 2024, consumers might be able to take full advantage of the online platform and the European Repair Information Form (ERIF) by approximately 2030.

If we leave aside amendment to the choice of remedies within the legal guarantee (repair if cheaper than replacement), the main new features are the national online platform to find repairers, and the ERIF, which

[18] The Proposal on Ecodesign set the following schedule: 'review, between 2022 and 2026, 33 Commission regulations and adopt 5 new measures under the current Ecodesign Directive, which cannot be carried out by staff currently working on implementation of the Directive;

- prepare and adopt up to 18 new delegated acts between 2024 and 2027; 12 new delegated acts would also be adopted between 2028 and 2030, with staff and budget implications in 2025–2027.
- prepare implementing acts (on average one per year as from 2024) when this is needed to ensure uniform conditions for the implementation of this Regulation.' (COM(2022) 142 final, p. 11).

would strengthen the R2R beyond the guarantee period. In line with the CEAP 2020 motto of 'empowering consumers', the ERIF 'facilitates consumer choice of repair services' by allowing comparison of 'repair opportunities in order to choose the most suitable' (Recital 18 of the proposal). The online national platform 'enables consumers to search' and 'directly request that form' (Recital 21 and 25 of the proposal). The option for an EU platform was discarded because 'a national platform is closer to the consumer's needs', and the key requirements are granted at the EU level, allowing the same results across the EU (SWD (2023, 59 final, 71).

However, both are merely information tools that are consistent with the latest trends in EU environmental law,[19] where mandatory tools are losing ground and information measures are taking the lead, placing the responsibility for advancement towards sustainability on to consumers. A primary focus on 'consumer choice' is a key feature of neo-liberalism in law.[20] It is also consistent with the three trends in EU environmental policy identified by Bouwma et al.:[21] 'a movement from compulsory settings towards [a] "due diligence system" (DDS), a movement from regulatory to information and agreement-based instruments and an increasing reliance on self-governance'. The Commission put it in black and white, stating that 'the majority of Member States did not support imposing obligations to repair on economic operators', and that even those supportive of the obligation wanted it to be limited to the producer, not the seller (COM(2023)155 final, 6). Business stakeholders also had a preference for voluntary commitments, something that half of consumer organisations have found ineffective (COM(2023)155 final, 5).

The proposed regulation for the ERIF and the national online platform contains several shortcomings that should be addressed. For a start, the ERIF is not directly accessible, but is supplied to the consumer 'upon request', and can only be provided by 'producers' (or their authorised representatives or importers in the EU) with an obligation to repair, as established in Article 5 of the proposal (Art. 4.2 of the proposal). The form has clear limitations in scope, with regard to the subjects under obligation, and accessibility. Moreover, a fee might be charged before facilitating the form, if the repairer needs to assess the product to provide the information included in the ERIF (Art. 4.3). In any case, the information included in the form (Art. 4.4: data on the repairer, price, estimated time of repair, type of repair suggested, etc.) is not binding for

---

19 Nogueira, supra, note 2, p. 1.

20 D.S. Grewal and J. Purdy, 'Law and Neoliberalism', *Law and Contemporary Problems*, (2015) 77, pp. 1–23, p. 13, https://scholarship.law.duke.edu/lcp/vol77/iss4/1.

21 I.M. Bouwma, A.L. Gerritsen, D. Kamphorst and F.H. Kistenkas, *Policy instruments and modes of governance in environmental policies of the European Union; past, present and future*, Statutory Research Tasks Unit for Nature & the Environment (WOT Natuur & Milieu), WOt-technical report 60, 2015, p. 27.

Table 1. Own authorship based on the legal texts of the EU institutions' proposals

Comparation of the negotiation positions. Key issues	Commission	Parliament	Council
Scope of goods covered (art.1), Annex II		Annex II. + Bicycles	1.3."Articles 5 and 6 shall only apply to goods for which and to the extent that reparability requirements are provided for by Union legal acts as listed in Annex II".
Definitions (art.2)		New definition: "1a. 'repair' means returning a defective product or waste to a condition where it fulfils its intended use" New definitions of 'independent operator' and 'fulfilment service provider'	Change "producer" to "manufacturer". Definition of "Repair" by reference to the Ecodesign Regulation Definition of "Durable médium" as in Directive (EU) 2019/771.
European Repair Information Form (art.4)	Mandatory and limited to goods under art.5 obligation to repair.	Voluntary. On a durable medium"	Mandatory and limited to goods under art. 5 obligation to repair.
	"2. Repairers other than those obliged to repair by virtue of Article 5 shall not be obliged".	Delete 4.2.	"on a durable medium (…)and within a reasonable period of time"
	If the price cannot reasonably be calculated in advance, the manner in which the price is to be calculated and the *maximum price* for the repair;	*The maximum price expected for the repair including but not limited to costs for spare parts, labour costs, costs for the freight, delivery or postal charges or, if either the total* price or *any of its subparts* Voluntary additional information might be included	Free of charge Voluntary additional information might be included

Obligation to repair (art.5)	1. Member States shall ensure that upon the consumer's request, the producer shall repair, for free or against a price or another kind of consideration, goods for which and to the extent that reparability requirements *are provided for by Union legal acts as listed in Annex II*. The producer shall not be obliged to repair such goods where repair is impossible. The producer may sub-contract repair in order to fulfil its obligation to repair.	1. Member States shall ensure that upon the consumer's request, the producer shall repair, goods which are listed in Annex II, *whether or not reparability requirements for those goods are provided for by Union legal acts*. The producer shall not be obliged to repair such goods where repair is *factually or legally* impossible. *The producer shall not refuse the consumer's request purely due to economic considerations such as the costs.* The producer may sub-contract repair in order to fulfil its obligation to repair. *In such cases, the producer shall provide the repairer with all relevant information to allow the repairer to fulfil his obligations.* Conditions for repair and possibility of a replacement good.	Within reasonable time and price 3a. Without prejudice to the obligation to repair under this article, consumers may seek repair from any repairer of their choice.
Online platform (art.7)	National platforms	National platforms Promote private initiatives Inclusion of repair led- communities and repair cafés and crossborder services	EU platform
Penalties (art.11)	National penalties should be "effective, proportionate and dissuasive". Notification to the Commission of the rules 24 months after entry into force.	Detailed criteria to impose penalties. Alignment with Regulation (EU) 2017/2394 on enforcement of consumer protection. Fines being at least 4% of the seller's or producer's annual turnover or, if the information is not available, 2 m. euros. Notification of the rules 18 months after entry into force.	No changes to the Commission proposal.

(continued)

Table 1 *continued*

Comparation of the negotiation positions. Key issues	Commission	Parliament	Council
Information/Promotion of repair (art.9, recital)		New recital 26.a. calling for amendment of value added tax to at least to those mentioned in Annex II. Measures as repair vouchers, national repair funds or other actions and incentives. Banning anti-repair practices through software or hardware or because of previous repairs by non-authorised repairers.	
Choice of remedies/Legal guarantee (art.12)	Always repair first if it is cheaper.	Repair if it is cheaper "unless the repair is factually or legally impossible or would create significant inconvenience to the consumer."' + 1 year liability if repair is chosen.	Maintains consumer choice. + 6 months liability period if repair takes place. Minimum harmonization Seller's obligation to inform of the right to choose.
Transposition (art.16,17)			+6 months for business adaptation

Source: Produced by the author.

the repairer, and is not considered to be a contractual offer.[22] Repairers 'remain free to decide not to conclude such a contract' (Recital 10 of the proposal), and they could even alter the repair conditions of the form by simply waiting to conclude the contract until after the 30-day period within which those conditions cannot be modified has elapsed (Art. 4.5 of the proposal).

On late November 2023 both the European Parliament and the Council fixed their negotiating positions for the trilogue on the Right to Repair Proposal.[23] The European Parliament amendments try to push for a wider scope of goods with a repair obligation, to strengthen repair rights and ban anti-repair practices (software/hardware limiting repair and limitations to non-authorised repairers). It also mentions measures to promote repair, asks for a change in VAT rules and proposes a detailed regulation of the penalties. The Council wants to keep the obligation to repair tied to the previous existence of legal acts that provide for repair requirements for certain types of goods. The Council differs on the Commission and Parliament positions because it prefers an EU level Online platform. Both the Parliament and the Council provide for extra liability periods for repaired products (+1year/+6months).

6. UNEVEN RIGHT TO REPAIR STEMMING FROM THE ECODESIGN REGULATION PROPOSAL

As discussed above, the core legal decisions on extending the right to repair are contingent upon on the scope of the Ecodesign Regulation now under discussion, since Article 5 of the R2R proposal essentially limits repair obligations to products subject to reparability requirements under eco-design regulations. Analysing the provisions of the proposal for a Regulation of the European Parliament and of the Council establishing a framework for setting ecodesign requirements for sustainable products and repealing Directive 2009/125/EC (COM(2022) 142 final) gives a more complete picture of what the EU is going to push for with regard to the right to repair: what type of obligations, for which products, for how long, and with what limitations.

---

22 M. López and M. Jesús, *Hacia una regulación europea sobre la reparación de bienes de consumo: la propuesta de Directiva de 22 de marzo de 2023*, Centro de Estudios de Consumo, 2023, https://manueljesusmarin.es/wp-content/uploads/2023/05/cesco_78.pdf.

23 P9_TA(2023) ADOPTED. Common rules promoting the repair of goods Amendments adopted by the European Parliament on 21 November 2023. https://www.europarl.europa.eu/doceo/document/TA-9-2023-0400_EN.pdf.
Council of the European Union, Mandate for negotiations with the European Parliament, 2023/0083(COD), Brussels, 17.11.2023, https://data.consilium.europa.eu/doc/document/ST-15408-2023-INIT/en/pdf.

6.1. PRODUCTS POTENTIALLY COVERED BY REPARABILITY REQUIREMENTS

The Ecodesign Regulation proposal says that it 'shall apply to any physical good that is placed on the market or put into service, including components and intermediate products' (Art. 1.2), but excludes food, medicine, veterinary products, living plants, animals or products of human origin. The long-awaited decision to extend eco-design requirements to all capital goods – not only energy-related goods, or those with a long lifespan, but also non-energy goods and fast-use goods that generate a lot of waste[24] – is a step in the right direction.

However, enlarging the scope of eco-design regulation has two major constraints. Firstly, the proposed Regulation does not establish any directly applicable, specific obligation for issues relevant to ensuring reparability and durability, in the eco-design phase. The following will be defined through delegated acts that develop eco-design requirements for each goods category:

> ease of repair and maintenance as expressed through: characteristics, availability and delivery time of spare parts, modularity, compatibility with commonly available spare parts, availability of repair and maintenance instructions, number of materials and components used, use of standard components, use of component and material coding standards for the identification of components and materials, number and complexity of processes and tools needed, ease of non-destructive disassembly and re-assembly, conditions for access' (Annex I, COM(2022) 142 final,1).

There is no general mandate on the availability of spare parts, accessibility of tools or instructions, or who (i.e. independent or authorised repairers) will have access to those parts, instructions and tools. The Commission is empowered to adopt the delegated acts referred to above (Art. 4 of the proposal), or to decide that no performance and/or information requirements are needed. If they are needed, Member States cannot restrict or impede relevant products from being placed on the market for reasons of non-compliance with national rules (Art. 3 of the proposal). More stringent national rules would not limit the free movement of goods that comply with EU requirements.

Moreover, questions about product categories; the extent to which requirements for reparability and information about repair apply; whether spare parts are available, and for how long; whether access to spare parts is limited to authorised repairers; and the type of information about repair deemed necessary, and where it will be made available, will all be decided in delegated acts. This could

24 M. Calisto Friant, W.J.V. Vermeulen and R. Salomone, 'Analysing European Union circular economy policies: words versus actions', *Sustainable Production and Consumption*, (2021) 27, p. 347.

lead to an uneven right to repair, with varying reparability obligations for each type of goods.

Secondly, the proposed Regulation establishes both procedural provisions and criteria that might *de facto* limit eco-design regulations and reparability requirements to the categories of products that already have eco-design regulations. Expanding the scope to new goods depends on the approval of delegated acts, which the Commission says will take until at least 2030 (COM (2022) 142 final, 11). Also, the direct involvement of those representing corporate interests, in defining the requirements, through the RSB, as explained above, and the Ecodesign Forum (Art. 17 of the proposal) might further dilute the proposals. The eco-design proposal also establishes criteria for prioritising which products should have eco-design requirements (Art. 16). Significantly, these criteria identify, as the first issue to be assessed, the potential for improvement without 'entailing disproportionate costs', taking into account 'the absence or insufficiency of Union law or failure of market forces or self-regulation measures … to address the objective properly'. The representativity of the product in Union trade (sales) is the second criterion, and only the third criterion assesses 'the distribution of the environmental impacts, energy use and waste generation across the value chain, in particular whether they take place within the Union'. Finally, even if a decision is taken to promote eco-design requirements, they must fulfil certain criteria, related mainly to assessment of economic efficiency (Art. 5.5):

> no significant negative impact on the functionality of the product, no adverse effect on the health and safety of persons; no significant negative impact on consumers in terms of the affordability of relevant products, also taking into account access to second-hand products, durability and the life cycle cost of products; no disproportionate negative impact on the competitiveness of economic actors, at least of SMEs; no proprietary technology imposed on manufacturers or other economic actors; no disproportionate administrative burden on manufacturers or other economic actors.

The combination of postponed enforceability, uneven requirements, and corporate-oriented criteria and procedures, pushes back the horizon of a fully deployed, comprehensive right to repair.

6.2. SOME PREVIOUS STEPS TOWARDS REPARABILITY AND DURABILITY

The 2018–19 revision of the eco-design rules for energy-related products (for example, refrigerators, washing machines, light sources) took a first step towards reparability, by providing for the existence of spare parts, information about them, replacement using simple tools, etc., but also revealed the drawbacks of the initial proposals, on corporate-sensitive issues such as accessibility to spare parts and repair information for non-professional and non-registered users (professional installers can even be charged to access this information). Similarly, there were proposals to facilitate dismantling operations for repair purposes, but these were toned down to relate to recycling only. However, in almost all of the revised rules, the period of existence of spare parts was generally extended, from the seven years proposed in the initial drafts, to ten years in the approved regulations.

As regards planned obsolescence and durability, although the latter was included in the European Commission's proposal for the revision of Directive 2010/30/EU on product energy labelling, it did not appear in the final version – Regulation (EU) 2017/1369 of 4 July 2017 establishing a framework for energy labelling and repealing Directive 2010/30/EU – or in the eco-design regulations that were updated in 2018–19. This seems to be a real Achilles heel on the road to circularity. Providing consumers with information about durability and planned obsolescence was postponed, for eventual study in a 'long-term roadmap', to be presented by the Commission (Recital 36, EU Regulation 2017/1369). However, the EU Omnibus Regulation 2021/341 of 23 February 2021 represents a step in the right direction. It contains multiple amendments to all the eco-design regulations revised just two years earlier,[25] and introduces a provision to penalise software that distorts obsolescence testing carried out by market surveillance authorities. It also requires that the performance and energy consumption parameters listed in the declaration of conformity should not worsen after a software or firmware update. Although it only affected energy related products, this is probably the first time that European legislation has established binding rules to limit some form of obsolescence. The Ecodesign Regulation proposal also prohibits products with applicable delegated acts concerning eco-design from being placed on the market if they are designed to have software or firmware updates that alter their performance when tests are being carried out (Art. 33).

7. LEGAL INTERSECTIONS WITH CORE EU POLICIES

A more complete picture of the legal approach to reparability involves a closer look at other areas of corporate law and standards. Reparability and longer-lasting

[25] Regulations (EU) 2019/424, (EU) 2019/1781, (EU) 2019/1782, (EU) 2019/2019, (EU) 2019/2020, (EU) 2019/2021, (EU) 2019/2022, (EU) 2019/2023 and (EU) 2019/2024 were amended as regards eco-design requirements for enterprise servers and data storage products, electric motors and variable speed drives, refrigeration appliances, light sources and stand-alone control gear, external power supplies, electronic displays, household dishwashers, domestic washing machines and domestic washer-dryers and refrigeration appliances with a direct vending function.

products are not only an environmental issue, but could also imply major changes in business models, consumer behaviour and the economic system. The fact that the Ecodesign Regulation and R2R proposals both have Article 114 of the TFEU, aiming at the establishment and functioning of the internal market, as their legal basis, gives a hint as to the importance – and probably predominance – of the constraints arising from other EU corporate/private legislation.

7.1. THE ROLE OF CORPORATE-DRIVEN VOLUNTARY STANDARDISATION

The first Circular Economy Action Plan (2015) mentioned the need to promote technical standardisation in relation to materials efficiency. Standardisation regarding life expectancy or reparability could be better implemented at the EU level.[26] In fact, the European Commission mandated the European standardisation organisations to develop generic standards on durability and the possibility of reusing and recycling certain products. Of the more than twenty standards this work aims to create, only eight have been drawn up. These are limited to energy-related products, and some of them deal with reparability and durability.[27] The key features of the regulatory agenda are developed by voluntary, corporate-driven standards. Once the impossibility of avoiding standards became clear, the initial reluctance of companies gave way to active involvement in developing them.[28]

The central role of privately based self-regulation can also be seen in the recent Ecodesign Regulation proposal, which would enable economic operators to develop alternative eco-design requirements to those developed by the European Commission.[29] The criteria for assessing whether a self-regulation

---

26 C. Dalhammar and J.L. Richter (eds.) et al., *Promoting the Repair Sector in Sweden*, The International Institute for Industrial Environmental Economics, Centre for Environmental and Climate Science, 2020, p. 54.

27 EN 45552:2020: General method for the assessment of the durability of energy-related products; EN 45553:2020: General method for the assessment of the ability to remanufacture energy-related products; EN 45554:2020: General methods for the assessment of the ability to repair, reuse and upgrade energy-related products; EN 45555:2019: General methods for assessing the recyclability and recoverability of energy-related products; EN 45556:2019: General method for assessing the proportion of reused components in energy-related products; EN 45557:2020: General method for assessing the proportion of recycled material content in energy-related products; EN 45558:2019: General method to declare the use of critical raw materials in energy-related products; EN 45559:2019: Methods for providing information relating to material efficiency aspects of energy-related products.

28 F. Mathieux, F. Ardente and S. Bobba, 'Ten years of scientific support for integrating circular economy requirements in the EU ecodesign directive: Overview and Lessons Learnt', *Procedia CIRP*, (2020) 90, p. 141.

29 Article 18 Self-regulation measures. 1. Two or more economic operators may submit a self-regulation measure establishing ecodesign requirements for products to the Commission as an alternative to a delegated act adopted pursuant to Article 4(…).

measure is 'a valid alternative to a delegated act' consists of having a 'market share in terms of volume of the signatories to the self-regulation measure in relation to the products covered by that measure [that] is at least 80% of units placed on the market or put into service'. This allowing of companies that enjoy a predominant market share to decide the scope of reparability and eco-design requirements might harm a comprehensive right to repair.

Some authors argue that, for the circular economy to advance at the pace and level of ambition expected by its proponents, it needs to confront orthodox neo-liberal environmental governance, and rethink instruments, such as standardisation instruments, to challenge existing market relationships.[30] This concern is consistent with a recent European Commission statement on the weight of corporate interests in decision-making for standardisation:

> Today's decision-making processes within the European standardisation organisations, in particular in ETSI, allow an uneven voting power to certain corporate interests: some multinationals have acquired more votes than the bodies that represent the entire stakeholder community. This is why the Commission believes that administrative and good governance principles need to be put in place when the European standardisation organisations act upon European standardisation requests and develop standards used to show compliance with rules imposed in the interest of EU citizens' (COM (2022) 31 final: 4–5).

A balance must be struck between the technical needs of standardisation for reparability, and a transparent, public-driven definition of the goals to be pursued by the standardisation process.

7.2. INDUSTRIAL PROPERTY CONSTRAINTS: OPEN ACCESS vs. FIRM-CONTROLLED INFORMATION AND REPAIR SERVICES

Industrial property also hinders the fight against planned obsolescence and an ambitious push for repair, which is a flagship measure of CEAP 2020. Companies have lobbied intensively against R2R, and seek to protect their interests, under industrial property law, in various ways. Branding all components of their devices, including tiny ones, makes it difficult to replace them with parts from other providers. The tech giant Apple uses this strategy to ensure control over its products, and prevent repair by unauthorised technicians. It has denounced non-brand components as counterfeits in the highest courts, including in a

30 A. Flynn and N. Hacking, 'Setting standards for a circular economy: A challenge too far for neoliberal environmental governance?', *Journal of Cleaner Production*, (2019) 212, p. 1266, https://doi.org/10.1016/j.jclepro.2018.11.257.

case decided by the Norwegian Supreme Court in June 2020.[31] Companies also seek to block the importation of reconditioned parts,[32] which limits product durability and complicates repairs. There is strong corporate activism against the attempts of several US states[33] and the European Commission (COM2015, 614 final) to regulate the right to repair.

Companies also obstruct repair work by preventing 'odd-jobber' consumers or independent repair technicians from accessing disassembly information, product instructions, or the tools needed for disassembly or repair. Here, again, intellectual property issues and allegations of safety risks from product mishandling make repair more difficult. The many recent EU eco-design regulation reforms show how this has prevailed in limiting access to information for a wider range of repair workers. Such restrictions undermine the objectives of repairing, remanufacturing, refurbishing or recycling products. In a globalised market, it is difficult (and costly) for manufacturers to provide repair services for all their products worldwide. Using intellectual property barriers to prevent independent repair can turn products with a potentially longer lifespan into unusable waste.

Similarly, patents are being used to prevent access to software that enables product repair and refurbishment, or to directly protect programming that shortens the lives of products and accelerates planned obsolescence. In the groundbreaking decision in *Impression Products Inc. v. Lexmark International Inc.*,[34] in which Lexmark sought to prevent reuse and refilling of its ink cartridges by other companies, the US Supreme Court ruled in favour of patent exhaustion once the product has been sold. However, with no hint of criticism or reflection on these issues in the CEAP 2020, the European Commission is promoting 'an intellectual and industrial property strategy that will ensure that intellectual property is defended as a key factor in boosting the circular economy and the development of new business models' (COM(2020) 98 final, 20).

In the US, the COVID-19-induced shortage of parts and repair services in rural areas, particularly for agricultural equipment, has revitalised the pro-repair movement that is pushing for 'right to repair' state legislation. The US Congress and Senate commissioned the Federal Trade Commission (FTC)

---

31 Supreme Court of Norway, HR-2020–1142-A, case no. 19-141420SIV-HRET, 2.6.2020, https://www.domstol.no/globalassets/upload/hret/decisions-in-english-translation/hr-2020–1142-a.pdf https://repair.eu/news/apple-crushes-one-man-repair-shop/.

32 Right to Repair, Apple uses trademark law to strengthen its monopoly on repair, 11.6.2020, https://repair.eu/news/apple-uses-trademark-law-to-strengthen-its-monopoly-on-repair/.

33 L. Chan Grinvald and O. Tur-Sinai, 'Intellectual Property Law and the Right to Repair', 88 *Fordham Law Review* 63 (2019), https://ir.lawnet.fordham.edu/flr/vol88/iss1/3.

34 United States Supreme Court, IMPRESSION PRODUCTS, INC. v. LEXMARK INTERNATIONAL, INC. (2017). Docket No: No. 15-1189. Argued: March 21, 2017. Decided: May 30, 2017, https://supreme.justia.com/cases/federal/us/581/15-1189/.

to conduct a report on 'how manufacturers – particularly mobile and auto manufacturers – can limit consumer repairs and repair services and how those limitations can increase costs, limit choice, and impact consumers'.[35] In a report detailing the practices that hinder repair, and the conflicting positions of industry and the pro-repair movement, the FTC has proposed measures to update competition and consumer rights, to reflect the new repair challenges. These would overturn the Magnuson–Moss Warranty Act, almost 50 years old, which is insufficient in today's consumer scenarios. The proposed measures seek to facilitate repairs by consumers themselves, or by independent repairers, in the face of increasingly common practices involving product designs that complicate or impede repair; unavailability of parts and repair information; designs that make independent repairs less safe; policies or statements that direct consumers to the manufacturer's repair networks; enforcement of patent rights and trademarks; disregard for non-genuine parts and independent repair; and software lockouts and firmware upgrades or end-user licensing agreements.[36] The report calls for reinvigorated regulation and enforcement, expressing scepticism regarding the effectiveness of self-regulation for such a wide range of companies, in light of so few successful precedents. Finally, it points out the contrast between the new European eco-design standards for certain electrical and electronic products and those of the US, particularly the European restriction of access to certain parts and repairs to authorised repairers only.[37]

7.3. THE IMPACT OF THE SERVICES DIRECTIVE ON PROXIMITY AND ACCESSIBILITY TO REPAIR SERVICES

Competition rules do not favour the CEAP 2020 proposal[38] of exploring complementary legislation to 'incentivize "products as services" or other similar models where producers retain ownership of the product or responsibility for its performance throughout its life cycle'. Cases before state and European competition authorities and the Court of Justice of the European Union (CJEU) have shown inconsistencies.

Limitations on the access of independent repair shops to repair activities and spare parts might be seen as territorial restrictions, leading to fines for anti-competitive practices (*Vaillant Group*, repair of gas boilers CNMC 2019).[39]

---

35 Federal Trade Commission, *Nixing the Fix: An FTC Report to Congress on Repair Restrictions*, FTC, 2021, https://www.ftc.gov/system/files/documents/reports/nixing-fix-ftc-report-congress-repair-restrictions/nixing_the_fix_report_final_5521_630pm-508_002.pdf, p. 3.

36 Ibid., p. 6.

37 Ibid., pp. 6–7, 49.

38 Ibid.; CEAP, supra, note 1, p. 4.

39 https://www.cnmc.es/prensa/multa-reparacion-calderas-cnmc-20191126.

In some cases, however, the CJEU did not find anti-competitive practices when independent repairers were prevented from accessing spare parts (Case *Confédération européenne des associations d'horlogers-réparateurs v. European Commission*).[40] In fact, any regulations requiring companies to offer repair services for their products, or to have repair shops within a certain proximity to consumers, would be subject to evaluation under Article 15.2 (a) and (h) of the Services Directive[41] and could be considered territorial restrictions or discriminatory requirements.

In short, European competition authorities have been resistant to including sustainability issues in their assessments.[42] However, aspects linked to collaborative agreements, the right to repair, and new models of consumption and ownership, should lead to a circularity-attuned redefinition of competition law. Accordingly, circularity would be considered an overriding public interest that could justify imposing conditions on the free establishment and movement of services.

7.4. CONSUMER EMPOWERMENT WITH SLIGHT LEGAL CHANGES

In the EU, the key measures of consumer empowerment and ensuring R2R, contained in the second CEAP, have had little impact, to date, on the parallel processing of EU consumer legislation. The EU seems to prefer nudging consumers to change their lifestyles, through information measures, rather than forcing them to reduce consumption through mandatory rules that discourage unsustainable or misleading practices. Keirsbilck and Rousseau[43] point out that 'access to information is necessary, but not sufficient to foster sustainable consumption choices. Importantly, recent studies show that consumers are often overwhelmed with information'. In fact, consumer rights are conceived of mainly as a question of price and increasing choice, but not as a matter of having access to more sustainable products and sales practices. Making consumption easy, rather than limiting unsustainable consumer habits, aligns consumer law and consumer rights with an economic model based on permanent growth and consumerism.

---

40 Case T-712/14 *Confédération européenne des associations d'horlogers-réparateurs (CEAHR) v. European Commission*, CJEU 23 October 2017, https://curia.europa.eu/juris/document/document.jsf;jsessionid=07CA73772BD75E85F63BC7ADADAD766AE1?text=&docid=195810&pageIndex=0&doclang=EN&mode=lst&dir=&occ=first&part=1&cid=219510.

41 Directive 2006/123/EC of the European Parliament and of the Council of 12 December 2006 on services in the internal market.

42 A. Gerbrandy, 'Solving a Sustainability-Deficit in European Competition Law', *World Competition*, (2017) 40(4), 539–562.

43 B. Keirsbilck and S. Rousseau, 'The Marketing Stage: Fostering Sustainable Consumption Choices in a "Circular" and "Functional" Economy' in B. Keirsbilck and E. Terryn (eds.), *Consumer Protection in a Circular Economy*, Intersentia, 2019, pp. 93, 103.

The adoption of Directives 2019/770, 2019/771 and 2019/2161 confirms the 'light-touch' approach to the relationship between consumer law and sustainability.[44] Consumer law could play a decisive role in encouraging more circular behaviour, given that Directive 2011/83/EU on consumer rights[45] is a directive of maximum harmonisation that does not allow Member States to introduce different provisions. However, its provisions do not sufficiently reflect sustainability objectives. In relation to the supply of goods, for example (Art. 18), the Directive does not prevent aggressive e-commerce competition practices, such as express deliveries, deliveries to wherever the consumer chooses (last-mile delivery), or deliveries of several goods separately (basket-splitting), which have considerable environmental impact by increasing emissions.[46] Terryn and Van Gool[47] criticise the Directive's provisions on passing of risk (Art. 20) and the right of withdrawal (Arts. 9–16). While these are very favourable to consumers (in terms of deadlines, possibility of picking where goods are to be delivered, etc.), they mean that consumers do not bear the environmental costs of failed deliveries, and can too easily return long-distance purchases. They suggest solutions for a sustainable approach that includes extending the exceptions to the right of withdrawal, limiting this right in relation to goods already used, making it compulsory to provide information on the environmental impact of different delivery options, and prohibiting free returns or removing the mandatory nature of this right.

The Sales of Goods Directive[48] contains some steps forward that, although still insufficient, are more coherent with the commitment to circularity. The provisions regarding remedies, the burden of proof – with respect to second-hand goods, as well as goods sold at public auctions – and the producer's commercial guarantee of durability have all been postponed, to be reviewed five years after the Directive's entry into force (Recital 71). Indeed, Recital 33 of the Directive notes that:

---

44 V. Mak and E. Terryn, 'Circular economy and consumer protection: The consumer as a citizen and the limits of empowerment through consumer law', *Journal of Consumer Policy*, (2020) 43(1), p. 230.

45 Directive 2011/83/EU of the European Parliament and of the Council of 25 October 2011 on consumer rights, amending Council Directive 93/13/EEC and Directive 1999/44/EC of the European Parliament and of the Council and repealing Council Directive 85/577/EEC and Directive 97/7/EC of the European Parliament and of the Council Text with EEA relevance.

46 M. García Goldar, 'The inadequate approach of Directive (EU) 2019/771 towards the circular economy', *Maastricht Journal of European and Comparative Law*, (2021) 29(1), 9–24, https://doi.org/10.1177/1023263X211051827.

47 E. Terryn and E. Van Gool, 'The Role of European Consumer Regulation in Shaping the Environmental Impact of e-commerce', 18 November 2020, EuCML 2021(3), pp. 89–100, https://doi.org/10.2139/ssrn.3732911.

48 Directive (EU) 2019/771 of the European Parliament and of the Council of 20 May 2019 on certain aspects concerning contracts for the sale of goods.

> while this Directive should not impose an obligation on sellers to ensure the availability of spare parts for a period as an objective requirement of conformity, this should not affect other provisions of national law which oblige the seller, producer or other person constituting a stage in the chain of transactions to ensure the availability of spare parts or to inform the consumer of such availability.

The Directive introduces 'a promising conformity criterion not covered by the previous Directive 1999/44/EC', although Article 2(13) has a rather narrow definition ('the ability of goods to maintain their required functions and performance under normal conditions of use') that does not refer to a period for which the consumer may reasonably expect a product to last.[49] However, here also, the Directive has been criticised, because the objective conformity criteria (Art. 7) requires product compliance with the principle of average quality ('which goods of the same type normally present, and which the consumer can reasonably expect'). Thus, if planned obsolescence is common to all suppliers of a type of products, durability would not act as an objective conformity criterion. Also, legal liability in the event of non-conformity still has a two-year time limit that may hinder anti-obsolescence policies, particularly for goods that should reasonably last longer (refrigerators, washing machines etc.). This issue is no longer subject to maximum harmonisation, so some Member States are extending liability periods.

Finally, the Proposal for a Directive on the right to repair makes a slight amendment to the Sales of Goods Directive (EU) 2019/771: in a case of non-conformity 'where the costs for replacement are equal to or greater than the costs for repair, the seller shall repair the goods in order to bring those goods in conformity' (Art. 12). This amendment would put an end to the equivalence of available remedies in cases of non-conformity, which has been criticised in terms of sustainability and circularity.[50] Thus, the proposed amendment is a positive step for promoting reparability, and prolonging product life, even if it is subject to a cost evaluation.

In short, small steps have been taken to encourage product-life extension and repair, but there is still room for recent consumer legislation reforms to align with the paradigm shift that is needed to fulfil the CEAP 2020 sustainable consumption goals.

8. CONCLUSION

The right to repair is a flagship measure of the second CEAP (2020). Closing the loop – or being circular – has a lot to do with changes in consumption

49 Ibid.; García Goldar, supra, note 46, p. 14.

50 E. Terryn, 'A Right to Repair? Towards Sustainable Remedies in Consumer Law' at B. Keirsbilck and E. Terryn (eds.), supra, note 37, pp. 127–147, pp. 133–135.

patterns, and product durability and reparability. It also has a clear impact on our economic system and business models. The tardiness and shortcomings of the Proposal for a Directive that was finally presented in March 2023 reveals that we are in troubled waters. Most of the measures and funding under the circular economy umbrella are still about waste rather than the circular design and durability of products.[51] No single universal right to repair arises from the proposal, as specific obligations on reparability (accessibility of spare parts, tools, or information on repair, length of time on which parts' availability, etc.) will depend on the future eco-design regulations for each product category, to be approved in delegated acts, as the negotiating positions of both the Council and the Commission in the trilogue show. The Commission's legislative agenda will delay the drafting of those delegated acts until 2030, so there is still a long way to go before a robust right to repair might emerge. Also, the fragmented approval procedure of those delegated acts, with no uniform legal reparability requirements arising from the Proposal for an Ecodesign Regulation (2022), makes it likely that the right to repair will vary for different categories of goods.

The proposals might be passed before the next European elections, but the fact that the directly applicable tools mainly provide information (for example, the online national repairers' platform, and ERIF), and that mandatory rules on reparability seem to been postponed, are consistent with the neo-liberalist drift of EU environmental law.[52] The increasing role of corporate interests in proposal design (the RSB, the Ecodesign Forum, standards) and the criteria for deciding the scope of future legislation is not counterbalanced by environmentally oriented assessment and criteria.

Additionally, intersections with other areas of corporate law that function according to a narrow and mainly market-oriented interpretation of the European project make the push for sustainable consumption more difficult. The provisions of competition law, the Services Directive, industrial property law, and consumer law, along with the relevance given to private standards, should be aligned in pursuit of sustainability.

---

51 Ibid.; Nogueira, supra, note 2, p. 1; European Court of Auditors, *Circular economy: Slow transition by member states despite EU action*, EU, 2023, https://www.eca.europa.eu/ECAPublications/SR-2023-17/SR-2023-17_EN.pdf, p. 5.

52 L. Krämer, *EU Environmental Law*, Sweet & Maxwell, 2011, p. 425; N. De Sadeleer, *EU Environmental Law and the Internal Market*, Oxford University Press, 2014, pp. 216–217; Bouwma et al., supra, note 18, p. 27; Nogueira, supra, note 2, p. 1.

THE RELATION BETWEEN EU CHEMICALS, PRODUCT AND WASTE LEGISLATION GOVERNING PLASTIC PACKAGING AND THE TRANSITION TOWARDS A MORE CIRCULAR PLASTIC PACKAGING CHAIN IN THE EU

Ida Mae DE WAAL

ABSTRACT

The EU is in transition towards a circular economy (CE). Two of the sectors on which there is a specific focus are plastic and packaging. Plastic packaging is governed by an extensive legal framework consisting of both sector-specific and general EU chemicals, product and waste legislation, which together regulate its life cycle. Since the first Circular Economy Action Plan (CEAP), the European Union (EU) has taken several steps to better align this legislation with the transition towards a CE and multiple revisions of existing legislation are currently taking place, to contribute to the EU's CE objectives. This chapter analyses to what extent the current EU chemicals, product and waste legislation governing plastic packaging aligns with the transition towards a more circular plastic packaging chain. The relation between the current legislation governing the life cycle of plastic packaging, on the one hand, and the CE transition, on the other, seems weak, but the many revisions seem promising, and could make a positive contribution to the transition towards a more circular plastic packaging chain.

1. INTRODUCTION

The European Union (EU) is in transition towards a circular economy (CE), which is described by the EU as an economy 'where the value of products, materials and resources is maintained in the economy for as long as possible, and the generation of waste is minimized'.[1] In its Circular Economy Action Plans (CEAPs), the EU has named both plastics and packaging as key product groups.[2] Currently, plastic packaging is the main application of plastic (approximately 40 per cent), and also constitutes the majority of plastic waste (around 60 per cent).[3] The use of plastic packaging is increasing, and so is the generation of plastic packaging waste.[4] As only 45 per cent of the EU's plastic packaging waste is being recycled, large amounts of plastic packaging waste are still being landfilled or incinerated.[5] This not only causes a significant loss of materials and value,[6] but also causes environmental harm, because of, *inter alia*, (marine) litter.

---

1 European Commission, 'Closing the loop – An EU action plan for the Circular Economy', COM(2015) 614 final, p. 2. This is the definition used by the European Commission. However, there is no undisputed definition for the CE. See, e.g. J. Kirchherr, D. Reike and M. Hekkert, 'Conceptualizing the circular economy: An analysis of 114 definitions', *Resources, Conservation and Recycling*, (2017) 127, pp. 221–232.

2 European Commission, 'A new Circular Economy Action Plan: For a cleaner and more competitive Europe', COM(2020) 98 final, pp. 8–10.

3 Plastics Europe, *The Circular Economy for Plastics – A European Overview*, Plastics Europe, 2022; Commission Staff Working Document, 'A European Strategy for Plastics in a Circular Economy', SWD(2018) 16 final, pp. 19–20; Commission Staff Working Document, 'Measuring progress towards circular economy in the European Union – Key indicators for a monitoring framework', SWD(2018) 17 final, p. 24; E. de Tandt et al., 'A recycler's perspective on the implications of REACH and food contact material (FCM) regulations for the mechanical recycling of FCM Plastics', *Waste Management*, (2020) (119), p. 316; European Commission, 'A European Strategy for Plastics in a Circular Economy', COM(2018) 28 final, pp. 11–12.

4 European Commission, COM(2020) 98 final, p. 8. See also Eurostat, Packaging waste statistics, 2023 on: https://ec.europa.eu/eurostat/statistics-explained/index.php?title=Packaging_waste_statistics#Waste_generation_by_packaging_material.

5 Plastics Europe, *The Circular Economy for Plastics – A European Overview*, Plastics Europe, 2022, pp. 29, 31, 41.

6 E. Watkins and J.-P. Schweitzer, *Moving towards a circular economy for plastics in the EU by 2030*, Think 2030, Institute for European Environmental Policy (IEEP), 2018, p. 5; COM(2018) 28 final, p. 6; J.N. Hahladakis and E. Iacovidou, 'Closing the loop on plastic

The transition towards a CE, including the transition towards a more circular plastic packaging chain, ideally requires that the legal framework does not hamper the transition, but is instead conducive to it.[7] This is especially true for the legislation governing the life cycles of materials and products: EU chemicals, product and waste legislation.[8] The life cycle of plastic packaging is governed by both sector-specific and general EU chemicals, product and waste legislation, such as Regulation 10/2011 on plastic materials and articles intended to come into contact with food (Plastics Regulation),[9] and the Packaging and Packaging Waste Directive (PPWD),[10] as well as the REACH Regulation,[11] and the Waste Framework Directive (WFD).[12]

Since the first CEAP, the EU has already taken action to better align this legislation with the CE transition. For example, the Plastic Bags Directive[13] was introduced in 2015, the PPWD and the WFD were amended in 2018,[14] and the Single-use Plastics (SUP) Directive was introduced in 2019.[15] More recently, the

---

packaging materials: What is quality and how does it affect their circularity?', *Science of the Total Environment*, (2018) 630, p. 1398; A. Tenhunen-Lunkka et al., 'Greenhouse Gas Emission Reduction Potential of European Union's Circularity Related Targets for Plastics', *Circular Economy and Sustainability*, (2023) 3, pp. 475–478. See also European Parliament, 'Plastic waste and recycling in the EU: fact and figures', 2023, on: https://www.europarl.europa.eu/news/en/headlines/priorities/circular-economy/20181212STO21610/plastic-waste-and-recycling-in-the-eu-facts-and-figures.

7 COM(2015) 614 final, p. 2.

8 T.J. de Römph, 'The legal transition towards a Circular Economy' (dissertation), KU Leuven and Hasselt University, 2018, pp. 27, 267–277; European Commission, 'Communication on the implementation of the circular economy package: options to address the interface between chemical, product and waste legislation', COM(2018) 32 final; I.M. de Waal, 'The Legal Transition towards a More Circular Electrical and Electronic Equipment Chain – A Case Study of The Netherlands', *Sustainability*, (2023) 15, p. 2.

9 Commission Regulation (EU) No. 10/2011 of 14 January 2011 on plastic materials and articles intended to come into contact with food, OJ 2011 L 12/1.

10 European Parliament and Council Directive 94/62/EC of 20 December 1994 on packaging and packaging waste, OJ 1994 L 365/10.

11 Regulation (EC) No. 1907/2006 of the European Parliament and of the Council of 18 December 2006 concerning the Registration, Evaluation, Authorisation and Restriction of Chemicals (REACH), establishing a European Chemicals Agency, amending Directive 1999/45/EC and repealing Council Regulation (EEC) No. 793/93 and Commission Regulation (EC) No. 1488/94 as well as Council Directive 76/769/EEC and Commission Directives 91/155/EEC, 93/67/EEC, 93/105/EC and 2000/21/EC, OJ 2006 L 396/1.

12 Directive 2008/98/EC of the European Parliament and of the Council of 19 November 2008 on waste and repealing certain Directives, OJ 2008 L 312/3.

13 Directive (EU) 2015/720 of the European Parliament and of the Council of 29 April 2015 amending Directive 94/62/EC as regards reducing the consumption of lightweight plastic carrier bags, OJ 2015 L 115/11.

14 Directive (EU) 2018/851 of the European Parliament and of the Council of 30 May 2018 amending Directive 2008/98/EC on waste, OJ 2018 L 150/09; Directive (EU) 2018/852 of the European Parliament and of the Council of 30 May 2018 amending Directive 94/62/EC on packaging and packaging waste, OJ 2018 L 150/141.

15 Directive (EU) 2019/904 of the European Parliament and of the Council of 5 June 2019 on the reduction of the impact of certain plastic products on the environment, OJ 2019 L 155/1.

European Commission (EC) presented, amongst other things, a proposal for a new Packaging and Packaging Waste Regulation, in November 2022. As previous research has shown that, in general, EU chemicals, product and waste legislation does not (yet) fully support the transition towards a CE,[16] the question can be asked to what extent the current and upcoming EU chemicals, product and waste legislation governing plastic packaging take into account the CE transition, as well as to what extent they reflect CE aspects and life-cycle thinking, and are thus aligned with the transition towards a more circular plastic packaging chain.

This chapter is structured as follows. Section 2 elaborates upon the relevance of plastic packaging and the EU's objectives regarding a more circular plastic packaging chain. Section 3 examines the relevant EU chemicals, product and waste legislation, in light of the CE transition in the EU. Section 4 analyses this legislation, including future developments regarding these three areas of law, to answer to what extent the legislation that governs the life cycle of plastic packaging is in line with the transition towards a more circular plastic packaging chain. Finally, section 5 contains the chapter's conclusion.

2. PLASTIC PACKAGING AND THE TRANSITION TOWARDS A CE IN THE EU

The EU aims to transform its linear economy into a CE. Instead of an economy based on a take-make-waste approach, a CE aims to maintain the value of materials and products in the economy for as long as possible, and to minimise the generation of waste. In a CE, the focus is on the environmental impact of materials and products throughout their life cycles.[17] In other words, life-cycle thinking is central to the concept of a CE.[18] Life-cycle thinking is mentioned as a guiding principle in EU circular economy law and policy,[19] and is also reflected in the waste hierarchy, which provides a priority order in waste prevention and management.[20]

---

16 I.M. de Waal, 'Coherence in law: A way to stimulate the transition towards a circular economy? A critical analysis of the European Commission's aspiration to achieve full coherence between chemicals legislation and waste legislation – and product legislation', *Maastricht Journal of European and Comparative Law*, (2021) 28 (6), pp. 760–783.

17 T.J. de Römph and G. van Calster, 'REACH in a circular economy: The obstacles for plastics recyclers and regulators', *Review of European, Comparative & International Law (RECIEL)*, (2018) 27, p. 277; T.J. de Römph, 'The legal transition towards a Circular Economy', above n. 8, p. 36.

18 T.J. de Römph, 'The legal transition towards a Circular Economy', above n. 8, p. 36.

19 T.J. de Römph and J.M. Cramer, 'How to improve the EU legal framework in view of the circular economy', *Journal of Energy & Natural Resources Law*, (2020) 38(3), p. 247.

20 Art. 4, Directive 2008/98/EC of the European Parliament and of the Council of 19 November 2008 on waste and repealing certain Directives, OJ 2008 L 312/3. See, more extensively, T.J. de Römph, 'The legal transition towards a Circular Economy', above n. 8, pp. 50–55.

In its CEAPs, the EC states that it aims 'to establish the right regulatory framework for the development of the CE',[21] and to ensure that 'the regulatory framework is streamlined and made fit for a sustainable future'.[22] To achieve this aim, and to ensure that the interactions between all life-cycle stages, and along the entire value chain, are taken into account, certain key product value chains, such as plastics and packaging, are given priority.[23] As stated in the introduction above, packaging is the main application of plastic, and both this application and the generation of waste keep increasing. However, the recycling rate of 45 per cent, which is low compared with other packaging materials,[24] means that significant amounts of materials, as well as 95 per cent of the value of plastic packaging, are being lost to the economy.[25]

Following up on the CEAP 2015, the EU Plastics Strategy was announced in 2018, containing the EU's vision for a circular plastics economy. It *inter alia* aims to improve the economics and quality of plastics recycling, by focusing on improving product design, recycled content, and separate collection of plastic waste, and also aims to curb plastic waste and littering, by tackling single-use plastics, microplastics and compostable and biodegradable plastics.[26] Specifically with regard to plastic packaging, it aims to ensure that all plastic packaging is reusable or cost-effectively recyclable by 2030.[27] The EU Plastics Strategy is also the first EU policy framework to adopt a material-specific life-cycle approach, and integrates all life-cycle stages into the plastic value chain, namely circular design, use, reuse and recycling.[28] In the subsequent Green Deal and CEAP 2020, the EC also announced several follow-up measures to the EU Plastics Strategy and the actions set out therein. Looking specifically at the legislation governing plastic packaging, these actions include introducing mandatory requirements for recycled content and waste-reduction measures, developing further requirements to ensure all packaging is reusable or recyclable by 2030, and focusing on a timely implementation of the SUP Directive.[29] These actions show an increased focus on the recycling and reuse of plastic packaging (waste). In short, multiple measures that will have implications for the legislation governing the life cycle of plastic packaging have been announced.

---

21 COM(2015) 614 final, p. 2.

22 COM(2020) 98 final, p. 3.

23 Ibid., pp. 6–10.

24 SWD(2018) 16 final, p. 20.

25 E. Watkins and J.-P. Schweitzer, above n. 6, p. 5; COM(2018) 28 final, p. 6; J.N. Hahladakis and E. Iacovidou, above n. 6, p. 1398; A. Tenhunen-Lunkka et al., above n. 6, pp. 475–478.

26 Commission Staff Working Document, 'On the implementation of the Circular Economy Action Plan', SWD(2019) 90 final, p. 10.

27 COM(2018) 28 final, p. 9.

28 European Commission, 'On the implementation of the Circular Economy Action Plan', COM(2019) 190 final, pp. 6–7.

29 European Commission, 'The European Green Deal', COM(2019) 640 final, pp. 7–8; COM(2020) 98 final, pp. 8–10.

3. EU CHEMICALS, PRODUCT AND WASTE LEGISLATION GOVERNING PLASTIC PACKAGING IN LIGHT OF THE CE TRANSITION

Plastic packaging is governed by both general and sector-specific EU chemicals, product and waste legislation. Together, this legislation governs the whole life cycle of plastic packaging. The main legal acts within these three areas of legislation are the REACH Regulation, CLP Regulation,[30] Persistent Organic Pollutants (POPs) Regulation,[31] the Packaging and Packaging Waste Directive, the SUP Directive, the Ecodesign Directive, the EU Ecolabel Directive, the WFD and the WSR.[32] In addition, there are several sector-specific legal acts that focus specifically on certain applications of plastic packaging, such as plastic packaging that is intended to come into contact with food (so-called food contact materials (FCMs)), i.e. the Plastics Regulation and Regulation on recycled plastic food-contact materials and articles,[33] and the Cosmetic Products Regulation.[34] Table 1 contains a brief overview of these legal acts, after which the legislation will be discussed in more detail, keeping in mind the objectives of the CEAPs and the EU Plastics Strategy.

Table 1. Overview of EU chemicals, product and waste legislation governing plastic packaging

The legislation marked with an asterisk (*) is currently being revised.

Legislative instrument	Focuses on: use of chemicals (C), and/or product stage (P) and/or waste stage (W)	Objective of the legislation
REACH Regulation*	C	Regulates chemicals in the EU, by setting up a system for registration, evaluation, authorisation and restriction.[35]

(continued)

30 Regulation (EC) No. 1272/2008 of the European Parliament and of the Council of 16 December 2008 on classification, labelling and packaging of substances and mixtures, amending and repealing Directives 67/548/EEC and 1999/45/EC, and amending Regulation (EC) No. 1907/2006, OJ 2008 L 353/1.

31 Regulation (EU) 2019/1021 of the European Parliament and of the Council of 20 June 2019 on persistent organic pollutants (recast), OJ 2019 L 169/45.

32 Regulation (EC) No. 1013/2006 of the European Parliament and of the Council of 14 June 2006 on shipments of waste, OJ 2006 L 190/1.

33 Commission Regulation (EU) 2022/1616 of 15 September 2022 on recycled plastic materials and articles intended to come into contact with foods, and repealing Regulation (EC) No. 282/2008, OJ 2022 L 243/3.

34 Regulation (EC) No. 1223/2009 of the European Parliament and of the Council of 30 November 2009 on cosmetic products (recast), OJ 2009 L 342/59.

35 Art. 1(1), Regulation (EC) No. 1907/2006 of the European Parliament and of the Council of 18 December 2006 concerning the Registration, Evaluation, Authorisation and

Table 1 *continued*

Legislative instrument	Focuses on: use of chemicals (C), and/or product stage (P) and/or waste stage (W)	Objective of the legislation
CLP Regulation*	C	Establishes the system of classification, labelling and packaging of chemical substances and mixtures in the EU.[36]
POPs Regulation	C	Lays down rules on prohibiting, phasing-out or restricting the manufacturing and the placing on the market of POPs.[37]
Regulation on materials and articles to come into contact with food*	C P	Lays down rules for the placing on the market of materials and articles intended to come into contact with food, as well as providing the basis for securing a high level of protection of human health and interests of consumers.[38]
Plastics Regulation	C P	Establishes requirements for the manufacture and marketing of plastic materials and articles that are to come into contact with food.[39]
Regulation on recycled plastic food-contact materials and articles	C P W	Lays down rules for the placing on the market and use of recycled plastic, as well as the development and operation of recycling technologies, processes and installations.[40]
Regulation on cosmetic products*	C P	Establishes rules on cosmetic products made available on the EU market, to ensure both the functioning of the internal market and a high level of protection of human health.[41]

(continued)

Restriction of Chemicals (REACH), establishing a European Chemicals Agency, amending Directive 1999/45/EC and repealing Council Regulation (EEC) No. 793/93 and Commission Regulation (EC) No. 1488/94 as well as Council Directive 76/769/EEC and Commission Directives 91/155/EEC, 93/67/EEC, 93/105/EC and 2000/21/EC, OJ 2006 L 396/1.

36 Art. 1(1), Regulation (EC) No. 1272/2008 of the European Parliament and of the Council of 16 December 2008 on classification, labelling and packaging of substances and mixtures, amending and repealing Directives 67/548/EEC and 1999/45/EC, and amending Regulation (EC) No. 1907/2006, OJ 2008 L 353/1.

37 Art. 1, Regulation (EU) 2019/1021 of the European Parliament and of the Council of 20 June 2019 on persistent organic pollutants (recast), OJ 2019 L 169/45.

38 Art. 1(1), Regulation (EC) No. 1935/2004 of the European Parliament and of the Council of 27 October 2004 on materials and articles intended to come into contact with food and repealing Directives 80/590/EEC and 89/109/EEC, OJ 2004 L 338/4.

39 Art. 1(2), Commission Regulation (EU) No. 10/2011 of 14 January 2011 on plastic materials and articles intended to come into contact with food, OJ 2011 L 12/1.

40 Art. 1(2), Commission Regulation (EU) 2022/1616 of 15 September 2022 on recycled plastic materials and articles intended to come into contact with foods, and repealing Regulation (EC) No. 282/2008, OJ 2022 L 243/3.

41 Art. 1, Regulation (EC) No. 1223/2009 of the European Parliament and of the Council of 30 November 2009 on cosmetic products (recast), OJ 2009 L 342/59.

Table 1 *continued*

Legislative instrument	**Focuses on: use of chemicals (C), and/or product stage (P) and/or waste stage (W)**	**Objective of the legislation**
Packaging and Packaging Waste Directive* (incl. Plastic Bags Directive)	P W	Lays down measures on preventing the production of packaging waste, and reusing, recycling or recovery of packaging waste.[42]
Single-use Plastics Directive	P W	Contains rules for the ten single-use plastic items most commonly found on European beaches, in order to prevent and reduce the negative impact of single-use plastic on the environment and human health.[43]
Ecodesign Directive*	(C) P (W)	Establishes a framework for setting eco-design requirements for energy-related products, which are implemented through product-specific implementing regulations.[44]
EU Ecolabel	P	Lays down the rules for establishing and applying the voluntary EU Ecolabel scheme.[45]
WFD*	(C) (P) W	Provides the general framework for waste management in the EU, including the waste hierarchy.
Waste Shipment Regulation*	W	Establishes procedures and control regimes for shipments of waste between MSs, imported from or exported to third countries.[46]

Source: Produced by the author.

3.1. EU CHEMICALS LEGISLATION

Plastic packaging, or, to be precise, the monomers and polymers of which the plastic is composed,[47] is governed by the REACH Regulation and CLP

42 Art. 1, European Parliament and Council Directive 94/62/EC of 20 December 1994 on packaging and packaging waste, OJ 1994 L 365/10.

43 Art. 1, Directive (EU) 2019/904 of the European Parliament and of the Council of 5 June 2019 on the reduction of the impact of certain plastic products on the environment, OJ 2019 L 155/1.

44 Arts. 1(1) and (2), Directive 2009/125/EC of the European Parliament and of the Council of 21 October 2009 establishing a framework for the setting of ecodesign requirements for energy-related products (recast), OJ 2009 L 285/10.

45 Art. 1, Regulation (EC) No. 66/2010 of the European Parliament and of the Council of 25 November 2009 on the EU Ecolabel, OJ 2010 L 27/1.

46 Art. 1(1) and (2), Regulation (EC) No. 1013/2006 of the European Parliament and of the Council of 14 June 2006 on shipments of waste, OJ 2006 L 190/1.

47 Plastic consists of a chain of monomers, which together form a polymer. These can be derived from non-renewable fossil feedstock, such as oil, but also from renewable biomass, such as sugar cane or corn. See SWD(2018) 16 final, p. 5; W. Leal Filho et al., 'An Overview of the Problems Posed by Plastic Products and the Role of Extended Producer Responsibility in Europe', *Journal of Cleaner Production*, 2019 (214), p. 550.

Regulation.[48] The REACH Regulation aims to protect human health and the environment by setting up a process of registration, evaluation, authorisation and restriction of chemicals. REACH is applicable to substances until they enter the waste stage, as REACH excludes waste from its scope.[49] However, REACH does have an impact on the waste stage of substances. When a safety assessment has to be carried out for a substance, the manufacturer must take into account the whole life cycle of the substance, including the waste stage.[50] Furthermore, REACH is important during the recycling process as well, as the recycled polymer will re-enter the scope of the REACH Regulation when it ceases to be waste.[51] The recycler whose recovery process leads to the creation of these substances, mixtures or articles, is thus considered a manufacturer under REACH.[52] As such, the recycler will also have to comply with the registration, evaluation, authorisation and restriction requirements under REACH. Although the REACH Regulation applies to the chemical substances of plastic packaging, polymers – both new and existing – are currently exempted from the Regulation's registration and evaluation requirements.[53]

---

48 Arts. 1 and 2, Regulation (EC) No. 1907/2006 of the European Parliament and of the Council of 18 December 2006 concerning the Registration, Evaluation, Authorisation and Restriction of Chemicals (REACH), establishing a European Chemicals Agency, amending Directive 1999/45/EC and repealing Council Regulation (EEC) No. 793/93 and Commission Regulation (EC) No. 1488/94 as well as Council Directive 76/769/EEC and Commission Directives 91/155/EEC, 93/67/EEC, 93/105/EC and 2000/21/EC, OJ 2006 L 396/1; Art. 1, Regulation (EC) No. 1272/2008 of the European Parliament and of the Council of 16 December 2008 on classification, labelling and packaging of substances and mixtures, amending and repealing Directives 67/548/EEC and 1999/45/EC, and amending Regulation (EC) No. 1907/2006, OJ 2008 L 353/1.

49 Art. 2(2), Regulation (EC) No. 1907/2006 of the European Parliament and of the Council of 18 December 2006 concerning the Registration, Evaluation, Authorisation and Restriction of Chemicals (REACH), establishing a European Chemicals Agency, amending Directive 1999/45/EC and repealing Council Regulation (EEC) No. 793/93 and Commission Regulation (EC) No. 1488/94 as well as Council Directive 76/769/EEC and Commission Directives 91/155/EEC, 93/67/EEC, 93/105/EC and 2000/21/EC, OJ 2006 L 396/1.

50 E. de Tandt et al., above n. 3, p. 318; D. Jepsen et al., *Reach and the recycling of plastics: Reference manual for an appropriate implementation of the REACH requirements for the operators of recycling plants*, Umweltbundesamt, 2012, p. 9; T.J. de Römph and G. van Calster, above n. 17, p. 268. See: Arts. 3.37 and 18(4)(a), Annex I, Annex II, and Annex XII, Regulation (EC) No. 1907/2006 of the European Parliament and of the Council of 18 December 2006 concerning the Registration, Evaluation, Authorisation and Restriction of Chemicals (REACH), establishing a European Chemicals Agency, amending Directive 1999/45/EC and repealing Council Regulation (EEC) No. 793/93 and Commission Regulation (EC) No. 1488/94 as well as Council Directive 76/769/EEC and Commission Directives 91/155/EEC, 93/67/EEC, 93/105/EC and 2000/21/EC, OJ 2006 L 396/1.

51 I.e. when one of the conditions of Art. 3(1), Directive 2008/98/EC of the European Parliament and of the Council of 19 November 2008 on waste and repealing certain Directives, OJ 2008 L 312/3, is met. See also T.J. de Römph and G. van Calster, above n. 17, p. 270.

52 E. de Tandt et al., above n. 3, pp. 318–319; T.J. de Römph and G. van Calster, above n. 17, pp. 270–271.

53 Art. 2(9), Regulation (EC) No. 1907/2006 of the European Parliament and of the Council of 18 December 2006 concerning the Registration, Evaluation, Authorisation and

This is because polymer molecules are argued to represent a low concern. However, the components of the polymer – the monomers and substances to improve its performance – can be subject to the registration requirements of REACH,[54] unless they have already been registered.[55] Registration is also not required when the conditions of the so-called registration exemption are met: these conditions include that the substances have already been registered, that the substance resulting from the recovery process is the same as the substance already registered, and that the required information on the safety of the registered substance is available to the recycler.[56] Irrespective of the registration, recyclers will have the obligation to determine the risk and hazard profiles of their recycled substances, which information may need to be communicated down the supply chain.[57]

Manufacturers of plastics also have to comply with the rules for classification, labelling and packaging contained in the CLP Regulation. Classification and labelling requirements apply to polymers that are classified as hazardous according to the CLP Regulation, and which are manufactured as a pure substance, or contained in a mixture above a certain classification threshold.[58]

Restriction of Chemicals (REACH), establishing a European Chemicals Agency, amending Directive 1999/45/EC and repealing Council Regulation (EEC) No. 793/93 and Commission Regulation (EC) No. 1488/94 as well as Council Directive 76/769/EEC and Commission Directives 91/155/EEC, 93/67/EEC, 93/105/EC and 2000/21/EC, OJ 2006 L 396/1.

54 That is, when the requirements of Art. 6(3) of the REACH Regulation are met, meaning that the polymer consists of 2% weight by weight (w/w), or more, of such monomer substance(s) or other substance(s) in the form of monomeric units and chemically bound substance(s), and when the total quantity of such monomer substance(s) or other substance(s) makes up one tonne or more per year. See also European Chemicals Agency (ECHA), *Guidance for monomers and polymers, version 3.0*, ECHA, 2023, p. 8.

55 Art. 6(3), Regulation (EC) No. 1907/2006 of the European Parliament and of the Council of 18 December 2006 concerning the Registration, Evaluation, Authorisation and Restriction of Chemicals (REACH), establishing a European Chemicals Agency, amending Directive 1999/45/EC and repealing Council Regulation (EEC) No. 793/93 and Commission Regulation (EC) No. 1488/94 as well as Council Directive 76/769/EEC and Commission Directives 91/155/EEC, 93/67/EEC, 93/105/EC and 2000/21/EC, OJ 2006 L 396/1.

56 ECHA, *Guidance for monomers and polymers*, above n. 50, p. 19. See, more elaborately, T.J. de Römph and G. van Calster, above n. 17, pp. 271–272.

57 Art. 31, Regulation (EC) No. 1907/2006 of the European Parliament and of the Council of 18 December 2006 concerning the Registration, Evaluation, Authorisation and Restriction of Chemicals (REACH), establishing a European Chemicals Agency, amending Directive 1999/45/EC and repealing Council Regulation (EEC) No. 793/93 and Commission Regulation (EC) No. 1488/94 as well as Council Directive 76/769/EEC and Commission Directives 91/155/EEC, 93/67/EEC, 93/105/EC and 2000/21/EC, OJ 2006 L 396/1. Also, Art. 32 contains the duty to communicate information down the supply chain when a safety data sheet is not required, and Art. 33 contains a duty to communicate information on substances in articles. See also ECHA, *Guidance for monomers and polymers*, above n. 50, p. 21; ECHA, *Guidance on waste and recovered substances, version 2*, ECHA, 2010, pp. 13–15.

58 Art. 39, Regulation (EC) No. 1272/2008 of the European Parliament and of the Council of 16 December 2008 on classification, labelling and packaging of substances and mixtures,

Furthermore, plastic packaging containing hazardous substances or mixtures has to meet certain packaging requirements under the CLP Regulation.[59] None of these CLP requirements distinguish between virgin and recycled plastics.

In addition to the REACH and CLP Regulations, the POPs Regulation can also be of importance for the production and recycling of plastic packaging. The use of persistent organic pollutants (POPs) in plastic packaging is prohibited, and when POPs happen to be present in plastic (packaging) waste streams, and the set content thresholds are exceeded, the waste should be disposed or recovered in such a way as to destroy the POP content.[60]

Plastic packaging is often used for food or beverages, i.e. as food contact material (FCM). Regulation 1935/2004 on materials and articles intended to come into contact with food aims to preclude substances from being transferred from materials and articles to the food itself.[61] As well as imposing general requirements, such as on the safety of the materials and articles,[62] it states that specific measures can be adopted for groups of materials or articles. The specific measure for plastic materials and articles intended to come into contact with food, including packaging, is Regulation 10/2011, also called the Plastics

---

amending and repealing Directives 67/548/EEC and 1999/45/EC, and amending Regulation (EC) No. 1907/2006, OJ 2008 L 353/1. These requirements also apply when a substance requires registration under REACH, but as polymers are generally exempted from registration, only the second prerequisite is important for polymer manufacturers: see Art. 39(b), Regulation (EC) No. 1272/2008 of the European Parliament and of the Council of 16 December 2008 on classification, labelling and packaging of substances and mixtures, amending and repealing Directives 67/548/EEC and 1999/45/EC, and amending Regulation (EC) No. 1907/2006, OJ 2008 L 353/1. Art. 23(d) of the CLP Regulation contains an exemption for the labelling requirement for mixtures containing polymers that meet the condition set out in s. 1.3.4.1 of Annex I, Regulation (EC) No. 1272/2008 of the European Parliament and of the Council of 16 December 2008 on classification, labelling and packaging of substances and mixtures, amending and repealing Directives 67/548/EEC and 1999/45/EC, and amending Regulation (EC) No. 1907/2006, OJ 2008 L 353/1.

59 Art. 35, Regulation (EC) No. 1272/2008 of the European Parliament and of the Council of 16 December 2008 on classification, labelling and packaging of substances and mixtures, amending and repealing Directives 67/548/EEC and 1999/45/EC, and amending Regulation (EC) No. 1907/2006, OJ 2008 L 353/1.

60 Art. 7, Regulation (EU) 2019/1021 of the European Parliament and of the Council of 20 June 2019 on persistent organic pollutants (recast), OJ 2019 L 169/45. See also M. Crippa et al., *A Circular Economy for Plastics: Insights from research and innovation to inform policy and funding decisions*, European Commission, 2019, pp. 43–44.

61 Recital 3, Regulation (EC) No. 1935/2004 of the European Parliament and of the Council of 27 October 2004 on materials and articles intended to come into contact with food and repealing Directives 80/590/EEC and 89/109/EEC, OJ 2004 L 338/4; Art. 1(1), Regulation (EC) No. 1935/2004 of the European Parliament and of the Council of 27 October 2004 on materials and articles intended to come into contact with food and repealing Directives 80/590/EEC and 89/109/EEC, OJ 2004 L 338/4.

62 E.g. Art. 3(1) of Regulation 1935/2004 requires that materials and articles do not transfer their constituents to food in quantities that could endanger human health, unacceptably change the food's composition or bring about a deterioration of the food's organoleptic characteristics.

Regulation.[63] The Plastics Regulation includes requirements on composition, migration limits,[64] multi-layer and multi-material multi-layer materials and articles,[65] and on a written declaration of compliance in order to enable an easy identification of used materials and substances.[66] Under the Plastics Regulation, only risk-assessed and authorised materials and substances that are included in the positive list or Union list may be used intentionally.[67]

In the recitals of Regulation 1935/2004, it is stated that the use of recycled materials and articles should be favoured for environmental reasons, but that strict requirements should be established to ensure consumer protection and food safety.[68] This has resulted in Regulation 2022/1616 on recycled plastic materials and articles intended to come into contact with foods.[69] This Regulation aims to ensure that recycled plastics intended to come into contact with food are chemically and microbiologically safe, and, to that end, regulates all recycled plastic materials and articles. It ensures the safety of recycled plastics by regulating the suitability of recycling technologies, by authorising recycling processes, and by setting requirements for recycling installations.[70] At the moment, only post-consumer mechanical polyethylene terephthalate

63 Art. 1, Commission Regulation (EU) No. 10/2011 of 14 January 2011 on plastic materials and articles intended to come into contact with food OJ 2011 L 12/1, Art. 5 and Annex I Regulation (EC) No. 1935/2004 of the European Parliament and of the Council of 27 October 2004 on materials and articles intended to come into contact with food and repealing Directives 80/590/EEC and 89/109/EEC, OJ 2004 L 338/4.

64 Arts. 11 and 12, Commission Regulation (EU) No. 10/2011 of 14 January 2011 on plastic materials and articles intended to come into contact with food, OJ 2011 L 12/1.

65 Ibid., Arts. 13 and 14.

66 Ibid., Arts. 15 and 16, & Art. 16, Regulation (EC) No. 1935/2004 of the European Parliament and of the Council of 27 October 2004 on materials and articles intended to come into contact with food and repealing Directives 80/590/EEC and 89/109/EEC, OJ 2004 L 338/4.

67 Art. 5 & Annex I, Commission Regulation (EU) No 10/2011 of 14 January 2011 on plastic materials and articles intended to come into contact with food, OJ 2011 L 12/1. See also C. Matthews, F. Moran and A.K. Jaiswal, 'A review on European Union's strategy for plastics in a circular economy and its impact on food safety', *Journal of Cleaner Production*, (2021) 283, p. 3; E. de Tandt et al., above n. 3, p. 322.

68 Recital 24, Regulation (EC) No. 1935/2004 of the European Parliament and of the Council of 27 October 2004 on materials and articles intended to come into contact with food and repealing Directives 80/590/EEC and 89/109/EEC, OJ 2004 L 338/4. The legal basis for these requirements is Art. 5 of Regulation (EC) No. 1935/2004 of the European Parliament and of the Council of 27 October 2004 on materials and articles intended to come into contact with food and repealing Directives 80/590/EEC and 89/109/EEC, OJ 2004 L 338/4.

69 Commission Regulation (EU) 2022/1616 of 15 September 2022 on recycled plastic materials and articles intended to come into contact with foods, and repealing Regulation (EC) No. 282/2008, OJ 2022 L 243/3. This Regulation recently replaced Commission Regulation (EC) No. 282/2008 of 27 March 2008 on recycled plastic materials and articles intended to come into contact with foods and amending Regulation (EC) No 2023/2006, OJ 2008 L86/9, which was not applicable to all recycling technologies.

70 Recitals 7 and 8 & Art. 3, Commission Regulation (EU) 2022/1616 of 15 September 2022 on recycled plastic materials and articles intended to come into contact with foods, and repealing Regulation (EC) No. 282/2008, OJ 2022 L 243/3.

(PET) recycling, and recycling from product loops which are closed and controlled, are listed as suitable recycling technologies.[71] Finally, the recycled plastics that are to be used in FCM packaging have to comply with the Plastics Regulation.[72] The reason for this is that the same level of safety should be ensured for both new and recycled plastics.[73]

Plastic packaging used for cosmetics is regulated by Regulation 1223/2009. This Regulation requires that cosmetic products are safe for human health, which includes taking into account migration of prohibited substances from packaging.[74] In order to demonstrate that a cosmetic product is indeed safe, it has to undergo a safety assessment prior to being placed on the market. This safety assessment has to take into account information about the relevant characteristics of the packaging material, in order to assess the interaction between the product and the packaging material, the barrier properties of the packaging material, and the substances migration from/to the packaging material.[75]

3.2. EU PRODUCT LEGISLATION

Plastic packaging can be seen as a stand-alone product,[76] for which both the PPWD and the SUP Directive contain provisions that qualify as product requirements. The PPWD covers the management of all plastic packaging and plastic packaging waste. It aims to prevent or reduce the impact of packaging and packaging waste on the environment, as well as to ensure the functioning of the internal market, and, to that end, it lays down measures to prevent the production of packaging waste, and for the reuse, recycling or recovery of packaging.[77] In addition to the waste management of (plastic) packaging, the PPWD also focuses on product requirements for packaging. To prevent the generation of packaging waste, and to minimise the environmental impact of

---

71 Ibid., Recitals 8 and 14 & Art. 3 & Annex I.

72 Ibid., Art. 4(2).

73 Ibid., Recital 16.

74 Art. 3. and Art. 17, Regulation (EC) No. 1223/2009 of the European Parliament and of the Council of 30 November 2009 on cosmetic products (recast), OJ 2009 L 342/59.

75 Ibid., Art. 10 & Annex I.

76 The PPWD defines packaging as 'all products made of any materials of any nature to be used for the containment, protection, handling, delivery and presentation of goods, from raw materials to processed goods, from the producer to the user or the consumer': see Art. 3(1), European Parliament and Council Directive 94/62/EC of 20 December 1994 on packaging and packaging waste, OJ 1994 L 365/10.

77 Ibid., Art. 1. See also Recital 27, Directive (EU) 2018/852 of the European Parliament and of the Council of 30 May 2018 amending Directive 94/62/EC on packaging and packaging waste, OJ 2018 L 150/141.

packaging,[78] MSs have to take measures to ensure that packaging complies with certain essential requirements, which relate to its manufacturing and composition, and reusable and recoverable nature. Specific requirements include minimising the weight and volume of packaging and the presence of hazardous substances, and ensuring that it is designed for reuse or recovery.[79]

Several types of plastic packaging also fall within the scope of the SUP Directive, which was introduced in 2019, following upon the EU Plastics Strategy. The SUP Directive covers the ten single-use plastic items most often found on the EU's beaches, which include food packaging, beverage containers and cups, plastic carrier bags, and packets and wrappers.[80] The Directive's objectives are threefold: preventing and reducing the negative impact of single-use plastic on the environment and human health, promoting the transition towards a CE, and contributing to the functioning of the internal market.[81] It particularly aims to contribute towards curbing marine litter, as 50 per cent of EU marine litter consists of single-use plastic items.[82] In order to achieve its objectives, the SUP introduces multiple product requirements for different single-use plastic items, including for plastic packaging.[83] It prohibits certain packaging made of expanded polystyrene, and all packaging made of oxo-degradable plastics.[84] For food containers and beverage cups, MSs are also to take measures to achieve a consumption reduction.[85] Product requirements will, furthermore,

---

78 Art. 4(1) & Art. 9, European Parliament and Council Directive 94/62/EC of 20 December 1994 on packaging and packaging waste, OJ 1994 L 365/10. See also Recital 21, Directive (EU) 2018/852 of the European Parliament and of the Council of 30 May 2018 amending Directive 94/62/EC on packaging and packaging waste, OJ 2018 L 150/141.

79 Art. 9 & Annex II, European Parliament and Council Directive 94/62/EC of 20 December 1994 on packaging and packaging waste, OJ 1994 L 365/10. See also SWD(2018) 16 final, pp. 56–57.

80 Art. 2(1) and Annex, Directive (EU) 2019/904 of the European Parliament and of the Council of 5 June 2019 on the reduction of the impact of certain plastic products on the environment, OJ 2019 L 155/1. See also Recital 7, Directive (EU) 2019/904 of the European Parliament and of the Council of 5 June 2019 on the reduction of the impact of certain plastic products on the environment, OJ 2019 L 155/1.

81 Art. 1., Directive (EU) 2019/904 of the European Parliament and of the Council of 5 June 2019 on the reduction of the impact of certain plastic products on the environment, OJ 2019 L 155/1. See also Recitals 2, 29 and 36, Directive (EU) 2019/904 of the European Parliament and of the Council of 5 June 2019 on the reduction of the impact of certain plastic products on the environment, OJ 2019 L 155/1.

82 European Commission, *Turning the tide on single-use plastics*, EU Publications Office, 2021. See also Recitals 1, 5 & 6, Directive (EU) 2019/904 of the European Parliament and of the Council of 5 June 2019 on the reduction of the impact of certain plastic products on the environment, OJ 2019 L 155/1.

83 See also M. Hüttler, J.C. Schmitt and M. Gall, '120 Circular Design Standards for Plastic Packaging – A Comprehensive Analysis', 20th European Round Table on Sustainable Consumption and Production, 2021, pp. 2–3.

84 Art. 5, Directive (EU) 2019/904 of the European Parliament and of the Council of 5 June 2019 on the reduction of the impact of certain plastic products on the environment, OJ 2019 L 155/1. See also ibid., Recital 15.

85 Ibid., Art. 4.

apply to beverage containers, requiring that lids and caps have to stay on; and for PET bottles there is a minimum recycled content requirement.[86] Lastly, labelling and marking requirements apply to beverage cups as well.[87]

Plastic packaging can also be seen as part of the life cycles of the products they contain,[88] making more general EU product legislation relevant as well. The main legal framework in this regard is the Ecodesign Directive. While currently only applying to energy-related products, the packaging of these products has been named as part of the life cycle which should be taken into account to reduce the environmental impact of products.[89] Packaging can, thus, play a role as an eco-design parameter for the preparation of implementing measures laying down eco-design requirements for products.[90] At the moment, however, there are no eco-design regulations setting specific requirements with regard to the (recycled) materials used in, or composition of, product packaging. For the sake of completeness, it should be mentioned that such requirements can, however, be found in some EU Ecolabel criteria. Despite being a voluntary instrument, the EU Ecolabel aims to minimise the environmental impacts of products over their entire life cycles, and therefore includes requirements regarding plastic packaging for some products.[91]

---

86 Ibid., Arts. 6 (1) and (5). See also ibid., Recital 17.

87 Ibid., Art. 7. This is further set out in Commission Implementing Regulation (EU) 2020/2151 of 17 December 2020 laying down rules on harmonised marking specifications on single-use plastic products listed in Part D of the Annex to Directive (EU) 2019/904 of the European Parliament and of the Council on the reduction of the impact of certain plastic products on the environment, OJ 2020 L 428/57.

88 See, *inter alia*, Commission Staff Working Document, 'Sustainable Products in a Circular Economy – Towards an EU Product Policy
Framework contributing to the Circular Economy', SWD(2019) 91, pp. 24–25, where it is stated that (plastic) packaging itself is not a product, but is strongly connected with products.

89 Annex I, Part 1, 1.1(c), & Art. 15(6), Directive 2009/125/EC of the European Parliament and of the Council of 21 October 2009 establishing a framework for the setting of ecodesign requirements for energy-related products (recast), OJ 2009 L 285/10, and also Recital 13 of this Directive.

90 Ibid., Annex I, Part 1, 1.1(c) & Art. 15(6).

91 Commission Decision (EU) 2021/1870 of 22 October 2021 establishing the EU Ecolabel criteria for cosmetic products and animal care products (notified under document C(2021) 7500), OJ 2021 L 379/8, including recitals 7 and 8). See also Commission Decision (EU) 2017/1214 of 23 June 2017 establishing the EU Ecolabel criteria for hand dishwashing detergents (notified under document C(2017) 4227), OJ 2017 L 180/1); Commission Decision (EU) 2017/1215 of 23 June 2017 establishing the EU Ecolabel criteria for industrial and institutional dishwasher detergents (notified under document C(2017) 4228), OJ 2017 L 180/16; Commission Decision (EU) 2017/1216 of 23 June 2017 establishing the EU Ecolabel criteria for dishwasher detergents (notified under document C(2017) 4240), OJ 2017 L 180/31); Commission Decision (EU) 2017/1217 of 23 June 2017 establishing the EU Ecolabel criteria for hard surface cleaning products (notified under document C(2017) 4241), OJ 2017 L 180/45; Commission Decision (EU) 2017/1218 of 23 June 2017 establishing the EU Ecolabel criteria for laundry detergents (notified under document C(2017) 4243), OJ 2017 L 180/63; Commission Decision (EU) 2017/1219 of 23 June 2017 establishing the EU

3.3. EU WASTE LEGISLATION

Plastic packaging that is (intended to be) discarded becomes plastic packaging waste and, therefore, falls within the scope of EU waste legislation. As stated above, both the PPWD and SUP Directives contain provisions on the waste management of plastic packaging. In addition to the essential requirements already discussed, the PPWD requires MSs to take measures to prevent the generation of packaging waste, specifically to reduce the consumption of lightweight plastic bags,[92] and to encourage the reuse of packaging.[93] Among other things, these measures have to be included, in a specific chapter on packaging and packaging waste, in national waste management plans.[94] MSs also have to ensure that there are systems in place for the collection and reuse, recycling or recovery of plastic packaging waste.[95] In this regard, they are required to establish Extended Producer Responsibility (EPR) schemes by the end of 2024.[96] By making producers responsible for the end-of-life phase of packaging, the aim is to reduce the generation of packaging waste, and to increase separate collection and recycling,[97] attaining at least the targets specified in Table 2 below.[98] Also, EPR is supposed to incentivise resource-efficient design, as the EPR fees paid by producers are based on the weight of the packaging.[99] Furthermore, fee modulation, which has to be applied, where possible, in case of collective fulfilment of EPR obligations, has to take into account aspects

Ecolabel criteria for industrial and institutional laundry detergents (notified under document C(2017) 4245), OJ 2017 L 180/79.

92 Art. 4(1a)–(1c), European Parliament and Council Directive 94/62/EC of 20 December 1994 on packaging and packaging waste, OJ 1994 L 365/10, which is the implementation of Directive (EU) 2015/720 of the European Parliament and of the Council of 29 April 2015 amending Directive 94/62/EC as regards reducing the consumption of lightweight plastic carrier bags, OJ 2015 L 115/11. See also Recitals 2, 4, 5 & 10, Directive (EU) 2015/720 of the European Parliament and of the Council of 29 April 2015 amending Directive 94/62/EC as regards reducing the consumption of lightweight plastic carrier bags, OJ 2015 L 115/11.

93 Art. 5, European Parliament and Council Directive 94/62/EC of 20 December 1994 on packaging and packaging waste, OJ 1994 L 365/10.

94 Ibid., Art. 14 & Art. 28 Directive 2008/98/EC of the European Parliament and of the Council of 19 November 2008 on waste and repealing certain Directives, OJ 2008 L 312/3.

95 Art. 7(1), European Parliament and Council Directive 94/62/EC of 20 December 1994 on packaging and packaging waste, OJ 1994 L 365/10.

96 Ibid., Art. 7(2), & Arts. 8 and 8a, Directive 2008/98/EC of the European Parliament and of the Council of 19 November 2008 on waste and repealing certain Directives, OJ 2008 L 312/3. See also Recital 20 Directive (EU) 2018/852 of the European Parliament and of the Council of 30 May 2018 amending Directive 94/62/EC on packaging and packaging waste, OJ 2018 L 150/141.

97 Recital 20, Directive (EU) 2018/852 of the European Parliament and of the Council of 30 May 2018 amending Directive 94/62/EC on packaging and packaging waste, OJ 2018 L 150/141.

98 Art. 8a(1)(b), Directive 2008/98/EC of the European Parliament and of the Council of 19 November 2008 on waste and repealing certain Directives, OJ 2008 L 312/3.

99 SWD(2018) 16 final, pp. 56–57.

like reusability and recyclability.[100] With regard to the recycling and recovery of packaging waste, the PPWD sets increasingly stringent targets. Specifically with regard to plastic packaging, a minimum of 50 per cent by weight of all plastic packaging waste will have to be recycled by the end of 2025, and a minimum of 55 per cent by the end of 2030 (see Table 2).[101]

Table 2. Minimum percentage by weight of the packaging waste that is to be recycled, as required by Article 6 PPWD

Deadline	Packaging waste	Plastic packaging waste
No later than 31 December 2008	55% as a minimum & 80% as a maximum	22.5% (exclusively material that is recycled back into plastics)
No later than 31 December 2025	65%	50%
No later than 31 December 2030	70%	55%

Source: Produced by the author.

Similarly to the PPWD, the SUP Directive also concerns waste management, but only for certain single-use plastic packaging. The SUP Directive complements the existing obligation for MSs to establish EPR schemes for single-use plastic packaging, as it requires producers not only to cover these costs, but also the costs of awareness-raising measures, the waste collection of products discarded in public collection systems, and the costs of cleaning up the litter from those products.[102] MSs are also required to take measures related to consumers, including making them aware of reusable alternatives and the impact of incorrect disposal, and to influence their behaviour, to reduce litter.[103] Specifically with regard to plastic packaging consisting of beverage bottles, the Directive,

[100] Art. 8a (4)(b), Directive 2008/98/EC of the European Parliament and of the Council of 19 November 2008 on waste and repealing certain Directives, OJ 2008 L 312/3. See also SWD(2019) 91, pp. 24–25.

[101] Art. 6(1)(g)(i) and Art. 6(1)(i)(i), European Parliament and Council Directive 94/62/EC of 20 December 1994 on packaging and packaging waste, OJ 1994 L 365/10. Commission Implementing Decision (EU) 2019/665 of 17 April 2019 amending Decision 2005/270/EC establishing the formats relating to the database system pursuant to European Parliament and Council Directive 94/62/EC on packaging and packaging waste (notified under document C(2019) 2805), OJ 2019 L 112/26, contains the formats on the database system of the PPWD and the calculation of the achievement of the targets.

[102] Art. 8(2) and Annex, Part E, s. I. These are food containers, beverage bottles and cups, packets and wrappers, and lightweight plastic carrier bags. See also Recitals 21 and 22, Directive (EU) 2019/904 of the European Parliament and of the Council of 5 June 2019 on the reduction of the impact of certain plastic products on the environment, OJ 2019 L 155/1.

[103] Art. 10, Directive (EU) 2019/904 of the European Parliament and of the Council of 5 June 2019 on the reduction of the impact of certain plastic products on the environment, OJ 2019 L 155/1.

furthermore, sets additional separate collection targets: 77 per cent by 2025, and 90 per cent by 2029.[104]

The WFD provides the general framework for waste management in the EU, and aims to prevent or reduce the generation of waste and its adverse impacts, as well as to reduce the overall impacts of resource use, and improve the efficiency of such use.[105] This general framework for waste management includes, among other things, the waste hierarchy, rules on by-products, end-of-waste criteria, the framework and minimum requirements for EPR schemes, and measures on preparingfor reuse and recycling. Of specific relevance for plastic packaging are the fact that the WFD requires MSs to take measures to prevent waste generation, by setting measures to encourage reuse of (plastic) packaging;[106] mentions plastic as one of the waste streams that require national separate collection schemes;[107] and contains a preparing for reuse and recycling target for household waste, which also explicitly covers plastic (packaging).[108]

Lastly, the WSR also plays a role with regard to plastic packaging, as plastic packaging waste is regularly being shipped for processing within the EU, as well as to countries outside the EU.[109] Since 2020, new rules have been introduced to ban, or more strictly control, the export and import of plastic waste.[110] These new rules aim to improve the control of (illegal) transboundary shipments of plastic waste, and thereby to encourage the environmentally sound management of plastic waste.[111]

4. ANALYSIS: THE LEGAL FRAMEWORK GOVERNING THE LIFE CYCLE OF PLASTIC PACKAGING: IN LINE WITH THE CE TRANSITION?

The previous section discussed the legislation governing each life-cycle stage of plastic packaging. As stated in the Introduction, the EU has already taken steps to better align its chemicals, product and waste legislation with the CE

---

104 Ibid., Art. 9. See also ibid., Recital 27.

105 Art. 1, Directive 2008/98/EC of the European Parliament and of the Council of 19 November 2008 on waste and repealing certain Directives, OJ 2008 L 312/3.

106 Ibid., Art. 9(1)(d).

107 Ibid., Art. 11(1.

108 Ibid., Art. 11(2)(a). See also T.J. de Römph and G. van Calster, above n. 17, p. 269; SWD(2019) 90 final, p. 6.

109 European Court of Auditors, *Review no. 4/2020: EU action to tackle the issue of plastic waste*, pp. 36–37.

110 Commission Delegated Regulation (EU) 2020/2174 of 19 October 2020 amending Annexes IC, III, IIIA, IV, V, VII and VIII to Regulation (EC) No 1013/2006 of the European Parliament and of the Council on shipments of waste, OJ 2020 L 433/11.

111 Commission Delegated Regulation (EU) amending Annexes IC, III, IIIA, IV, V, VII and VIII to Regulation (EC) No. 1013/2006 of the European Parliament and of the Council on

transition. Since the first CEAP, several of the above-mentioned legal acts have been amended or reviewed. This section will analyse to what extent the legal framework governing the life cycle of plastic packaging aligns with the objectives of the transition towards a more circular plastic packaging chain, as outlined in the CEAPs and EU Plastics Strategy. It will not only analyse to what extent the legislation explicitly pays attention to the CE transition, but also to what extent the provisions reflect life-cycle thinking, or are aligned with the waste hierarchy. The possible implications of the many revisions of the plastic packaging legislation currently taking place will also be covered in this analysis. The legislation will be discussed in the order of the perceived extent to which it aligns with the CE transition in the plastic packaging chain, starting with legislation that clearly expresses this in its objectives, followed by legislation in which CE aspects or life-cycle thinking seem to be reflected, and, finally, legislation where this would only seem to be the case following the upcoming revisions.[112]

4.1. PLASTIC PACKAGING LEGISLATION AND THE TRANSITION TOWARDS A MORE CIRCULAR PLASTIC PACKAGING CHAIN

As shown in section 3 above, the PPWD, SUP and WFD all explicitly mention that their aims are to contribute to the CE transition, as they were all amended or introduced following the first CEAP.

The PPWD and SUP Directive both contain provisions on the product stage, as well as the waste stage, of plastic packaging. According to the objective of the PPWD, these measures follow the order of the waste hierarchy, in order to contribute to the transition towards a CE.[113] The SUP Directive also has, as one of its objectives, the promotion of the transition to a CE, but with innovative and sustainable business models, products and materials.[114] It also has, as

---

shipments of waste – Explanatory Memorandum, COM(2020) 7091. See also European Court of Auditors, above n. 105, pp. 36–37.

112 See also, about this, I.M. de Waal, 'The Legal Transition Towards a More Circular Plastic Packaging Chain: A Case Study of the Netherlands', *European Energy and Environmental Law Review*, (2023) 32(5), pp. 226–247.

113 Art. 1(2), European Parliament and Council Directive 94/62/EC of 20 December 1994 on packaging and packaging waste, OJ 1994 L 365/10 reads: '2. To that end, this Directive lays down measures aimed, as a first priority, at preventing the production of packaging waste and, as additional fundamental principles, at reusing packaging, at recycling and other forms of recovering packaging waste and, therefore, at reducing the final disposal of such waste in order to contribute to the transition towards a circular economy'.

114 Art. 1, SUP Directive reads: 'The objectives of this Directive are to prevent and reduce the impact of certain plastic products on the environment, in particular the aquatic environment, and on human health, as well as to promote the transition to a circular economy with

its main focus, preventing the generation of waste – the highest step in the waste hierarchy.[115] These objectives seem to be reflected in the structure and provisions of both directives, which seem to indicate that they do, in fact, follow the waste hierarchy, and also pay attention to the whole life cycle of plastic packaging, as they each address multiple life-cycle stages in the waste hierarchy's order.[116] The recitals of both directives further clarify their links with their intended contributions to the CE transition. For example, the recitals of the PPWD explain that the recovery and recycling targets were increased, in the 2018 amendment, to better reflect the transition towards a CE.[117] And the SUP Directive's recitals state that it stimulates the circular use of plastics, as it promotes the market uptake of recycled materials by means of the mandatory minimum recycled content requirement for PET bottles,[118] and underlines the importance of taking into account the whole life cycle of plastic products, mentioning specifically the importance of a life-cycle assessment, and design for circularity of packaging.[119]

Nevertheless, in achieving their objectives, both directives seem to fall short in some respects. For instance, the PPWD only sets targets for recycling and recovery, and does not contain measurable aims for measures that are higher in the waste hierarchy. Also, the essential requirements, in their current form, are considered a weakness, and are said not to support the transition towards a more circular plastic packaging chain, as it is argued that they do not reflect, amongst other things, the prioritisation of the waste hierarchy, and, as a result, do not align well with other waste legislation, such as the targets in the PPWD, and the recycled content requirements in the SUP Directive.[120] A similar

innovative and sustainable business models, products and materials, thus also contributing to the efficient functioning of the internal market.'

115 Recital 2, Directive (EU) 2019/904 of the European Parliament and of the Council of 5 June 2019 on the reduction of the impact of certain plastic products on the environment, OJ 2019 L 155/1. See also European Environment Agency, *Preventing plastic waste in Europe*, EEA Report No. 02/2019, 2019, p. 11.

116 The PPWD starts with provisions that require MSs to ensure that measures, together with the essential requirements, are implemented to prevent the generation of packaging waste and minimise its environmental impact (Art. 4), and subsequently features provisions that require MSs to take measures to encourage the increase of reusable packaging, and systems to reuse packaging (Art. 5). The SUP Directive lays down measures ranging from consumption reduction (Art. 4), and product requirements (Arts. 5 and 6), to consumer awareness (Arts. 7 and 10) and waste management.

117 Recitals 2 and 9, Directive (EU) 2018/852 of the European Parliament and of the Council of 30 May 2018 amending Directive 94/62/EC on packaging and packaging waste, OJ 2018 L 150/141.

118 Recitals 2 and 17, Directive (EU) 2019/904 of the European Parliament and of the Council of 5 June 2019 on the reduction of the impact of certain plastic products on the environment, OJ 2019 L 155/1.

119 Ibid., Recital 18.

120 This legislation includes the WFD and the SUP Directive, as well as the PPWD itself. See European Commission, *Effectiveness of the Essential Requirements for Packaging and Packaging Waste and Proposals for Reinforcement*, EU Publications Office, 2020, para. E.1.0, pp. 47–49.

situation occurs with regard to the SUP Directive. For example, it seems that the provision focusing on the highest step in the waste hierarchy – prevention – lacks most of the substance required to achieve its goal. The restrictions on placing on the market cover only oxo-degradable plastic packaging and certain plastic packaging items made of expanded polystyrene. Although it does require MSs to take necessary measures to achieve a measurable quantitative consumption reduction, which may include national consumption targets, or measures ensuring that reusable alternatives are available,[121] the SUP Directive itself only suggests, but does not impose, measures, and does not itself set any targets.[122] Furthermore, the provisions in the SUP Directive that do focus on the higher waste hierarchy steps also often have only a limited scope of application. For example, the marking requirements apply only to beverage cups,[123] targets for separate collection apply only to beverage bottles, and the product requirements and minimum recycled content requirements are also limited to (PET) beverage bottles.[124] In summary, the provisions of the PPWD could, thus, be better aligned with its objectives, and there also seems room for improvement with regard to the impact of the SUP Directive on the CE transition.

It seems that this situation might be improved, however, by the Proposal for the Packaging and Packaging Waste Regulation (PPWR). The objectives of the PPWR are to reduce the negative environmental impact of packaging and packaging waste, and, more specifically, to reduce packaging waste generation, promote a CE for packaging in a cost-effective way, and promote the use of recycled content in packaging. The proposal aims for a shift from a directive to a regulation, which aims to contribute to harmonising the existing rules. It aims to further stimulate the transition to a CE by covering the entire life cycle of packaging, as well as by improving existing regulatory instruments, such as the essential requirements, and introducing several new ones.[125] These include criteria for design for recyclability,[126] mandatory recycled content

---

121 Art. 4(1), Directive (EU) 2019/904 of the European Parliament and of the Council of 5 June 2019 on the reduction of the impact of certain plastic products on the environment, OJ 2019 L 155/1.

122 This will be part of the evaluation of the SUP Directive, which will be carried out by July 2027. See ibid., Art. 15.

123 Ibid., Art. 7.

124 Ibid., Art. 6. The limited scope of application of the recycled content requirement is, however, in line with the fact that, under the Recycled Plastics Regulation, only post-consumer mechanical PET recycling is currently listed as a suitable recycling technology for FCMs.

125 Proposal for a Regulation of the European Parliament and of the Council on packaging and packaging waste, amending Regulation (EU) 2019/1020 and Directive (EU) 2019/904, and repealing Directive 94/62/EC, COM(2022) 677 final. This research did not take into account any developments regarding this proposal after 1 May 2023.

126 Ibid., Art. 6.

requirements,[127] bans on certain packaging applications,[128] mandatory reuse and refill targets,[129] and targets for packaging waste reduction.[130] This shows an increased focus on the higher steps in the waste hierarchy. Moreover, considering the fact that single-use packaging also falls within the scope of the PPWR, this proposal will complement the requirements for single-use packaging, and amend the SUP Directive too,[131] as well as addressing above-mentioned criticisms by introducing consumption reduction targets, and by applying to (single-use) packaging in general, instead of just plastics.

Since its amendment, the objective of the WFD has also stated that the measures it lays down, which prevent or reduce waste generation and the adverse impacts thereof, as well as the fact that it reduces the impacts of resource use, and improves the efficiency of such use, are crucial for the CE transition.[132] The amendment introduced the CE concept, and updated several provisions on prevention, preparing for reuse and recovery of waste, including increased targets, and minimum requirements for EPR,[133] thereby impacting, to some extent, on the life-cycle stages preceding the waste stage. However, the amendment focused mainly on strengthening reuse and recovery.[134] More generally, and similarly to the PPWD and SUP Directive, the WFD has, despite its objective, been criticised for not paying enough attention to waste prevention, i.e. the highest step in the waste hierarchy.[135] The revision of the WFD might change things for the better though, as it aims to improve the alignment of waste management with the waste hierarchy, with specific attention also given to waste prevention, including considering regulatory measures such

127 Ibid., Art. 7.

128 Ibid., Art. 22.

129 Ibid., Art. 26.

130 Ibid., Art. 38.

131 See, for the amendments, ibid., Art. 61 and Recital 134.

132 And Art. 1 of Directive 2008/98/EC of the European Parliament and of the Council of 19 November 2008 on waste and repealing certain Directives, OJ 2008 L 312/3 reads: 'This Directive lays down measures to protect the environment and human health by preventing or reducing the generation of waste, the adverse impacts of the generation and management of waste and by reducing overall impacts of resource use and improving the efficiency of such use, which are crucial for the transition to a circular economy and for guaranteeing the Union's long-term competitiveness.'

133 Recitals 3, 43 and 44, Directive (EU) 2018/851 of the European Parliament and of the Council of 30 May 2018 amending Directive 2008/98/EC on waste, OJ 2018 L 150/09.

134 B. Puentes Cocina, 'An Analysis of the Circular Economy Legislative Package: A New Paradigm vs The Old Waste Law' in M. Boeve et al. (eds.), *Environmental Law for Transitions to Sustainability*, Intersentia, 2021, p. 57; C. Backes and M. Boeve, 'Envisioning the Future of the Circular Economy: A Legal Perspective', *Environmental Policy and Law*, (2022) 52, pp. 253–263.

135 T.J. de Römph, 'Waste in European waste law: the Waste Framework Directive explained' in M. Faure (ed.), *Elgar Encyclopedia of Environmental Law, vol. XII*, Edward Elgar Publishing, 2023, p. 459.

as overall or product-specific waste reduction targets.[136] Furthermore, the current development of EU-wide end-of-waste criteria for plastic waste[137] might improve the situation regarding the demarcation between waste and non-waste, including issues regarding polymer waste recycling.[138]

In addition to the PPWD, SUP and WFD, the Recycled Plastics Regulation and the WSR also aim to contribute to the CE transition through their provisions, even though it is not explicitly mentioned in their objectives themselves. The recitals of the Recycled Plastics Regulation make clear that it aims to contribute to increasing the recycled content in plastic packaging while maintaining a high level of protection for human health. In this way, the Regulation contributes to achieving the objective of the EU Plastics Strategy, and thereby ultimately to increasing plastic recycling in general, which has been identified as an essential prerequisite for the CE transition.[139] Similarly, although this is not explicitly mentioned, as such, in the legal text itself, the WSR has been amended several times to contribute to the CE objectives and EU Plastics Strategy, including the recent tightening of the WSR legislation with regard to shipment of plastic waste.[140] By aiming, among other things, to facilitate waste shipments for reuse and recycling in the EU, and because of an export ban on plastic waste that was recently adopted by the European Parliament, the recent proposal for the revision of the WSR could expand the WSR's contribution to the CE.[141]

The Ecodesign Directive and EU Ecolabel also do not aim explicitly to contribute to the CE transition, according to their objectives, but their potential is being explored to improve their contribution to CE objectives.[142] At the moment, there are already Ecolabel criteria for several products that promote

---

136 European Commission, 'Call for evidence for an impact assessment, Environmental impact of waste management – revision of EU waste framework', Ref. Ares(2022)577247, 25.01.2022. See also Directorate-General for Environment, 'Call for Evidence: Revision of the Waste Framework Directive' 14 February 2022, on: https://environment.ec.europa.eu/news/waste-framework-directive-revision-2022-02-14_en.

137 ECHA, *Guidance for monomers and polymers*, above n. 50, p. 19. See also Directorate-General for Environment, 'The Commission starts to develop end-of-waste criteria for plastic waste', 5 April 2022, on: https://environment.ec.europa.eu/news/commission-starts-develop-end-waste-criteria-plastic-waste-2022-04-05_en.

138 ECHA, *Guidance for monomers and polymers*, above n. 50, p. 19.

139 Recitals 1 and 2, Commission Regulation (EU) 2022/1616 of 15 September 2022 on recycled plastic materials and articles intended to come into contact with foods, and repealing Regulation (EC) No. 282/2008, OJ 2022 L 243/3.

140 https://environment.ec.europa.eu/news/plastic-waste-shipments-new-eu-rules-importing-and-exporting-plastic-waste-2020-12-22_en. See also Commission Delegated Regulation (EU) amending Annexes IC, III, IIIA, IV, V, VII and VIII to Regulation (EC) No. 1013/2006 of the European Parliament and of the Council on shipments of waste – Explanatory Memorandum, COM(2020) 7091.

141 Proposal for a Regulation of the European Parliament and of the Council on shipments of waste and amending Regulations (EU) No. 1257/2013 and (EU) No. 2020/1056, COM(2021) 709 final, p. 2; https://www.europarl.europa.eu/news/en/press-room/20230113IPR66627/waste-shipments-meps-push-for-tighter-eu-rules.

142 SWD(2019) 91, pp. 12, 21–23.

CE aspects for packaging, such as being refillable, minimising material use, or design for recyclability.[143] Despite being a voluntary instrument, in this way the EU Ecolabel aims to stimulate market actors to consume and produce more sustainably, as well as to engage them in the CE transition,[144] and it could thereby help exploit the potential for the CE transition in the plastic packaging chain.[145]

The Ecodesign has similar potential to establish product-specific requirements on plastic packaging that could contribute to the CE transition, as it focuses on, and regularly mentions, the importance of the whole life cycle of products,[146] including (plastic) packaging. However, as stated previously, currently none of the implementing measures laying down eco-design requirements contain CE aspects for plastic packaging. This may change, however, with the Proposal for Ecodesign Regulation, which will establish a framework to set eco-design requirements, potentially for almost all physical goods on the EU market, including their packaging, in order to improve their sustainability and circularity.[147] This proposal states that it may complement the PPWD in setting

143 Commission Decision (EU) 2021/1870 of 22 October 2021 establishing the EU Ecolabel criteria for cosmetic products and animal care products (notified under document C(2021) 7500), OJ 2021 L 379/8, including Recitals 7 and 8. See also Commission Decision (EU) 2017/1214 of 23 June 2017 establishing the EU Ecolabel criteria for hand dishwashing detergents (notified under document C(2017) 4227), OJ 2017 L 180/1; Commission Decision (EU) 2017/1215 of 23 June 2017 establishing the EU Ecolabel criteria for industrial and institutional dishwasher detergents (notified under document C(2017) 4228), OJ 2017 L 180/16; Commission Decision (EU) 2017/1216 of 23 June 2017 establishing the EU Ecolabel criteria for dishwasher detergents (notified under document C(2017) 4240), OJ 2017 L 180/31;
Commission Decision (EU) 2017/1217 of 23 June 2017 establishing the EU Ecolabel criteria for hard surface cleaning products (notified under document C(2017) 4241), OJ 2017 L 180/45; Commission Decision (EU) 2017/1218 of 23 June 2017 establishing the EU Ecolabel criteria for laundry detergents (notified under document C(2017) 4243), OJ 2017 L 180/63; Commission Decision (EU) 2017/1219 of 23 June 2017 establishing the EU Ecolabel criteria for industrial and institutional laundry detergents (notified under document C(2017) 4245), OJ 2017 L 180/79. See also COM(2018) 28 final, pp. 11–12; SWD(2018) 16 final, p. 29; SWD(2019) 91, pp. 24–25.

144 European Commission, *Strategic EU Ecolabel Work Plan 2020–2024*, EU, 2020, p. 3.

145 SWD(2019) 91, pp. 24–25. See also C. Fayole et al. (eds.), *For Better Not Worse: Applying Ecodesign Principles to Plastics in the Circular Economy*, ECOS, 2019, p. 21.

146 This is, e.g. already evident in the definition of ecodesign: Art. 2(23), Directive 2009/125/EC of the European Parliament and of the Council of 21 October 2009 establishing a framework for the setting of ecodesign requirements for energy-related products (recast), OJ 2009 L 285/10. See, more extensively, C. Dalhammar, 'The Application of "life cycle thinking" in European environmental law: theory and practice', *Journal of European Environmental & Planning Law*, (2015) 12(2), pp. 97–127.

147 In contrast to, e.g. the PPWD, which focuses on the packaging as a product in itself. See also Commission Staff Working Document, 'Proposal for a Regulation of the European Parliament and of the Council establishing a framework for setting ecodesign requirements for sustainable products and repealing Directive 2009/125/EC', SWD(2022) 82 final, p. 65.

product-based requirements on packaging, to contribute to minimising the amount of packaging, and thereby the generation of packaging waste.[148] Both the weight and volume of the packaging, as well as the plastic waste and packaging waste, are mentioned as product parameters that may be used as a basis for improving aspects of the product by means of eco-design requirements.[149] Furthermore, following the approach of the proposed Ecodesign Regulation, the revised Construction Products Regulation (CPR) will also set sustainability criteria for construction products and their packaging,[150] thereby becoming relevant for the transition towards a circular plastic packaging chain too.[151]

Next to the legislation that may or may not explicitly aim to contribute to the CE transition, there is also legislation governing the life cycle of plastic packaging that does not explicitly refer to its contribution to the CE, but does contain provisions in which CE aspects or life-cycle thinking are expressed. This is the case, for example, with the REACH Regulation, in which the importance of considering the whole life cycle of chemicals is underlined with regard to safety assessments.[152] However, the obligation that relates and refers to the life cycle and supply chain ends with the waste stage; the use of

---

148 Recital 21, Proposal for a Regulation of the European Parliament and of the Council establishing a framework for setting ecodesign requirements for sustainable products and repealing Directive 2009/125/EC, COM(2022) 142 final.

149 Annex I, (i) and (p), Proposal for a Regulation of the European Parliament and of the Council establishing a framework for setting ecodesign requirements for sustainable products and repealing Directive 2009/125/EC.

150 More specifically, the CPR will require manufactures not only to design and manufacture, but also to package, their products in such a way that their overall environmental and climate sustainability reaches the state-of-the-art level, to give preference to recyclable and recycled materials, and to design products in such a way that reuse, remanufacturing or recycling are facilitated, amongst other things. See Art. 22(2), Proposal for a Regulation of the European Parliament and of the Council laying down harmonised conditions for the marketing of construction products, amending Regulation (EU) 2019/1020 and repealing Regulation (EU) 305/2011, COM(2022) 144 final. See also, about inherent product environmental requirements, Annex I, Part C, s. 2.

151 Recital 20, Proposal for a Regulation of the European Parliament and of the Council laying down harmonised conditions for the marketing of construction products, amending Regulation (EU) 2019/1020 and repealing Regulation (EU) 305/2011; COM(2022) 144 final, pp. 2, 6.

152 See, e.g. Annex I 0.3, Regulation (EC) No. 1907/2006 of the European Parliament and of the Council of 18 December 2006 concerning the Registration, Evaluation, Authorisation and Restriction of Chemicals (REACH), establishing a European Chemicals Agency, amending Directive 1999/45/EC and repealing Council Regulation (EEC) No. 793/93 and Commission Regulation (EC) No. 1488/94 as well as Council Directive 76/769/EEC and Commission Directives 91/155/EEC, 93/67/EEC, 93/105/EC and 2000/21/EC, OJ 2006 L 396/1. See also, e.g. Annex XII, Annex I 5.0, Art. 3.37, Annex I 0.7, Art. 18(4)(a), Annex I 5.1.1 and 5.2.2, and Annex II, s. 13 Regulation (EC) No. 1907/2006 of the European Parliament and of the Council of 18 December 2006 concerning the Registration, Evaluation, Authorisation and Restriction of Chemicals (REACH), establishing a European Chemicals Agency, amending Directive 1999/45/EC and repealing Council Regulation (EEC) No. 793/93 and Commission Regulation (EC) No. 1488/94 as well as Council Directive 76/769/EEC and Commission Directives 91/155/EEC, 93/67/EEC, 93/105/EC and 2000/21/EC, OJ 2006 L 396/1.

recovered substances does not have to be included in these assessments.[153] Moreover, REACH requirements disadvantage recyclers in comparison with producers of new plastics, particularly in terms of collecting the required information.[154] The supply of information is already complicated, as polymers are being exempted from the registration and evaluation requirements,[155] but the information required under REACH also fails to reach the waste stage, which creates barriers for recyclers with regard to determining the risk and hazard profiles of their recycled substances, and with regard to complying with the registration exemption for the monomers and other substances that do fall under the registration requirement.[156] In other words, the current REACH set-up hampers plastic recyclers, and thereby the transition towards a more circular plastic chain. While the recently introduced SCIP database already aims to contribute to closing the information gap,[157] the forthcoming revision of the REACH Regulation could also bring about a change, as one of the measures being considered is a revision of the registration requirements, including registration for certain polymers.[158] Other measures under consideration relate to simplifying communication in the supply chain, and reforming the evaluation, authorisation and restriction processes.[159]

Finally, some of the legal acts governing plastic packaging seem neither to pay attention to nor reflect CE aspects at all: these are the CLP Regulation, Regulation 1935/2004 on FCMs, and the Cosmetics Regulation. Again, however, the upcoming revisions of these legal acts may be able to contribute positively to the CE transition in the plastic packaging chain. For example, the proposal for the revised CLP Regulation contains rules for refillable containers for chemicals, which has the potential to reduce packaging waste and facilitate

153 ECHA, *Guidance on waste and recovered substances*, above n. 53, p. 10.

154 T.J. de Römph, 'Waste in European waste law', above n. 131, p. 456. See, more extensively, on barriers for plastic recyclers under REACH, T.J. de Römph and G. van Calster, above n. 17.

155 European Commission, 'Chemicals Strategy for Sustainability: Towards a Toxic-Free Environment', COM(2020) 667 final, p. 20. See also section 3 above.

156 See, more extensively, about barriers for plastic recyclers, T.J. de Römph and G. van Calster, above n. 17. See also COM(2018) 32 final.

157 Art. 9(2), Directive 2008/98/EC of the European Parliament and of the Council of 19 November 2008 on waste and repealing certain Directives, OJ 2008 L 312/3. See also ECHA, *Chemical Recycling of Polymeric Materials from Waste in the Circular Economy*, ECHA, 2021, p. 61; E. de Tandt et al., above n. 3, p. 320. See, further, section 3 above.

158 See also Art. 138(2), Regulation (EC) No. 1907/2006 of the European Parliament and of the Council of 18 December 2006 concerning the Registration, Evaluation, Authorisation and Restriction of Chemicals (REACH), establishing a European Chemicals Agency, amending Directive 1999/45/EC and repealing Council Regulation (EEC) No. 793/93 and Commission Regulation (EC) No. 1488/94 as well as Council Directive 76/769/EEC and Commission Directives 91/155/EEC, 93/67/EEC, 93/105/EC and 2000/21/EC, OJ 2006 L 396/1, which already gives the EC the possibility to present a legislative proposal for the registration of polymers.

159 European Commission, 'Inception Impact Assessment', Ref. Ares(2021)2962933, 04.05.2021.

more sustainable sales forms.[160] Also, Regulation 1935/2004, which recognised, in its recitals, that the use of recycled materials and articles should be favoured, but is said to provide no basis itself to develop rules for supporting and encouraging sustainable and safe alternatives for packaging,[161] is being revised. Its revision aims to support sustainable packaging solutions, to contribute to the CE transition, and, more specifically, to make plastic packaging reusable and recyclable, and to encourage alternatives to plastic packaging and reduce waste.[162] The Plastics Regulation and Recycled Plastics Regulation are both based on Regulation 1935/2004, so the revision of the latter might also affect these two regulations. Lastly, a revision of the Cosmetics Regulation has also been announced, but the impact on cosmetic packaging in particular is not yet clear.[163]

4.2. GENERAL THEMES AND OUTLOOK

From the above analysis of plastic packaging legislation in light of the CE transition, two overarching themes could be observed.

First, it should be noted that most of the legislation that governs plastic packaging predates the CE transition and, therefore, neither the CE nor circularity aspects are explicitly mentioned in most of the legal texts themselves. This is not the case for the PPWD, SUP Directive and WFD, for which the CE transition is even part of their objectives. However, it appears that even these pieces of legislation, which explicitly aim to contribute to the CE transition, have room for improvement regarding the extent to which their provisions are in line with the CE objectives, for instance by focusing on higher steps in the waste hierarchy, or by better reflecting life-cycle thinking. It turns out, therefore, that including the CE transition in the objectives of a legal act does not guarantee that the provisions themselves will realise this objective. In addition, and building on the above, it also seems that, in multiple instances, the potential of provisions or legal act is not fully utilised in favour of the CE transition, regardless of any objectives that explicitly refer to the CE transition.

---

160 Art. 35 & Annex II, s. 3.4, Proposal for a Regulation of the European Parliament and of the Council amending Regulation (EC) No. 1272/2008 of the European Parliament and of the Council on classification, labelling and packaging of substances and mixtures, COM(2022) 748 final; Recital 15 Proposal for a Regulation of the European Parliament and of the Council amending Regulation (EC) No. 1272/2008 of the European Parliament and of the Council on classification, labelling and packaging of substances and mixtures.

161 European Commission, 'FCM Inception Impact Assessment', Ref. Ares(2020)7731375, 18.12.2020.

162 Ibid.

163 European Commission, 'Cosmetic Product Regulation Inception Impact Assessment', Ref. Ares(2021)6011962, 04.10.2021.

As discussed above, this can be seen with regard to the essential requirements in the PPWD, and the fact that multiple provisions in the SUP Directive, such as the requirement on recycled content, have only a limited scope of application. EPR is another example of an instrument that, arguably, is not being used to its full potential, as it, for instance, only makes producers responsible for achieving *at least* the targets in the PPWD,[164] and as fee modulation is not mandatory. This can also be seen with regard to the Ecodesign Directive and EU Ecolabel, which are said to be able to contribute to the CE transition, but whose potential to do so has not yet been fully utilised, despite the fact that, for some products, there are Ecolabel criteria promoting CE aspects for (plastic) packaging. As has also been pointed out above, provisions that (could) contribute to the CE transition or focus on higher steps in the waste hierarchy regularly lack concrete measures or measurable objectives. For example, besides preparing for reuse, recycling and recovery, neither the PPWD nor the WFD contain any targets focusing on higher steps in the waste hierarchy, and the SUP Directive does so only to a limited extent. However, with regard to both existing and potentially new or different targets, their effectiveness in contributing to the CE transition, their relation to broader sustainability benchmarks, and their interrelationship, should be kept in mind.[165] In short, the extent to which the legal framework governing plastic packaging focuses on the CE could be improved, paying particular attention to ensuring that the provisions themselves adequately contribute to, and align with, CE objectives, and that their potential is fully utilised with a view to achieving the CE transition.

Second, and more generally, it appears that, within the legal framework governing the life cycle of plastic packaging, multiple legal acts focus on multiple life-cycle stages of packaging simultaneously. This is, first and foremost, evident in the Ecodesign Directive and EU Ecolabel, both of which focus on the environmental impacts of products over their entire life cycles. This can also be seen in the PPWD and SUP, which contain provisions on, and thus focus on, both the product and waste stages of packaging. Even the WFD contains provisions that focus on multiple life-cycle stages, such as EPR,[166] or the list of measures to prevent waste generation. From this seems to follow that the boundaries between EU chemicals, product and waste legislation, as areas of law, are frequently blurred. For example, provisions on either consumption

164 Art. 8a(1)(b), Directive 2008/98/EC of the European Parliament and of the Council of 19 November 2008 on waste and repealing certain Directives, OJ 2008 L 312/3.

165 See, more extensively, C. Backes and M. Boeve, above n. 130.

166 Especially Art. 8(2) of Directive 2008/98/EC of the European Parliament and of the Council of 19 November 2008 on waste and repealing certain Directives, OJ 2008 L 312/3, which states that MSs 'may take appropriate measures to encourage the design of products and components of products in order to reduce their environmental impact and the generation of waste in the course of the production and subsequent use of products'.

reduction or waste prevention show that similar measures can be adopted from a different angle, and labelling and marking requirements show how product requirements can be used to influence the end-of-life stage. While these examples from the PPWD and SUP Directive can be argued to demonstrate a less strict division between product and waste legislation, the Plastics Regulation and Recycled Plastics Regulation can, similarly, be said to contain both chemicals and product legislation, as they concern substances as well as the composition of packaging.[167] The SCIP database, whose basis is in the WFD, serves to inform recyclers about the presence of hazardous substances, and thereby shows a clear link between chemicals and waste legislation. In other words, the fact that multiple legal acts focus on multiple life-cycle stages, and that the boundaries between EU chemicals, product and waste legislation, which can be said to more or less represent separate life-cycle stages, are more blurred, can be seen as a step towards more life-cycle thinking within the legal framework governing plastic packaging. However, the issues that exist with regard to the current REACH set-up, and the information gap between the chemicals and product stage and the waste stage, show that there is still room for improvement at the interface between these three areas of law.[168]

Looking to the future, the many revisions currently taking place will likely increase the extent to which explicit attention will be paid to the CE transition in the legal framework governing plastic packaging. At the time of writing, only the proposals for the PPWR, Ecodesign Regulation, WSR and CPR have been published. These show that the extent to which the actual provisions will be in line with the CE transition will also improve, including in the extent to which the provisions reflect the waste hierarchy, as well as the extent to which provisions will be substantiated or have a wider scope of application. This is the case with regard to, *inter alia*, the proposals for the PPWR, Ecodesign Regulation and CPR, and likely for the revision of the WFD as well. As for the other revisions, some of the impact assessments, such as that for the WFD, seem to indicate a similar trend. Nevertheless, it remains to be seen to what extent the revised legislation will contribute to achieving a more circular plastic packaging chain, in practice. The same goes for the more recently introduced legislation, such as the Recycled Plastics Regulation, which is said to contribute to the CE transition, but for which the actual contribution has yet to be proven. In any event, the many developments will, in all likelihood, contribute to improving harmonisation, and levelling the playing field for plastic packaging stakeholders, as both the revisions of the PPWD and Ecodesign Directive are proposals for regulations.

---

167 See also K. Syberg et al., 'Regulation of plastic from a circular economy perspective', *Current Opinion in Green and Sustainable Chemistry*, (2021) 29, p. 3.

168 See also T.J. de Römph, 'Waste in European waste law', above n. 131, p. 456.

Furthermore, the extent to which the legal framework focuses on multiple life-cycle stages is also expected to increase further with the upcoming revisions. The proposals already published show that, for example, the PPWR focuses explicitly on the whole life cycle of packaging, and therefore contains several product requirements, such as design for recyclability criteria, minimum recycled content requirements, and requirements for reusable packaging. Similarly, the Ecodesign Regulation, which may complement the PPWD or the PPWR by setting product-based packaging requirements, also considers all life-cycle stages when establishing such eco-design requirements.[169] It thus seems that, with the PPWD at least, life-cycle thinking will become more integrated, and the legislation will, therefore, become more in line with the CE transition, but attention should be paid to ensure that this will not lead to inconsistencies, gaps or overlaps within the legal framework. The proposals for both the PPWR and Ecodesign Regulation, as well as the current SUP Directive, address potential overlaps between, and the need to ensure consistency among, these pieces of legislation, as well as with other chemicals, product and waste legislation.[170] Nevertheless, continuous attention will have to be paid to guarantee proper interaction between the parts of, and coordination within, the legal framework, to prevent unintentional barriers for its implementation, and to ensure an effective contribution to the transition towards a more circular packaging chain.

5. CONCLUSION

Plastic packaging is one of the product chains the EU is focusing on in its transition towards a CE. Its life cycle is governed by an extensive legal framework consisting of EU chemicals, product and waste legislation. The analysis in this chapter shows that this legal framework appears to align, to varying degrees, with the transition towards a more circular plastic packaging chain. However, notwithstanding the explicit focus on a legal act's contribution to the CE, it is especially important that the provisions themselves adequately

---

169 See, *inter alia*, Art. 5 and Recital 21, Proposal for a Regulation of the European Parliament and of the Council establishing a framework for setting ecodesign requirements for sustainable products and repealing Directive 2009/125/EC.

170 See, *inter alia*, Proposal for a Regulation of the European Parliament and of the Council on packaging and packaging waste, amending Regulation (EU) 2019/1020 and Directive (EU) 2019/904, and repealing Directive 94/62/EC, including Recitals 9, 48 and 102; Proposal for a Regulation of the European Parliament and of the Council establishing a framework for setting ecodesign requirements for sustainable products and repealing Directive 2009/125/EC, including Recitals 17, 21, 22; Art. 2(2) and Recitals 10 and 17, Directive (EU) 2019/904 of the European Parliament and of the Council of 5 June 2019 on the reduction of the impact of certain plastic products on the environment, OJ 2019 L 155/1.

contribute to, and align with, CE objectives, as well as that their potential is fully utilised. Furthermore, the analysis shows that, within the legal framework governing plastic packaging, there is often a focus on multiple life-cycle stages simultaneously, and frequently the boundaries between chemicals, product and waste legislation, as areas of law, are indistinct. This could be argued to reflect life-cycle thinking, and thus to be in line with the CE transition. With regard to both these outcomes, the many revisions of the legal framework governing plastic packaging seem promising, and thus could have a positive impact on the extent to which the legislation aligns with the CE transition. Nevertheless, this chapter did not address the implementation of the legislation, and its contribution to the CE transition in the plastic packaging chain, in practice. Further research on this is necessary, and will continue to be necessary, given the many legal developments that are currently taking place. It remains to be seen to what extent the revisions will actually improve the relation between the EU chemicals, product and waste legislation governing plastic packaging, and the transition towards a more circular plastic packaging chain, in practice.

MULTI-LEVEL INCENTIVES FOR THE RECOVERY OF VALUABLE RESOURCES FROM BIOWASTE

Balancing Competence for Circularity

Matija KAJIĆ*

ABSTRACT

In the context of rethinking environmental law, the present chapter looks at which competence obstacles, if any, are hampering the circular management of valuable organic resources from biowaste (vegetable, fruit and garden (VFG) waste) in the European Union (EU). It does so by looking at the doctrinal and empirical findings from a biowaste case study in Den Haag (in its EU and Dutch national legal context), to highlight any competence issues that may be creating power gaps and blocking the achievement of a circular material cycle. This case study illustrates that the transition to a circular agri-food system should not only depend on the development of new technologies, but also on an appropriate balancing of power between private actors and different institutions, throughout the relevant materials' life cycles.

* This chapter is based on findings from the fourth and fifth chapters of the author's upcoming PhD dissertation.

1. INTRODUCTION

Present-day agricultural practices in the European Union (EU) are a strain on non-renewable resources and planetary health.[1] Nutrients, like nitrogen, phosphorus and potassium, as well as other valuable organic matter, are key ingredients in fertilisers and other agricultural products, but their overuse has created concerns around scarcity.[2] The EU legal and policy framework surrounding the circular economy encourages recovery of this valuable organic matter from several waste streams, including biowaste. However, though the biotechnological methods for this recovery exist, they are mostly not applied on a major commercial scale.

Biowaste is a good source of these valuable organic resources, because it accounts for the largest fraction – 40 per cent – of European municipal solid waste.[3] At present, only 30 per cent of biowaste across Europe is collected separately and recycled.[4] This means there is a large untapped source of valuable organic matter in our waste reserves. The EU's Waste Framework Directive (WFD) defines biowaste as biodegradable garden and park waste; food and kitchen waste from households, restaurants, caterers and retail premises; and comparable waste from food-processing plants.[5] The present chapter focuses on a part of this biowaste stream: VFG (vegetable, fruit and garden) waste. The contents of the stream are rather self-explanatory, consisting largely of food (vegetables and fruit) and various types of garden waste (grass clippings, hedge cuttings, leaves, wood, soil and stones). As with most waste streams, the EU is currently aiming to move towards more sustainable management of the biowaste stream, and VFG waste within that. The goal of policy and legislation in this area is to reduce the amount of VFG waste being landfilled, and to increase the amount being treated and re-processed into new products.[6]

The life cycle of VFG waste (after it has been discarded by consumers) can be viewed as comprising three phases: collection in the form of biowaste, treatment for recovery, and creation of new material streams (new products). Treatment of VFG waste that includes the recovery of valuable organic matter

1 C.M. Mehta et al., 'Technologies to Recover Nutrients from Waste Streams: A Critical Review', *Critical Reviews in Environmental Science and Technology*, (2015) 45(4), pp. 385 *et seq*.

2 M. de Boer et al., 'An Assessment of the Drivers and Barriers for the Deployment of Urban Phosphorus Recovery Technologies: A Case Study of The Netherlands', *Sustainability*, (2018) 10(6), pp. 1790 *et seq*.

3 European Compost Network, 'Biowaste in the Circular Economy', Workshop Report, 2017, https://cor.europa.eu/hr/events/Pages/Bio.aspx.

4 Ibid.

5 European Parliament and Council Directive 2018/851 of 30 May 2018 amending Directive 2008/98/EC on waste (Waste Framework Directive, WFD) [2018] OJ L 150/109, Art. 3(4).

6 European Commission, 'Closing the loop – An EU action plan for the Circular Economy', COM(2015) 614 final.

offers a series of benefits, through the conversion of 'waste' into a hygienic product, diversion from landfills, and the provision of valuable materials, as well as possible revenue.[7] Furthermore, such treatment helps avoid the loss of natural resources (both material and energy) that went into production, as well as helping to avoid potential environmental harm (like environmental pollution and greenhouse gas emissions), through the diversion of VFG waste from landfills.[8]

Treatment of VFG waste can result in three types of products to close the material loop. These are fertiliser products, platform chemicals (bioplastics), and bioenergy. Bioenergy is excluded from the scope of this chapter, because it is the least desirable treatment method, according to the bio-based value pyramid and the EU's waste hierarchy.[9] The easiest way to convert biomass into a product is to combust it and produce energy. While this may be the easiest example of a bio-based practice, it is not ecologically desirable or hugely profitable.[10] This is why it is placed at the bottom of the pyramid. Other more desirable practices are depicted higher up on the pyramid.[11]

Various public institutions have competence in these three phases of the life cycle, however due to the absence of a closed-loop system in this sector, it can be hypothesised that, somewhere in the life cycle of these materials, there is a power gap, resulting in valuable resources being lost. This leads us to ask whether a rebalancing of competence is required, to manage valuable organic resources from biowaste in a circular manner in the EU.

'Competence', in this context, is taken to mean 'the power to act', and the chapter will begin with a descriptive discussion on the power to act at each institutional level (EU, national and regional/local). Following this, it will look at a case study from Den Haag, to understand how competences plays out in practice.

---

7 C.R. Lohri et al., 'Treatment technologies for urban solid biowaste to create value products: a review with focus on low-and middle-income settings', *Reviews in Environmental Science and Bio/Technology*, (2017) 16(1), pp. 81 *et seq.*

8 Ibid.

9 The bio-based value pyramid is a concept from the bio-based economy, which seeks to encourage the use of the most valuable parts of biomass to create products with the greatest added value. The value pyramid approach requires optimal value utilisation, meaning that those substances or materials that can be used in high-quality products are isolated first: Centre of Biobased Economy, 'The basic principles of a biobased economy', 2018, https://maken.wikiwijs.nl/51426/Introduction_to_the_Biobased_Economy#!page-839681.

10 Ibid.

11 Ibid.; The value pyramid approach requires optimal value utilisation, meaning that those substances or materials that can be used in high-quality products are isolated first. In the case of VFG waste, for instance, the valuable materials should be reused for nutrition first (in the form of products made from fruits and vegetables, for human consumption, or as feed). The remaining components of the VFG waste (nutrients and other valuable organic matter) can then be recovered and used as chemicals and materials. Lastly, the remaining VFG biomass can be used to create biogas. This is the lowest value application in the pyramid.

All these components are brought together into a descriptive and normative methodology. First, a descriptive doctrinal methodology is applied, to describe which institutions hold competence over each of the three relevant phases, and how competences are shared. Secondly, considering that this chapter is based on the author's PhD research, an empirical component is added, on the basis of the semi-structured interviews performed for the PhD research. The results of these interviews are qualitative, and are not intended to be representative of an entire population. Instead, they provide a practical, local context to the legal findings, and illustrate some of the real-life considerations that have to be made in the transition to a circular agri-food system in which organic resources are recovered and reused.

2. COMPETENCE AT THE EU LEVEL

The core objectives of circularity, minimising waste and ensuring reuse of valuable resources come from the EU's 2015 Circular Economy Package (CE Package), which is 'a set of policy documents and legislative proposals on waste aimed at stimulating the transition towards a Circular Economy'.[12] One of the central objectives of the CE Package is to build an appropriate regulatory regime that would allow the circular economy to develop. This objective is further supplemented by the EU Green Deal,[13] and particularly the Farm to Fork Strategy.[14]

---

12 Communication from the Commission to the European Parliament, the European Council, the Council, the European Economic and Social Committee and the Committee of the Regions, 'A new Circular Economy Action Plan for a cleaner and more competitive Europe', COM/2020/98 final, 12.

13 Communication from the Commission to the European Parliament, the European Council, the Council, the European Economic and Social Committee and the Committee of the Regions, 'The European Green Deal', COM/2019/640 final, ss. 2.1.3 and 2.1.6. S. 2.1.3 states: 'A key aim of the new policy framework will be to stimulate the development of lead markets for climate neutral and circular products, in the EU and beyond.' S. 2.1.6 states: 'By shifting the focus from compliance to performance, measures such as eco-schemes should reward farmers for improved environmental and climate performance, including managing and storing carbon in the soil, and improved nutrient management to improve water quality and reduce emissions'. S. 2.1 states: 'To achieve these aims, it is essential to increase the value given to protecting and restoring natural ecosystems, to the sustainable use of resources and to improving human health'.

14 Communication from the Commission to the European Parliament, the Council, the European Economic and Social Committee and the Committee of the Regions, 'A Farm to Fork Strategy for a fair, healthy and environmentally-friendly food system', COM/2020/381 final, s. 2.3: 'The Commission will take action to scale-up and promote sustainable and socially responsible production methods and circular business models in food processing and retail, including specifically for SMEs, in synergy with the objectives and initiatives put forward under the new CEAP. The deployment of a circular and sustainable EU Bioeconomy provides business opportunities, for instance linked to making use of food waste.'

EU competence around VFG waste management (and the management of other biowaste) comes from Article 191 of the Treaty on the Functioning of the European Union (TFEU), according to which Union policy on the environment 'shall contribute, among other things, to protecting and improving the quality of the environment, protecting human health, ensuring prudent and rational utilisation of natural resources, and combating climate change'.[15] Particularly relevant for the present chapter are the words 'ensuring of prudent and rational utilisation of natural resources', as this is linked to conserving raw materials on Earth, by methods such as the recovery of materials from waste.

Union competence in waste management further derives from two key Union obligations that have been developing and deepening since the first Single European Act, in 1987.[16] These obligations are, first, balancing the requirements of market integration with those of environmental protection, and, second, the enforcement of EU environmental policy.[17] Both of these involve complex political and economic considerations, in which Union legislation typically holds a wide margin of discretion, even outside the fields of waste and environmental law.[18] The environmental objectives at the core of these Articles give the EU competence to act in each of the three phases of the VFG life cycle (collection, treatment and products), as long as the actions are proportional. On the topic of waste, it remains a contested issue whether this wide margin of discretion is warranted and valuable in resolving issues that are largely national, or even local, in nature, such as collection, treatment and use of materials recovered from waste.

Regarding subsidiarity, the TFEU's Article 5(3) justifies action at the EU level 'if the objective of the proposed action cannot be sufficiently achieved by the Member States either at central level or at regional and local level, but can rather … be better achieved at Union level'.[19] While action at the EU level

---

15 Consolidated version of the Treaty on the Functioning of the European Union [2012] OJ C 326/12 (hereinafter 'TFEU'), Art. 191.

16 F. Jacobs, 'The Role of the European Court of Justice in the Protection of the Environment', *Journal of Environmental Law*, (2006) 18(2), pp. 195 *et seq.*

17 Case C-2/90 *(Walloon Waste) Commission of the European Communities v. Kingdom of Belgium*, [1992] ECLI 310; Case C-28/09 *European Commission v. Republic of Austria*, [1992] ECLI 854; Case 302/86 *(Danish Bottles) Commission of the European Communities v. Kingdom of Denmark*, [1988] ECLI 421; Case 240/83 *(ADBHU) Procureur de la République v. Association de défense des brûleurs d'huiles usagées (ADBHU)*, [1985] ECLI 51. The *Walloon Waste* case, decided in July 1992, confirmed that waste is to be regarded as a 'good'. *Commission v. Austria* confirmed that accumulation of waste constitutes a danger to the environment. The *Danish Bottles* and *ADBHU* cases confirmed that 'the protection of the environment constitutes one of the Community's essential objectives and that it also constitutes one of the acceptable "mandatory requirements" which national authorities could rely on to restrict the entry of goods from other Member States'.

18 Jacobs, supra, note 15.

19 TFEU, supra, note 14, Art. 5(3).

is typically considered to increase efficiency, this comes at the risk of creating democratic voids and lacking broad support.[20] Subsidiarity, therefore, attempts to ensure that EU action is in line with the EU's democratic principles, and that decisions are taken as closely as possible to the citizen.[21] This gives rise to subsidiarity tensions between the assumed efficient action at the supranational EU level, and the potentially less efficient but more democratic action at the national and regional levels.[22] This was underlined in a 2014 reasoned opinion on the WFD from Austria, which made the argument that the EU should focus on helping Member States comply with existing substantive norms, rather than continually developing new ones.[23]

As with most waste streams, this tension is present around the topic of VFG waste collection and reprocessing. The EU is building pressure for more circular waste collection and treatment. For example, Article 11(1) of the WFD sets the requirements for EU Member States to promote high-quality recycling through their waste collection systems. Article 11(2)(c) makes this more concrete, by setting a target for a 55 per cent increase in recycling and preparation for reuse of municipal waste, by 2025.

Alongside Article 11, the revisions of Article 22 call for Member States to implement a system whereby biowaste is either separately collected or recycled at its source, by 31 December 2023,[24] as well as calling upon the Commission to 'carry out an assessment on the management of bio-waste', and to set 'minimum requirements for bio-waste management and quality criteria for compost and digestate'.[25] When it comes to the enforcement of these new requirements, there are EU-wide standards on inspection and reporting. The inspection standards are outlined in Article 34 of the WFD, with Article 34(2) in particular requiring that inspections concerning collection and transport operations cover the origin, nature, quantity and destination of the waste collected and transported. Article 35 further requires waste holders at various stages of the waste treatment chain (transporters, dealers and brokers) to track

---

20 I. Wanzenböck and K. Frenken, 'The subsidiarity principle in innovation policy for societal challenges', *Global Transitions*, (2020) 2, pp. 55 *et seq.*

21 Consolidated Version of the Treaty on European Union [2008] OJ C115/13 (hereinafter 'TEU'), Art. 10(3); PP Craig, 'Subsidiarity, a Political and Legal Analysis', *Journal of Common Market Studies* (2012) 50, pp. 72–87 *et seq.*

22 TEU, supra, note 20, Art. 10(3); O. Pimenova, 'Subsidiarity as a "regulation principle" in the EU', *Theory and Practice of Legislation* (2016) 4(3), pp. 381–398.

23 C. Jackson and E. Watkins, 'EU waste law: the challenge of better compliance', *Institute for European Environmental Policy*, May 2021, https://ieep.eu/publications/eu-waste-law-the-challenge-of-better-compliance/, pp. 3 *et seq.*

24 European Parliament and Council Directive 2018/851 of 30 May 2018 amending Directive 2008/98/EC on waste [2018] OJ L150/109, Art. 22.

25 Ibid.; European Commission, 'Accompanying document to the Communication from the Commission on future steps in biowaste management in the European Union', SEC(2010) 577 final, pp. 17 *et seq.*

and report a series of waste characteristics (the quantity, nature and origin of that waste; the quantity of products and materials resulting from preparing for reuse, recycling or other recovery operations; frequency of collection; treatment method foreseen in respect of the waste, etc.). In addition to inspection, Member States have various reporting obligations concerning the implementation of waste legislation, with the two main ones being: (1) reporting on targets; and (2) submitting implementation reports.[26]

Article 16 of the WFD requires Member States to have an integrated and adequate network of waste disposal and recovery installations for the recovery of mixed municipal waste collected from private households, but Article 16(4) clarifies that this does not mean that each Member State has to possess the full range of final recovery facilities within its borders. Such a requirement does not exist for the VFG waste stream, even in Article 22, which specifically deals with biowaste.

Articles 23 to 26 of the WFD set out the basic framework for permits and registration, including what ought to be contained in a permit, and the responsibilities of national competent authorities in relation to the issuing, exemptions from, and extension of, permits. Article 27 promises that the Commission shall adopt delegated Acts supplementing the WFD, by setting out technical minimum standards for treatment activities (including for the recycling of waste that requires a permit), but no such delegated Acts have so far been adopted. What have been published and assessed by the Commission are the waste management plans that Member States are required (by Article 28 WFD) to submit to the Commission. The plans, which are to be evaluated and reviewed by the Member States at least every six years, ought to reflect on the types of waste collected on national territory, existing disposal and recovery installations, measures attained, and general waste management policies (national and local), and can also discuss organisation aspects, instruments and programmes for waste prevention, and public awareness campaigns. When it comes to reporting and enforcement, the WFD refers only to required inspections, reporting, record-keeping, enforcement, and penalties for uncontrolled management of waste as they relate to waste collectors and transporters. There is no mention of enforcement requirements for reprocessing installations that actually treat waste. Despite this, it can be seen that waste and resource management in this area certainly includes EU action and facilitation.

As with most environmental protection matters, this involvement of the EU level is legitimised by the transboundary effects of environmental overuse and resource conservation.[27] However, it can also be seen that implementation

26 European Commission, 'Reporting on implementation of waste legislation', *EC Website*, 2020, https://ec.europa.eu/environment/waste/reporting/index.htm.

27 Jacobs, supra, note 15.

of EU waste legislation at the Member State level has remained patchy.[28] Additionally, some possible community actions, like the creation of a 'supra-waste inspection authority', have been unpopular with Member States.[29] Both of these factors confirm a lack of wide support for Union action in this area.

This second tension present at the EU level relates to proportionality.[30] The Member States have committed themselves to a series of complex and unfamiliar objectives in the transition to a circular economy, as part of a commitment to overall environmental conservation. According to former Advocate General Francis Jacobs, 'whether a measure is proportionate to achieve a certain objective, environmental or other, depends, first and foremost, on the standard set by the objective to be achieved'.[31] Large overarching environmental goals allow for even drastic measures to seem potentially proportional. Following this logic, it can be argued that the circularity commitments involve a high level of protection, and thereby imply a readiness to accept more restrictive measures, including new targets and requirements, potentially before old ones have been fully achieved. Especially considering the widening bounds of proportionality in rulings of the European Court of Justice (ECJ), in relation to measures that protect the environment, it is unsurprising that this is an area in which Member States feel uncomfortable allowing a further stretching of subsidiarity and proportionality.[32] The balancing act between these subsidiarity and proportionality tensions remains a point of contention as the circular economy transition proceeds.

While the setting of new, stricter substantive requirements, under the justification of environmental protection, can be proportional and respectful of subsidiarity, this does not mean that the Union could not do more to emphasise and encourage solutions at the national or subnational levels.

---

28 Total waste generation is increasing (and varies extremely between Member States). Additionally, the treatment methods used vary (making it difficult to track whether targets are being met); Jackson and Watkins, supra, note 22.

29 Jackson and Watkins, supra, note 22.

30 T. van den Brink, 'Proportionality Beyond the Constitution: The Impact of the Principle on EU Digitalization Legislation' in U. Bernitz, X. Groussot, J. Paju and S. A. de Vries (eds.), *General Principles of EU Law and the EU Digital Order*, Wolters Kluwer, 2019, p. 103.

31 Jacobs, supra, note 15.

32 It is somewhat clear from the ECJ case law that the bounds of proportionality can be stretched for the purposes of an objective like the environment. This claim is supported by cases like the *ADBHU* case from 1985, the *Danish Bottles* case from 1988 (both supra, note 16), and the more recent 2001 case *PreussenElektra* (Case C-379/98 (PreussenElektra) *PreussenElektra AG v. Schhleswag AG* [2001] ECLI 160). In both *ADBHU* and *Danish Bottles*, the Court confirmed that the protection of the environment constitutes one of the EU's essential objectives, and also constitutes one of the acceptable mandatory requirements which national authorities can rely on to restrict the entry of goods from other Member States. Meanwhile, in *PreussenElektra*, the ECJ confirmed that a measure that essentially imposed a 'buy local' obligation on German electricity consumers was not a measure having equivalent effect to a quantitative restriction. No analysis of whether the provision respected proportionality was applied.

3. COMPETENCE AT THE DUTCH NATIONAL AND REGIONAL LEVEL

In the Netherlands, the EU's WFD is transposed into domestic law mainly by the Environmental Management Act (Wet Milieubeheer or Wm, 1979).[33] Chapter 10 of the Wm deals with waste substances, with Article 10.21(2) calling specifically for the separate collection of various waste streams, including biowaste. This puts Dutch national law in compliance with the WFD, but there are some deviations specific to Articles 11 and 22 of the WFD. For instance, in the WFD, Article 11(1) states that, 'by 2015 separate collection shall be set up for at least the following: paper, metal, plastic and glass', but this has not been transposed into Dutch national legislation. In the Netherlands, specific rules governing collection are laid down in provincial and municipal by-laws, rather than in national frameworks.[34] As such, instead of direct transposition, the Netherlands ensures that these requirements are met through framework contracts between municipalities, industry and the government.[35]

In addition to the Wm, any work relating to waste streams, including VFG waste, starts with the National Waste Management Plan (the LAP), which is the policy framework for waste in the circular economy. The most recent version is the LAP3, from 2017. The general policy framework in the LAP is further elaborated by the various sector plans for specific waste streams. Sector plan 6 discusses '[s]eparately collected/delivered vegetable, fruit and garden waste from households (kitchen and garden waste)'.

3.1. COLLECTION

The Netherlands is pushing to be a step ahead of the EU when it comes to separation of waste for collection, having set the national target for separately collected waste at 75 per cent by 2020, including a reduction in how much residual waste every inhabitant is permitted per year (100 kilogrammes). These requirements are outlined in the Dutch government's 'Household Waste Implementation Program' (VANG 2019–2023).[36]

Certain intricate topics, like the living environment (and waste therein), are mentioned broadly in provincial by-laws (Provinciale Omgevingsverordening), and then implemented more concretely through municipal waste policies and

---

33 European Commission, 'National factsheet on separate collection: Netherlands', https://www.municipalwasteeurope.eu/sites/default/files/NL%20National%20factsheet.pdf.

34 Ibid.

35 Ibid.

36 The Dutch Ministry of Infrastructure and Water Management, *Circular Economy Implementation Programme 2019–2023*, https://hollandcircularhotspot.nl/wp-content/uploads/2019/09/Circular-Economy-Implementation-Programme-2019–2023.pdf.

waste collection plans. The provincial by-laws are intended to be a bit more distant from content-based topics like separate collection, instead dealing with broader, safety-related waste issues. This means that most of the substance-oriented work regarding VFG waste collection is left to municipalities. An example of how VFG waste collection is addressed at the municipal level is discussed later in this chapter, in the case study of Den Haag.

3.2. TREATMENT FOR RECOVERY

In the Dutch legislative landscape, the legislation and policies most relevant to reprocessing installations are the LAP3, the Environmental Management Act (Wet milieubeheer, or Wm) and the General Provisions Environmental Law Act (Wet algemene bepalingen omgevingsrecht, or Wabo).[37] The Wm is relevant because it is the implementing legislation for the European WFD. Specifically regarding new installations, the Wm sets the environmental protection requirements, and places limitations on the environmental consequences of installations, like noise, light and odours.

When it comes to permits, Dutch law is in compliance with the WFD's requirements.[38] Previous reports on this topic have identified that a major concern in the Dutch reprocessing system is that, 'when striving to contribute to circularity, it is possible that risks are [being] underestimated, or that not all aspects of the processing are [being] properly analysed'.[39] As such, it is up to the competent authority to make a proper assessment before granting a permit for a waste treatment installation. Which authority has the competence to grant a permit is dependent on the types of activities that are to be carried out at the installation, and this is not regulated in the Wm, but in the Wabo. According to Article 2 of the Wabo, the permit requirement applies to all projects that consist wholly or partly of founding, changing or altering a facility's operation.[40] Most waste reprocessing operations, therefore, require an environmental permit *(omgevingsvergunning)*. Regarding the competent authority, the basic rule is that the competent authority is the municipality *(burgemeester en wethouders)*,[41] however the province can be the competent authority in relation to projects deemed to be 'of provincial importance', whereas the environment minister has competence on projects deemed to be of 'national importance'.[42]

---

37 Dutch Implementing Decree No. 645 of 2005 implementing provisions of the Fertilizing Substances Act (Uitvoeringsbesluit Meststoffenwet).

38 Dutch Environmental Management Act 1993 (Wet milieubeheer), Art. 13.2 11.

39 I. Bisschops et al., *Kleinschalige verwekingsmethoden voor gft en swill*, LeAF Report, 2020, p. iii.

40 Dutch General Provisions Act, 2023 (Wet algemene bepalingen omgevingsrecht), Art. 2.1(e).

41 Ibid., Art. 2.4(1).

42 Ibid., Art. 2.4(2, 4).

These requirements from the Wabo are implemented by the Environmental Law Decree (Besluit omgevingsrecht), which specifies exactly which installation activities the environmental permits apply to. Annex 1 (Part A) of this Environmental Law Decree indicates that establishments that work with biomass require an environmental permit, and that the competent authority is not the municipality.[43] The general methods are listed in Annex I, Part C of this Decree, but the more specific treatment methods are mentioned in the EU Industrial Emissions Directive (IED).

If a treatment method or installation is mentioned in the IED, then the competent authority is the province and not the municipality, while if it is not mentioned, then the competent authority is the municipality.[44] Recovery installations for both biological treatments and physicochemical treatments of non-hazardous waste are mentioned in the IED (provided that the installations exceed a capacity of 75 tonnes per day), meaning that the province is the competent authority for these installations.[45] Composting and anaerobic digestion installations definitely meet this capacity, as the Netherlands treats a total of around 1,763,000 tonnes of VFG waste per year, with even the smallest installations treating more than 29,523 tonnes per year (around 80 tonnes per day).[46] Most installations treat much more.

In addition to the permit requirements relating to the provincial authorities, there are also requirements for treatment at the national level. A concern with EU regulations in this area is that EU reuse and recycling targets do not distinguish between various recovery processes, meaning that resource-efficient and environmentally safe recovery does not have to be given priority. For Member States wanting to ensure that treatment is as environmentally friendly and circular as possible, standards more relevant to these types of goals have to be implemented at the national level. In the Netherlands, an example of these types of standards can be found in the 'minimum standard for processing' set out in the LAP3.[47] These requirements set the minimum required quality of reprocessing for each respective waste stream, and exist to prevent waste reprocessing at a lower than desirable level, in accordance with the EU's waste hierarchy. For instance, if the minimum standard for a waste stream is recycling, then that waste stream cannot be incinerated. For the VFG waste stream, the

---

43 Dutch Environmental Law Decree (Besluit omgevingsrecht), Annex 1 (Part A and C).

44 European Parliament and Council Directive 2010/75/EU of the 24 November 2010 on industrial emissions (integrated pollution prevention and control), OJ L 334.

45 European Parliament and Council Directive 2010/75/EU of the 24 November 2010 on industrial emissions (integrated pollution prevention and control), OJ L 334, Annex I, Clause 5 'Waste Management'.

46 Rijkwaterstaat, 'Afval monitor' 2023, https://afvalmonitor.databank.nl/jive/.

47 Dutch National Waste Management Plan (LAP3), 'Sectorplan 06; Gescheiden ingezameld/afgegeven groente-, fruit- en tuinafval van huishoudens', p. 1, Art. II.

same minimum standard applies to both separately collected VFG waste from households, and such waste from industry. The minimum standards are composting, with the aim of recycling, or fermentation, using the biogas formed as fuel.[48]

3.3. PRODUCTS RECOVERED FROM VFG WASTE TREATMENT

At the Dutch national level, most attention is geared towards the treatment of VFG waste for recovery of products to be used in agricultural applications (mainly as compost to be used as fertiliser). In fact, the reprocessing of VFG waste (and swill) into compost is currently the only legally permitted reprocessing method, against which any other proposed methods are compared.[49] Stable compost is currently the only product from the VFG waste stream that may be applied to the soil as fertiliser, and stable compost can only be achieved with a sufficiently long processing time that allows the compost to reach a sufficiently high temperature.

Although a legal framework has been developed for only a limited number of recovered products, the present review of competences demonstrates that each relevant part of the life cycle is accounted for at the national level. This means that, in theory, the desired materials should be making a full feedback loop to recovery and reuse.

4. COMPETENCE AT THE MUNICIPAL LEVEL

As explained above, topics like waste are mentioned broadly in provincial by-laws, but are regulated and implemented in more detail through municipal waste policies and waste collection plans. Considering that so much responsibility for VFG waste collection rests with municipalities, it is useful to look into how they approach collection. The present chapter takes the Dutch municipality of Den Haag as a case study. Den Haag is the provincial capital of the province of South Holland. It is definitely a relevant urban waste management case study, as Den Haag is the third-largest city in the Netherlands, with a population of over half a million citizens, and a population density of $6{,}644/km^2$.[50]

Dutch municipalities each draw up a plan for how to approach waste collection (including VFG waste collection), and often also a supporting policy.

---

48 Ibid, p. 1.

49 Dutch Environmental Management Act 1993, supra, note 37.

50 CityPopulation, 'Netherlands: Administrative Division', https://www.citypopulation.de/en/netherlands/admin/.

In Den Haag, the 'Waste policy in the municipality of Den Haag' was drawn up in 2008.[51] This plan is still in force, and it puts organic waste and VFG waste centre stage. The policy was used as a basis for the 'Household Collection Plan' for the period from 2016 to 2020, which focused explicitly on separate collection.[52] Although 2020 has passed, this is still the plan used by Den Haag to guide its waste collection plans, and is continually referenced, even in newer policy documents like 'Program for a Clean City 2021–2022'.[53]

Den Haag faces many challenges when it comes to VFG waste collection because it is densely populated, with many high-rise buildings (which are known to cause collection issues in separate collection systems). To deal with these challenges, the municipality does implement many of the common policy measures used to improve collection (access to information for citizens, door-to-door collection, conveniently located waste drop-off points, etc.), to encourage separate waste collection.

Even though policy documents and EU legislation both place an emphasis on source-separated waste, this is becoming less of a practice across Dutch municipalities, including Den Haag. Since citizens were not effectively separating their waste into streams, many municipalities (for example, Amsterdam, Utrecht and Den Haag) have started to move away from source separation, and have begun sending their waste to be separated by machines at the facilities of various processing businesses.[54] Many municipalities are now moving to this method, to ensure a higher quality of collected waste, leading to better opportunities for recovery, and higher-quality recovered material streams. It seems this does not come into conflict with the requirements of Article 22 of the WFD, because the biowaste is still being separated; it is just not being collected separately.[55]

When it comes to treatment of VFG waste, it is mainly the regional and national authorities that have competence, meaning that municipalities like Den Haag have less influence on this part of the life cycle. This makes sense,

---

51 Haags Milieucentrum, *Afvalbeleid in de gemeente Den Haag*, 2008, https://denhaag.raadsinformatie.nl/document/3352490/1/RIS160008a.

52 Den Haag Council, *Afval scheiden, gewoon apart! – Huishoudelijk Afvalplan Den Haag 2016–2020*, https://denhaag.raadsinformatie.nl/document/3338658/1/RIS288629_bijlage%20Afval%20scheiden,%20gewoon%20apart%20-%20Huishoudelijk%20Afvalplan%20Den%20Haag%202016–2020.

53 Den Haag Council, *Programma voor een Schone stad, Den Haag 2021–2022*, https://denhaag.raadsinformatie.nl/document/9527083/1/RIS307053_Bijlage.

54 Den Haag Council, *Grondstoffenplan Den Haag*, 2021, https://denhaag.raadsinformatie.nl/document/10656926/1/RIS310285_Bijlage_Grondstoffenplan_gewijzigde_versie_12-10; Den Haag Council, *Circulair Den Haag*, 2018, https://denhaag.raadsinformatie.nl/document/6291317/1/RIS299353_Bijlage_1.

55 European Parliament and Council Directive 2018/851 of 30 May 2018 amending Directive 2008/98/EC on waste [2018] OJ L150/109, Art. 22.

considering that the waste treated in these installations does not come from only one municipality.

An area relevant to the valuable raw materials contained within VFG waste, and in which municipalities do have some influence, is resource conservation. Municipalities in the Netherlands draw up resource management plans, with which they influence how the resources belonging to the city will be used. This includes the valuable raw organic materials contained within waste streams like VFG waste. Den Haag is quite progressive in this area, and the municipality has committed itself to keeping valuable resources within the city as much as possible, so that they can be reprocessed into new products by local entrepreneurs.[56] In this way, cities attempt to control how resources are used, in the hope of closing feedback loops and creating circularity.

However, the extent to which this is effective, in practice, has been brought into question by the empirical interviews performed in the course of the present author's research. An interview with an expert from the municipal authorities in Den Haag revealed that the current collection and treatment practices lead to much of the power over these resources ending up with waste processing companies, at the very end of this material life cycle.[57] Since Dutch municipalities are slowly moving away from source-separated collection, waste processing companies are doing the bulk of separating waste into streams. Through this, the competence – the power to act – is handed over to private actors, who may not share the same circularity objectives as the institutional actors that preceded them in the life cycle. Once waste processing companies become holders of the waste, it is up to them how the materials are treated, and where the treated material streams end up. Although this could be solved simply through legal obligations, the development of such obligations is often slow, especially in parts of the sector where such novel treatment methods are being applied. There is significant pushback to such obligations in new, innovative markets, such as those of materials recovered from VFG waste.[58]

The situation described above represents a power gap in the material life cycle. Although Dutch municipalities are tasked with drafting and implementing resource management plans and waste plans, they have little control (under the current system) over the resources created from their city's waste. The municipal authorities in Den Haag have proposed a solution to this loss of control over resources, via green public procurement contracts.[59] This would entail maintaining some degree of control over the recovered materials, by including clauses in contracts with processing businesses that require them

56 Ibid.

57 Interview with expert from the municipality in Den Haag (Netherlands, 11 May 2022).

58 Interview with expert from a bio-based plastics producer (Netherlands, 17 November 2022).

59 Supra, note 57.

to, for example, cycle a certain percentage of the recovered materials back into the city from which the waste originated.[60] As such, cities would have greater control over the feedback loops at the end of the material life cycle, abide by circularity objectives, and cycle the valuable materials back into municipal entrepreneurial ventures.

Literature on this topic indicates that there are opportunities to include green and circular objectives in the public procurement process, but there are considerations that have to be made before embracing this as a solution, including a weighing of competing objectives.[61] The requirements calling for materials to be treated in a specific way, or for certain percentages to be returned to the city, could be included either as contractual conditions, or as award criteria in an open tender. In both instances, adding such a clause can be beneficial, because it becomes a requirement that must be fulfilled. Be they contractual conditions, or award criteria in relation to a tender, from a public procurement perspective it is essential that the minimum competitive procedural requirements (equality, transparency, non-discrimination and proportionality) are met.

In the case of an award criterion (or criteria), there is the added benefit of businesses competing for the contract. Interviews with experts at the EU, national and local levels have indicated that this could improve the possible results (for example, because companies will push themselves to demonstrate that they can treat larger quantities of waste, and provide higher-quality material streams),[62] as well as increasing the likelihood that companies will work together, combine know-how, and apply collaboratively in response to invitations to tender (to increase their chances of getting the contracts).

When it comes to competing objectives, an array of issues can arise. For example, if the principle of non-discrimination is followed in a tendering process, the call must be open to companies across the whole of the EU (not just Dutch companies, or companies in the vicinity of Den Haag). Although this would meet the EU free-market objective of non-discrimination, it would run counter to the circular economy and waste management objectives of treating and processing waste as close as possible to its source. This would further add to the complicated balancing of objectives that takes place in the process of transitioning to a circular economy, and lead to potentially fragmented solutions across different municipalities and Member States.

---

60 Ibid.

61 S.D. Sönnichsen and J. Clement, 'Review of Green and Sustainable Public Procurement: Towards Circular Public Procurement', *Journal of Cleaner Production*, (2020) 245, pp. 2 *et seq.*

62 Supra, note 57 and 58; Interview with an expert from the Ministry of Infrastructure and Water Management (Netherlands, 23 January 2022); Interview with an expert from the European Phosphorus Network (Netherlands, 9 February 2023).

5. CONCLUSION

The case study from Den Haag demonstrates a bottom-up drive for change on competence balancing relevant to the circular management of valuable organic resources. It shows that this is an area in which local governments and businesses have begun to require solutions, and possibly an area in which more local governments will be seeking solutions in the future (as recycling targets, and targets to minimise landfilling, continue to increase at the EU and national levels). In the absence of a top-down, unified approach to resource management at the end of the material cycle, a fragmented landscape of solutions at the municipal level will continue to develop.

From a legislative perspective, it can be seen that competence is clearly defined in two phases of the materials' life cycle (collection and treatment), but not clearly defined at the very end of the cycle, when it comes to actually creating a circular system and looping the materials back into markets – into a circular economy. The present division of competences has created a public/private gap in the final phase of the materials' cycle. The law places the power to act in this area with municipalities and regional governments: municipalities have the power to draft policies around waste collection and resource management, and regional governments are largely the competent authorities when it comes to permits for, and control of, treatment plants and processing facilities. Despite this, in practice, control of the resources, and the power to act, in the final stages of the cycle, currently lie with the private sector – with the processing businesses.

This points to a need to rebalance competence in this last phase of the cycle, to ensure that valuable organic resources from biowaste are treated in a circular manner, in line with the overarching circularity objectives outlined at the EU level. The proportionality and subsidiarity assessment in section 2 of this chapter illustrated that Union action is possible in this area, and could increase efficiency in reaching the relevant circularity objectives. However, it also illustrated that this is not necessarily a preferred route, because of the resistance Member States have shown to further Union action on such a locally specific issue. As such, this barrier to circularity requires a careful balancing of competence. On the one hand, it is not necessarily desirable for a fragmented landscape to continue developing at the municipal level, with diverse municipal actions on a broad, Union-wide objective; on the other hand, Member States have shown resistance to an overextension of Union competences in this area.

This leaves us with the Member States' national level. We have seen how some Member States (like the Netherlands) do go beyond EU law, to meet environmental and circularity objectives. An example of this can be found in the Dutch minimum treatment standards in the LAP3, which turn a waste hierarchy recommendation into a requirement. This could be extended to VFG waste, as from the perspective of institutional power it seems that national authorities are best placed to provide guiding standards in this area, by harmonising some of the fragmented solutions currently on the table, for example through the adoption of public procurement legislation or the strengthening of legal requirements for public actors in this sector. At the EU level, this type of national drive to meet the circularity objectives could be supported and further facilitated, not necessarily through more legislation, but rather through topic-specific guiding opinion documents for Member State and local actions in this area. In this way, the EU could help Member States comply with existing substantive targets and circularity objectives.[63]

[63] Jackson and Watkins, supra, note 22, pp. 3 *et seq.*

PART II

CONFLICTS AND FRICTIONS

THE RELATIONSHIP BETWEEN THE LEGAL SYSTEM AND TECHNOLOGICAL INNOVATIONS IN FRESHWATER MANAGEMENT

Understanding Potential Points of Friction

Sophie MELCHERS*

ABSTRACT

Freshwater management is becoming increasingly complex, with climate change having profound effects on our water system. Legal developments, such as climate adaptation and circular economy measures, at the international,

* This research was performed within the framework of the research program AquaConnect, funded by the Dutch Research Council (NWO, grant-ID P19-45) and public and private partners of the AquaConnect consortium and coordinated by Wageningen University and Research.

European and national levels, aim to create and maintain a livable world. At the same time, technological innovations aim to optimise our freshwater use, to ensure that the right quantity and quality of water is available at the right times and places. The relationship between the legal system and technological innovations in the field of freshwater management will be clarified with practical and legal examples, particularly with reference to the 2020 European Union (EU) Regulation on minimum requirements for water reuse. By understanding this relationship and the potential points of friction, this contribution shows that technological innovations need the legal system, and that the legal system manages to balance technological innovation and other interests well. The legal system helps to manage uncertainty around innovation, helps to balance an array of interests, and clarifies certain responsibilities. The flexibility the legal system provides should, however, be used to implement and maintain technological innovations, in order to facilitate the climate adaptation and circular economy goals.

1. INTRODUCTION

In response to climate change, a plethora of theories, concepts and strategies have emerged. Some deal with climate change head-on, others deal with reducing risks from the realities of climate change. Climate change mitigation is the umbrella term for any action that deals with tackling climate change head-on, and, notably, actions which lower greenhouse gas emissions. One such strategy is the circular economy. A circular economy would see a stark decrease in greenhouse gas emissions, and a decrease in dependence on resources such as water.[1] The need to face the risks associated with climate change – floods and droughts, to name just two – has also given rise to scholarship on climate adaptation. In short, climate adaptation strategies seek to adjust society to climate change, in order to reduce harm.[2] Ideas on the circular economy and climate adaptation have made their way into concrete European Union (EU) goals: decoupling economic growth from resource use,[3] and climate resilience by 2050,[4] respectively. This chapter deals primarily with the circular economy and climate adaptation.

---

1 European Commission, 'A new Circular Economy Action Plan: For a cleaner and more competitive Europe' (Communication), COM(2020) 98 final (2020) (hereinafter 'EU Circular Economy Action Plan'), p. 4.

2 Intergovernmental Panel on Climate Change, 'Annex I: Glossary', in Masson-Delmotte et al. (eds), *Global Warming of 1.5°C – An IPCC Special Report* (Cambridge University Press 2018), under 'adaptation'.

3 These are two of the key goals of the European Green Deal: see European Commission, 'The European Green Deal' (Communication), COM(2019) 640 final (2019).

4 See European Commission, 'Forging a climate-resilient Europe: The new EU Strategy on Adaptation to Climate Change' (Communication), COM(2021) 82 final (2021) (hereinafter the 'EU Strategy').

The relatively broad climate adaptation and circular economy goals have been concretised into separate policies in different domains. One such domain is freshwater management. Freshwater management has a strong presence in EU climate adaptation policies, as the EU has noted that both nature-based solutions and technological innovations are necessary in various areas of freshwater management, including agriculture and drinking water production.[5] Similarly, freshwater management is part of the EU's circular economy policies, especially in the domain of water reuse to reduce the reliance on natural water sources for economic production.[6] Water reuse is, in a way, the circular economy applied to freshwater management; instead of a 'take-make-use' approach, water reuse allows freshwater of different qualities to be reused for different purposes, at different times and places.[7]

To meet water-related climate adaptation and circularity goals, technological innovation will be necessary. For example, it will be necessary to construct a landscape resilient to both floods and droughts (climate adaptation), and to create infrastructure capable of advanced water reuse (circular economy). Most technological innovations central to freshwater management are somewhat different to most of those central to the larger law and technology discourse. The latter focus mostly on emerging, often digital, technologies, such as information and communication technologies, nanotechnologies, robotics, and surveillance technologies.[8] Technological innovations in freshwater management are often physical, build on existing technologies rather than disruptive technologies, and involving changes to the physical landscape. These include wastewater treatment technologies, detailed real-time mapping of surface water and groundwater, and brine, concentrate and sludge management technologies, including reuse. Unlike the above-mentioned classic law-and-technology technologies, most freshwater technologies do not have an intangible and immediate widespread, or Internet-based, effect.[9]

Technological innovations in freshwater management are situated within a vast legislative and regulatory system.[10] Technological innovations for

---

5 Ibid, pp. 16–17.

6 EU Circular Economy Action Plan, supra, note 1, p. 15; Council Directive 2000/60/EC of 23 October 2000 establishing a framework for Community action in the field of water policy, [2000] OJ L 327/1, Annex VI, Part B, (x); Council Directive 91/271/EEC of 21 May 1991 concerning urban waste water treatment, [1991] OJ L135/40, Art. 12(1).

7 P. Morseletto, C.E. Mooren and S. Munaretto, 'Circular Economy of Water: Definition, Strategies and Challenges', (2022) 2 *Circular Economy and Sustainability*, pp. 1463, 1463–1464.

8 G.E. Marchant, 'The Growing Gap between Emerging Technologies and the Law' in G.E. Marchant, B.R. Allenby and J.R. Herkert (eds.), *The Growing Gap Between Emerging Technologies and Legal-Ethical Oversight: The Pacing Problem*, Springer, 2011, p. 19.

9 Geoengineering technologies are a different species of innovation altogether, see, e.g. H. Du, *An International Legal Framework for Geoengineering*, Routledge, 2018, pp. 7–20.

10 C. Termeer et al., 'The regional governance of climate adaptation: A framework for developing legitimate, effective, and resilient governance arrangements', (2011) 2 *Climate Law*, p. 159.

freshwater-related climate adaptation and the circular economy cannot be fully examined without also examining the legal system at hand,[11] be it national, regional or international.[12] The introduction of technological innovations into a given legal system highlights two main functions of the legal system. First, the legal system must enable and incentivise innovation, to meet the policy goals of climate adaptation and the circular economy. This can be done with market-based approaches, such as environmental taxes on business.[13] Such taxes, on water-related activities, like wastewater production and subsequent pollution of public waters, have shown positive effects on the reduction of such polluting activities.[14] The legal system can also use legal instruments, such as applying liability law, which could deter certain behaviour deemed harmful for the environment, and could provide redress where harm is nonetheless done.[15] Market-based approaches and the liability regime alone have shown to be unsuccessful in spurring along the necessary technological innovations for climate adaptation and circular economy goals; strict and ambitious environmental targets are often necessary.[16] Second, the legal system must manage the uncertainties that come with technological innovations, safeguard other rights and interests, and point out which party is responsible for damages, in the event that innovations cause damage.

The legal system, with these incentivising and safeguarding functions, can be a source of friction when technological innovations are introduced.[17] The question of the points of friction between advancing technological innovations and protecting other interests has attracted considerable academic attention in many fields, including the vast body of literature on the precautionary principle.[18] However, with the consequences of climate change becoming ever clearer, and with the deadlines for climate adaptation and circular economy policy goals rapidly approaching, the relation between technologies in freshwater management and the legal system must be thoroughly examined. This chapter makes a first attempt at understanding the relationship and points of intersection between technologies in freshwater management and the legal system. To do so, elements from the extensive body of literature on law and technology, water

11 Ibid.

12 T. de Gier, J. Gupta, and M. van Rijswick, *State of the art on the Legal and Policy Literature on Adaptation to Climate Change: Towards a research agenda*, Knowledge for Climate, 2009.

13 M.G. Faure and R.A. Partain, *Environmental Law and Economics: Theory and Practice*, Cambridge University Press, 2019, pp. 132–138.

14 Ibid.

15 G.T. Schwartz, 'Mixed Theories of Tort Law: Affirming Both Deterrence and Corrective Justice', (1997) 75 *Texas Law Review*, p. 1801.

16 J. Verschuuren, 'Innovatie en milieuregelgeving', (2015) 42 *Milieu en Recht*, pp. 596, 599–600.

17 E.R. de Jong, 'Een kroniek van ontwikkelingen op het snijvlak van aansprakelijkheid en innovatie op drie niveaus' (2020), 7 *Nederlands Tijdschrift voor Burgerlijk Recht*, pp. 202, 203.

18 See, for examples in environmental law, Verschuuren, supra, note 16; Faure and Partain, supra, note 13. There also exist also entire bodies of such literature in other academic disciplines, such as intellectual property law or digital technology regulation.

governance, and climate adaptation and circularity laws and policies, will be analysed and combined to create new insights.

Throughout this chapter, EU Regulation 2020/741 on minimum requirements for water reuse (the 'EU Water Reuse Regulation'), and occasional Dutch examples of freshwater innovations, will be used illustratively. In the Netherlands, the centuries-long quest to deal with water surplus is now complemented by a need to deal with water shortages. These developments will require technological innovations, and a refreshed outlook on the role of the legal system in incentivising these technological innovations while safeguarding other interests.

2. CLIMATE ADAPTATION AND CIRCULAR ECONOMY GOALS NEED LAWS AND POLICIES

Laws and specific policies must be created in order to meet broader policy goals, such as those in the EU Green Deal, and particularly climate adaptation and the circular economy.[19] This section first briefly outlines how climate adaptation and circular economy goals in relation to freshwater management are formulated under EU law and policy, with an emphasis on the EU Green Deal and its strategies. These two strands of policy have inspired many technological innovations, as well as legal change at the EU and national levels. A better understanding of these policy goals will allow us to better understand the relationship between technological innovations in freshwater management and the legal system, later in this chapter.

2.1. CLIMATE ADAPTATION UNDER THE EU GREEN DEAL

The most recent definition of climate adaptation, by the Intergovernmental Panel on Climate Change (IPCC), the leading research body on climate change, is as follows:

> Adjustment in natural or human systems in response to actual or expected climatic *stimuli* or their effects, which moderates harm or exploits beneficial opportunities.[20]

Climate adaptation is emphasised in the main text of the Green Deal as follows:

> The Commission will adopt a new, more ambitious EU strategy on adaptation to climate change. This is essential, as climate change will continue to create significant

[19] These goals can be as broad as the United Nations Sustainable Development Goals, or as specific as those laid out in the previously mentioned EU Water Reuse Regulation.

[20] Supra, note 2.

> stress in Europe in spite of the mitigation efforts. Strengthening the efforts on climate-proofing, resilience building, prevention and preparedness is crucial. Work on climate adaptation should continue to influence public and private investments, including on nature-based solutions. It will be important to ensure that across the EU, investors, insurers, businesses, cities and citizens are able to access data and to develop instruments to integrate climate change into their risk management practices.[21]

In other words, the EU acknowledges climate adaptation as a strategy, alongside climate mitigation measures. Moreover, under the 2021 EU Climate Law, both the Commission and the Member States are obligated to create climate adaptation strategies.[22] Climate adaptation was further expanded in the 2021 EU Strategy on Adaptation to Climate Change (the 'EU Strategy').[23] Particularly notable in this strategy is the emphasis on so-called 'no-regret measures', which are those measures worth pursuing regardless of the exact climatic changes. These measures promote action when uncertainty about the exact consequences of climate change could otherwise stifle any action.[24] Nature-based solutions are mentioned in the EU Strategy as such no-regret measures.[25]

Besides no-regret measures, the topic of uncertainty – which will be revisited in section 4.1. below – is dealt with throughout the EU Strategy. The document urges further development of our understanding of climate adaptation, to foster knowledge exchange between scientists and policymakers, and to improve the collection and sharing of data on climate-related risks and losses.[26] These strategies, however, deal only with reducing uncertainty by increasing knowledge. Other than encouraging no-regret measures, the EU Strategy does not give guidance on how to move forward against a background of uncertainty; in other, more technical, words, the EU emphasises reducing epistemic uncertainty, but the EU Strategy does not deal with uncertainty stemming from unpredictability or multiple knowledge frames, i.e. multiple understandings of how to manage the issue at hand.[27]

Freshwater management in relation to extreme weather events occupies a fairly strong position in the EU Strategy. First, it uses the droughts experienced across Europe in 2018, 2019 and 2020 as examples of a problem suitable for no-regret measures.[28] It lists numerous examples of technological innovations

---

21 EU Green Deal, p. 5.

22 Regulation (EU) 2021/1119 of 30 June 2021 establishing the framework for achieving climate neutrality and amending Regulations (EC) No. 401/2009 and (EU) 2018/1999 ('European Climate Law'), [2021] OJ L243/1, Arts. 5(2) and (4).

23 EU Strategy, supra, note 4.

24 Ibid., p. 2.

25 Ibid., p. 11.

26 Ibid., pp. 4–7.

27 M. Brugnach et al., 'Toward a Relational Concept of Uncertainty: about Knowing Too Little, Knowing Too Differently, and Accepting Not to Know', (2008) 13 *Ecology and Society*, p. 30.

28 EU Strategy, supra, note 4, pp. 2–3.

which create a resilient society, such as sustainable (re)use of water in agriculture, and the creation of additional drinking water supply and storage infrastructure.[29] Second, it refers to the need for both nature-based solutions and technological innovations, to ensure the availability and sustainability of freshwater.[30] Notably, water-related EU legislative instruments, such as the Water Framework Directive and the Floods Directive, do not mention climate adaptation.[31] The EU Water Reuse Regulation on minimum requirements for water reuse does mention adaptation to climate change as one of its purposes.[32]

2.2. CIRCULAR ECONOMY UNDER THE EU GREEN DEAL

The circular economy occupies a strong position in the EU Green Deal, but it is a particular type of circularity that is emphasised. Under the EU Green Deal, the circular economy is strongly linked to economic development. This is, in part, because the term 'circular economy', which inherently links it with industry, is preferred over 'circularity'. Moreover, circular economy measures often deal with the life cycles of products, i.e. making product life cycles circular rather than linear. The EU Green Deal states that such circular economy measures will focus on resource-intensive sectors, such as textiles, construction, electronics and plastics.[33] Unlike climate adaptation, circular economy measures in freshwater management, such as water reuse, are notably absent from the EU Green Deal.

The subsequent 2020 Circular Economy Action Plan does, however, include ideas and policies on the circular economy in freshwater management. First, it links freshwater with resource extraction:

> As half of total greenhouse gas emissions and more than 90% of biodiversity loss and water stress come from resource extraction and processing, the European Green Deal launched a concerted strategy for a climate-neutral, resource-efficient and competitive economy.[34]

Second, it sees freshwater as a resource in itself, and classifies it as a 'biological resource'.[35] For freshwater specifically as a resource, the 2020 Circular Economy

29 Ibid., p. 3.
30 Ibid., pp. 16–17.
31 Directive 2000/60/EC establishing a framework for Community action in the field of water policy, 2000 (hereinafter 'Water Framework Directive'); Directive 2007/60/EC of 23 October 2007 on the assessment and management of flood risks, 2007.
32 Council Regulation (EU) 2020/741 of 25 May 2020 on minimum requirements for water reuse, (2020) OJ L 177/32 (hereinafter 'EU Water Reuse Regulation'), Art. 1(2).
33 EU Green Deal, supra, note 21, pp. 7–9.
34 EU Circular Economy Action Plan, supra, note 1, p. 4.
35 Ibid., pp. 14–15.

Action Plan mentions the EU Water Reuse Regulation as a stimulus for water reuse in agriculture, and mentions that '[t]he Commission will facilitate water reuse and efficiency, including in industrial processes'.[36] The EU Water Framework Directive also allows Member States to use water reuse technologies in industry.[37] Directive 91/271/EEC concerning urban waste water treatment, equally, states that 'treated waste water shall be reused whenever appropriate'.[38] Reuse of the nutrients dissolved or suspended in the wastewater, argued to be useful for fertiliser recovery and reuse,[39] is also mentioned as a possibility in the Directive concerning urban waste water treatment, but no further legal guidance is given.[40]

Lastly, the EU Water Reuse Regulation is a fitting example of how the EU emphasises the circular economy of water, or more simply 'water reuse', even though it seems hidden from view in the EU Water Framework Directive, and is absent from the Green Deal. The EU Water Reuse Regulation has, as one of its purposes, promotion of the circular economy,[41] including the reuse of nutrients.[42]

It should be noted here that water, including freshwater, lends itself extremely well to circular economy measures. Water is circular to begin with: it follows an infinite cycle of evaporation and precipitation. It is the specific needs in terms of water quality and quantity, for certain purposes, at certain places and times, that make it a resource, and bring challenges if the available water and its intended purpose do not align. By making freshwater management circular within the climatic water cycle, the available water and the purpose can once again be aligned. For example, reusing wastewater from agricultural processes for cooling water in industry will allow for an overall reduction of water extraction, and a reduction in the discharge of wastewater, and associated discharges, into the environment. Therefore, even though freshwater in the circular economy does not take up much space in the EU Green Deal, it lends itself very well to such circular economy measures. Moreover, creating and executing these measures is in the spirit of the EU Green Deal, and assists in reaching other EU Green Deal goals, such as achieving climate neutrality and halting biodiversity loss.

---

36 Ibid., p. 15.

37 Water Framework Directive, supra, note 31, Annex VI, Part B, (x).

38 Council Directive 91/271/EEC of 21 May 1991 concerning urban waste water treatment, (1991) OJ L135/40 (hereinafter 'EU Urban Waste Water Directive'), Art. 12(1).

39 E.g. A. Rosemarin et al., 'Circular nutrient solutions for agriculture and wastewater – a review of technologies and practices', (2020) 45 *Current Opinion in Environmental Sustainability*, p. 78.

40 EU Urban Waste Water Directive, supra, note 38, preambles 11 and 12.

41 EU Water Reuse Regulation, supra, note 32, Art. 1(2).

42 Ibid., preambles 11 and 12.

2.3. REMAINING CHALLENGES WITH INCORPORATING CLIMATE ADAPTATION AND CIRCULAR ECONOMY GOALS INTO THE LEGAL SYSTEM

Climate adaptation and circular economy policies from the EU Green Deal and other related communications and legal instruments must make their way into the national legal systems of the Member States. Even regulations, which have direct binding force, need to be implemented somehow in the national legal systems. Directives give even more decision-making freedom to Member States. The above-mentioned EU legal instruments, and any others, bring some characteristics of national legal systems to the forefront. These are legal rigidity, legal hierarchy, and the involvement of private actors. Each of these may complicate the transposition of policy goals into law.

First, climate adaptation and circular economy laws and policies must fit the general legal system, which can be understood as the sum of all fields of law and legal institutions, and the network of interactions between them.[43] This includes all corners of the legal system, including international, European, national and local laws and institutions. Any new or existing laws and policies must operate within at least the outer boundaries of the existing legal system, and must, therefore, operate in a system which serves other goals as well, such as safeguarding human rights and the economy. The legal system can also be adapted to make room for new laws and policies, for example by creating a new environmental ombudsperson, a court specific to environmental issues, or more room for environmental experimentation. However, these are heavily dependent on political will. Therefore, more often, the legal system is reinterpreted to incentivise practical change without requiring legal change.[44] This can include reinterpretation of the scope of specific rules or of certain norms, obligations or the division of responsibility, etc. The caveat here is that these rules have enough flexibility, whether intentionally or unintentionally, to allow for such reinterpretation.

Second, the legal system consists of multiple levels, whereby the higher levels, such as the international and EU levels, establish overarching obligations in certain areas of the law, which the lower levels, mainly the national and local levels, such as provinces and municipalities, must abide by. In turn, national and local jurisdictional levels often give concrete interpretations to these higher-level obligations, and execute them.

---

43 J. Wenta and J. McDonald, 'The role of law and legal systems in climate change adaptation policy' in E.C.H. Keskitalo and B.L. Preston (eds.), *Research Handbook on Climate Change Adaptation Policy*, Edward Elgar Publishing, 2019, p. 70.

44 A. Garmestani et al., 'Untapped capacity for resilience in environmental law', (2019) 116 *Proceedings of the National Academy of Sciences of the United States of America*, p. 19899.

Especially important in the field of climate adaptation are the stark differences in environmental challenges, both between and within countries. This is due to regional differences in how climate change expresses itself in combination with regional vulnerabilities.[45] It is also often the local or regional governments that are responsible for making changes in the physical environments to meet climate adaptation or circular economy goals. For example, it is up to the provinces, municipalities and regional water authorities in the Netherlands to protect the regional water systems and infrastructure, including certain surface water bodies and flood defense structures, to organise rainwater collection and wastewater purification and to maintain groundwater levels.[46] Regional differences and regional duties of care require that higher-level (national or EU) laws have the right amount of flexibility.

Such regional action, based on flexible higher-level laws, fits with EU approaches to climate adaptation, most notably the principle of subsidiarity.[47] This flexibility of interpretation, by lower-level governments, is also present in the EU Water Reuse Regulation, which states:

> This Regulation should be flexible enough to allow the continuation of the practice of water reuse and at the same time to ensure that it is possible for other Member States to apply those rules when they decide to introduce this practice at a later stage. Any decision not to practise water reuse should be duly justified based on the criteria laid down in this Regulation and reviewed regularly.[48]

This Regulation's flexibility is slightly different from the regulatory flexibility described above. Note that this envisioned flexibility applies when EU Member States introduce water reuse (either before or after the introduction of the Regulation (sentence 1), and provides the possibility for Member States not to introduce water reuse (sentence 2).

A third key factor is the necessary involvement of private actors, in both urban and non-urban areas.[49] For example, climate adaptation and circular economy policies, such as green roofs, often target many properties owned by many different private actors, in a small area.[50] But, equally important agricultural or

45 Termeer et al., supra, note 11, p. 162.
46 Dutch Water Law (Waterwet), Arts. 3.2, 3.2a, 3.4, 3.5 and 3.6.
47 Consolidated Treaty on the Functioning of the European Union [2012] OJ C326/47, Art. 5 and e.g. N. de Sadeleer, 'Principle of Subsidiarity and the EU Environmental Policy', (2012) 9 *Journal of European Environmental and Planning Law*, p. 63.
48 EU Water Reuse Regulation, supra, note 32, preamble 7.
49 H.K. Gilissen et al., *Op weg naar een handreiking voor de implementatie van klimaatadaptatie-lessen uit het project 'Klimaatbestendige Woonwijken Regio Utrecht'*, Centre for Water, Oceans and Sustainability Law, Utrecht University, 2021, pp. 17–18.
50 H. Mees et al., 'Who governs climate adaptation? Getting green roofs for stormwater retention off the ground', (2013) 56(6) *Journal of Environmental Planning and Management*, p. 802.

industrial reforms require actions to be taken by private actors. For example, reusing household wastewater for agricultural purposes, as promoted by the EU Water Reuse Regulation, requires the involvement of wastewater treatment facilities, farmers or farmers' collectives, and other private or partially private actors, in the development and execution of such reuse.[51]

There are indications from research that the public–private relationship in climate adaptation policies is most effective when there is a strong presence of the local or regional government in the entire policy process, from creating to implementing to evaluating.[52] An important social factor also appears to be the involvement of citizens in the process of designing climate adaptation and circular economy policies, in order to ensure democratic legitimacy, improve public support, and create the most effective measures for specific locales.[53] When the procedure for citizen engagement is explicitly communicated, the objectives of the climate adaptation plan are also more likely to be met.[54]

In conclusion, to create effective climate adaptation and circularity laws and policies, it is necessary to navigate an intricate web of legal rigidity, legal hierarchy, and both public and private stakeholders. The creation of such laws and policies, therefore, faces dilemmas in every phase of the creation and implementation process.

3. CLIMATE ADAPTATION AND CIRCULAR ECONOMY GOALS REQUIRE TECHNOLOGICAL INNOVATIONS

Climate adaptation and circular economy goals require laws and policies to be propelled into action, but these goals also need innovation to be achieved. There is a need for innovative infrastructure and technologies to make the freshwater system circular and resilient to climate change. Technological innovations in freshwater management can be incredibly varied, from creating drinking water through reverse osmosis, to decreasing the burden on urban infrastructure during flash rains by increasing the water storage capacity of buildings. This section will briefly outline the need for technological innovations to meet climate adaptation and circularity goals, as well as some often-heard critiques.

The need for technological innovations in freshwater management, for climate adaptation and circularity policies, has been emphasised by multiple international and EU institutions. For example, the IPCC has argued that the

51 EU Water Reuse Regulation, supra, note 32, preamble 18.
52 Mees et al., supra, note 50, pp. 818–819.
53 Mees et al., supra, note 50.
54 C.J. Uittenbroek et al., 'The Design of Public Participation: Who Participates, When and How? Insights in Climate Adaptation Planning from the Netherlands', (2019) 62 *Journal of Environmental Planning and Management*, p. 2529.

rapid diffusion of technological innovations is part of the solution towards a sustainable future.[55] In the United Nations Framework Convention on Climate Change, multiple provisions urge for the transfer of technologies which combat climate change, and which adapt societies to climate change.[56] In the EU, multiple laws and policies explain the need for technological innovations, to meet climate adaptation and circular economy policies. As mentioned in section 2.1. above, the EU Strategy relates climate adaptation in the freshwater sector to technological innovations.[57] The EU Circular Economy Action Plan also relates the circular economy to technological innovations.[58] Even though the Action Plan does not explicitly link freshwater management with technological innovations, it does link innovations to 'resources'[59] and 'primary materials',[60] both of which can be interpreted to include (fresh)water.

It is important to note here the critique, often heard in the field of technological innovations for climate adaptation, that reducing consumption should be the focal point of our efforts, not finding ways to maintain or increase existing consumption. There are merits to this point, which are also applicable to the argument of this chapter. However, a circular freshwater system does reduce consumption of groundwater and surface water, because a circular system relies less and less on these 'original sources'.[61] Instead, the extracted groundwater and surface water is utilised to the highest degree. In essence, it is possible to decrease consumption of raw materials and increase the utility or lifespan of the extracted resources at the same time, as long as the focal point is waste reduction. This applies both to the water itself and the materials suspended in the wastewater.

Questions can also be raised, rightfully, about what direction technological innovations should take.[62] Innovation comes with uncertainty: both inherent scientific uncertainty about the technological innovations themselves, and uncertainty about the exact climatic changes. Also, these technological innovations, and the changes in infrastructure they can cause, affect other

---

55 G. Blanco et al., 'Innovation, Technology Development and Transfer' in P.R. Shukla et al. (eds.), *Climate Change 2022: Mitigation of Climate Change – Contribution of Working Group III to the Sixth Assessment Report of the Intergovernmental Panel on Climate Change*, Cambridge University Press, 2022.

56 Framework Convention on Climate Change (adopted 9 May 1992, entered into force 21 March 1994) 1771 UNTS 107, Arts. 4.1(h), 4.3, 4.4, 4.5 and 4.7.

57 See, e.g. the EU Strategy, supra, note 4, Box 1 on pp. 2–3.

58 EU Circular Economy Action Plan, supra, note 1, pp. 13–14 and 17.

59 Ibid., p. 6.

60 Ibid., p. 2.

61 H.K. Gilissen and A. Outhuijse, 'Naar een optimale beheersing van waterschaarsterisico's in 2030: Meer aandacht voor zelfvoorzienendheid en de verkleining of verandering van de waterbehoefte' in C. Backes, E. Brans and H.K. Gilissen (eds.), *2030: Het juridisch instrumentarium voor mitigatie van klimaatverandering, energietransitie en adaptatie in Nederland*, Boom Juridisch, 2020, p. 396.

62 Supra, note 55, pp. 1655–1657.

interests, such as nature conservation, or economic interests such as shipping routes. There must always be a balance found between interests, but sometimes one interest must make way for another. Lastly, technological innovations cannot be created or maintained without an understanding of responsibility, especially when the innovation causes damage. These topics form the subject of the next section, on the points of friction between law and innovation.

4. THE POTENTIAL FRICTION BETWEEN THE LEGAL SYSTEM AND TECHNOLOGICAL INNOVATIONS

The previous two sections highlighted the importance of the translation of climate adaptation and circular economy goals into law, and the necessity of technological innovations to meet these goals. Further scrutiny shows that there is uncertainty which needs to be managed, an array of interests which need to be balanced, and unclear responsibilities which need to be clarified. The legal system can help with all of these issues.

4.1. SCIENCE, EXPERIMENTATION AND UNCERTAINTY

Uncertainty can accidentally lead us to the wrong course of action, or lead us to completely freeze any action at all. Uncertainty about the future of our environment can be mediated by the advances of science. Virtually every scientific discipline now discusses climate change and how to face it.[63] Science has given us some of the greatest insights into how climate change works, how to slow it down, and how to adapt to it. These scientific insights usually promote change, technological innovations, radical changes in behaviour, changes in legislation, etc. However, the legal system is notoriously slow – stagnant, even – compared with how rapidly science gives us these new insights. This section deals with three ways in which science and the legal system are related.

Changing the law requires some form of governmental majority, depending on the political system and type of legislative change. The drafting of the law, which often precedes legal change, is done by a diverse group of lawmakers and judges, with an equally diverse set of backgrounds and interests. Most laws, such as advanced economic legislation or spatial planning laws, require a thorough scientific understanding. For freshwater management, for example, it is necessary to bring together people with an understanding of all facets of the socio-ecological system, including hydrology, geohydrology, ecology,

63 H. Du et al., 'Enriching the concept of solution space for climate adaptation by unfolding legal and governance dimensions', (2022) 127 *Environmental Science and Policy*, p. 253.

ecotoxicology, city planning, economics, etc. This requires that many public servants integrate their different disciplines on paper, and that science has its rightful place in this legal drafting process.[64] For example, when the EU Water Framework Directive was drafted, scientific experts played an important role in the wording of the text and the content of the annexes.[65] Moreover, the EU Water Reuse Regulation recognises that new scientific knowledge may require alterations to the legal minimum water quality standards. It therefore allows for legislative amendments to its text, if 'new scientific developments and technical process so require'.[66]

Another way in which science influences legislation is through the execution of legislation, rather than the lawmaking process itself. One such way is through the 'best available techniques' (BATs) doctrine, a doctrine in which those techniques which are best at preventing or minimising emissions and impacts on the environment are favoured. The technique which is considered 'best' is, therefore, the one which is most successful at preventing or minimising emissions and environmental impacts, but taking into account reasonable (economic) accessibility to the operator.[67] Science influences which techniques become BATs, through the Sevilla Process, a dialogue between Member States, industries concerned, and non-governmental organisations.[68] These BATs then form the basis of the BAT conclusions, which are essentially summary documents of the Sevilla Process, including a detailed explanation of the BAT itself, its workings, and its emissions. These BAT conclusions are legally binding, and form the basis for setting permit conditions.[69] This ensures that the BAT really does become the technique which should be used throughout the EU for its specific activity or industry. Only in certain cases are legislators allowed to choose a different technique.[70] When environmental norms are so ambitious that existing BATs cannot meet them, legislators can even force innovation.[71]

64 H.F.M.W. van Rijswick, 'The Road to Sustainability: How Environmental Law Can Deal with Complexity and Flexibility', (2012) 8 *Utrecht Law Review*, pp. 1, 1–2.

65 N. Valin and D. Huitema, 'Experts as policy entrepreneurs: How knowledge can lead to radical environmental change', (2023) 142 *Environmental Science and Policy*, p. 21.

66 EU Water Reuse Regulation, supra, note 32, preamble 36.

67 Council Directive 2010/75/EC of 24 November 2010 on industrial emissions (integrated pollution prevention and control) (recast), [2010] OJ L334/17 (hereinafter 'EU Industrial Emissions Directive'), Art. 3(10).

68 See ibid., Art. 13, and Commission Implementing Decision 2012/119/EU of 10 February 2012 laying down rules concerning guidance on the collection of data and on the drawing up of BAT reference documents and on their quality assurance referred to in Directive 2010/75/EU of the European Parliament and of the Council on industrial emissions (2012) OJ L63/1.

69 EU Industrial Emissions Directive, supra, note 67, Art. 14(3).

70 Ibid., Art. 15(4).

71 Supra, note 16, pp. 599–600.

There is also a way in which the legal system stimulates science by allowing for uncertainty. Uncertainty is part of science, especially in the creation of technological innovations, where real-world experimentation is necessary. Legislators can create spaces in the law to allow for such technological innovations to be introduced, to see whether or not they work. These are called experimentation clauses.[72] Such experimentation clauses can be part of, or an impetus for, so-called 'regulatory sandboxes'. These are regulatory frameworks where experimentation is facilitated in a particular area, for a particular time period, while ensuring that appropriate safeguards are in place.[73] Regulatory sandboxes have been discussed in academic literature as a suitable tool for the regulation of financial technologies ('fintech').[74] Some EU Member States allow for regulatory sandboxes in the energy sector.[75] For example, the Dutch executive order 'experiments decentralised, sustainable electricity production' allows homeowners' associations and cooperatives to propose projects which would otherwise be prohibited by existing legislation.[76] Underlining the difficulty of finding the right amount of flexibility, however, the inclusion of experimentation clauses in the new Dutch Electricity Law and Gas Law was rejected.[77] It was argued that this type of legal flexibility would come with great uncertainty for citizens and companies, about the future of energy policy, and that it could compromise a cohesive, nationwide approach to energy.[78]

In the field of EU freshwater management, there does not seem to exist the possibility for regulatory sandboxes, despite the EU's push for regulatory sandboxes 'in the face of high uncertainty and disruptive challenges'.[79] There is also an experimentation clause – not a complete regulatory sandbox – in the EU Water Reuse Regulation: research or pilot projects in relation to urban wastewater reclamation facilities can be exempted from the scope of the Regulation if the project is not carried out in a zone where water is abstracted

---

72 Council of the European Union, Outcome of Proceedings, 'Council Conclusions on Regulatory sandboxes and experimentation clauses as tools for an innovation-friendly, future-proof and resilient regulatory framework that masters disruptive challenges in the digital age', 13026/20 (16 November 2020), p. 5.

73 Ibid., p. 4.

74 See, e.g. H.J. Allen, 'Regulatory Sandboxes', (2019) 87 *George Washington Law Review*, p. 579.

75 A Veseli et al., 'Practical necessity and legal options for introducing energy regulatory sandboxes in Austria', (2021) 73 *Utilities Policy*, p. 101296.

76 For a detailed overview of this executive order and its pros and cons, see E.C. van der Waal, A.M. Das and T. van der Schoor, 'Participatory Experimentation with Energy Law: Digging in a "Regulatory Sandbox" for Local Energy Initiatives in the Netherlands', (2020) 13 *Energies*, p. 458.

77 Raad van State, (Besluit experimenten Elektriciteitswet 1998 en Gaswet), 2020, Bijlage bij Kamerstukken I 2020/21, 34627, F.

78 Ibid.

79 Council of the European Union, Outcome of Proceedings, supra, note 72, p. 4.

for human consumption, is appropriately monitored, and runs for a maximum of five years.[80] Any successfully grown crops irrigated with reused wastewater are not allowed to be placed on the market.[81]

These three ways of incorporating science into the making or execution of the law allow for science to generate successes, while acknowledging the inherent risk of failure. The uncertainty that comes with scientific experiments and their conclusions should not, and does not, hinder their uses in a legal context. Science and uncertainty go hand in hand, and the legal system accommodates this uncertainty, in order to realise its goals. In other words, science needs the legal system to incorporate scientific conclusions into legislation, to ensure that the best available techniques become standard practice, and to ensure that experimentation in the real world is possible and safe.

4.2. BALANCING RIGHTS AND INTERESTS IN A LEGAL SYSTEM

Creating and maintaining a technological innovation often influences other protected rights or interests. For example, economic rights may be affected when a new filtration technique for drinking water production becomes the new BAT; a new water storage facility may cast a shadow over a solar panel farm for a certain time during the day; or a protected nature area might be affected when it is reassigned as a potential floodplain during one-in-a-hundred-year floods. Such situations might deal with unforeseen situations, unusual cases not fully crystalised in the law, specific local circumstances, or a combination of these factors. In these cases, the relevant legislative authority may add to existing rules, create requirements which are stricter or less strict than the original rules, or deviate from a generic prohibition. These deviations allow for legislative authorities to make choices between conflicting interests, in order to act in line with broader goals, and to prevent inaction.

Of course, such deviations from legislation are exceptional. They are only granted to certain authorities and governing bodies in relation to certain topics, and their reasoning must meet a myriad of demands.[82] It is also possible for government bodies to operate within the existing legal framework, i.e. without making any legal deviations. Government bodies such as regional water authorities, provinces, or municipalities can tackle environmental challenges by changing the way they cooperate, and by using the lessons learnt from experiments with technological innovations or other types of innovations

---

80 EU Water Reuse Regulation, supra, note 32, Art. 2(3).

81 Ibid.

82 For a detailed explanation of such deviations (*maatwerk*) under the Dutch Environment and Planning Act, see K.J. de Graaf and H.D. Tolsma, 'Flexibiliteit in de Omgevingswet: Maatwerk, gelijkwaardigheid en experimenten', (2014) 41 *Milieu en Recht*, p. 635.

(regulatory innovations, social innovations, etc.). In the literature, this is called 'adaptive governance' or 'adaptive co-management'.[83] Explaining the entire scholarly thinking about adaptive governance exceeds the scope of this chapter, but explaining its constituent parts is necessary in order to understand why adaptive governance can be successful in tackling environmental challenges within a democratic system, and, in particular, why it can be successful in balancing rights and interests.

The first element of adaptive governance is 'polycentric governance', in which multiple governmental actors operate in the same legal space, with partially overlapping and partially different scales, and without an absolute hierarchy between them.[84] The Dutch water governance model is an example of polycentric governance, since provinces, municipalities and regional water authorities all operate in roughly the same geographical and legal space. Although a hierarchy does exist between these entities, cooperation towards the same goal is the main component of their relationship. Such polycentric governance, in which absolute control is exchanged for flexibility, is also helpful in managing uncertainties.[85]

The second element is public participation.[86] While there can be discussion on the meaning of both 'public' and 'participation', the key component of public participation is cooperation between governmental and non-governmental stakeholders;[87] in other words, those actors, both public and private, that have a stake in the environmental issue at hand are included in the decision-making to a certain degree. This could include different governmental actors, (drinking) water companies, wastewater treatment facilities, and even citizens.

The third element is experimentation.[88] The adaptive governance literature does not speak of technological or scientific experimentation, as is the focus of this chapter, but of experimentation of different management styles, to find the one that best fits the environmental issue at hand;[89] it is experimentation with governance itself, not with science to aid governance. This allows governments to be flexible, and to find a form of cooperation that works best for the issue at hand.

---

83 B.C. Chaffin, H. Gosnell and B.A. Cosens, 'A decade of adaptive governance scholarship: synthesis and future directions', (2014) 19 *Ecology and Society*, pp. 3, 56 and D. Huitema et al., 'Adaptive Water Governance: Assessing the Institutional Prescriptions of Adaptive (Co-)Management from a Governance Perspective and Defining a Research Agenda', (2009) 14 *Ecology and Society*, p. 26.

84 D. Huitema et al., 'Adaptive Water Governance: Assessing the Institutional Prescriptions of Adaptive (Co-)Management from a Governance Perspective and Defining a Research Agenda', (2009) 14 *Ecology and Society*, pp. 28–30.

85 Supra, note 27, p. 30.

86 Huitema et al., supra, note 83, pp. 30–32.

87 Ibid.

88 Ibid., pp. 32–34.

89 Ibid.

The fourth element is the focus on bioregions,[90] or regions which have an environmental similarity, such as river basins or the habitat of a certain species of flora or fauna. If such bioregions cross administrative boundaries, then the governance will have to include all governmental bodies which cover that bioregion; the bioregion will not be split up. In water governance specifically, river basins are often the bioregion within which governmental bodies cooperate.[91] Importantly, focusing on bioregions reduces the chance that (experimental) action in one administrative area will cause damage in another administrative area; such areas are urged to cooperate.

Adaptive governance is a flexible way to deal with the rigidities of the legal system.[92] It allows for deep cooperation, whereby all relevant stakeholders are involved in the decision-making process, and the focus lies on a specific bioregion. Such deep cooperation and interaction specifically in freshwater management and water reuse has also been identified by the EU as an important strategy. The EU Water Reuse Regulation mentions such cooperation and interaction between the parties involved as a precondition for water reuse, as well as a necessity for planning the supply of reused water in line with the demand from end users.[93] Adaptive governance, together with the possibility to experiment with different governance types, allows for all rights and interests involved to have a place at the table, and for these rights and interests to be weighed against each other to find a balance that all parties can agree upon. Adaptive governance, therefore, is a suitable alternative when legal deviation is not possible or desirable.

Lastly, the financial side of technological innovations in freshwater management should also be mentioned here. Technological innovations in freshwater management, such as water reuse technologies, are often still expensive investments. While this does not mean that economic rights are automatically violated, it does raise the question whether the legal system should incentivise innovation by lowering the cost of such technological innovations. The EU Water Reuse Regulation mentions that the 'high investment needed to upgrade urban waste water treatment plants and the lack of financial incentives for practising water reuse in agriculture have been identified as being among the reasons for the low uptake of water reuse in the Union'.[94] It then states that '[i]t should be possible to address those issues by promoting innovative schemes and economic incentives to appropriately take account of the costs and the socioeconomic and environmental benefits of water reuse'.[95] It should be noted,

---

90 Ibid., 34–36.
91 See, e.g. the EU Water Framework Directive, supra, note 31.
92 Of course, if the relevant law(s) is/are non-discretionary, then the possibilities for any flexibility, even in the form of adaptive governance, are limited.
93 EU Water Reuse Regulation, supra, note 32, preamble 18.
94 Ibid., preamble 13.
95 Ibid.

however, that it does not mention what such schemes and incentives should look like, or who should make them.

4.3. RESPONSIBILITY, ACCOUNTABILITY AND LIABILITY

A final piece of the puzzle towards creating and maintaining technological innovations in freshwater management is responsibility for the risks inherent to technological innovations. When technological innovations are first put out into the world, in the form of experiments, it is important to know which party is responsible for any damage that may occur if the experiment fails. Again, uncertainty arises when responsibility is not clear from the outset. At a later stage, responsibility is still relevant to determining who should implement the innovation, who is responsible for its maintenance or monitoring, who can reap the profits, etc.

The EU answered part of the responsibility question in the context of the EU Water Reuse Regulation. The Regulation clearly states that the 'reclamation facility operators'[96] are primarily responsible for the quality of reclaimed water at the point of compliance – when the water is handed over to the next party[97] – as well as for the water quality monitoring.[98] After the point of compliance, the responsibility for water quality passes on to the next party.[99] Responsibility for the distribution, storage and use of reused water is not assigned to a specific actor by the EU Water Reuse Regulation. However, the mandatory risk-management plan, which is made by the reclamation facility operators, other responsible parties, and end users, must identify, where relevant, which parties are responsible for these actions.[100]

5. CONCLUSION

The legal system and technological innovations in freshwater management have a complex relationship. Whereas the former seems apprehensive, and even slow at times, technological innovations are characterised by their newness and rapid development. With challenges ahead as urgent and all-encompassing as climate adaptation and the circular economy, this chapter sought to point out exactly

96 The natural or legal persons behind the water treatment facility, who can be the same as those that treat the wastewater for reuse (ibid., Art. 3(5) and (6)).
97 Ibid., Art. 3(11).
98 Ibid., preamble 19.
99 European Commission, 'Guidelines to support the application of Regulation 2020/741 on minimum requirements for water reuse' (Information) 2022/C 298/01 (2022), para. 2.4.2.
100 Ibid.

what the relationship is between the legal system and technological innovations in freshwater management.

The EU legal system, including the EU Water Reuse Regulation, finds a good balance between stimulating technological innovations in freshwater management and protecting other interests. Uncertainties inherent to scientific discovery and technological innovations are minimised through inclusion of science in the lawmaking process, in the execution of the law, and through experimentation clauses. The possibility to deviate from the law, although exceptional, allows the regulator to make a choice between conflicting rights and interests. And, where deviations from the law are not possible or desirable, adaptive governance can create the flexibility required by certain situations. Where finances are an obstacle to the implementation of water reuse innovations, the EU Water Reuse Regulation allows for the creation of economic incentives. Allocation of responsibilities for damage and risk is, in many ways, 'the final obstacle'. The EU Water Reuse Regulation places the bulk of the responsibility, especially for the quality of the reused water, on the reclamation facility operators. Allocation of the remaining responsibility must be agreed upon by the parties involved themselves.

All in all, the legal system and technological innovations in freshwater management may seem to be in conflict, but the legal system needs technological innovations to meet its policy goals, and technological innovations need a legal system to ensure safety, fairness and responsibility. Much is left to be explored in this relationship, especially the question of responsibility for technological innovations in freshwater management.

REDUCING PEAT OXIDATION AND GREENHOUSE GAS EMISSIONS IN DUTCH PEATLANDS

Bridging the Gap between Interconnected Environmental Challenges and the Fragmented Legal and Governance System

Martijn van Gils

ABSTRACT

Environmental challenges are interconnected, both in their causes and their solutions. At the same time, the legal and governance system is fragmented: different authorities are responsible for different environmental policy domains, such as water management, nature conservation and spatial planning. The resulting 'gap' makes it more difficult for public authorities to develop environmental policies aligned across policy domains, and to implement them effectively. This chapter explores this gap in the context of reducing peat oxidation and greenhouse gas (GHG) emissions from peatlands in the Netherlands. It examines how this gap makes it more difficult for public authorities to reduce peat oxidation and GHG emissions effectively, and how public authorities can use their policy and legal instruments to bridge this gap.

1. INTRODUCTION

Nine per cent of the Netherlands is covered by peatlands. As a result of wide-scale drainage of these areas for agricultural purposes, peat oxidation occurs, which, besides soil subsidence, causes the emission of substantial amounts of CO2 and other greenhouse gases, such as methane and nitrous oxide, into the atmosphere. Peat oxidation also has several other adverse effects, such as the deterioration of water quality and biodiversity. To effectively reduce these greenhouse gas emissions (hereinafter 'GHG emissions') and mitigate other adverse effects, public authorities must reduce the drainage of peatlands. This requires public authorities to act in the policy domains of both water management and spatial planning, departing considerably from current policies and practices, which are mostly aimed at maintaining the drainage of peatlands, so that they can continue to be used for intensive dairy farming.

One of the main obstacles for the effective reduction of peat oxidation and GHG emissions from peatlands in the Netherlands is the 'gap' between the interconnected environment and the fragmented legal and governance system.[1] The challenges to the environment are interconnected, both in their causes and their solutions. The legal and governance system, however, is fragmented: different public authorities are responsible for different environmental policy domains, such as water management and spatial planning, and exercise their responsibilities to promote different, sometimes conflicting, environmental interests. The resulting 'gap' makes it more difficult for public authorities to address environmental challenges effectively.

This chapter examines this gap in the context of reducing peat oxidation and GHG emissions from peatlands in the Netherlands, and answers the following research question: how does the gap between the interconnected environment and the fragmented legal and governance system make it difficult for public authorities to reduce peat oxidation and GHG emissions from peatlands, and how can public authorities use their policy and legal instruments to bridge this gap?

The chapter first discusses the causes, processes and adverse effects of soil subsidence and oxidation in Dutch peatlands, including GHG emissions (section 2). It then describes the legal obligations to reduce peat oxidation and GHG emissions, both at the EU and the national level (section 3). Thereafter, it outlines the measures that public authorities can take to reduce oxidation and GHG emissions from peatlands, in the policy domains of both water management and spatial planning and land use (section 4). Consequently, the chapter describes the legal responsibilities of public authorities to reduce peat oxidation and GHG emissions from peatlands, and the (legal) instruments they can use to exercise their responsibilities (section 5). It then discusses the gap between the interconnected environment and the fragmented legal and governance system, in the context of reducing peat oxidation and GHG emissions from peatlands. It first describes how this gap makes it difficult for public authorities to effectively address this environmental challenge, and then how public authorities can use the policy and legal instruments available to them to bridge this gap (section 6). The chapter ends with a conclusion (section 7).

---

1 For a governance perspective, see M. van den Ende, 'Wicked problems and creeping crises: A framework for analyzing governance challenges to addressing environmental land-use problems', *Environmental Science & Policy*, (2023) 141, pp. 168–177.

2. SOIL SUBSIDENCE, PEAT OXIDATION AND GHG EMISSIONS FROM DUTCH PEATLANDS

Peat oxidation is the process by which the organic matter in peat bogs biodegrades ('burns') and is released into the air as methane and, mainly, CO_2. This happens when the peat soil dries out and is exposed to oxygen from the air. The main cause of the desiccation and subsequent oxidation of the peat soil is drainage. To keep the soil suitable for agriculture, especially grassland for dairy farming, the water level in the surrounding surface waters (ditches and canals) is kept low. This ensures a lower groundwater level and prevents excessively wet soil conditions, so that intensive agricultural use remains possible. However, the consequence of this drainage process is that the groundwater level can drop sharply, especially in dry summers, sometimes to more than a metre below ground level. As a result, a significant portion of the upper peat soil dries out and oxidises.

Dutch peatlands are caught in a vicious circle of drainage, peat oxidation and soil subsidence. As a result of the drainage, the soil subsides. Over time, this causes the ground level to move closer to the groundwater table, which in turn makes the soil wetter. To keep the peat soil suitable for intensive agricultural use, the land must then be drained further, causing more oxidation and subsidence. This 'vicious cycle' of drainage, peat oxidation and subsidence has been ongoing for approximately 1,000 years, and has resulted in many metres of soil subsidence.[2]

One of the main adverse effects is the emission of greenhouse gases in the atmosphere. The annual emission of CO_2 from peatlands in agricultural use is estimated at 4.2Mt; the annual emission for the entire peatland area is 7Mt. That represents 2 per cent and 4 per cent, respectively, of the total annual emission of CO_2 in the Netherlands.[3] The volume of greenhouse gases emitted varies by area, and depends on several factors. Among other things, the amount of drainage, the agricultural land use (for example, grassland or arable farming) and soil composition (peat, clay on peat, or sand on peat) play a role.

The vicious cycle of drainage, oxidation and subsidence has several other adverse effects: as a result of peat oxidation, nutrients such as nitrates, phosphates and sulphates end up in surface waters, causing the deterioration of groundwater and surface waters and/or affecting habitats and/or species; nature-conservation areas can dry up, as the surrounding agricultural areas subside faster, relative to the natural area, and groundwater flows away to surrounding agricultural

---

2 Council for the Environment and Infrastructure, *Stop Land Subsidence in Peat Meadow Areas: The 'Green Heart' Area as an Example*, Report, 2020, pp. 8–10, rli.nl/sites/default/files/advisery_report_stop_land_subsidence_in_peat_meadow_areas.pdf.

3 Wageningen University and Research & Statistics Netherlands, *The SEEA EEA carbon account for the Netherlands*, Report, 2017.

parcels, thereby affecting habitats and/or species; and flood risks and water management costs increase as more engineering measures are needed to prevent flooding in the increasingly low-lying area.[4]

3. LEGAL OBLIGATIONS TO REDUCE PEAT OXIDATION AND GHG EMISSIONS FROM PEATLANDS

Both EU and national legislation require that peat oxidation and GHG emissions from peatlands be reduced, for the purpose of climate change mitigation. In certain situations, EU legislation also requires the reduction of peat oxidation to mitigate other adverse effects thereof, such as the negative impact on habitats and species (Habitats and Birds Directive), and on the status of groundwater and surface waters (the Water Framework Directive). Furthermore, the Nature Restoration Act, if enacted, would directly oblige the Netherlands to rewet the peatlands.

This section will discuss these legal obligations at the EU and national levels. It provides a short overview of these obligations, without discussing in detail the legal provisions from which these requirements derive.

3.1. OBLIGATIONS AT THE EU LEVEL

3.1.1. The LULUCF Regulation

The LULUCF (land use, land-use change and forestry) Regulation, which restricts GHG emissions from land use, land-use change and forestry, applies to most of the peatland areas in the Netherlands.[5] The Regulation obliges Member States to ensure that, for the period from 2021 to 2025, emissions from land use, including emissions from peatlands in agricultural use, do not exceed removals from other land-use sectors.[6] It also sets out a Union target of net GHG removals in the LULUCF sector for 2030, which is 310 Mt of CO2 equivalent.[7] The Member State targets are set out in Annex IIa of the LULUCF Regulation, based

[4] See ibid., chs. 1 and 2, for an extensive overview of the causes, processes and adverse effects of soil subsidence.

[5] Regulation (EU) 2018/841 of the European Parliament and of the Council of 30 May 2018 on the inclusion of greenhouse gas emissions and removals from land use, land use change and forestry in the 2030 climate and energy framework, and amending Regulation (EU) No. 525/2013 and Decision No. 529/2013/EU (Text with EEA relevance), OJ 2018 L156/61 ('LULUCF Regulation'). Art. 2(1)(c) and (d) states that the Regulation applies to 'managed cropland' and 'managed grassland', which includes all Dutch peatlands in agricultural use.

[6] Ibid., Art. 4(1).

[7] Ibid., Art. 4(2).

on based on the average of its greenhouse gas inventory data for the years 2016, 2017 and 2018. For the Netherlands, the net removal target is 435 kt of CO2 equivalent.[8]

The reduction of CO2 emissions from peatlands is likely necessary to achieve these targets, although further action is not needed: it is projected that current policies, including the reduction of CO2 emissions from peatlands by 1 Mt by 2030 as set out in the Climate Agreement, are sufficient to meet the targets of the LULUCF.[9] Furthermore, the Regulation does provide for several flexibility mechanisms, such as the transfer of net removals to other Member States, which the Netherlands could use to reduce the amount of removals it has to achieve in the land use sector, including the reduction of CO2 emissions from peatlands.[10] The Netherlands could also offset CO2 emissions in peatlands with additional measures in other land use sectors, such as forestry.

3.1.2. The Habitats Directive, Birds Directive and Water Framework Directive

The norms and objectives of the Habitats and Birds Directives could also require Member States to reduce soil subsidence and peat oxidation, because of the negative impact thereof on habitats and/or species in Natura 2000 areas.[11] First, these areas could dry up as a result of groundwater flowing to the surrounding peatlands in agricultural use, which are lower-lying due to subsidence. Second, peat oxidation causes the leaching of nutrients, such as nitrates, phosphates and sulphates, into surrounding surface waters. This could lead to the deterioration of habitats and/or the disturbance of species in the Natura 2000 areas, which Member States, pursuant to Article 4(4) of the Birds Directive and Article 6(2) of the Habitats Directive, should take appropriate steps to avoid. It could also make it more difficult to maintain or restore the habitats and species in these Natura 2000 areas at or to a favourable conservation status, for which Article 6(1) of the Habitats Directive and Articles 3(1) and 4(1) of the Birds Directive require Member States to take the necessary measures.

The Water Framework Directive might also require Member States to reduce peat oxidation, as peat oxidation causes the leaching of nutrients in surface and groundwaters, and can, therefore, affect the quality of surface waters and/or

---

8 Ibid., Annex IIa, Column C. The Netherlands is one of only four Member States that are allowed to have net GHG emissions by 2030, together with Denmark, Ireland and Malta.

9 Netherlands Environmental Assessment Agency (PBL), *Climate and Energy Outlook of the Netherlands 2023*, Report, 26 October 2023.

10 Ibid., Arts. 4(3), 12 and 13b.

11 Directive 2009/147/EC of the European Parliament and of the Council of 30 November 2009 on the conservation of wild birds, OJ 2010 L 20/53 (Birds Directive) and Art. 6(1), Council Directive 92/43/EEC of 21 May 1992 on the conservation of natural habitats and of wild fauna and flora, OJ 1992 L 206/35 (Habitats Directive), specifically Arts. 3(1), 4(1) and 4(4) of the Birds Directive Arts. 6(1) and 6(2) of the Habitats Directive.

groundwater.[12] Under the Directive, Member States are obliged to implement the necessary measures to prevent deterioration of the status of all bodies of surface water and groundwater, which includes the ecological and/or chemical status of these bodies of water.[13] The Directive also obliges Member States to achieve good surface water and groundwater status, by 2027 at the latest.[14] However, the extent to which the raising of water levels can contribute to improving water quality is limited: pollution of surface waters and groundwater is mostly caused by agricultural and industrial activities, not by peat oxidation.[15]

3.1.3. The Nature Restoration Law

The Nature Restoration Law could, if adopted, have significant consequences for the agricultural use of Dutch peatlands. Since its proposal by the European Commission,[16] both the Council and the European Parliament have drafted their own versions of the regulation. In this chapter, the provisional agreement of the Council and the European Parliament on the Nature Restoration Law, agreed upon on 22 November 2022, will be discussed.[17]

The proposed regulation aims to contribute to the continuous, long-term and sustained recovery of biodiverse and resilient nature across the EU's land and sea areas by restoring ecosystems, including peatlands, and to contribute towards achieving the EU climate mitigation and climate adaptation objectives. The restoration of various ecosystems serves both aims: these ecosystems can, if restored into good condition, remove and store large amounts of CO2. The proposed regulation includes a specific provision for *peatlands*:.[18]

'*Member States shall put in place measures which shall aim to restore organic soils in agricultural use constituting drained peatlands. Those measures shall be in place on at least:*

(a) 30% of such areas by 2030, of which at least a quarter shall be rewetted;
(b) 40% of such areas by 2040, of which at least a third shall be rewetted;
(c) 50% of such areas by 2050, of which at least a third shall be rewetted.'

---

12 Directive 2000/60/EC of the European Parliament and of the Council of 23 October 2000 establishing a framework for Community action in the field of water policy, OJ 2000 L 327/43 (Water Framework Directive).

13 Ibid., Arts. 4(a)(i) and (b)(i).

14 Ibid., Arts. 4(a)(ii) and (b)(ii), in accordance with Arts. 4(4)(c) and 13(7).

15 Council for the Environment and Infrastructure, *Soils for Sustainability*, Report 2020, https://dev.en.rli.nl.overboord.nl/sites/default/files/rli_2020-02_vitale_bodem_eng_interactief.pdf.

16 Proposal for a Regulation of the European Parliament and of the Council on nature restoration, COM(2022) 304.

17 General Chair of the Council, Proposal for a Regulation of the European Parliament and of the Council on nature restoration – Letter to the Chair of the European Parliament Committee on the Environment, Public Health and Food Safety (ENVI), 15907/23.

18 Ibid., Art. 9(4).

Measures to restore and rewet peatlands (the distinction between them is not entirely clear) will have considerable impact on the agricultural use of peatlands in the Netherlands. Although the regulation does not define what these measures exactly entail,[19] farmers will have to change to alternative farming practices, such as paludiculture (see section 4).[20] However, certain flexibility mechanism exist: Member States may put in place restoration measures to rewet organic soils that constitute drained peatlands under land uses other than agricultural use and count those rewetted areas as contributing, up to a maximum of 40%, to the achievements of the rewetting targets.[21] Furthermore, the extent of the rewetting of peatland under agricultural use may be reduced to less than these targets by a Member State if such rewetting is likely to have significant negative impacts on infrastructure, buildings, climate adaptation or other public interests and if rewetting cannot take place on other land than agricultural land.[22]

The provision also states that Member States shall incentivise rewetting to make it an attractive option for farmers and private landowners, and foster access to training and advice for farmers and other stakeholders on the benefits of rewetting peatland and on the options of subsequent land management and related opportunities. Finally, the provision states that the obligation for Member States to achieve the rewetting targets '*does not imply an obligation for farmers and private landowners to rewet their land, for whom rewetting on agricultural land remains voluntary*'.[23] This provision would, in my view, be useless: since Member States have to achieve the rewetting targets set out above, the rewetting of agricultural land will most likely *not* remain voluntary, since the economic and technical viability of alternative agriculture use of peatlands remains very uncertain, making it unlikely that farmers will be incentivised to rewet their land (see section 4 below)

3.2. NATIONAL OBLIGATIONS

The Dutch Climate Act, which, among other things, elaborates on the objectives of the Paris Climate Agreement, requires a 95 per cent reduction in GHG

---

19 According to preamble 54, '*Member States can choose from a wide range of restoration measures for drained peatlands in agricultural use spanning from converting cropland to permanent grassland and extensification measures accompanied by reduced drainage, to full rewetting with the opportunity of paludicultural use, or the establishment of peat-forming vegetation.*'.

20 This is apparent from preamble 55, which states that '*[r]estored and rewetted peatlands can continue to be used productively in alternative ways*', such as '*paludiculture, the practice of farming on wet peatlands*'.

21 Proposal for a Nature Restoration Law, supra, note 21, Art. 9(4). Member States may put in place restoration measures, including rewetting, in areas of peat extraction sites and count those areas as contributing to achieving those targets, although that is not particularly relevant for the Netherlands, as it has very few peat extraction sites.

22 Ibid.

23 Ibid.

emissions in the Netherlands by 2050, compared with 1990 levels.[24] The Act also requires the national government to aim for a 49 per cent reduction in GHG emissions by 2030, in order to achieve the 2050 target.[25] In the Dutch Climate Agreement, (an agreement between the national government, decentralised public authorities and companies to meet the 2030 target of a 49 per cent reduction in GHG emissions, as stated in the Dutch Climate Act), it was agreed that CO2 emissions from peatlands must be reduced by 1Mt by 2030. The provinces which contain peatlands will each adopt a policy programme (a 'regional peat meadow strategy'), setting out the overall mix of measures per peatland area to achieve this objective.[26] However, this reduction target is most likely insufficient to meet future climate targets. If CO2 emissions from peatlands are only reduced by 1Mt, it will, ultimately, be difficult to meet the target of a 95 per cent reduction of GHG emissions by 2050, as set in the Climate Act. Although the GHG emissions from peatlands will most likely not exceed the remaining 5 per cent of emissions, very little room remains for residual emissions from other sectors. Thus, it is likely that further reductions in GHG emissions from peatlands will be necessary.

4. MEASURES TO REDUCE PEAT OXIDATION AND GHG EMISSIONS FROM PEATLANDS

Reducing peat oxidation and GHG emissions from peatlands requires public authorities to take measures in multiple policy domains, in particular water management and spatial planning. The most important measure is to raise the levels of the surface waters in peatlands, such as ditches and canals, which will eventually lead to a higher groundwater table. This is technically feasible, as the low-lying peatlands of the Netherlands have a highly artificial water system, in which surface water levels can be maintained very well by weirs and pumps. For most surface waters in these areas, the water level which should be maintained is laid down in an administrative decision, known as a *water level decision* (see, further, section 5.2.1. below). In addition, farmers and other landowners can install submerged drainage systems, which enable them to influence groundwater levels more directly.

Although wetter soil conditions can reduce peat oxidation and GHG emissions, they also affect the economic viability of the current agricultural use of peatlands, which is primarily dairy farming. Wetter soil conditions reduce the

---

24 Art. 2(1), Dutch Climate Act (*Staatsblad (Dutch National Register)* 2019, 253).

25 Ibid., Art. 2(2).

26 Dutch Climate Agreement, ch. C4, 'Agriculture and Land Use', C.4.5.1., 'Peat Meadow Areas'. https://www.klimaatakkoord.nl/documenten/publicaties/2019/06/28/national-climate-agreement-the-netherlands.

production of grass, which is used as livestock feed, and make it more difficult to cultivate peat soils. Although agriculture will still be possible in wetter conditions, farmers will need to switch to other agricultural uses of peatlands. These include a less intensive form of dairy farming (less animals, lower grass production) or paludicultural use of peatlands, such as the cultivation of various types of reeds, sphagnum or cranberries. In certain areas, it will be necessary to transform agricultural land into nature-conservation areas.[27]

5. RESPONSIBILITIES AND INSTRUMENTS OF PUBLIC AUTHORITIES TO REDUCE PEAT OXIDATION AND GHG EMISSIONS FROM PEATLANDS

5.1. THE RESPONSIBILITIES AND INSTRUMENTS OF PUBLIC AUTHORITIES FOR THE PROTECTION OF THE ENVIRONMENT IN THE NETHERLANDS

The protection of the environment is listed as a public responsibility – a duty of care – in the Dutch Constitution. Article 21 of the Constitution states that '[i]t shall be the concern of the authorities to keep the country habitable and to protect and improve the environment'. The responsibilities of different public authorities for the protection of specific environmental policy domains, as well as the (legal) instruments available to public authorities to exercise these responsibilities, are laid down in sectoral legislation, such as the Spatial Planning Act, the Nature Protection Act and the Water Act. These Acts will be integrated into the new Environment and Planning Act, which will enter into force on 1 January 2024.[28]

As the Netherlands has a multi-level governance and legal system, environmental policymaking and decision-making are carried out by four geographically distinct levels of government: the national government, the provinces, the municipalities, and the regional water authorities. The national government, as well as the provinces and municipalities, which are decentralised public authorities, have a wide range of public competencies, including the regulation of land use and the protection of the environment. Regional water authorities (hereinafter 'RWAs') are functionally decentralised authorities. In contrast to provinces and municipalities, the RWAs only have specific public responsibilities, primarily regional water management.[29] The responsibility for

27 Council for the Environment and Infrastructure, *Stop Land Subsidence in Peat Meadow Areas*, supra, note 2.

28 Environment and Planning Act (*Staatsblad (Dutch National Register)* 2016, 156).

29 Arts. 1(1) and (2), Regional Water Authorities Act (*Staatsblad (Dutch National Register)* 1991, 444). For an extensive overview of the public competencies of RWAs, see H. Havekes et al., *Water Governance: The Dutch Water Authority Model*, Dutch Water Authorities, 2017, ch. 2;

the management of 'national waters', which includes the sea, and the main rivers, estuaries and lakes of the Netherlands, lies with a specific agency of the national government, called Rijkswaterstaat.[30]

The national government, as well as the decentralised public authorities, have several policy and legal instruments at their disposal, to exercise their responsibilities. These include developing public policies, enacting (decentralised) legislation and general administrative rules, making administrative decisions, and performing factual acts. Public authorities can use the (legal) instruments at their disposal *only* to exercise the responsibilities assigned to them.

Citizens affected by administrative decisions or factual acts can seek judicial protection against such decisions, before an administrative or, in some cases, a civil court, if they perceive the decision or act as unlawful. Decentralised legislation and general administrative rules cannot be directly challenged in court, but can be reviewed by a court as part of the judicial review of an administrative decision.[31]

5.2. WHICH PUBLIC AUTHORITIES ARE RESPONSIBLE, AND WHICH LEGAL INSTRUMENTS CAN THEY USE TO REDUCE PEAT OXIDATION AND GHG EMISSIONS FROM PEATLANDS?

Although reducing peat oxidation and GHG emissions from peatlands is not listed as a public responsibility in Dutch environmental legislation, both EU and Dutch law require public authorities to do so (see section 3 above). Reducing peat oxidation and GHG emissions from peatlands requires measures in the policy domains of both water management and spatial planning, to be taken by the public authorities responsible for these policy domains, primarily RWAs and municipalities. To allow them to do so, these public authorities have various policy, financial and legal instruments at their disposal. Although policy instruments, such as environmental strategies and programmes of measures, and financial instruments, such as subsidies, are important tools for reducing peat oxidation and GHG emissions, this section will focus primarily on the relevant *legal* instruments. It will discuss the legal instruments relating to water management, and those relating to spatial planning and land use.

H. van Rijswick and H. Havekes, *European and Dutch Water Law*, Europa Law Publishing, 2012.

30 Art. 3.1(1), Water Act (*Staatsblad (Dutch National Register)* 2009, 489).

31 This is called indirect review (*exceptieve toetsing*). See also K. de Graaf, B. Marseille and M. Wever, 'Rebalancing indirect judicial review of administrative action in the Netherlands' in M. Eliantonio and D. Dragos (eds.), *Indirect Judicial Review in Administrative Law*, Routledge, 2022, pp. 117–136.

5.2.1. Water Management

As outlined in section 4 above, reducing peat oxidation and GHG emissions requires a higher groundwater table, which can be effectuated by raising the water levels of surface waters in peatlands. To raise surface water levels, water level decisions *(peilbesluiten)* must often be amended. The Minister of Infrastructure and Water Management establishes water levels for designated national waters.[32] RWAs establish water level decisions for designated regional surface waters, as part of their responsibility for the management of regional water systems.[33] The raising of the levels of regional surface waters is especially important to reducing peat oxidation and GHG emissions, as regional surface waters have a much greater influence than national surface waters on the groundwater table in peatlands.

In a water level decision, the water levels, or parameters within which water levels may vary, are established for the surface waters in specific, often very small, geographical areas, which are called 'water level areas'. The determined water levels are maintained as much as possible, during the periods, or in the conditions, indicated.[34] For non-designated regional waters, for example in areas with higher elevations, RWAs can establish target levels, which are not legally binding.

RWAs are functional decentralised public authorities and can exercise the (legal) instruments at their disposal *only* to exercise the specific responsibilities assigned to them. As set out in the Water Act, they must exercise their responsibilities for the management of regional water systems, which includes the establishment of water level decisions, for the purpose(s) of:

a. *preventing and, where necessary, limiting floods, excess water and the scarcity of water*
b. *protecting and improving the chemical and ecological quality of water systems and*
c. *fulfilling the societal functions assigned to water systems.*[35]

This statutory limitation of the purposes for which RWAs can exercise their (legal) instruments for the management of regional waters will not change under the new Environment and Planning Act.[36]

---

32 Art. 5.2(1), Water Act, supra, note 36.
33 Ibid., Arts. 1.1(1) and 5.2(1), and Art. 1.1(2), Regional Water Authorities Act, supra, note 35.
34 Art. 5.2(2), Water Act, supra, note 36.
35 Ibid., Art. 2.1(1).
36 Arts. 2.17(1)(a)(i) and 2.41, Environment and Planning Act, supra, note 34.

5.2.2. *Spatial Planning and Land Use*

To ensure that the agricultural use of peatlands changes to be better suited to wet conditions, municipalities can enact general rules, in their zoning plans or environmental by-laws, in which they prohibit or prescribe certain agricultural uses. They could also lay down provisions, in their zoning plans and/or by-laws, which require a permit for certain agricultural uses, in combination with assessment rules for the granting of these permits. In so far as these rules are enacted in the interests of spatial planning, they must be included in the municipal zoning plans.[37] If these rules serve other environmental interests, such as the reduction of GHG emissions, municipalities should include them in their environmental by-laws.

Municipal zoning plans also assign functions, such as agriculture, nature conservation and residential areas, to locations in the municipal territories. The assignment of these functions is legally relevant, as different (sets of) environmental rules will apply to different functions: for example, in a nature-conservation area, environmental rules will often restrict activities that would be allowed in agricultural areas. If it is necessary for the agricultural use of peatlands to be terminated in certain areas, municipalities can amend zoning plans to change the agricultural function currently assigned to a particular area, to, for example, a nature-conservation or residential area, for which the applicable rules will prohibit or severely restrict agricultural activities. When a provincial interest is involved, provinces can enact similar general environmental rules, which take precedence over municipal rules. Provincial rules about spatial planning, as well as the assignment of spatial functions, are laid down in provincial zoning plans. Other environmental rules are laid down in the provincial environmental regulations.[38]

Under the Environment and Planning Act, all municipal rules on the environment, spatial planning and land use will be integrated into the physical environment plan, which each municipality has to enact.[39] All provincial rules relating to the environment will be integrated into the environmental regulation, to be enacted by all provinces.[40]

5.2.3. *Proportionality and Fundamental Rights*

The general rules and assignments of functions, in zoning plans and environmental by-laws, as well as water level decisions, should be in conformity

---

37 Art. 3.1(1), Spatial Planning Act *Staatsblad (Dutch National Register)* 2007, 105).

38 Ibid., Art. 3.26, and Art. 1.2, Environmental Management Act (*Staatsblad (Dutch National Register)* 1979, 442).

39 Art. 2.4, Environment and Planning Act, supra, note 34.

40 Ibid., Art. 2.6.

with general legal principles, particularly the principle of proportionality, and the fundamental rights enshrined in the Dutch Constitution. They should also be in conformity with EU law and the fundamental rights enshrined in the European Convention of Human Rights; the Netherlands is a monist legal order, in which provisions of international law, which may be binding on all persons by virtue of their contents, have direct effect, and take precedence over domestic law.[41] If the function assigned to a location in a zoning plan is changed away from agricultural use and re-assigned to, for example, a nature function, the farmer needs to be bought out by a public authority or to be expropriated with appropriate compensation. Similarly, if a general rule is enacted which restricts the agricultural use of peatlands, and thereby affects certain farmers disproportionately, their losses will be compensated.[42]

6. THE GAP BETWEEN THE INTERCONNECTED ENVIRONMENT AND THE FRAGMENTED LEGAL SYSTEM, AND HOW TO BRIDGE IT

6.1. THE GAP BETWEEN THE INTERCONNECTED ENVIRONMENT AND THE FRAGMENTED LEGAL AND GOVERNANCE SYSTEM

As outlined in section 5 above, environmental law and governance in the Netherlands are organised on a sectoral basis: different public authorities are responsible for different components of the environment, and exercise their responsibilities to protect different, possibly conflicting, environmental interests. Although the new Environment and Planning Act integrates most sectoral environmental legislation into a single environmental code, the fragmentation of environmental law will remain. Although some instruments in the new Act are aimed at providing an integrated approach to the protection of the environment, such as the physical environment plan, which will contain all municipal rules on the environmental (see already section 5.2.2),[43] the sectoral organisation of environmental law will mostly remain in place.

There are good reasons for this sectoral organisation of environmental law. A fully integrated approach, in which public authorities develop a comprehensive set of integrated policies which address all environmental challenges in a particular area, is not always desirable or even possible. A solution for one

41 The direct effect and primacy of EU law was established in Case 26/62, *Van Gend & Loos*, ECLI:EU:C:1963:1 and Case 6/64, *Costa v. ENEL*, ECLI:EU:C:1964:66.

42 Supreme Court, 18 January 1991, ECLI:NL:HR:1991:AC4031.

43 Art. 4.1, Environment and Planning Act, supra, note 34.

environmental challenge can negatively impact on the solution for another challenge, which makes it very difficult, if not impossible, to come up with a comprehensive set of policies that satisfies all actors and interests involved.[44]

At the same time, this means that environmental policymaking and decision-making is *fragmented*. Fragmentation is commonly defined as a situation in which the 'legal and governance architecture' is marked by a 'patchwork' of public institutions that are different in, *inter alia*, their spatial scope and subject matter.[45] Fragmentation, especially a high degree thereof, is also undesirable: the resulting gap between the integrated environment and the fragmented legal and governance system makes it more difficult for public authorities to effectively develop and implement policies aligned across policy domains.[46]

6.2. THE GAP IN THE CONTEXT OF REDUCING PEAT OXIDATION AND GHG EMISSIONS FROM PEATLANDS

The reduction of peat oxidation and GHG emissions from peatlands provides a good example of how the gap between the interconnected environment and the fragmented legal and governance system makes it (more) difficult for public authorities to effectively address environmental challenges. As described in section 5 above, reducing peat oxidation requires the exercise of (legal) instruments in the policy domains of both water management and spatial planning, for which different public authorities, primarily RWAs and municipalities, are responsible. Public authorities can only exercise these (legal) instruments to promote certain environmental interests. For example, RWAs can only exercise their responsibilities for the management of regional water systems, such as amending water level decisions, for the purposes set out in the Water Act.

This considerably limits the ability of RWAs to raise the groundwater level in peatlands. Although raising surface water levels to reduce peat oxidation could

44 Council for the Environment and Infrastructure, *The Sum of the Parts: Converging National and Regional Challenges*, Report, 2019. See also, in the context of environmental legislation, I. de Waal, 'Coherence in law: A way to stimulate the transition towards a circular economy? A critical analysis of the European Commission's aspiration to achieve full coherence between chemicals legislation and waste legislation – and product legislation', *Maastricht Journal of European and Comparative Law*, (2021) 28(6), pp. 760–783.

45 H.K. Gilissen et al., 'Bridges over Troubled Waters: An Interdisciplinary Framework for Evaluating the Interconnectedness within Fragmented Flood Risk Management Systems', *Journal of Water Law*, (2016) 25(1), pp. 12–26; F. Biermann et al., 'The Fragmentation of Global Governance Architectures: A Framework for Analysis', *Global Environmental Politics*, (2009) 9(4), pp. 14–40.

46 S.Wuijts, P.P.J. Driessen and H.F.M.W. van Rijswick, 'Governance Conditions for Improving Quality Drinking Water Resources: the Need for Enhancing Connectivity', *Water Resources Management* (2018) 32, pp. 1245–1260.

serve various environmental interests, including reducing GHG emissions, protecting species and habitats, and improving water quality, RWAs cannot amend water level decisions to promote those interests, as they are outside the scope of the Water Act. This complicates policymaking and decision-making and could prevent public authorities from addressing the challenges of soil subsidence, peat oxidation and GHG emissions from peatlands effectively. This section will further discuss the (im)possibility of RWAs amending water level decisions to raise water levels.

6.2.1. Raising Water Levels to Reduce GHG Emissions from Peatlands

It is impossible for RWAs to use their legal instruments to amend water level decisions *solely* for the purpose of reducing GHG emissions. This would serve the environmental interest of mitigating climate change, which is not an interest that RWAs can take into account in the exercise of their public responsibilities.

It could be argued that, by amending water level decisions to raise surface water levels, RWAs serve one of the purposes of the Water Act, namely *the fulfilment of the societal functions assigned to water systems*. This is because the reduction of GHG emissions, in order to mitigate climate change, can certainly be considered a societal need to which water systems can contribute. However, it follows from both the explanatory memorandum to the Water Act, and from case law, that 'societal function' must be interpreted narrowly, to concern only the function of the water system itself (for example, fisheries or shipping) or the facilitation of the surrounding land use (for example, agriculture or nature conservation). In practice, the water levels established in water level decisions mostly facilitate the surrounding agricultural land use.[47] Since the reduction of GHG emissions is neither a function of the water system itself nor an environmental interest bound to a specific type of land use, it is not considered a 'societal function' under the Water Act.

RWAs cannot, therefore, exercise their legal instruments, including the establishment or amendment of water level decisions, solely to reduce GHG emissions from peat. This is prohibited, as it would result in *détournement de pouvoir* (exercising a responsibility for a different purpose than that for which it was conferred).[48] This was also stated by the Council of State, the Netherlands' highest administrative court on environmental matters, in a judicial decision in 2021, which concerned an appeal by a non-governmental organisation against a water level decision, on the grounds, among others, that it violated the Paris

47 For an elaborate analysis in Dutch, see M. van Gils and F. Groothuijse, 'Juridisch instrumentarium voor de reductie van CO2-emissie uit veengebieden: gefundeerd op slappe bodem?', *Tijdschrift voor Bouwrecht*, (2021/115), para. 5.

48 Art. 3:3, General Administrative Law Act (*Staatsblad (Dutch National Register)1993, 693)*.

Agreement, because the decision maintained the current extent of drainage of a peatland area, and did not, therefore, do enough to mitigate climate change. However, the court decided that the decision was not disproportionate, since 'the reduction of CO_2 emissions does not belong to the duties of the regional water authority'.[49]

6.2.2. *Raising Water Levels to Protect Species and Habitats*

Only in certain conditions can RWAs use their legal instruments to raise water levels *solely* for the purpose of protecting species and/or habitats. For surface waters in or surrounding Natura 2000 areas or nature-conservation areas protected under domestic law, RWAs should exercise their responsibilities to facilitate these areas to *fulfil the societal functions assigned to water systems*. These areas have a specific 'nature-conservation function', and the water system should be aimed at facilitating this type of land use. These areas typically require high water levels, as the protected habitats and species there require wet conditions.

However, nature protection interests which are not bound to a specific area, such as the protection of birds outside protected areas,[50] or the biodiversity of peatlands in general, are not considered a 'societal functions' under the Water Act. Notwithstanding that the Netherlands *should* comply with its obligations under European nature protection legislation, this does preclude RWAs, as decentralised public authorities, from exercising their responsibilities, including amending water level decisions, for the purpose of these interests.

6.2.3. *Raising Water Levels for Water-Related Purposes*

RWAs could also amend water level decisions to raise surface water levels in order to serve the other purposes set out in the Water Act. First, RWAs could raise water levels for *preventing and, where necessary, limiting floods and excess water*. This would reduce soil subsidence, and contribute to climate change mitigation, and, in turn, reduce the risk of flooding, or at least prevent it from increasing. However, the effect on flood prevention and water safety would only be modest and indirect. In the short term, raising water levels would even decrease water safety, as raising water levels reduces the water storage capacity of ditches and canals. This makes it very difficult for RWAs to justify raising water levels for the purposes of limiting flood risks and enhancing water safety.

It could also be argued that raising surface water levels could *limit the scarcity of water* in peatlands, as the peat soil would not dry out as much as it currently does. However, raising water levels in peatlands also leads to fewer

---

49 Judicial Division of the Council of State, 15 September 2021, ECLI:NL:RVS:2021:2077.
50 Art. 5(d), Birds Directive, supra, note 14.

water resources in other areas. Furthermore, in periods when fresh water is scarce, it is allocated according to a 'priority of needs' list, enacted in the Water Decree, which designates how the available fresh water should be prioritised.[51] Preventing subsidence of peatlands is ranked as a high-priority interest, but is not the only such interest (these also include, *inter alia*, guaranteeing the supply of drinking water, and ensuring the stability of flood defences). As a result, it might not even be possible to maintain high water levels in drier periods, as the water might be required for other purposes.

Finally, raising water levels to reduce peat oxidation could also serve to *protect and improve the chemical and ecological quality of water systems*. Since peat oxidation leads to a deterioration of the quality of groundwater and surface water, reducing oxidation will improve water quality, which is also important considering the objectives of the Water Framework Directive. However, the extent to which the raising of water levels can contribute to improving water quality is limited (see section 3.1.2. above). Protecting and improving water quality would not, therefore, justify RWAs raising water levels substantially.

6.3. BRIDGING THE GAP

6.3.1. *The Integration or Alignment of Public Policymaking*

The statutory limitation, described above, of the purposes for which RWAs can exercise their (legal) instruments, including amending water level decisions, is a good example of the gap between the interconnected environment and the fragmented legal and governance system. Although raising surface water levels could serve interests that are not water-related, such as enhancing biodiversity and mitigating climate change, RWAs cannot amend water level decisions to raise water levels in view of these interests, as they are outside the scope of the purposes listed in the Water Act. This is a result of the sectoral organisation of environmental law and governance, in which the responsibilities for different components of the environment are strictly divided between different public authorities.

However, this gap can be bridged. This requires public authorities to integrate or align public policymaking and decision-making, both at the strategic level, at which comprehensive, long-term environmental policies are developed, and at the implementation level, at which strategic policies are translated into concrete measures and administrative decisions.

At the strategic level, public authorities could bridge this gap by integrating, or at least aligning, their policies to deal with the interrelated challenges of soil

---

51 Art. 2.9, Water Act, supra, note 36 and Art. 2.1, Water Decree (*Staatsblad (Dutch National Register)* 2009, 548).

subsidence, peat oxidation and GHG emissions from peat.[52] This should ensure that these environmental challenges are addressed similarly in the policy domains of both water management and spatial planning and land use, resolving, as far as possible, the underlying, potentially conflicting interests of these policy areas.

At the implementation level, bridging the gap can be achieved through coordination of (the exercise of) policy and legal instruments.[53] It should be clear which public authority is responsible for implementing which measures, and how they should use the (legal) instruments at their disposal for implementing them. The province would be the most obvious public authority for coordinating the exercise of (legal) instruments by public authorities, as it stands between the national government, which operates on the strategic level, and the municipality and RWAs, which operate primarily on the implementation level. Furthermore, under the Environment and Planning Act, the province is specifically assigned the responsibility for the area-focused coordination of the exercise of the responsibilities of municipalities and RWAs.[54] For this purpose, the province could establish operational policy documents (under the Environment and Planning Act, these are called 'programmes'), in which it describes which measures should be implemented by which public authorities, within what time frame, and using which (legal) instruments.

6.3.2. The Alignment of Legal Instruments to Change Water Levels and Land Use

The alignment of the *legal* instruments to raise water levels, particularly the amendment of water level decisions, and the assignment of functions and general rules about (agricultural) land use in zoning plans and other (decentralised) environmental legislation, should be based on the principle of '*function decides water level*'.[55] Since it is difficult for RWAs to change water levels *solely* to reduce peat oxidation and/or reduce GHG emissions, except in certain cases to protect and improve water quality, the land use itself first needs to change. Municipalities and provinces (if a provincial interest is involved) can do so by enacting general rules which prohibit or prescribe certain agricultural uses, or require a permit for them, so that the agricultural land use is better suited to wet conditions. They can also change the function of agricultural land to nature-conservation areas or residential areas. Since water level decisions are mostly aimed at facilitating land use to fulfil the 'societal

---

52 Van den Ende, supra, note 1.

53 Also see Gilissen, supra, note 51; Wuijts, Driessen and Van Rijswick, supra, note 52.

54 Art. 2.18(1)(a), Environment and Planning Act, supra, note 34.

55 M. van Gils, E. Stouthamer and F. Groothuijse, 'Towards a legal strategy fitting today's challenge of reducing impacts of subsidence in the Netherlands', *Proceedings of the International Association of Hydrological Sciences*, 2020(382), pp. 825–829.

functions' of water systems, RWAs must amend these decisions to raise water levels, as this is necessary to facilitate the new functions or changed agricultural uses of the peatland area.

7. CONCLUSION

One of the main obstacles to the effective reduction of peat oxidation and GHG emissions from peatlands in the Netherlands is the 'gap' between interconnected environmental challenges and the fragmented legal and governance system. Environmental law and governance are organised on a sectoral basis, in which the responsibilities for different components of the environment are divided between different public authorities. In such a fragmented system, it is difficult for public authorities to develop and implement effective policies for the interconnected challenges faced by the environment.

In the context of reducing peat oxidation and GHG emissions from peatlands, this gap is particularly apparent. The environmental challenges of soil subsidence, oxidation and GHG emissions from peatlands are very interconnected, and require measures in the policy domains of both water management and spatial planning. However, because of the fragmentation of environmental law and policies, these measures must be taken by different public authorities, primarily RWAs and municipalities, who have limited decision-making scope. This is particularly true for RWAs, who can exercise their responsibilities *only* to serve water-related purposes, which considerably limits their ability to amend water level decisions to raise water levels in peatlands. This complicates policymaking and decision-making and could prevent public authorities from effectively addressing the interconnected challenges of soil subsidence, peat oxidation and greenhouse gas emissions from peatlands.

The gap can, however, be bridged, both at the strategic and the implementation level. At a strategic level, public authorities should develop integrated policies, or at least align their policies with one another, to deal with these interrelated challenges in the different policy areas involved, particularly water management, and spatial planning and land use. At the implementation level, this can be achieved through coordination of (the exercise of) policy and legal instruments. The alignment of the use of legal instruments should be based on the principle of '*function decides water level*'. Since it is difficult for RWAs to raise water levels to reduce peat oxidation and GHG emissions, the land use itself first needs to change. To do so, municipalities and/or provinces should enact general rules that prohibit, prescribe, or require a permit for, certain agricultural uses of peatlands, or assign a different function to areas currently in agricultural use. RWAs must then amend water level decisions to raise water levels, as this is necessary to facilitate the new function or changed agricultural use of the peatland area.

Thus, by developing integrated policies and aligning the exercise of legal instruments, public authorities can bridge the 'gap' between the interconnected environment and the fragmented legal and governance system. This would enable them to deal effectively with interrelated environmental challenges, such as reducing soil subsidence, oxidation and GHG emissions from peatlands.

UNVEILING THE LOOPHOLE OF COMPENSATORY RESTORATION AFTER DAMAGE IN THE EU

Francesca LEUCCI

ABSTRACT

Equivalency analysis methods, such as the habitat equivalency analysis, were introduced in the European Union (EU) to assess the interim losses of environmental damages, i.e. the losses occurring between environmental accidents and full recovery therefrom. More precisely, they allow restoration projects to be measured, so that the value of benefits equals the value of lost ecological services. Yet, whether environmental liability laws can prevent and remedy environmental damages depends on various factors, including how accurate such analyses can be. By illustrating the law and practice of the habitat equivalency analysis, in the EU and the United States (US), this chapter seeks to unveil the hidden loophole that can lead to partial compensation of damage, and thus inefficient prevention of environmental accidents in the EU.

1. INTRODUCTION

The primary goals of the European Union (EU) Environmental Liability Directive (Directive 2004/35/CE) (ELD) are to return damaged environments to the condition they were in prior to the damage, and to remedy the lost natural resources and services during the period of recovery – the so-called interim losses. Indeed, even if injured natural resources are fully restored to their baselines, society also needs compensation for the losses of natural resources and their services, between the moment of the injury and the moment of full recovery. Moreover, if injured natural resources cannot be fully restored, society needs compensation for permanent losses. The activity of addressing and compensating interim and permanent losses goes by the name 'compensatory restoration', and the process 'to ensure that compensatory restoration neither over-compensates nor under-compensates for service losses'[1] is called 'scaling'.

The aims of this chapter are to illustrate the peculiarities of the law and practice of compensatory restoration in the EU, in comparison with the United States (US), and to determine whether full internalisation of environmental costs is being achieved in both jurisdictions. This is essential with a view to determining whether environmental liability laws are likely to achieve not only restoration, but also efficient prevention of environmental accidents, by making polluters pay for the full cost of the harms they caused.

2. COMPENSATORY RESTORATION IN THE EU

In the EU, the declared goal of compensatory restoration measures, under the ELD, is to address and compensate for the interim losses of natural resources and services until full recovery.[2] Moreover, the primary techniques to scale compensatory remedial measures are the 'service-to-service' or the 'resource-to-resource' equivalence approaches.[3] Therefore, actions to provide resources and/or single services of the same type, quality and quantity should be given priority over monetary payments. Only where these kinds of resources and/or services are not available will alternative natural resources and/or services have to be provided, in which case, for instance, a reduction in quality may be offset by an increase in quantity.[4]

Lastly, if it is not possible to use the service-to-service approach, the competent authority may prescribe the employment of monetary valuation of

[1] W.H. Desvousges et al., 'Habitat and resource equivalency analysis: a critical assessment', *Ecological Economics*, (2018) 143, pp. 74, 75.

[2] It must be kept in mind that interim losses occur over an infinite period of time if primary restoration is not possible. The magnitude of interim losses depends on the primary restoration options, and the time taken until full recovery.

[3] Directive 2004/35/CE of the European Parliament and of the Council of 21 April 2004 on environmental liability with regard to the prevention and remedying of environmental damage, OJ 2004 L 143/56 (hereinafter 'ELD'), Annex II, para. 1.1.3.

[4] Ibid., para. 1.2.2.

natural resources, to scale compensatory measures. This differs from physical measurements of losses, as it relies on traditional non-market valuation methods, such as market prices or contingent valuation methods (i.e. surveys to estimate how much people would be willing to spend to avoid a certain damage to the environment). If the monetary valuation of lost resources/services is practicable, but valuation of replacement resources/services requires excessive time or money ('cannot be performed at a reasonable time-frame or at a reasonable cost'), the Directive prescribes that the competent authority can choose remedial measures whose cost is equivalent to the monetary value of lost resources or services.[5]

This resembles the third scaling approach in the US (value-to-cost), as the next section will illustrate. Moreover, it implies that the goal of monetary valuation should, first, be to equate the value of the damage with the value of the replacement resources and/or services (value-to-value). Only when this is not practicable then the value-to-cost approach comes in. Whether this sequence is effectively followed in practice will be the subject of section 7 below.

3. COMPENSATORY RESTORATION IN THE US

Under US law, there are three main approaches to scaling compensatory restoration options.[6]

The first is the 'service-to-service' approach (resource-to-resource method), which is based on a one-to-one trade-off, meaning that the lost service is replaced by a new one that provides the same quantity of services. Whenever possible, public authorities should apply this approach. If the injured and the replaceable natural resources are of the same type, quality and value, this approach is the most appropriate.

The habitat equivalency analysis (hereinafter 'HEA') is the most common service-to-service approach. Under US law, the HEA entails three main steps:

1. Quantifying the present (discounted) value of service losses.
2. Quantifying the present value of service gains (provided by compensatory restoration projects).
3. Calculating the quantity of restoration needed to equate losses and gains.[7]

---

5 Ibid., para. 1.2.3.

6 The first guidance document on scaling restoration projects under the Oil Pollution Act of 1990 was issued by the NOAA in 1997. It recommended scaling restoration through the habitat equivalency analysis (HEA), and that the cost of the project is considered to be the measurement of the damage.

7 National Oceanic and Atmospheric Administration, Damage Assessment and Restoration Program, 'Habitat equivalency analysis: an overview', 1995, p. 24.

In order to quantify service losses, it is important to take into account the following: the starting moment of the injury, the per cent service level prior to the accident (baseline), the service decline function, the per cent service level decrease, the extent of injury (hectares of habitat or number of individual organisms), the starting moment of recovery, the service recovery function (time-path), and the maximum per cent service provision after restoration.

In order to quantify the benefits of compensatory projects, the following factors need to be assessed: the initial percent service of a compensatory site, the starting moment of provision of services in the compensatory site, the service provision function (time-path), the duration of the compensatory project, and the relative value of the compensatory resource compared with the injured one.

After discounting service gains and losses, restoration is scaled by dividing the number of restoration units needed to compensate the public for lost natural resources by the number of units lost.

If the service-to-service approach is not feasible, i.e. a one-to-one match is not possible, the second scaling approach is the 'value-to-value' approach. It differs from the previous approach because it is based on the economic value (obtained through non-market valuation methods) of the damage,[8] rather than a physical measurement of the services provided. Its aim is to identify a restoration option such that the benefit of the compensatory option is equal to the economic value of the lost services.[9] In the US, when scaling a restoration action, public bodies have to discount all service quantities and/or values to the date of the claim, and to evaluate the uncertainties of restoration actions. The criteria to follow when selecting the appropriate restoration action include the capability of returning the resource to its baseline in an 'expeditious and cost-effective'[10] manner, while involving the interested parties in the administrative process (cooperative approach).

A third possible approach to scaling is the value-to-cost approach. According to the law, this should be the least-preferred approach, but it is in fact the most common. Here, the value of the lost services and/or resources is weighted against the cost of restoration, instead of measuring the benefits of restoration. While this approach ensures equivalency between the value of the loss and the cost

---

8 The value of damage to the environment can be achieved through economic valuation techniques that measure public preferences for an environmental state. These techniques include stated preference mechanisms and revealed preference mechanisms, aimed at eliciting people's preferences through surveys, in the first case, or by using data from actual markets, in the second case. By contrast, costs of clean-up and restoration do not need to previously identify a damage and damaged parties. They are based on technical options available, rather than on public preferences.

9 Under US law, public authorities have to measure the value of injured natural resources or services, and then 'select the restoration action that has a cost equivalent to the lost value' (National Oceanic and Atmospheric Administration, supra, note 7).

10 15 CFR §990.10 – Purpose.

of the compensatory restoration project, there is no guarantee that this value will be equivalent to the social benefits.[11] Apparently, this is the most common approach in the US,[12] because it is convenient for all the parties cooperating in the natural resource damage assessment (NRDA): public authorities can save funds and staff resources, the polluter has fewer assessment costs to reimburse, and the public can benefit sooner from the completion of restoration.

To sum up, the cooperative nature of the NRDA in the US allows the limitations of the more accurate value-to-value approach to be overcome.

4. DISCUSSION

In light of the above, if one had to respect the sequence of valuations for scaling in the order in which they appear under both EU and US laws, remediation should primarily be based on physical measurement of the damage, and the economic valuation of damages should come into play every time that the service-to-service match is not possible. Under EU law, economic (monetary) valuations are explicitly mentioned as 'alternative valuation techniques' for compensatory restoration. However, the wording of the ELD is not detailed and precise like the US laws, when it comes to scaling restoration, nor is economic valuation made mandatory if the service-to-service approach is not possible. More exactly, the equivalence between the economic value of the loss, on the one hand, and the benefit of the alternative restoration option, on the other, is not mentioned very clearly, as it is under the US law. But even more can be said on the service-to-service approach, which represents the most common scaling technique everywhere. Therefore, the rest of this chapter needs to focus on the HEA, as the main tool to compensate for environmental damages through the service-to-service approach. Seemingly, economic and ecological scholars have largely discussed the HEA, on both sides of the Atlantic. The first debated issue is whether or not compensatory restoration measures can, theoretically, achieve the declared goal of compensating society for the (interim) losses. The second fundamental issue is whether this goal has been effectively attained, in the practice of damage compensation. After examining the emergence of the HEA from a historical perspective (section 5), the following three sections (sections 6, 7 and 8) summarise, in turn, the main literature on, and the practice of, the HEA, in the US and the EU. The last section (section 8) draws some conclusions on the efficiency of compensatory restoration measures, as part of the environmental damage assessment process.

---

11 On this point, see R.E. Unsworth and R.C. Bishop, 'Assessing natural resource damages using environmental annuities', *Ecological Economics*, (1994) 11, p. 35.

12 S.M. Thur, 'Resolving Oil Pollution Liability with Restoration-based Claims', *Océanis*, (2006) 32, pp. 375, 382.

5. THE EMERGENCE OF THE HABITAT EQUIVALENCY ANALYSIS

'Equivalency analysis methods including habitat equivalency analysis (HEA) and resource equivalency analysis (REA)[13] were developed to facilitate restoration scaling',[14] i.e. to make sure that the value of ecological services gained through compensatory restoration is equal to the value of the lost services, prior to the environmental injury.

The conceptual basis of HEA/REA was developed in the 1990s, in a few seminal papers by King and Adler,[15] Mazzotta et al.,[16] Unsworth and Bishop,[17] Jones and Pease,[18] and Unsworth et al.[19] These authors discussed and suggested a paradigm shift in NRDAs, from monetary assessments of environmental damages to the analysis of the adequate scale of restoration projects that can 'make the public whole', i.e. compensate for the loss caused by an environmental accident.

According to all these scholars, the need for such a shift was rooted in one main reason: equivalency analyses could avoid the controversies often associated with monetary valuations of passive or non-use values.[20] In this way, they allow the ultimate goal of environmental damage assessments – restoration – to be achieved in a more cost-effective manner.

After these early theoretical works, compensatory restoration started being used in some environmental damage assessments in the US, in the 1990s.[21] By the beginning of the 2000s, the 'paradigm shift' was considered complete,[22] and in the early 2000s (when the ELD in the EU was about to be born) the

---

13 REA is conceptually the same as HEA, but service losses are not calculated in terms of habitat area, but through biological metrics, such as the number of organisms lost and gained. HEA is used for habitat losses, and REA for resource losses.

14 Desvousges et al., supra, note 1, p. 75.

15 D.M. King and K.J. Adler, 'Scientifically defensible compensation ratios for wetland mitigation', US Environmental Protection Agency' (1991).

16 M.J. Mazzotta, J.J. Opaluch and T.A. Grigalunas, 'Natural resource damage assessment: the role of resource restoration', *Natural Resources Journal*, (1994) 34, p. 153.

17 Unsworth and Bishop, supra, note 11.

18 C.A. Jones and K.A. Pease, 'Restoration-based compensation measures in natural resource liability statutes', *Contemporary Economic Policy*, (1997) 15, p. 111.

19 R.E. Unsworth, M.D. Barash and M.T. Huguenin, 'A proposed framework for developing and selecting compensatory restoration projects under federal natural resource damage assessment statutes', Industrial Economics Incorporated, 1999.

20 On this point, see also A. Randall, 'Whose losses count? examining some claims about aggregation rules for natural resources damages', *Contemporary Economic Policy* (1997) 15, p. 88.

21 See, for instance, Texas General Land Office, Texas Parks and Wildlife Department, Texas Natural Resource Conservation Commission, NOAA, US Fish and Wildlife Service, and US Department of the Interior, 'Draft damage assessment and restoration plan and environmental assessment for the point comfort/lavaca bay npl site recreational fishing service losses', 1999.

22 N.E. Flores and J. Thacher, 'Money, who needs it? Natural resource damage assessment', *Contemporary Economic Policy*, (2002) 2, p. 171.

employment of HEA became largely widespread in the US practice. On the one hand, US public authorities seemed much more inclined to use equivalency analyses, in order to save time and money,[23] and, on the other, equivalency analyses facilitated the early conclusion of liability lawsuits, by providing a basis for settlements.[24] Within a few years, in the early 2000s, the HEA/REA became the primary method for the calculation of environmental damages in the US. Since 2004, and drawing on the American model, it has also been explicitly incorporated in the EU ELD. However, unlike other non-market monetary valuation methods, the growing use of equivalency analysis methods was not accompanied by a deep level of academic and legal scrutiny. As notably stated, 'the principle of equivalency analysis may have been lost or ignored in the rush to find a simple method of analysis'.[25] Considering that HEA and REA were originally introduced for relatively simple situations, such as seagrass and coral reef losses,[26] their extensive use caused some scholars to ask whether equivalency analyses were also likely to compensate for the total social loss in cases of more complex injured environments. An overview of this literature is needed, to determine under which conditions HEA and REA can be considered an appropriate and efficient method to compensate for environmental losses.

6. EQUIVALENT COMPENSATION OF ENVIRONMENTAL LOSSES OR NOT?

The bulk of scholarship on equivalency analysis is focused on its policy and legal contexts, rather than on its welfare implications.[27] The latter point has been often overlooked, in both the economic and the ecological scholarship. Only a few fundamental works have investigated to what extent the HEA (or REA) may, theoretically, compensate for the social losses caused by environmental accidents.[28]

23 D.B. Thompson, 'Valuing the environment: Courts' struggles with natural resources damages', *Environmental Law*, (2002) 32, p. 62.

24 On the NOAA website, it is possible to find plenty of cases of NRDA plans based on HEA.

25 Desvousges et al., supra, note 1, p. 75.

26 The most cited cases in which the NOAA originally employed the HEA, and the courts approved its use, are *United States v. Fisher*, 1997 [Case No. 92-10027-CIVIL-DAVIS], and the case of a coral reef grounding in Florida. See, on the latter, K. Banks, R.E. Dodge, L. Fisher, D. Stout and W. Jaap, 'Florida Coral Reef Damage from Nuclear Submarine Grounding and Proposed Restoration', *Journal of Coastal Research*, (1998) 26, p. 64. See also *United States v. Great Lakes Dredge and Dock Co.*, 1999 [Case No. 97-10075].

27 M. Zafonte and S. Hampton, 'Exploring welfare implications of resource equivalency analysis in natural resource damage assessments', *Ecological Economics*, (2007) 61, pp. 134, 135.

28 Compensatory restoration differs from primary restoration because the aim of the latter is to improve the recovery, and to shorten the duration of the injury, while compensatory restoration can occur off-site, and concerns losses occurring until primary restoration has been fully achieved. Even if primary remedial measures help return the environment to 100% baseline conditions, compensation for past and interim losses is still required.

The next subsection (section 6.1) reviews the main literature on the HEA, while the following subsection (section 6.2) draws some conclusions from this review.

6.1. THE ECONOMIC SCHOLARSHIP ON THE HEA

Flores and Thacher[29] tried to answer the basic question of whether monetary valuations can be effectively avoided when NRDAs are based on compensatory restoration. They found that failing to consider money when measuring preferences does not ensure adequate compensation for social welfare losses, because of heterogenous preferences,[30] and value changes over time. Money would, instead, help the assessment of the relative costs and benefits of restoration projects, in order to identify the least-cost option, but also the potential redistributional effects which need to be considered, beyond welfare economic principles.

Strange et al.[31] examined the application of the HEA to determine the amount of restoration required to compensate for habitat loss, in the case of a salt marsh[32] damaged after an oil spill. According to the ecological literature, structural attributes (for example vegetation) fully recover within short times, whereas functional attributes (for example nutrient cycling) require more years to return to a fully functioning salt marsh: 'As a result, 100% recovery of some ecological services may represent only partial recovery of the system as a whole'.[33] Each of the marsh services may be measured through different metrics.[34] For instance, the service of fish production may be measured by looking at the species composition, its density, the biomass and the population demographics. Each of these metrics requires a different number of years to achieve maximum level of services (full recovery).[35] For this reason, if the selected metric for scaling the required amount of restoration is based only on *some* of all the marsh services and/or some of the metrics available for that service, it might be inaccurate.

---

29 N.E. Flores and J. Thacher, supra, note 22, p. 171.

30 This is likely to occur when social groups from different geographical areas value natural resources. Plausibly, locals value injuries as affecting a natural resource of limited size, thus having a larger effect on its marginal value. Conversely, those living far away may perceive the injury to be on a larger resource supply, thus having a negligible or null effect on its marginal value.

31 E. Strange et al., 'Determining ecological equivalence in service-to-service scaling of salt marsh restoration', *Environmental Management*, (2002) 29, p. 290.

32 A salt marsh (also known as a '*shorre*' in French, and a '*palude salmastra*' in Italian) is a coastal ecosystem between land and open water, regularly flooded by tides, and dominated by salt-tolerant terrestrial plants which are essential for providing nutrients to the water, and for coastal protection. Their importance for biodiversity conservation has been particularly emphasised with reference to the impacts of climate change on coastal erosion.

33 Strange et al., supra n. 31, p. 297.

34 Ibid., p. 293.

35 Ibid., p. 294.

Table 1. Ecological services of salt marsh and associated metrics

Marsh services	Examples of metrics
Primary production	Above-ground biomass, below- ground biomass, stem density
Habitat for biota	Canopy architecture of vegetation
Soil development and biogeochemical cycling	Soil and porewater nutrients, soil organic matter content, substrate particle size, soil moisture content, nitrogen fixation rates, denitrification rates
Food chain support	Density and biomass of vegetation, infauna, macrophyte detritus, and benthic algae
Fish and shellfish production	Density, species composition, diversity, biomass, population demographics

Source: E. Strange et al, 'Determining ecological equivalence in service-to-service scaling of salt marsh restoration', Environmental Management, (2002) 29, p. 293.

Table 2. Years to achieve maximum level of services for different metrics and services

Ecological service	Metric	Time (yr.)	Recovery (%)	Type of project	Location of marsh	Source
Primary production	Above-ground biomass	2–3	100	Created	NC	Craft and others (1999)
	Below-ground biomass	3	100	Restored	NC	Broome and others (1986)
	Stem density	5–6	100	Restored	NC	Broome and others (1986)
Soil development and biogeochemical	Soil organic matter	24	29	Created	TX	Lindau and Hossner (1981)
cycling	Soil nitrogen	24	50	Created	TX	Lindau and Hossner (1981)
	Soil carbon	5	8	Created	NC	Craft and others (1991)
	Macroorganic matter	15–30	100	Created	NC	Craft and others (1988)
	Dissolved organic C	5	34	Created	NC	Craft and others (1991)
	Dissolved organic N	5	60	Created	NC	Craft and others (1991)
	NH4-N	5	25	Created	NC	Craft and others (1991)
Invertebrate food supply	Infauna density and species richness	15–25	100	Created	NC	Craft and others (1999)
	Infauna community composition	1–17	100	Created	NC	Sacco and others (1994)

(continued)

Table 2 *continued*

Ecological service	Metric	Time (yr.)	Recovery (%)	Type of project	Location of marsh	Source
Secondary production	Shellfish density	3–15	93	Created	TX	Minello and Webb (1997)
	Fish density	3–15	41	Created	TX	Minello and Webb (1997)
	Shellfish density	5	20	Created	TX	Minello and Zimmerman (1992)
	Fish density	5	100	Created	TX	Minello and Zimmerman (1992)

Source: E. Strange et al., 'Determining ecological equivalence in service-to-service scaling of salt marsh restoration', Environmental Management, (2002) 29, p. 294.

Furthermore, short-term recovery, based on population-based metrics, does not imply long-term sustainability, and the lack of long-term data increases the uncertainties. Lastly, natural variations can make recovery trajectories even more difficult to predict.

For all these reasons, the HEA only theoretically represents an optimal tool for scaling restoration, since 'it reflects ecological variability and complexity'.[36] Yet, in practice, its reliability critically depends on its assumptions, and the data available, including in the long term. Therefore, Strange et al. recommended the employment of a flexible approach to the HEA that compares results using multiple metrics, and assesses equivalence based on evidence. Monitoring activities should then allow restoration results to be evaluated and adjusted.

Dunford et al.[37] investigated the sensitivity of the REA methodology under several price-change scenarios, with changes in the baseline, and with different metrics. For instance, changes in the baseline specifically made the service loss increase or decrease, or stay constant. Because of this, an approach based on historical data, (so-called, before-and-after approach) would be more recommended than one based on baseline ecological conditions (so-called, reference-location approach). Regarding the metric, they criticised the fact that the HEA often relies on single metrics (for example, number of fish or number of acres) to compare lost and gained services, because habitats provide many different services, and the choice of the metric should depend on the complexity of the damaged ecosystem. Also, metrics based on bio-indicators (population metrics) often overestimate the effect of injuries on the public benefit, or may provide almost no information about the change in the 'high-level' habitat

36 Ibid., p. 298.

37 R.W. Dunford, T.C. Ginn and W.H. Desvousges, 'The use of habitat equivalency analysis in natural resource damage assessments', *Ecological Economics*, (2004) 48, p. 49.

services. The unlikelihood of a single metric accurately reflecting services is a significative limitation of the HEA.

Zafonte and Hampton[38] delved more into the two issues of heterogenous preferences and price changes. The basic resource equivalency problem can be formulated in an equation between the value of the injured resource (time, space and magnitude of the injury) and the value of the restored resource (time, space and magnitude of benefits).[39] Since the REA was originally introduced to restore resources 'of the same type, quality and of comparable value',[40] the values attributed to each injured and restored resource unit are assumed to be equivalent, and to drop out of the equation. Once the equation is satisfied, it is possible to determine the cost of conducting the restoration project using the assessed scale. The cost of the restoration project is, ultimately, the measure of the damage. Therefore, with the REA, the question for environmental agencies is no longer how much society values the benefits of the restoration project (what amount of money makes society indifferent), but how much it costs to provide a compensating amount of the injured resource (what amount of restoration makes society indifferent).[41]

The authors represented the common multi-period REA problem by showing that restoration projects normally begin after the initial injury, and are supposed to provide less than a 100 per cent gain in resource service value.[42]

Figure 1. Conceptual representation of the REA problem

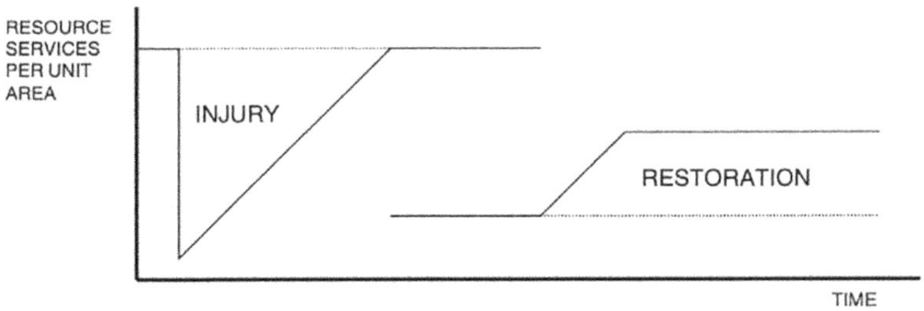

Source: M. Zafonte and S. Hampton, 'Exploring welfare implications of resource equivalency analysis in natural resource damage assessments', Ecological Economics, (2007) 61, p. 136.

According to Zafonte and Hampton, the values of the injured and restored resources may not cancel each other out in the equation, in three main cases:

- When the injured and restored resources are different (problem of substitutability).[43]

38 Supra, note 27.
39 Ibid., p. 135.
40 NOAA, 'Habitat equivalency analysis: an overview', 1995.
41 Jones and Pease, supra, note 18, p. 114.
42 Zafonte and Hampton, supra, note 27, p. 136.
43 Even similar ecosystems may provide different types of services.

- When the per-unit value of the injured and restored resources can change over time (for example, the baseline supply changes over time).[44]
- When people place heterogeneous preferences on the injured/restored natural resources, even in cases of perfect substitutability.[45]

With all these cases having in common the imperfect substitutability of injured and restored resources, it is uncertain whether the REA can help in scaling, in such a way that society is indifferent. By simulating two scenarios of: (1) long-term shifts in the baseline supply, resulting in a value change, over time, of the resource; and (2) market-level effects only at the local level, Zafonte and Hampton found that the REA, under traditional assumptions,[46] may overcompensate society by more than 25 per cent, except for permanent injuries,[47] in case (1), and may undercompensate society by almost 50 per cent, in case (2).

Zafonte and Hampton concluded that the inclusion of monetary values in the REA can, theoretically, provide a 'close approximation' of the welfare change. In line with Flores and Thacher, they found that monetary valuations are particularly needed to achieve full compensation when different subsets of the population place different values on the affected resources.[48]

Borrego and Riera[49] analysed an interesting issue in scaling, using the value-to-value approach under the ELD: the distance-decay function in off-site remediation projects. They investigated what amount of compensatory remediation is required to offset the environmental damage when off-site restoration projects are located far away from the damaged environment, by looking at the case study of environmental damage following a forest wildfire in Catalonia (Spain). Based on welfare losses determined by contingent valuation, they found that the efficient amount of compensatory remediation represented by off-site projects should be higher.

---

44 For instance, the wetland acreage has declined considerably from historical levels, in the US. Conversely, restoration projects aimed at increasing the wetland supply have more than doubled the area of wetlands in California: see Zafonte and Hampton, supra, note 27, p. 137.

45 This is the point already raised by Flores and Thacher, supra, note 22.

46 Where the value of the injured resource is equal to the value of the restored resource.

47 This is because the long-term increase in value affects both injured and restored resources, unless the decline in the resource quantity is severe, and it does not affect the success of restoration. If the decline of natural resources over time is severe, and it does not affect the success of compensatory restoration, the project will stop producing benefits in the long term. This is the case of endangered or declining species.

48 The same limitation occurs with the other non-market valuation methods, such as contingent valuation.

49 A.D. Borrego and P. Riera, 'Forest fire compensation: a contingent valuation exercise with a fixed bid and varying environmental quality levels' in A. González-Cabán (ed.), *Proceedings of the third international symposium on fire economics, planning and policy: common problems and approaches*, US Department of Agriculture, Forest Service, 2010.

In the wake of the few EU-wide empirical studies on the equivalency analysis complemented by welfare considerations, Martin-Ortega et al.[50] investigated whether compensatory restoration measures offset environmental damages 'from a public perception viewpoint'.[51] They specifically looked at the Corredor Ecologico del Rio Guadiamar, also known as the 'Green Corridor', that was created after the breach of the tailings dam of a mine[52] owned by the Boliden Apirsa company, in Aznalcóllar, 50 kilometres north of the Doñana National Park (southern Spain), in 1998. The breach of the dam released 6 million cubic metres of toxic mud into the Guadiamar river. The damage to the National Park was promptly diverted away, thanks to dams built quickly to contain the mud, and the Green Corridor was created, as a 'protected landscape' under regional law, to recover part of the damaged river, and to create a new recreation area. Moreover, it created a green passage for animals, between the National Park and the other protected area of Sierra Morena, and an additional buffer zone for the protection of the National Park. While the first two goals provided primary and complementary restoration, the animal passageway and the buffer zone represented compensatory restoration measures (additional improvements to compensate for interim losses). Drawing on the examples of the *Exxon Valdez* and *Prestige* oil spills, Martin-Ortega et al. conducted a survey study, to elicit the willingness to pay (WTP) of people living in 25 municipalities in Andalusia (southern Spain), to prevent similar accidents in the future. The mean WTP value for preventing similar accidents was 10.11 euros per household per year, and the mean WTP for the compensatory remediation provided by the Green Corridor was 4.75 euros per household per year, while the perceived gain from the Green Corridor, for the few (5 per cent) people who had visited the Green Corridor, was 9.40 euros per household per year. The practical application of monetary valuation methods showed that, even though the Green Corridor has returned the area to the conditions prior to the accident, the benefit provided by its additional services was insufficient to offset the interim losses caused by the toxic spill, from a social perspective (it was less than half the perceived welfare loss). Moreover, the additional services were not perceived as offsetting the original damage. Also, the lower value given to the Green Corridor, due to its low visitation rate, suggested that non-use values might be more important, in the case of the Doñana National Park. The study confirmed the need to complement resource and service equivalency methods with more economic valuation, to

---

50 J. Martin-Ortega, R. Brouwer and H. Aiking, 'Application of a value-based equivalency method to assess environmental damage compensation under the European Environmental Liability Directive', *Journal of Environmental Management*, (2011) 92, p. 1461. The study was part of the EU DG Research Project 'Resource Equivalency Methods for Assessing Environmental Damage in the EU (REMEDE)', under the 6th Framework Programme.

51 Ibid., p. 1462.

52 Tailings dams are earth-fill embankment dams, created to store by-products of mining operations. In mining, tailings are toxic leftovers after extracting the valuable parts of rocks containing minerals.

make sure that decisions on compensatory measures compensate for the whole welfare loss, and do not cause losses to society. Unlike in the US, empirical literature on the economic valuation of environmental damages is quite scarce in the EU, and is mainly focused on welfare estimates of non-use values.[53] Martin-Ortega et al. found that equivalency methods were insufficient to compensate for the whole welfare loss, and that compensatory remediation measures need to be complemented by monetary valuations through traditional non-market methods.

Shaw and Wlodarz[54] provided additional arguments to prove that 'there is a potential misconception among some (including economists) that HEA is devoid of economics and that it replaces traditional economic valuation approaches as a method of estimating economic losses for injuries'. Conversely, non-market economic valuation methods may complement equivalency analyses, in the context of determining the appropriate scale of restoration. To support this conclusion, Shaw and Wlodarz focused on the role of the discount rate, and demonstrated how its inclusion in the HEA equation would say something about the 'optimal timing of replacement',[55] by drawing on various case studies. The first case study is an oil spill that occurred in 1997, in the US, damaging 50 acres of wetland. In this case, discounting interim service losses amounted to more than the initial loss, resulting in a total present discounted value of 195.8 acres. Including a social discount rate in the HEA would require a previous decision on the rate at which a society is willing to trade future for present resources. A positive rate would mean that the society preferred having a natural resource today rather than tomorrow. In the US, the National Oceanic and Atmospheric Administration (NOAA) recommended that public authorities employ discount rates for restoration costs, linked to annual rates of return, and to the specific time period; this rate is often 3 per cent. In the EU, the discount rate for restoration projects can range from 3 per cent to 6 per cent, with many differences across the EU Member States. In conclusion, for Shaw and Wlodarz, more careful consideration of discounting would significantly improve the results of restoration. Moreover, more cooperation between local ecologists and economists, in the HEA/REA, would be crucial to establishing appropriate habitat metrics, in line with the scientific knowledge available, and techniques in use.[56]

---

53 Martin-Ortega et al., supra, note 50, cites, as precedents, works in the EU: T.A. Grigalunas et al., 'Estimating the cost of oil spills: lessons from the *Amoco Cadiz* incident', *Marine Resource Economics*, (1986) 2, p. 239; K. Van Biervliet et al., 'A contingent valuation study on accidental oil spill along the Belgian coast' in F. Maes (ed.), *Marine Resource Damage Assessment: Liability and Compensation for Environmental Damage*, Springer, 2005, p. 165; M.L. Loureiro, J.B. Loomis and M.X. Vázquez, 'Economic valuation of environmental damages due to the *Prestige* oil spill in Spain', *Environmental and Resource Economics*, (2009) 44, p. 537.

54 W.D. Shaw and M. Wlodarz, 'Ecosystems, ecological restoration, and economics: does habitat or resource equivalency analysis mean other economic valuation methods are not needed?', *Ambio*, (2013) 42, p. 628.

55 Ibid., p. 634.

56 Ibid., p. 641.

6.2. TAKEAWAYS FROM THE LITERATURE

To summarise the review above, the HEA (or REA)[57] represents a service-to-service approach, relying on the assumption that the society sees an equivalency between the lost natural resource and the one provided through a compensatory restoration project or projects.[58]

The HEA has a reputation of being very convenient, because it avoids time-consuming and controversial economic valuations. Its basic idea is that, if a certain number of hectares of habitat have been destroyed, it is sufficient to provide a number of hectares of the same habitat equivalent to the present (discounted) value of what has been lost.

Despite these advantages, equivalency analyses might be grossly inaccurate for several reasons, such as the choice of a single or inappropriate metric, and the lack of ecological data on long-term restoration;[59] heterogenous preferences and changing values over time;[60] price-change scenarios;[61] or imperfect substitution between the injured and restored sites.[62]

As described by Dunford, the HEA relies on four fundamental but questionable assumptions:

1. The type, quality and quantity of services provided by the compensatory project are assumed to be comparable to those lost.[63]
2. The values of the injured and compensatory services are considered to be constant over time.[64]

---

57 Where the damaged environment is not a habitat, but another natural resource, e.g. loss of fish or other animals.

58 More precisely, the society is willing to accept a trade-off between the value of the lost natural resources and the value of the compensatory restoration projects.

59 Strange et al., supra, note 31.

60 Flores and Thacher, supra, note 22.

61 Dunford et al., supra, note 37.

62 Zafonte and Hampton, supra, note 27.

63 Unsworth and Bishop, supra, note 11. This allows to assume that the present value of losses is equal to the present value of gains. Moreover, the services should be equal from an economic point of view, meaning that their demand has to be equal, and that they are substitutes. For instance, if a wetland area has to offset the ecological losses of a similar wetland, then the demand and supply of these resources should be the same. It is important, therefore, to take account of the availability of substitutes, and the income effect on the demand and supply: the availability of substitutes makes the value for restoration lower. See also Desvousges et al., supra, note 1. Some scholars have argued that this assumption can be relaxed if resources are scaled, and thus HEA can be applied to services that are not of the same type and quality. Yet, as Desvousges makes clear, scaling requires prior knowledge of the value of the services, and relative demand and supply, to make sure that there is proportionality.

64 What Desvousges et al., supra, note 1, note 74, pinpointed in this regard is that 'the longer the time period involved in the HEA quantification, the less likely this assumption is to hold'. Despite this assumption, it seems that the value of environmental services is more plausibly expected to increase over time, because of technological changes and rising incomes that

3. Marginal changes in the value of the injured services are considered to be constant over time.[65]
4. Restoration costs are assumed to be equal to the value of lost services.[66]

For all these reasons, it is recommended to carefully check the conditions for equivalency, and especially whether:

1. The chosen metric (whether a single metric or an index aggregating multiple metrics) captures the full range of lost ecosystem services.
2. The quality and value of services at the damaged and restored sites are comparable with one another.
3. The 'market', i.e. the people valuing the services, is the same in relation to the damaged and the restored site; in other words, *are those injured also beneficiaries of the replacement resources?*

Many scholars have suggested avoiding inaccuracies by complementing equivalency analyses with economic valuation. Some have also put forward alternative models of HEA/REA which include monetary values.[67]

Now, with rocky shores, sandy beaches and intertidal mudflats (coastal wetlands), it is often the case that, even if primary restoration of these habitats is possible, interim service losses cannot be repaired through compensatory restoration projects, i.e. by creating additional habitats, because this would not be feasible. Therefore, it is common practice to restore a habitat of a different type, quality and value. But how should the compensatory habitat be scaled in such a case? It would be necessary to 'develop a relative value ratio' between the damaged and the compensatory resources, but there are no clear guidelines on this.[68] It would, thus, be natural to examine how public authorities are dealing

---

affect the future demand for environmental services. See A.C. Fisher, J.V. Krutilla and C.J. Cicchetti, 'The economics of environmental preservation: a theoretical and empirical analysis', *The American Economic Review*, (1972) 62, p. 605, and A.C. Fisher, J.V. Krutilla and C.J. Cicchetti, 'The economics of environmental preservation: further discussion', *The American Economic Review*, (1974) 64, p. 1030.

65 Marginal values are crucial in the economic valuation, because they depend on the amount of services already available, on shifts in demand due to substitutes, and on rising incomes. This observation is also in the literature on HEA, since it is common knowledge that, among the conditions for service-to-service scaling, changes in resources and services are sufficiently small, and the value per unit of service is expected to be independent of changes. See D. Chapman, N. Iadanza and T. Penn, *Calculating resource compensation: an application of the service-to-service approach to the Blackbird Mine hazardous waste site*, NOAA Damage Assessment and Restoration Program Technical Report 97-1, 1998.

66 If not, this would determine undercompensation or overcompensation. See Unsworth and Bishop, supra, note 11, fn. 74.

67 D.D. Pavanelli and N. Voulvoulis, 'Habitat Equivalency Analysis, A framework for forensic cost evaluation of environmental damage', *Ecosystem Services*, (2019) 38, p. 100953.

68 Thur, supra, note 12, p. 389.

with the assessment of compensatory restoration in practice, and this forms the subject of sections 7 and 8 below.

7. THE PRACTICE OF THE HEA IN THE US

In 2018, Jones and DiPinto conducted an empirical analysis of US cases on liability for damage to public natural resources and services with non-use values, over the 25 years since the Oil Pollution Act had been promulgated, to determine which approach was preferred by US public authorities when scaling compensatory restoration projects.[69] They found that they relied mostly on the service-to-service approach (HEA), rather than what they called a 'valuation' approach (i.e. surveys). This was mainly because the HEA 'simplifies complex ecosystems through the choice of representative ecological process or function metrics as proxies for the change in the quantity and quality of service levels at the injury and restoration sites in a particular case'.[70] Also, in the few cases that had been litigated, the courts had usually upheld the HEA.[71]

Specifically, the NOAA had started using the HEA for the calculation of environmental damages in the early 1990s, for ship grounding cases in Florida where small quantities of coral reefs and seagrass had been damaged. Subsequently, public authorities extended the use of the HEA to difficult-to-value environmental damages caused by oil spills, hazardous material releases and forest fires, and to a wide range of habitats and species, including wetlands, rivers, beaches, fish, aquatic birds and endangered species. The simplicity and flexibility of the HEA allowed assessments to be sped up, and provided a quick basis for restoration settlements, which are how most cases in the US are concluded. The parameters for measuring the service losses tend to be highly simplified: the baseline is assumed to be 100 per cent, the decline function is often taken to be instantaneous, and the extent of the injury is measured, but the restoration function and the service provision are the objects of subjective decisions based on previous restoration projects.[72]

---

69 C.A. Jones and L. DiPinto, 'The role of ecosystem services in USA natural resource liability litigation', *Ecosytem Services*, (2018) 29, p. 333. This study is quite relevant, given that Carol Adaire Jones was lead economist on the Oil Pollution Act regulations from 1990 to 1997, overseeing 36 NRDA claims, including the *Exxon Valdez* case, and Lisa DiPinto is current senior scientist for NOAA's Office of Response and Restoration, and was also coordinator for the *Deepwater Horizon* case of 2010.

70 Ibid., p. 340.

71 For instance, *US v. Fisher* et al. (1997) and *US v. Great Lakes Dredge and Dock Co.* (1999), supra, note 26. In both cases, federal courts awarded damages for the destruction of acres of seagrass. More recently, in 2008 and 2012, the use of HEA was upheld for valuing forest fire damages on US public land.

72 For a discussion on these parameters, see Thur, supra, note 12, p. 384, with many references.

In one of the largest settlements, to date, for hazardous waste pollution in the US, the Blackbird Mine case study (contamination from the Blackbird Copper Mine), public bodies decided to conduct a cost-effective damage assessment, to quantify the injury and establish the restoration goals.[73] They thus focused on just three ecological metrics: quality of surface waters, injury to food web, and injury to Chinook salmon (an endangered species). Based on these metrics, two restoration goals were identified: restoration of the salmon population, and restoration of fishery habitat for compensatory restoration. The recovery of the salmon population to its 'carrying capacity', i.e. 100 per cent service level, would also be an indicator of full recovery for other indicators, such as the water quality. Furthermore, salmon would guarantee the return of nutrients for the whole stream, and recreational and cultural services related to the fishery. The HEA was, instead, used to calculate the amount of fishery habitat required to compensate for interim losses in the damaged location, and to match it with the size and type of lost fishery habitat.

To assist with the appropriate scaling of compensatory restoration, the NOAA has supported the production of reports synthesising concepts, models and techniques that have developed since the early 1990s.[74] These documents provide references to case studies and primary ecological scholarship, and their primary aim is to provide guidance for restoration scaling, according to the type of damaged habitat and resources.[75]

As mentioned above, the HEA was, initially, applied mainly to vessel groundings and restoration of seagrass beds and coral reefs, which are relatively small incidents. Based on monitoring studies, the NOAA developed assessment and restoration planning protocols to quantify injuries, and to project recovery and restoration times. For marsh habitats, which are the habitats most often impacted by oil spills, public authorities tend to choose either a single metric, or a few metrics, linked to lost primary ecological services.

If replacement with habitats of the same type and quality, and comparable value, is not feasible or cost-effective, public bodies make habitat trade-off decisions, and often make more cost-effective use of restoration funds by replacing low-productivity habitats with high-value habitats. Generally speaking, there is no one best approach, but the aggregation approach should be tailored to the particular conditions of each case.[76] Moreover, assessments are usually

---

73 Ibid.

74 See, for instance, E.P. English, C.H. Peterson and C.M. Voss, 'Ecology and economics of compensatory restoration', NOAA Coastal Response Research Center (CRRC), 2009. This report is based on the division between ecological and human services. It describes concepts and methods of restoration scaling, including HEA, REA and survey-based valuations. However, the goal is not only to describe the state of the art, but mainly to provide a synthesis of techniques for specific habitats and resources.

75 See ibid., for a complete study of HEA techniques based on the type of injured ecosystem.

76 Jones and DiPinto, supra, note 69, p. 343.

cooperative, and the public works with responsible parties, to value data and develop 'consensus-based' parameters for the HEA. Lastly, restoration plans are subject to public review, which is an alternative and more cost-effective source of public preferences, rather than survey-based valuations.[77]

8. THE PRACTICE OF THE HEA IN THE EU

In the US, the equivalency analysis method has been employed for damage and remediation assessment for more than two decades, under various statutory laws, but it was never applied in the EU until its introduction by the ELD, entering into force in 2004.

The report on the *Use of Resource Equivalency Methods in Environmental Damage Assessment in the EU With Respect to the Habitats, Wild Birds and EIA Directives*,[78] within the REMEDE project,[79] revealed that the use of resource equivalency approaches among ecologists in the EU seemed to be almost unknown, but that principles and approaches from the US were mainly used within the compensation and mitigation framework associated with the EU Birds, Habitats and Environmental Impact Assessment Directives:

> At this stage, no prior experience could be found of the use of resource equivalency methods in identifying compensatory strategies for neutralising accidental environmental damage.[80]

However, within the REMEDE project, various case studies were considered as potential applications of the new REMEDE Toolkit principles, which were developed to estimate sufficient amounts of compensatory restoration.[81] It is

---

77 Several scholars have criticised the HEA in the US, because it does not correctly assess the benefits of restoration projects, and money may end up in projects for which there is limited demand. Yet, according to the US Department of the Interior (DOI), the fact that public participation is required at various stages of the assessment of restoration plans is more efficient than a time-consuming collection of information on benefits that would ultimately be paid by the polluter. See Jones and DiPinto, supra, note 69, pp. 345 and 347.

78 J. Cox, 'Use of resource equivalency methods in environmental damage assessment in the EU with respect to the habitats, wild birds and EIA Directives', Deliverable D6B, REMEDE, 2007.

79 The REMEDE project has been designed to support the implementation of Annex II of the ELD. It was established within the 6th Framework Programme of the European Commission, with the aim of testing and disseminating methods for determining the scale of remedial measures appropriate to offset accidental environmental damages. It draws on experiences and methodological issues from the US, and on the experience of the EU. It does not tackle the threshold of significant damage under the ELD, the estimation of how much primary remediation is needed, or the best baseline to consider. It focuses only on REA for compensatory remediation.

80 Cox, supra, note 78, p. 1.

81 See the EU DG Research Project 'Resource Equivalency Methods for Assessing Environmental Damage in the EU (REMEDE)', under the 6th Framework Programme. (2006).The cases are

worth providing an overview of at least one of these cases (the chemical spill in Helsingborg, Sweden), to illustrate the existing state of knowledge in the EU. The spill occurred on 4 February 2005, when a chemical tank in Kemira, near the municipality of Helsingborg, collapsed, releasing more than 16,000 tonnes of toxic acid into a harbour connected to the Baltic Sea. The release had lethal effects on sea organisms, animals, sea plants and sediments, affecting an area of up to 12 hectares, to a depth of 10 metres.[82] The spill was followed by a compensatory restoration project, at a cost of 100,000 euros, that could provide one discounted hectare of seagrass habitat services. Within REMEDE, Cole and Kriström tried instead to determine the total amount of (interim) environmental damage (debit), by using four different quantification metrics of habitat services (richness, abundance, biomass of invertebrates, and habitat quality). The resulting total interim loss for the society was 33.1 discounted service hectare years, during the four-year period needed to achieve full restoration. Then, three potential remediation options were identified, and the gain (credit) in habitat services from one of these remediation projects (planting of seagrass beds) was calculated. After obtaining the present (discounted) value of gains and credits of habitat services, the appropriate amount of remediation was scaled to offset the damage. Finally, the cost of the remediation option, including seagrass planting, project planning, the administrative and permitting process, and long-term monitoring costs, was calculated, as an indication of the magnitude of environmental liability associated with the oil spill, and based on a resource equivalency approach (100,000 euros).[83] Yet, this estimate was based on a previous US study, and it was uncertain whether costs would remain the same in the specific location of the Helsingborg harbour. Later, it was discovered that the 100,000-euro remediation project had not achieved the equivalency of lost and restored habitat services.[84]

Due to the scarce practice, it has been argued that remediation options in the EU should take into full account the lost services for human welfare.[85] Yet, as stressed by some EU experts, 'acceptable application of equivalency analyses requires technical knowledge (e.g. natural sciences, economics, law), data, stakeholder engagement, and sometimes a lengthy and costly negotiation process'.[86] Currently, the ELD does not provide public authorities with the

---

accessible at: http://web.archive.org/web/20140222151043/http://www.envliability.eu/docs/D12CaseStudies/D12CaseStudies.html.

82 S. Cole and B. Kriström, 'Tank collapse and chemical release (Helsingborg, Sweden) case study report, Deliverable D12, REMEDE, 2008, p. 1.

83 Ibid., p. 35.

84 S. Cole, 'Environmental compensation using the REMEDE toolkit: how much is enough?', Stockholm presentation, REMEDE, 2008.

85 E. Brans, 'Legal analysis: resource equivalency methods for assessing environmental damage in the EU, REMEDE Report, 2006.

86 J. Lipton et al. (eds.), 'Equivalency methods for environmental liability: assessing damage and compensation under the European Environmental Liability Directive', Springer, 2018, pp. 5, 18.

necessary amount of human and technical resources. A consensus-based approach to restoration seems possible, but there is no incentive to settle restoration plans for polluters and public authorities, nor is there any incentive for societal participation in the design of restoration projects, unlike in the US.[87] Moreover, the HEA does not encourage a dialogue between public authorities and groups with interests.[88]

9. CONCLUSION

This chapter analysed the remedies for environmental liability in the EU, in order to determine whether, compared to the US, interim losses are fully compensated and, in this way, whether the environmental costs of accidents can be totally internalised by liable parties.

In the US, polluters are liable for a well-defined list of removal costs, interim losses pending recovery, and costs of assessment.[89] Moreover, the environmental damage assessment often relies on the HEA, following guidelines based on 30 years of experience.[90] In addition, a number of factors facilitate the fast attainment of restoration, which in turn minimises environmental damages. When it comes to compensatory restoration measures, these factors are represented mainly by technical guidance, a consensus-based equivalency analysis, and public participation in the design of restoration plans. According to the US Department of the Interior (DOI), consensus-based approaches between the public and liable parties, clear guidelines on scaling techniques, and close coordination between various public authorities, rather than monetary damages, have proved to be the

87 This may lead to restoration not in line with the public demand: 'Une compensation hors site qui pourrait ne pas répondre à la demande de la population victime du préjudice n'est pas toujours satisfaisante'. See A. Bas et al., 'Méthodes d'équivalence et compensation du dommage environnemental', Revue d'Économie Politique, (2013) 143, pp. 127, 154. See also L. Krämer, 'The EU and the system of environmental loss and damage. liability, restoration and compensation' in B. Pozzo and V. Jacometti (eds.), Environmental Loss and Damage in a Comparative Law Perspective, Intersentia, 2021, pp. 3–28, emphasising that there is not even an incentive for the public (NGOs and individuals) to ask public authorities to intervene if they do not restore the injured environment, in the absence of liable parties. In the US and a few other countries, if national authorities do not comply with the public request to intervene, people can take the matter to court. This is not allowed under the ELD: 'Overall, the Directive does not offer effective means to protect the environment against illegal activities and hold the wrongdoer liable' (ibid., p.12).

88 A. Bas et al., supra, note 87, p. 152.

89 33 USC 2706(d)(1). Additionally, OPA provisions enable separate claims for private losses to real property, profits, earning capacity, public losses to revenues, and other costs.

90 HEA is also used in many countries to determine the amount of compensatory mitigation needed to approve economic projects *(ex ante)* with future negative impacts on the environment. For additional references on this point, see Shaw and Wlodarz, supra, note 54, pp. 630–631.

best strategy for attaining restoration more quickly, more efficiently, and more effectively.[91]

In the EU, polluters are liable for the costs of primary, complementary and compensatory restoration, plus assessment costs. Like in the US, the compensation of environmental damages through restoration has become the common remedy, because it is easier (based on fewer economic valuation methodologies), ensures that the environment is returned to its baseline state, and is flexible (it is possible to opt for compensatory restoration even if primary restoration is feasible).[92] However, a number of issues might reduce the likelihood of achieving both optimal deterrence and cost-effective restoration. As to deterrence, there are no precise time frames and guidelines on restoration and HEA, and the public is not involved in restoration plans. Moreover, compensatory restoration of interim losses and permanent losses cannot ensure full internalisation, due to the lack of expertise on HEA, and missing ecological data on ecosystem services. There is, therefore, room for a degree of doubt as to whether the EU ELD can achieve efficient deterrence in addition to cost-effective restoration, and so fully internalise the environmental costs of accidents, especially in the case of complex ecosystems for which resources of the same type, nature and quality do not exist.

---

91 Jones and DiPinto, supra, note 69, p. 345.

92 On the lack of a hierarchy of remedies in the ELD, see G.M. van den Broek, 'Environmental liability and nature protection areas: Will the EU Environmental Liability Directive actually lead to the restoration of damaged natural resources?', *Utrecht Law Review*, (2009) 5, pp. 117, 127.

WHAT ARE WE TALKING ABOUT WHEN WE DISCUSS THE RIGHTS OF FUTURE GENERATIONS IN CLIMATE LITIGATION?

Eva BALOUNOVÁ*

ABSTRACT

Although climate litigation concerning the rights of youth and future generations is on the rise, gaps in distinguishing between the rights of minors or young people, and future generations, as generations that will exist sometime in the future, appear. This chapter, therefore, aims to analyse two types of climate cases: first, climate cases involving both youth and future generations, where young people may be understood as a bridge between current and future generations; and, second, cases focused only on 'future generations', without being brought

* The research for this chapter was supported by the Lumina Quaeruntur award of the Czech Academy of Sciences for the 'Climate law' project, conducted at the Institute of State and Law.

especially by young plaintiffs. In particular, the focus is placed on the granting of standing in these two types of cases. In this regard, *Minors Oposa* is identified as a pilot case, in which standing was granted. Naturally, the chapter also addresses issues of incorporating intergenerational equity in positive law, and the link to sustainable development.

1. INTRODUCTION

Climate change litigation is growing in importance, and human rights-related claims are emerging as a dominant climate litigation strategy (the 'human rights turn' in climate litigation).[1] Overlapping trends are the involvement of young people in climate litigation (youth-led climate litigation), and the emphasis on future generations. However, these do not need to be identical, as cases involving minors do not need to address future generations, and vice versa. Although legal scholarship focuses on the role of children and young people in strategic climate litigation, confusion remains over the relationship between minors and future generations. Several articles have already analysed children's or youth-led climate litigation,[2] and this focus has culminated in a general comment on children's rights and the environment, with a special focus on climate change, drafted by the UN Committee on the Rights of the Child (CRC) in 2023, addressing intergenerational justice, and future generations as well. Several scholars have discovered intergenerational equity in climate litigation with an emphasis on the rights of future generations; others have focused on sustainable development as a principle protecting the rights of future generations.[3] Nevertheless, a clear distinction is missing between youth-led climate litigation, and climate litigation on behalf of future generations. Nolan concludes that the lack of clarity

---

1 J. Setzer and R. Byrnes, *Global trends in climate change litigation: 2020 snapshot*, Grantham Research Institute on Climate Change and the Environment/Centre for Climate Change Economics and Policy, p. 14; J. Peel and H.M. Osofsky, 'A Rights Turn in Climate Change Litigation?', *Transnational Environmental Law*, (2018) 7, pp. 37–67.

2 E. Donger, 'Children and Youth in Strategic Climate Litigation: Advancing Rights through Legal Argument and Legal Mobilization', *Transnational Environmental Law*, (2022) 11(2), pp. 263–289; L. Parker, J. Maestre, S. Jodoin et al., 'When the Kids Put Climate Change on Trial: Youth-Focused Rights-Based Climate Litigation around the World', *Journal of Human Rights and Environment*, (2022) 13(1), p. 64.

3 See D. Spentzou, 'Climate change litigation as a means to address intergenerational equity and climate change', *Queen Mary Law Journal*, (2021) 2, pp. 153–183; L. Slobodian, 'Defending the Future: Intergenerational Equity in Climate Litigation', *Georgetown Environmental Law Review*, (2020) 32, pp. 570–589; K.A. Emina, 'Sustainable Development and the Future Generations', *Social Sciences, Humanities and Education Journal (SHE Journal)*, (2021) 2(1), p. 57; R. Vasconcellos Oliveira, 'Back to the Future: The Potential of Intergenerational Justice for the Achievement of the Sustainable Development Goals', *Sustainability*, (2018) 10(2), p. 427.

vis-á-vis the definition of future generations and the relationship between future generations and children is also reflected in the relevant judgments.[4]

This chapter, therefore, analyses the relevant case law concerning the rights of minors, and those of future generations, in climate litigation. Regarding the rights of future generations, explicit incorporation of the principle of intergenerational equity in positive law may play a fundamental role. This chapter, therefore, first offers an overview of such incorporation in international law and national constitutions. A critical analysis of whether this explicit incorporation is a so-called game-changer is one of the aims of the chapter (see *Neubauer* and *People v. Arctic Oil*).[5] The chapter's focus is, likewise, the active legal standing of future generations, hence it categorises court approaches to this issue. The *Minors Oposa*[6] case is taken as a successful example of granting standing to future generations in environmental litigation, and by providing other more recent examples, this chapter argues that this success has already been replicated in climate litigation. When protecting the rights of future generations, several rights have already been the subjects of climate litigation – the rights to life, to a favourable environment, and to minority culture – for this reason, this chapter analyses the cases according to the rights claimed. Finally, the chapter aims to highlight case law that links the principles of intergenerational equity and sustainable development.

Section 2 of the chapter provides an overview of the concept of intergenerational equity, and its embeddedness in current positive law. Section 3 introduces climate litigation involving minors and the rights of future generations, with a relevant categorisation, and then offers an analysis of courts' approaches to granting standing to future generations. Thereafter, sections 4 and 5 provide a study of selected interesting cases, including cases from jurisdictions with explicit intergenerational protections and covering several fundamental rights (ecological and cultural), while section 6 focuses on cases involving the principle of sustainable development as a way of protecting the rights of future generations. Finally, section 7 presents some conclusions.

2. THE CONCEPT OF INTERGENERATIONAL JUSTICE IN (POSITIVE) LAW

In politics, the interests of future generations are often neglected, as politicians, driven by the interests of their re-election every four of five years, tend to focus

---

4 A. Nolan, 'Climate Justice Litigation, the Rights of Children and Future Generations and the Court', *Climate justice for children and future generations (webinar)*, Sabin Center for Climate Change Law, 3 March 2023.

5 See chapter 5.

6 *Minors Oposa v. Secretary of the Department of Environment and Natural Resources*, 33 I.L.M. 173 (1994).

on satisfying the needs and desires of their electorate – present citizens. For this reason, Tremmel calls for future ethics,[7] and Weiss proposes three basic principles of intergenerational equity: (1) conservation of options; (2) conservation of quality; and (3) conservation of access.[8] These should apply to a generation that is placed somewhere on the spectrum of time, but without knowing in advance where. Nolan offers a comprehensive overview of definitions of children and future generations.[9]

Tremmel argues that the interests of future generations should be safeguarded either through institutions or written law.[10] Slobodian distinguishes between duties to the future, and remedies across time. Duties to the future might be based on three key concepts: the public trust doctrine; the principle of non-discrimination; and the obligation to protect, respect and fulfil fundamental rights.[11] As remedies serving to protect the rights of future generations, Slobodian identifies three categories: institutional representation, planning for the future, and balancing needs.[12]

From the legal perspective, intergenerational justice is embedded in international, regional or national law. In international law, several multilateral environmental agreements (MEAs) explicitly refer to intergenerational justice. However, neither the Paris Agreement nor human rights law provide adequate protection for the rights of future generations.[13] The 1992 United Nations Framework Convention on Climate Change (UNFCCC)[14] calls for the protection of the climate system for the benefit of present and future generations of humankind (with no reference to children).[15] The 2015 Paris Agreement includes one preambular reference to human rights, involving a generalised reference

[7] J.C. Tremmel, 'Establishing intergenerational justice in national constitutions', in J.C. Tremmel (ed.), *Handbook of Intergenerational Justice*, Edward Elgar Publishing, 2006, p. 189.

[8] E.B. Weiss, Climate Change, Intergenerational Equity, and International Law, Georgetown Law Faculty Publications and Other Works, 2008, p. 616.

[9] A. Nolan, The Children are the Future – Or Not? Exploring The Complexities of the Relationship between the Rights of Children and Future Generations, *EJIL:Talk! Blog of the European Journal of International Law*, 5/2022.

[10] Tremmel, supra, note 6, p. 189.

[11] Slobodian, supra, note 3, p. 580.

[12] Ibid. Currently, institutional representations focus either on sustainable development (Germany, Canada, New Zealand and Australia), or on the future and future generations (or even children), such as in Finland, Wales, Israel, Norway and Hungary. See Network of Institutions for Future Generations.

[13] B. Lewis, 'The Rights of Future Generations within the Post-Paris Climate Regime', *Transnational Environmental Law*, (2018) 7(1), pp. 69–87.

[14] United Nations Framework Convention on Climate Change, May 9, 1992, S. Treaty Doc No. 102-38, 1771 U.N.T.S. 107.

[15] E.D. Gibbons, 'Climate Change, Children's Rights, and the Pursuit of Intergenerational Climate Justice', *Health and Human Rights Journal*, (2014) 16(1), p. 23.

to intergenerational equity.[16] Although the 1987 report *Our Common Future* focused significantly on sustainable development and intergenerational justice, the Sustainable Development Goals (UN SDGs) and their targets are also meagre on intergenerational justice concerns.[17] Nevertheless, the interplay between the rights of future generations and children, on the one hand, and climate change, on the other, is currently the focus of many scholars and international bodies. Recently, the UN CRC drafted the General Comment No. 26 on children's rights and the environment, with a special focus on climate change.[18] The rights of future generations, and specifically states' obligations towards them regarding climate change, were, furthermore, included in the questions raised by the United Nations General Assembly (UNGA) in the resolution requesting an advisory opinion from the International Court of Justice (ICJ), in March 2023.[19]

At the national level, explicit provisions on intergenerational justice appear either on a constitutional level, or in Acts, i.e. in some sort of framework climate law (national Climate Change Act or CCA). In 2021, over 80 constitutions worldwide (over 40 per cent) explicitly referred to future generations, which represents a significant rise since the late 1960s, when fewer than 10 did so.[20] The appearance of such clauses can be identified in many different countries across the world, including those in Europe, Latin America, Africa and Asia.

Tremmel distinguishes three types of clauses in constitutions for intergenerational justice: general clauses, ecological clauses and financial clauses.[21] Araújo and Koessler identify five themes of constitutional provisions mentioning future generations: future generations in *stricto sensu*, environment, natural resources, societal values and public finance. Environment and natural resources, together, constitute a dominant theme (over 90 per cent of clauses), and it is argued that this represents a new way of speaking about the environment: 'Instead of enshrining provisions protecting the environment per se, constitutions seem to have started to justify this protection in terms of a personified group of interest, i.e. humans in the future.'[22] Scholars talk about a new way of how constitutions frame rights, and describe the trend as part of the

16 Earlier drafts of the negotiated text had incorporated stronger language, consistent with Art. 3 of the UNFCCC, directly into the text, but this was later replaced by a provision on intergenerational equity, and, ultimately, resulted only in the preambular provision. See Lewis, supra, note 13.

17 R. Vasconcellos Oliveira, supra, note 3.

18 The Committee recognised the principle of intergenerational equity, and the interests of future generations. See General comment No. 26 (2023) on children's rights and the environment with a special focus on climate change, CRC/C/GC/26.

19 UNGA Resolution A/77/L.58 (initiative started by The Republic of Vanuatu).

20 R. Araújo and L. Koessler, 'The Rise of the Constitutional Protection of Future Generations', Legal Priorities Project, LPP Working Paper No. 7–2021.

21 Tremmel, supra, note 6, p. 191.

22 Araújo and Koessler, supra, note 19, p. 16.

expanding circle of the history of humanity's morality, including reflections on animals, among other things.[23]

The ecological clauses place a focus on either the environment or natural resources, or even on one particular resource (for example, water, in Uruguay). In most constitutions, the rights of future generations are designed as rights and the duty bearer does not have to be explicitly mentioned or is the state itself (for the opposite see Senegal[24]). The clauses may appear in the preamble of the constitution, or be directly embedded in its text. The risk of declaratory provisions not being reflected in reality arises, however, the countries with the most carbon emissions per capita, including Bahrain, Oman, Kuwait, Qatar, UAE, Canada, Saudi Arabia and the US, have not usually embedded any explicit provision on ecological intergenerational equity.[25]

Only a few countries explicitly connect intergenerational justice with the climate. Currently, 11 jurisdictions with an explicit provision on climate in their national constitutions have been identified: Algeria, Bolivia, Côte d'Ivoire, Cuba, Dominican Republic, Ecuador, Thailand, Tunisia, Venezuela, Vietnam and Zambia.[26] In these provisions, the way in which climate and intergenerational equity are connected varies.

3. INTERGENERATIONAL JUSTICE IN CLIMATE LITIGATION

Bogojevic identifies three reasons that have made the rise in youth-led human rights climate action possible: the constitutionalisation of environmental protection on a global scale, the greening of human rights, and the conceptualisation of environmental protection as a type of intrinsic right that exists independently of any legal provision.[27] In addition to these, the rise of intergenerational equity provisions in constitutions might be another reason for this trend, although it is closely connected to the other reasons.

---

23 Ibid.

24 In Senegal, the Constitution explicitly states that: 'Every citizen has the duty to preserve the natural resources and the environment of the country and to work for sustainable development for the benefit of the present and future generations.'

25 A. Deshmukh, 'Visualizing Global Per Capita CO_2 Emissions', *Visual Capitalist*, 1 December 2021, https://www.visualcapitalist.com/visualizing-global-per-capita-co2-emissions/.

26 'The 11 nations heralding a new dawn of climate constitutionalism', *Grantham Research Institute on Climate Change and the Environment, LSE*, 2 December 2021, https://www.lse.ac.uk/granthaminstitute/news/the-11-nations-heralding-a-new-dawn-of-climate-constitutionalism/.

27 S. Bogojevic, 'Human rights of minors and future generations: Global trends and EU environmental law particularities', *Review of European, Comparative and International Environmental Law*, (2020) 29(2), pp. 191–200, at pp. 193–194.

Even so, the relationship between youth-led climate litigation (including the rights of minors and young people) and the rights of future generations is unclear. Bogojevic gives an overview of cases in which minors were bundled with future generations, often mentioned jointly, and refers to these cases as 'actions about intergenerational equity and our responsibilities towards future generations, with the minors involved in the litigation standing as powerful symbols of a precarious future'.[28] In this way, she argues, as does Hilson, that minors form a temporal bridge between present and future generations.[29]

The landmark cases linking minors and future generations, in the context of environmental issues, are: *Minors Oposa*,[30] a Philippine case concerning deforestation; *Demanda Generaciones*,[31] a Colombian case challenging the deforestation of the Colombian Amazon rainforest; and, directly in relation to climate issues, *Juliana*,[32] a pioneering US case based on the public trust doctrine, and *Neubauer*, a German constitutional case from 2021.[33] Many more cases have been opened around the globe, including pending cases in front of the European Court of Human Rights.

Nevertheless, cases concerning the rights of future generations in relation to climate action do not necessarily need to involve minors or young people, and, therefore, do not need to overlap with youth-focused climate cases. Some youth-focused climate claims do not address the rights of future generations, yet some cases that do not look like typical youth-focused climate cases may address such rights.

Notably, Nolan concretises three types of climate litigation concerning intergenerational justice: litigation related to the short-term impacts on the rights of existing children; litigation related to the longer-term impacts on the rights of existing children as future adults; and litigation related to the impacts on the rights of not-yet-existing future generations.[34] However, in the latter type of case, clarity on who is entitled to assert those rights on behalf of those future generations is missing.

---

28 N. Rogers, '"If You Obey All of the Rules You Miss All the Fun": Climate Change Litigation, Climate Change Activism and Lawfulness', *New Zealand Journal of Public and International Law*, (2015) 13(1), p. 179, via ibid., p. 192.

29 C. Hilson, 'Framing Time in Climate Change Litigation', *Oñati Socio-Legal Series*, (2019) 9(3), pp. 361–379, via Bogojevic, supra, note 25, p. 192.

30 *Minors Oposa v. Secretary of the Department of Environment and Natural Resources*, 33 I.L.M. 173 (1994).

31 *Demanda Generaciones Futuras v. Minambiente*, 11001-22-03-000-2018–00319-00 (Supreme Court of Colombia, 5 April 2018).

32 *Juliana v. United States*, 217 F. Supp. 3d 1224, 1250 (D. Or. 2016).

33 *Neubauer, et al. v. Germany*, Bundesverfassungsgericht [BVerfG] [Federal Constitutional Court], 24 March 2021, Case No. BvR 2656/18/1, BvR 78/20/1, BvR 96/20/1, BvR 288/20, http://www.bverfg.de/e/rs20210324_1bvr265618en.html. The court's decision was made on four constitutional complaints, following previous proceedings at the Berlin Administrative Court. However, the case is commonly referred to as *Neubauer*.

34 Nolan, 'Climate Justice Litigation', supra, note 4.

In this chapter, several cases where the minors were acting as a 'bridge between the present and future' were analysed (see Table 1). Additionally, several other cases involving intergenerational equity, in the sense of future generations not yet existing, were examined (see Table 2). Generally, climate actions arguing for intergenerational justice have been brought on the basis of various provisions: on explicit constitutional protections (Germany, Norway); on public trust or non-discrimination provisions (US *(Juliana)*); and, occasionally, on the provisions of the UNFCCC and the Paris Agreement (*Carvalho*,[35] *Sacchi*[36] and *Plan B Earth*).[37]

Table 1. Youth-led climate claims addressing rights of future generations (decided)

Jurisdiction	Case (Year of filing)	Const. prov.	Outcome
Australia	*Youth Verdict v. Waratah Coal* (2020)	No	Positive on the merits
Canada	*ENVironnement JEUnesse v. Canada* (2018) *La Rose v. Her Majesty the Queen* (2018)	No	Dismissed Dismissed (for lack of justiciability and standing)
Colombia	*Demanda Generaciones Futuras v. Minambiente* (2018)	No	Positive on the merits
Germany	*Neubauer, et al. v. Germany* (2020)	Yes	Positive on the merits
India	*Pandey v. India* (2017)	No	Dismissed for lack of justiciability and standing
Norway	*Greenpeace Nordic Ass'n and Nature and Youth v. Ministry of Petroleum and Energy* (2016)	Yes	Negative on the merits
Sweden	*PUSH Sverige, Fältbiologerna och andra v. Sverige regering* (2016)	Yes	Dismissed for lack of justiciability and standing
Philippines	*Minors Oposa*		Positive on the merits
UK	*Plan B Earth and Others v. Prime Minister* (2021)	No	Dismissed for lack of justiciability and standing
Uganda	*Nisi Mbabazi et al v. AG* (2012)	Yes	Settled out of court
USA	*Juliana v. United States* (2015)	No	Dismissed for lack of justiciability and standing
UNCRC	*CRC Communication Sacchi et al. v. Argentina et al.* (2019)	No	Dismissed for lack of justiciability and standing
UNHRC	*Daniel Billy and Others v. Australia (Torres Strait Islanders Petition)*	No	Positive on the merits

(continued)

[35] CJEU Judgment: Case T-330/18, *Armando Ferrão Carvalho and Others v. The European Parliament and the Council* (People's Climate Case) (EU General Court, 24 May 2018, complaint).

[36] *Sacchi v. Argentina*, UNCRC, Decision adopted by the CRC under the Optional Protocol to the Convention on the Rights of the Child on a Communications Procedure in Respect of Communication No. 104/2019, CRC/C/88/D/104/2019 (8 October 2021).

[37] Judgment of the UK Supreme Court of 16 December 2020 in *Plan B Earth and Others v. Secretary of State for Transport*, [2020] EWCA Civ 214.

Table 1 *continued*

Jurisdiction	Case (Year of filing)	Const. prov.	Outcome
EU (CJEU)	*Armando Ferrão Carvalho and Others v. The European Parliament and the Council* (2018)	Yes	Dismissed for lack of justiciability and standing

Source: Produced by the author.

Table 2. Other climate cases addressing rights of future generations

Jurisdiction	Case (Year of filing)	Const. prov.	Outcome
Netherlands	*Urgenda Foundation v. State of the Netherlands* (2013)	No	Positive on the merits
Netherlands	*Milieudefensie et al. v. Royal Dutch Shell Plc* (2019)	No	Positive on the merits
South Africa	*Earthlife Africa Johannesburg v. Minister of Environmental Affairs, Thabametsi Case* (2016)	Yes	Positive on the merits
USA	*Massachusetts v. EPA* (2003)	No	Positive on the merits

Source: Produced by the author.

To a certain extent, these cases represent the 'typical' strategic climate litigation that aims to solve the climate crisis and support climate action (climate litigation aligned with climate goals).[38] On the other hand, some climate cases may directly aim at obstructing or opposing climate action,[39] hence affecting the rights of future generations. In *D.G. Khan Cement Company v. Government of Punjab*,[40] the company challenged new restrictions imposed by a provincial government on the expansion or establishment of cement plants, relying in part on alleged infringement of the company's constitutional right to freedom to trade. However, the court noted that, as climate resilience measures, the restrictions served the public interest, and upheld the government's restrictions. Regarding intergenerational justice, the court noted that 'the great silent majority of future generations is rendered powerless and needs a voice'. The court stated that it should be mindful that its decisions adjudicate upon the rights of future generations, and elaborated that 'we need to decolonize our future generations from the wrath of climate change, by upholding climate justice at all times'.[41]

---

[38] Setzer and Byrnes, supra, note 1.

[39] See *West Virginia v. Environmental Protection Agency*. Number 597 US _US Supreme Court; Washington, DC, USA; June 30, 2022); *RWE v. Kingdom of the Netherlands, ICSID Case No. ARB/21/4*.

[40] *DG Khan Cement*, C P1290-L/2019 (Supreme Court of Pakistan, 15 April 2021).

[41] *DG Khan Cement*, C P1290-L/2019 (Supreme Court of Pakistan, 15 April 2021), via Setzer and Byrnes, supra, note 1.

4. CASE STUDY: ON STANDING

The majority of youth-focused rights-based cases has been dismissed at a procedural stage, before being heard on the merits.[42] According to a study from 2022,[43] only three cases from twenty-three were heard on the merits: *Demanda Generaciones, Neubauer*, and *People v. Arctic Oil*.[44] The majority of cases – twenty in total – were dismissed at a preliminary stage, due to a lack of justiciability and standing.[45]

In existing literature, Johnston summarises theoretical arguments in favour of granting standing to future generations, including arguments concerning the unknown interests of future generations or non-existent legal personas.[46] Spentzou mentions the long-lasting effects of nuclear power, as an example of a previous discussion regarding the concept of intergenerational equity.[47]

The *Minors Oposa* case is usually cited as a landmark case, and a flagship example of a case in which the court granted standing to children and future generations, to challenge government action in environmental matters. In this case, in which timber licences and the extraction of natural resources were challenged, the Supreme Court of the Philippines stated, in 1993, that it '[found] no difficulty in ruling that they (the minors) can, for themselves, for others of their generation and for the succeeding generations, file a class suit'. In the court's view, 'every generation has a responsibility to the next to preserve that rhythm and harmony for the full enjoyment of a balanced and healthful ecology', and the 'minors' assertion of their right to a sound environment constitute[d], at the same time, the performance of their obligation to ensure the protection of that right for the generations to come'. This case was brought on behalf of future generations, and on behalf of the plaintiffs. Regarding the legal personality to sue on behalf of the succeeding generations, the court explained that this could only be based on the concept of intergenerational responsibility, in so far as the right to a balanced and healthful ecology was concerned. Slobodian argued, decades later (in 2020), that climate change cases were trying to replicate this success, in suits on behalf of future generations, who were often represented by young people.[48]

---

42 Parker, Maestre, Jodoin et al., supra, note 2, p. 80.

43 Parker, Maestre, Jodoin et al., supra, note 2, pp. 80–82.

44 *Greenpeace Nordic Ass'n and Nature and Youth v. Norway Ministry of Petroleum and Energy*, HR-2020–2472-P (Supreme Court of Norway, 22 December 2020).

45 Ibid., p. 82.

46 R. Johnston, 'Lacking Rights and Justice in a Burning World: The Case for Granting Standing to Future Generations in Climate Change Litigation', *Tilburg Law Review*, (2016) 21(1), pp. 36–40.

47 Spentzou, supra, note 3, p. 160. See also the International Court of Justice, *Legality of the Threat or Use of Nuclear Weapons*, Advisory Opinion of 8 July 1996.

48 Slobodian, supra, note 3, p. 577.

This chapter argues that this success has already been replicated in strategic climate litigation, although not based on legal provisions on intergenerational justice. Regarding the granting of standing to future generations, three main different positions have been taken by the courts: either a negative or a positive approach, or an approach that avoids addressing the issue.

As already mentioned, many climate actions have been dismissed for lack of justiciability and standing, regardless of the existence of the ecological intergenerational provision in the national constitution (see Table 1 above). For example, at the EU level, both climate lawsuits to date have been dismissed by the Court of Justice of the European Union (CJEU). In *Carvalho*, a case challenging the EU's original target of reducing greenhouse gas (GHG) emissions by 40 per cent by 2030, the claim was made on behalf of 'both current and future generations', invoking Articles 21 and 37 of the Charter of Fundamental Rights of the European Union[49] Article 3(3)(1) of the Treaty on European Union (TEU),[50] and Article 11 of the Treaty on the Functioning of the European Union (TFEU),[51] as well as Article 3(1) of the UNFCCC. In *Biomass*,[52] the grounds for action were to challenge the inclusion of forest biomass in the revised directive on the use of renewables,[53] thereby having damaging effects on the well-being of children. The CJEU declared both these cases inadmissible, in line with its previous case law, mainly due to the narrow standing rules for private applicants.[54]

In some rulings, the courts have decided to avoid addressing the granting of standing to future generations, focusing instead on granting standing to the current young generation, as in the decision of the federal district court in Oregon, in the 2016 case of *Juliana*, or the decision of the Hague Court of Appeal in the 2018 *Urgenda* case:

> After all, it is without a doubt plausible that the current generation of Dutch nationals, in particular but not limited to the younger individuals in this group, will have to deal with the adverse effects of climate change in their lifetime if global emissions of greenhouse gases are not adequately reduced.[55]

---

49 Charter of Fundamental Rights of the European Union [2012] OJ C326/391.

50 Consolidated version of the Treaty on European Union [2012] OJ C326/13.

51 Consolidated version of the Treaty on the Functioning of the European Union [2012] OJ C326/47.

52 Order of the General Court (Fourth Chamber) of 6 May 2020, *Sabo and Others v. Parliament and Council*, Order of the General Court, T-141/19, ECLI:EU:T:2020:179.

53 Renewable Energy Directive (known as RED II), Directive (EU) 2018/2001 of the European Parliament and of the Council of 11 December 2018 on the promotion of the use of energy from renewable sources [2018] OJ L328/82.

54 See Bogojevic, supra, note 25, p. 197.

55 Judgment of The Hague Court of Appeal from 9 October 2018, Case 200.178.245/01, *Urgenda Foundation v. Netherlands*, ECLI:NL:GHDHA:2018:2610, para. 37.

Both the US and the Netherlands lack constitutional ecological clauses on intergenerational justice.

In *Juliana*,[56] in which 21 youth plaintiffs filed a suit against the US federal government, claiming that the government's fossil fuel policies violated the federal public trust doctrine and their federal constitutional rights to due process and equal protection,[57] the federal district court in Oregon agreed that the plaintiffs had standing, and could, therefore, proceed to the substance of their claims. Nevertheless, the appellate court concluded, by a two-to-one majority, that the (youth) plaintiffs did not have standing, because they could not show that a decision in their favour would remedy their harm.[58]

The UN CRC, likewise, avoided addressing the issue of future generations, in the *Sacchi* case.[59] The Committee reasoned that, as children, the authors of the complaint were 'particularly impacted by the effects of climate change, both in terms of the manner in which they experience such effects as well as the potential of climate change to affect them throughout their lifetime, in particular if immediate action is not taken'.[60] The Committee, however, confirmed that the authors had established that they had personally experienced real and significant harm, to justify their victim status.

On the spectrum of positive outcomes, the courts tend to grant standing to 'transgenerational groups', or to address 'equity among living generations'. In *Massachusetts v. EPA*,[61] the US Supreme Court, in 2007, ruled that 'a state government can bring suit to contest harm that would occur over the next one hundred years as a result of climate change, based on the special interest of a sovereign state in all earth and air within its domain'.[62] Legal entities that exist now, and which will continue to exist beyond the lifetimes of their individual constituents, can hold rights and bring claims in a way that future people cannot, claims Slobodian, who offers additional examples of similar entities: an Arctic village facing melting sea ice and accelerating erosion, and a Nigerian community suffering health problems and loss of crops.[63]

Another group of cases deals with equity among living generations: equity between those who are making decisions today, and the generation of younger people who will face the future effects of those decisions.[64] In *Demanda*

56 *Juliana v. United States*, 217 F. Supp. 3d 1224, 1250 (D. Or. 2016).

57 M.C. Blumm and M.C. Wood, "No Ordinary Lawsuit": Climate Change, Due Process, and the Public Trust Doctrine', *American University Law Review*, (2017) 67, p. 1.

58 UN Environmental Programme, *Global Climate Litigation Report: 2020 Status Review*, UNEP, 2020, p. 39.

59 *Sacchi v. Argentina*, supra, note 31.

60 Ibid., para. 10.13.

61 Judgment of the US Supreme Court of 2 April 2007 in Case No. 05–1120, *Massachusetts et al. v. Environmental Protection Agency et al.*

62 Slobodian, supra, note 3, p. 579.

63 Ibid.

64 Ibid., p. 578.

Generaciones, the Supreme Court of Colombia, in 2018, found that 'future generations, including children who brought this action, will be directly affected, unless we presently reduce the deforestation rate to zero'.[65] Hence, the court qualified children as future generations. In this case, a group of 25 youth plaintiffs sued the Colombian government and several other entities, claiming that their failure to reduce deforestation violated the plaintiffs' fundamental rights. The Supreme Court of Colombia ordered the government to formulate and implement an action plan to halt deforestation, while recognising that the fundamental constitutional rights of life, health, minimum subsistence, freedom and human dignity were substantially linked to the environment and ecosystem.[66]

Quite similarly, in 2021, the Federal Constitutional Court of Germany ruled on *Neubauer*, a strategic climate litigation challenging the German Climate Act and its climate targets: 'The described risk of future restrictions on freedom gives rise to fundamental rights being presently affected because this risk is built into the current legislation'.[67] The court, recalling that there is a constitutional provision on intergenerational equity, reasoned that:

> Since future impairments of fundamental rights could potentially be set into irreversible motion today, and given that lodging a constitutional complaint to address the ensuing restrictions on freedom might be futile by the time the impairments have arisen, the complainants already have standing to lodge a constitutional complaint at the present time.[68]

These approaches grant standing to future generations, or in general to people who will live in the future, in so far as the current government activity is setting conditions that might affect future rights.

The Hague District Court went even further, in 2015, in *Urgenda*, when ruling that, '[i]n defending the right of not just the current but also the future generations to availability of natural resources and a safe and healthy living environment, it also strives for the interest of a sustainable society'.[69] In *Urgenda*, probably the most famous successful climate case, in which the Dutch courts ordered the state to lower its GHG emissions by at least 25 per cent by 2020, the Hague District Court held that Urgenda, the association, had standing on its own behalf, under a Dutch law specifically allowing class actions brought by interest groups, although the court rejected the argument that the 886 individual

---

65 *Demanda Generaciones*, supra, note 28, para. 11.2.

66 UNEP, supra, note 48, p. 39.

67 *Neubauer*, supra, note 28, para. 130.

68 Ibid.

69 Judgment of The Hague District Court of 24 June 2015 in Case C/09/456689 *Urgenda Foundation v. Netherlands*, ECLI:NL:RBDHA:2015:7196, para. 4.8.

claimants had standing, partly for practical reasons, as their claims could not result in a different outcome from the association's claim.[70]

In *Milieudefensie*,[71] the Hague District Court established that:

> the interests of current and future generations of Dutch residents and ... of the inhabitants of the Wadden Sea area ... as served in the alternative with the class actions, are suitable for bundling, even though in the Netherlands and in the Wadden region there are differences in time, extent and intensity to which the inhabitants will be affected by climate change caused by CO2 emissions.[72]

Although the Dutch jurisdiction does not have an explicit constitutional ecological intergenerational clause, standing for future generations to file a class suit in strategic climate litigation was recognised. Here, the court allowed the adherence of rights to the plaintiffs, and to future generations, as separate entities.

5. CASE STUDY: ON MERITS

5.1. ECOLOGICAL RIGHTS

Two countries with particularly strong constitutional protection of the ecological rights of future generations are Germany and Norway, and the relevant constitutional clauses were recently challenged in each country's highest courts. These cases will be considered in the following two subsections.

5.1.1. Neubauer

In the German Constitution (Basic Law, Grundgesetz or GG), Article 20a states that: 'Mindful also of its responsibility towards future generations, the state shall protect the natural foundations of life and animals by legislation and, in accordance with law and justice, by executive and judicial action, all within the framework of the constitutional order.'[73] This provision was inserted into the German Constitution in 1994, after a debate on whether the provision should list a right for individuals to a healthy environment or simply refer to a state

---

70 This decision was upheld by an appeal court, and was not disputed in the Supreme Court. See UNEP, supra note 48, p. 39.

71 Judgment of The Hague District Court of 26 May 2021 in Case C/09/571932 *Milieudefensie et al. v. Royal Dutch Shell Plc*, ECLI:NL:RBDHA:2021:5339.

72 Ibid., para. 4.2.4.

73 Basic Law for the Federal Republic of Germany in the revised version published in the Federal Law Gazette Part III, classification number 100-1, as last amended by the Act of 28 June 2022 (Federal Law Gazette I, p. 968).

duty – the latter was chosen.[74] Subsequently, Araújo and Koessler argued that this Article had little impact beyond government-related decisions on specific environmental disputes.[75] However, this changed in 2021, with the decision of the Federal Constitutional Court in the first German constitutional climate litigation, commonly referred to as *Neubauer*, in which the Federal Climate Protection Act was declared partly unconstitutional, because it did not sufficiently protect people against future infringements and limitations of freedom rights, in the wake of gradually intensifying climate change.[76] This surprising decision is viewed as the first successful constitutional complaint on environmental protection in Germany,[77] but for some it was a missed chance, as it was partly unsuccessful.[78]

The German Constitutional Court, in its decision, emphasised the principle of proportionality, and stated that Article 2 GG already encompassed the duty to protect freedom as a whole,[79] in connection with the state objective of environmental protection (Article 2 GG, Article 20a GG, the Paris Agreement, etc.).[80] The Constitutional Court found that the carbon budget allowed until the year 2030 has an 'advance interference-like effect' on the freedom of complaints, a freedom comprehensively protected under the Basic Law.[81] However, no violation of Article 20a GG could, ultimately, be ascertained, according to the Court, although the budget created disproportionate risks that freedom protected by fundamental rights would be impaired in the future, as it significantly narrowed the emission possibilities available after 2030.

---

74 Araújo and Koessler, supra, note 19, p. 37.

75 Ibid and L.J. Kotzé, '*Neubauer et al. versus Germany*: Planetary Climate Litigation for the Anthropocene?', *German Law Journal*, (2022) 22(8), p. 1424.

76 L.J. Kotzé, '*Neubauer et al. versus Germany*: Planetary Climate Litigation for the Anthropocene?', *German Law Journal*, (2022) 22(8), p. 1424.

77 F. Ekardt, 'Climate Revolution with Weaknesses', *Verfassungsblog*, 8 May 2021, https://verfassungsblog.de/climate-revolution-with-weaknesses/ or A. Buser, 'Of Carbon Budgets, Factual Uncertainties and Intergenerational Equity – The German Constitutional Court's Climate Decision' Forthcoming, *German Law Journal*, 21/8, https://ssrn.com/abstract=3919497 or http://dx.doi.org/10.2139/ssrn.3919497.

78 P. Schönberger, 'Germany's "Fair Share" of Climate Change Jurisprudence', *Völkerrechtsblog*, 17 May 2021, https://voelkerrechtsblog.org/germanys-fair-share-of-climate-change-jurisprudence/.

79 Article 2 "[Personal freedoms]:

(1) Every person shall have the right to free development of his personality insofar as he does not violate the rights of others or offend against the constitutional order or the moral law.
(2) Every person shall have the right to life and physical integrity. Freedom of the person shall be inviolable. These rights may be interfered with only pursuant to a law." (Art. 2 of the Basic Law for the Federal Republic of Germany, supra, note 63).

80 Ekardt, supra, note 68.

81 Although the court only required the legislator to set the reduction path for the period between 2030 and 2050 earlier and by other means (by the act of parliament not governmental ordinance), the legislator amended the KSG and strengthened the climate goals in it. See Buser, supra, note 80.

5.1.2. People v. Arctic Oil

Norway is a developed country that (like Hungary) refers to future generations in the context of natural resources.[82] Article 112 of its Constitution reads:

> Every person has the right to an environment that is conducive to health and to a natural environment the productivity and diversity of which are maintained. Natural resources shall be managed on the basis of comprehensive long-term considerations which will safeguard this right for future generations as well.
>
> In order to safeguard their right in accordance with the foregoing paragraph, citizens are entitled to information on the state of the natural environment and on the effects of any encroachment on nature that is planned or carried out.
>
> The authorities of the state shall take measures for the implementation of these principles.

Norway relies heavily on oil extraction and is well-known for progressive policies aimed at sharing the economic benefits of this activity, including a fund, created in 1990.[83] However, Norway only constitutionalised future generations in 2014, in the context of reform, the goal of which was to revitalise constitutional thinking in the country.[84]

This provision referred to above was relied upon by the plaintiffs in the first Norwegian climate case, commonly referred to as *People v. Arctic Oil*, in which several environmental non-governmental organisations claimed that the provision had been violated by licences for petroleum activity in the Barents Sea, issued by the Norwegian government (after Parliament had opened the area to petroleum extraction activity). Finally, on 22 December 2020, the Norwegian Supreme Court rejected the claim, upheld the decisions of lower-instance courts, and confirmed the validity of the petroleum licences. The Supreme Court ruled that, even though Article 112 of the Constitution protects citizens from environmental and climate harms, it only allows for judicial review under very limited conditions, which were not met in the present case.[85] The Supreme Court found that Article 112 establishes a legal duty for the government to adopt adequate and necessary environmental measures, but that judicial review is permitted only when this duty is grossly neglected. Hence, the Court established a very high threshold for setting aside legislative and other decisions that the Parliament has taken or consented to. Moreover, in this particular case, the

---

82 Araújo and Koessler, supra, note 19, p. 17.

83 See also Norges Bank Investment Management, The fund (2021), https://www.nbim.no/.

84 Ibid.

85 C. Voigt, 'The First Climate Judgment before the Norwegian Supreme Court: Aligning Law with Politics', *Journal of Environmental Law*, (2021) 33, pp. 697–710, p. 702.

threshold had, according to the court, not been passed, because Parliament had adopted several measures to reduce national emissions.[86] The Supreme Court concluded that no human rights had been violated, as the link between the decision to grant oil production licences and an increase in GHG emissions was too uncertain to constitute a 'real and immediate' threat to the right to life, or the right to respect for private and family life.[87]

As Voigt concludes, the relevance of Article 112 is, according to the Supreme Court, limited to:

> (i) providing guidance to the Parliament when acting as law-maker, (ii) providing guidance for the exercise of discretion in administrative decision-making, (iii) being an interpretation principle and (iv) being a standard for judicial review only in cases where the legislator was involved but had not taken a position on the environmental problem at stake.[88]

According to Voigt, the Norwegian Supreme Court missed the chance to establish the substantive content of Article 112 in light of the global challenge of climate change, when it failed to address the legal developments since 2014.[89] Four dissenting judges found procedural errors in granting the licences, and the case was brought to the European Court on Human Rights (ECHR) in June 2021.[90]

5.2. RIGHT TO MINORITY CULTURE: *TORRES STRAIT ISLANDERS* CASE

In the *Torres Strait Islanders* case, a petition by eight Torres Strait Islanders (Australian nationals), and on behalf of six of their children, submitted in May 2019, the UN Human Rights Committee (HRC) found, in September 2022, that Australia, by failing to adequately protect the indigenous peoples of Torres Strait Islands, had violated the petitioners' rights under Articles 17 and 27 of the International Covenant on Civil and Political Rights (right to privacy, family, home or correspondence, and right to minority culture, religion, and language, respectively).[91] The Covenant does not address intergenerational equity, thus the

---

86 Ibid.

87 Ibid.

88 Ibid., p. 703.

89 Ibid.

90 *Greenpeace Nordic and Others v. Norway* (no. 34068/21).

91 *Daniel Billy and Others v. Australia (Torres Strait Islanders Petition)*, CCPR/C/127/D/2728/2016, Human Rights Committee – Views adopted by the Committee under Art. 5(4) of the Optional Protocol concerning communication No. 2728/2016, 7 January 2020: see M. Feria-Tinta, 'Torres Strait Islanders: United Nations Human Rights Committee Delivers

petitioners recalled the wording of the Preamble of the Paris Agreement on, among other things, human rights, children and intergenerational equity, and claimed violation of Article 24 of the Covenant (protection of children), building a bridge between current children and future generations. The petitioners claimed that, concerning Article 24, 'the principle of intergenerational equity places a duty on current generations to act as responsible stewards of the planet and ensure the rights of future generations to meet their developmental and environmental needs'.[92] The HRC concluded that Australia's failure to adopt timely and adequate adaptation measures to protect the petitioners' collective ability to maintain their traditional way of life, and to transmit to their children and future generations their culture and traditions, and use of land and sea resources, disclosed a violation of the State Party's positive obligation to protect the petitioners' right to enjoy their minority culture. The HRC interpreted the right to a minority culture as a right to transmit the culture and traditional way of life to future generations.

6. CASE STUDY: SUSTAINABLE DEVELOPMENT AS A GUARANTEE FOR THE RIGHTS OF FUTURE GENERATIONS

In several climate cases, the courts have addressed the principle of intergenerational equity as being closely linked to the principle of sustainable development. In both *Urgenda* and *Milieudefensie*, Dutch courts referred to the relevant provisions of the UNFCCC proclaiming sustainability and intergenerational equity. Although the UNFCCC does not explicitly link these two principles, in *Urgenda* the Court of Appeal noted that '[t]he Convention seeks to protect the Earth's eco-systems and mankind and envisions a sustainable development for the protection of current and future generations'.[93] In *Milieudefensie*,[94] the court referred not only to the UNFCCC and UN SDG, but also to soft law, namely the *OECD Guidelines for Multinational Enterprises*, which contain provisions on sustainable development.[95]

Ground-Breaking Decision on Climate Change Impacts on Human Rights', *EJIL:Talk! Blog of the European Journal of International Law*, 27 September 2022, https://www.ejiltalk.org/torres-strait-islanders-united-nations-human-rights-committee-delivers-ground-breaking-decision-on-climate-change-impacts-on-human-rights/.

92 *Torres Strait Islanders Petition*, supra, note 79, para 5.8.

93 *Urgenda*, supra, note 45, para. 5.

94 Judgment of The Hague District Court of 26 May 2021 in Case C/09/571932 *Milieudefensie et al. v. Royal Dutch Shell Plc*, ECLI:NL:RBDHA:2021:5339.

95 See https://www.oecd.org/corporate/mne/.

6.1. THE *THABAMETSI* CASE

In South Africa, Article 24 of the Constitution provides a constitutional right to the environment, which is to be protected for the benefit of present and future generations. In the *Thabametsi* case,[96] South Africa's High Court considered the quality and form of climate change impact assessment required for environmental authorisation, in this case for a coal-fired power station. The power station had obtained the environmental authorisation in March 2015; however, none of the authorisation conditions related explicitly to climate change. After an appeal to the minister of environmental affairs, challenging the missing assessment of the project's potential contribution to further GHG emissions, the minister imposed the condition of undertaking a climate change impact assessment before the commencement of the project; in the meantime, EarthLife had launched judicial review proceedings. The High Court upheld the judicial review claim. It found errors in the original procedure, and also by the minister, who was supposed to send the matter back for reconsideration. As concluded by Humby,[97] the court's review of the prior decisions was framed by powerful statements associating the climate change impact assessment with sustainable development, intergenerational justice and the precautionary principle. Regarding Article 24 of the Constitution, the Court stated that:

> Sustainable development is at the same time integrally linked with the principle of intergenerational justice requiring the state to take reasonable measures to protect the environment 'for the benefit of present and future generations' and hence adequate consideration of climate change. Short-term needs must be evaluated and weighed against long-term consequences.[98]

6.2. *YOUTH VERDICT v. WARATAH COAL*

In *Youth Verdict*, an application challenging a new coal mine on human rights grounds, the Queensland Land Court, in November 2022, recommended rejecting the issuance of a mining lease.[99] The court pointed out that the principle of intergenerational equity is included in the National Strategy for Ecologically Sustainable Development (ESD), as it states that 'decision making processes

96 *Earthlife Africa Johannesburg v. Minister of Environmental Affairs*, 2 All SA 519 (High Court of South Africa, Gauteng Division, Pretoria (2017)).

97 T.-L. Humby, 'The *Thabametsi* Case: Case No 65662/16 *Earthlife Africa Johannesburg v. Minister of Environmental Affairs*', *Journal of Environmental Law*, (2018) 30(1), pp. 145–155.

98 *Earthlife Africa Johannesburg*, supra, note 82, para. 82.

99 *Youth Verdict v. Waratah Coal*, [2020] QLC 33; [2021] QLC 4; [2021] QLC 36; [2022] QLC 3; [2022] QLC 4.

should effectively integrate both long and short-term economic, environmental and equity considerations'. The court stressed that there is an intergenerational imbalance in climate change, because future generations will not have the same freedom that our generations have had, as their options for avoiding dangerous climate change will have been restricted, and they will experience the worst impacts of climate change and bear the legacy of decisions taken today. The Court interpreted the principle of intergenerational equity as placing a responsibility on today's decision-makers to make wise choices for future generations, and concluded that the best interests of future generations (and today's children) are not served by actions that narrow the options for achieving the Paris Agreement temperature goal. Consequently, while future generations would also experience some of the project's benefits, these would be disproportionately lower than those experienced by today's generations.

7. CONCLUSION

The courts have taken three main positions on granting standing to future generations: negative, avoiding and positive. These have been identified in jurisdictions with and without explicit constitutional provisions on (ecological) intergenerational justice. Although most youth-focused rights-based climate cases have been dismissed at a procedural stage, some were heard on the merits. Thus, the success of standing being granted in *Minors Oposa* has been replicated in climate litigation, in both *Neubauer* and *Demanda Generaciones*, where standing was granted to future generations, in so far as current activities create such conditions that rights might be affected in the future. The rights of future generations are linked to the rights of young people in these two cases: in *Demanda Generaciones*, the court referred to children and to future generations.

Interestingly, concerning *Neubauer* and *Demanda Generaciones*, only one of the jurisdictions involved explicitly enshrines ecological intergenerational justice in its constitution. The German Constitution, unlike the Colombian one, recognises the need for ecological intergenerational justice, in its Article 20a. However, in the German Constitutional Court's view, the provision on fundamental freedoms already provides sufficient protection against current measures with 'interference-like effects' that could violate these freedoms in the future. On the other hand, even an explicit constitutional provision on intergenerational justice does not ensure a ruling in favour of the (young) plaintiffs (in *People v. Arctic Oil*).

However, not all youth-led climate actions advocate for the rights of future generations. Furthermore, some cases not brought by young people aim to protect future generations. In the US, a jurisdiction with no explicit ecological intergenerational equity provision in its constitution, the Supreme Court recognised standing for transgenerational groups, such as states represented by the state government (in *Massachusetts v. EPA*). The UN HRC in the *Torres Strait Islanders* confirmed that the right to a minority culture may have been violated when the possibility of transmitting the culture/traditional way of life to future generations is endangered due to the failure to adopt adequate adaptation measures. In light of *Massachusetts v. EPA*, a minority and its culture, handed down from generation to generation, might be understood, in a way, as a transgenerational group: a legal entity that exists now, and which it is hoped will continue to exist beyond the lifetimes of its individual constituents.

In *Urgenda* and *Milieudefensie*, the courts recognised standing for future generations in class suits based on the principle of sustainability. In *Thabametsi* and *Youth Verdict*,[100] the courts linked provisions on sustainable development with the need to protect the climate for future generations, reasoning that states are obliged to take reasonable measures to protect the environment and climate for the benefit of future generations, and to find proportionality between short-term needs or benefits and long-term consequences. Ecological intergenerational equity enjoys protection under the South African Constitution, unlike in the constitutions of the Netherlands or Australia.

In conclusion, three ways of granting standing to future generations have arisen in climate litigation. First, standing might be granted when current activities create such conditions that rights might be affected in the future; second, an entity representing a transgenerational group can hold rights; and third, a successful claim could be made based on the principle of sustainable development. On these grounds, some courts have already confirmed climate change's intergenerational impacts, and ordered states to act accordingly. However, there is no evidence that explicit constitutional provisions on (ecological) intergenerational justice lead to greater success in climate litigation (regarding either standing or merits). Although such explicit provisions on ecological intergenerational equity tend to occur in countries with better climate performance (or, at least, such provisions do not correlate with the jurisdictions with the worst climate performance), the courts have upheld, as well as dismissed, the protection of future generations in countries with and without such provisions. Moreover, in Germany, a jurisdiction with such a provision, the court ruled in favour of future generations, but on the grounds of other constitutional provisions.

[100] Also in cases opposing climate action (see *DG Khan Cement*, supra, note 35).

UNCERTAIN CAUSATION IN CLIMATE CHANGE LIABILITY LITIGATION

Albert RUDA-GONZALEZ

ABSTRACT

In recent years, there has been an avalanche of court claims in connection with climate change liability, starting with the leading case *Urgenda* and its progeny. Recently, a claim has been filed before the Spanish Supreme Court to hold the Spanish government accountable regarding environmental policy related to climate change. This chapter analyses these claims against the background of tort liability. Such claims are usually framed in terms of liability of the state (or companies), but tort compensation is seldom claimed (or awarded). As is well known, for liability in tort to be established, there must be a causal link between damage, on the one hand, and the defendant's behaviour, on the other. However, causation is hardly analysed in these cases. Indeed, one of the major criticisms against the *Urgenda* decision was its poor causal analysis. Nevertheless, it is submitted that many of the evidentiary hurdles which plague environmental tort litigation, in general, are absent in the climate change litigation arena. Pollution-share liability, which is highly problematic in other scenarios, may prove to be a useful tool in this regard.

1. INTRODUCTION

In a landmark ruling issued in 2019, the Dutch Supreme Court (Hoge Raad) held the Dutch state accountable for its insufficient efforts in combating climate change.[1] The original decision, issued in June 2015 by a district court in The

1 Hoge Raad (HR) Decision (Arrest) 20.12.2019, no. 19/00135, ECLI:NL:HR:2019:2006, available in Dutch at https://uitspraken.rechtspraak.nl/#!/details?id=ECLI:NL:HR:2019:2006,

Hague,[2] upheld the claim filed by Urgenda, an environmental organisation, and was successively confirmed by the higher courts.[3] The Dutch courts determined that the Netherlands' actions were in violation of the principle of sustainable development, the prevention principle, and the precautionary principle, among other legal standards, and that they amounted to a violation of the rule of liability based on fault *(schuld)*, pursuant to the Dutch Civil Code (Burgerlijk Wetboek, or BW), Article 6:102. This ruling signifies a substantial departure from the expected conduct of the Dutch state, as it was deemed a case of negligence.[4]

The impact of this ruling extends far beyond the borders of the Netherlands, resonating both politically and legally on an international scale. It has emerged as a pivotal precedent in comparative environmental case law, serving as a template for similar lawsuits brought in other countries. Noteworthy examples include the *Klimaatzaak* case, in Belgium,[5] the claims made by *Greenpeace Norge* and *Natur og Ungdom*, in Norway,[6] and even the efforts of a Pakistani lawyer before the Lahore court (*Leghari* case),[7] among others.[8]

---

and in English (ECLI:NL:HR:2019:2007) at https://uitspraken.rechtspraak.nl/#!/details?id=ECLI:NL:HR:2019:2007.

2 Rechtbank Den Haag 24.6.2015, no. C/09/456689/HA ZA 13-1396, ECLI:NL:RBDHA:2015:7145, https://uitspraken.rechtspraak.nl/#!/details?id=ECLI:NL:RBDHA:2015:7145, and in English (ECLI:NL:RBDHA:2015:7196) at https://uitspraken.rechtspraak.nl/#!/details?id=ECLI:NL:RBDHA:2015:7196.

3 For the Court of Appeal decision, see Gerechtshof Den Haag, 09.11.2018, no. 200.178.245/01, ECLI:NL:GHDHA:2018:2591, https://uitspraken.rechtspraak.nl/#!/details?id=ECLI:NL:GHDHA:2018:2591, and in English (ECLI:NL:GHDHA:2018:2610) at https://uitspraken.rechtspraak.nl/#!/details?id=ECLI:NL:GHDHA:2018:2610.

4 On this case, it may truly be said that rivers of ink have been spilled. On the same, see A. Ruda Gonzalez, 'Perspectives de la litigació pel canvi climàtic arran del cas *Urgenda*', *Revista Catalana de Dret Ambiental*, (2018) (9–2), pp. 1–43, https://raco.cat/index.php/rcda/article/view/348630, with further references.

5 See the claimants' webpage, https://www.klimaatzaak.eu/nl. The first-instance court found for the claimants on 17 June 2021, but the court (Tribunal de première instance francophone de Bruxelles, Section Civile, 17.06.2021, no. 2015/4585/A) refused to set any concrete objectives as to greenhouse gas emission reduction levels. The case is currently under appeal. For the whole judicial evolution of the claim, see the résumé in https://www.klimaatzaak.eu/nl/the-case (in Dutch).

6 The environmental NGOs mentioned above judicially opposed the Norwegian government's oil drilling, to no avail. The claim was eventually dismissed by the Noregs Høgterett (Supreme Court of Norway), on 22.12.2020 (HR-2020–2472-P, no. 20-051052SIV-HRET). See the English translation of the decision, at https://www.greenpeace.org/static/planet4-norway-stateless/2022/05/d38444b5-annexes.pdf.

7 Higher Court of Lahore, 04.09.2015, W.P. No. 25501/2015, *Asghar Leghari v. Federation of Pakistan*. The text of the decision, in English, can be found at https://sys.lhc.gov.pk/appjudgments/2018LHC132.pdf. For a case overview in English, see https://judicialportal.informea.org/node/10. The decision can be described as a bold example of transformative adjudication in pursuit of climate justice, and is emblematic of the 'rights turn' in climate change litigation: see E.M. Barritt and B. Sediti, 'The Symbolic Value of *Leghari v. Federation of Pakistan*: Climate Change Adjudication in the Global South', *King's Law Journal*, 2019 (30–2), pp. 203–210, https://kclpure.kcl.ac.uk/portal/files/111826600/Barritt_and_Sediti_The_Symbolic_Value_of_Leghari_v_Federation_of_Pakistan_170619.pdf, p. 1.

Spain has not remained oblivious to this development. Greenpeace Spain[9] and other organisations have pursued a lawsuit against the Spanish state, and this has just been decided by the Tribunal Supremo (Spanish Supreme Court) (Administrative Chamber).[10] The lawsuit accuses the state, as is usual in these climate change litigation cases, of not having done enough to combat climate change.[11] However, in July 2023, the Spanish Supreme Court dismissed the claim, on the ground that the state plan to combat climate change meets Spain's commitments as a member of the EU.[12] Certainly, the Spanish court acknowledged that the state plan falls short, in that it does not allow for sufficient citizen participation; however, the Tribunal Supremo did not feel bound by the judicial decisions issued elsewhere to the contrary, such as the *Urgenda* case etc. One of the claimants' lawyers has decried that, in dismissing the claim, the Spanish Supreme Court has failed to keep up with its European counterparts.[13] However the truth is that there are also substantial differences between the way in which this claim was filed and, for instance, the *Urgenda* claim.[14]

The following discussion delves into the meaning and implications of the *Urgenda* case and its progeny, as regards tort liability for climate change. Such litigation will be examined against the background of environmental liability law. Using the *Urgenda* ruling as a starting point, the chapter explores the potential of climate change litigation to prompt changes in current tort liability law in general, and environmental liability law in particular. More specifically, and bearing in mind the usual causal hurdles faced by claimants in environmental liability cases, the chapter discusses whether use can be made of the doctrine

---

8 For an overview of climate change litigation around the world, see the web page of the Sabin Center for Climate Change, Columbia Law School (law projects listed under https://climate.law.columbia.edu/content/climate-change-litigation).

9 See Greenpeace España, 'Greenpeace inicia el primer litigio climático contra el Gobierno de España por inacción climática', 15.09.2020, https://es.greenpeace.org/es/noticias/greenpeace-litigio-climatico-gobierno-de-espana-por-inaccion-climatica/.

10 This decision remained unpublished at the time of submitting this chapter to the editor.

11 The claim emphasised the state's breach of its obligation to approve, and communicate to the European Commission, the comprehensive national plan of energy and climate, covering the period from 2021–30. See J. Doreste Hernández, 'El «juicio por el clima»: el litigio climático español', *Anuario de la Facultad de Derecho de la Universidad Autónoma de Madrid (AFDUAM)*, (2022) 26, pp. 383–406, https://www.boe.es/biblioteca_juridica/anuarios_derecho/abrir_pdf.php?id=ANU-A-2022-10038300406, p. 396.

12 See R. Rincón and M. Planelles, 'Primer litigio climático en España: el Tribunal Supremo da la razón al Gobierno frente a los ecologistas', *El País*, 27.07.2023, https://elpais.com/clima-y-medio-ambiente/2023-07-27/primer-litigio-climatico-en-espana-el-tribunal-supremo-da-la-razon-al-gobierno-frente-a-los-ecologistas.html.

13 See the comments of Lorena Ruiz-Huerta (in the news report cited in supra, note 12). See also Greenpeace España, 'El Tribunal Supremo ignora a la ciencia y los acuerdos internacionales y deja desprotegida a la ciudadanía', 27.07.2023, https://es.greenpeace.org/es/sala-de-prensa/comunicados/el-tribunal-supremo-ignora-a-la-ciencia-y-los-acuerdos-internacionales-y-deja-desprotegida-a-la-ciudadania/.

14 To start with, Urgenda's claim was filed as a liability claim in the private, non-administrative jurisdiction, while the Spanish case consisted of challenging a state plan.

of so-called 'pollution-share liability'. After explaining this doctrine in a succinct manner, it analyses the same in the highly specific scenario of climate change-related damage. Finally, the chapter tries to extract some conclusions as to whether and how notions discussed in the climate change litigation arena may impact on the practical application of existing liability frameworks. In this regard, while there have been some notable victories (*Urgenda* being the most prominent one), climate litigation as a whole may seem frustrating and disappointing, at least from the perspective of classic tort liability law. Thus, it may come as no surprise that such litigation has sometimes been described as 'much ado about nothing'.[15] It is, therefore, suggested that something more than posturing and aggressive public campaigns may be needed, to hold those responsible of climate change accountable for it.

2. CAUSAL UNCERTAINTY IN ENVIRONMENTAL LIABILITY

As observed above, causation is one of the most formidable hurdles with regard to climate change-related liability litigation. However, one of the most surprising aspects about such litigation is how little attention is paid to the issue of causation. If tort liability is about something – apart from damage, obviously – it is about causation. Indeed, tort is about making the one who has caused damage answer for it.

Generally speaking, causation is an unquestionably intricate issue within the realm of environmental responsibility. Countless authors have deemed it its weightiest burden, or, as some have occasionally remarked, its Achilles heel. On the other hand, some other scholars perceive causality rules as antiquated remnants from the early days of industrial society, unfit for grappling with the perils of our profoundly technological era. It is often remarked that chasms emerge between human action itself and the substantiation of said action,[16] in the sense of its consequences.

Indeed, the necessity of a causal connection, as a fundamental premise of tort liability, appears self-evident. However, if one looks at the regulatory framework, including the EU Directive on Environmental Liability (hereinafter 'ELD'),[17] as well as the national transposition statutes, such as those of Spain

---

15 See A. Ruda-González, 'Responsabilidad civil por daños climáticos: ¿mucho ruido y pocas nueces?', *Anuario de la Facultad de Derecho de la Universidad Autónoma de Madrid (AFDUAM)*, (2022) 26, pp. 312–338, https://www.boe.es/biblioteca_juridica/anuarios_derecho/abrir_pdf.php?id=ANU-A-2022-10032100346.

16 A paradigmatic position in this regard is that of U. Beck, *Políticas ecológicas en la Edad del Riesgo*, El Roure, 1998, p. 7.

17 Directive 2004/35/CE of the European Parliament and of the Council of 21 April 2004 on environmental liability with regard to the prevention and remedying of environmental

(Environmental Liability Act, hereinafter 'LRM')[18] or Portugal,[19] to name but a few, explicit regulations on this matter are often lacking.

As regards Portuguese law, for instance, the regulation at stake takes note of the difficulties of establishing causation in the environmental context. In the statute's explanatory statement, precisely emphasised as one of the elements that the legislature should into account, if it wants to avoid a 'statutory efficacy deficit', is a reference to 'the technical difficulty … [of] show[ing] that a given cause is apt to provoke damage (and subsequently, [of] attribute[ing] the same to its author)'.[20]

This is of twofold significance. Firstly, given the often strict nature of environmental liability, meaning that fault is not required as a liability condition, the causal link assumes paramount importance. If fault is not a prerequisite or condition for liability to be established, all the weight of the attribution to the author of the damage falls on the element of causation. Consequently, considering the complexity of the latter, it would be advisable for a legal system lacking a comprehensive statutory provision regarding the causal link – as is generally the case, and is certainly the case of Spanish law, among many others – to be equipped with such a statutory provision, to effectively address environmental liability issues. An illustration of this can be found in Swedish law. In Sweden, environmental liability is provided for in the Environmental Code (Miljöbalk, hereinafter 'MB'),[21] in particular in its Chapter 32, on 'Compensation for certain kinds of environmental damage and other private claims' *(Skadestånd för vissa miljöskador och andra enskilda anspråk)*. In view of the typical causal difficulties, proof of the causal link is to be decided on the balance of probabilities *(övrigt föreligger övervägande sannolikhet)*, after consideration of the circumstances of the case and other probable causes:

> Damage shall be deemed to have been caused by a disturbance referred to in the first paragraph[22] where, in view of the nature of the disturbance and its adverse

damage (Official Journal, OJ L 143, 30.04.2004), available at https://eur-lex.europa.eu/legal-content/EN/TXT/?uri=CELEX%3A02004L0035-20190626.

18 Act (Ley) 26/2007, of 23 October, de Responsabilidad Medioambiental (Official Gazette (Boletín Oficial del Estado, BOE) no. 255, 24.10.2007), https://www.boe.es/buscar/act.php?id=BOE-A-2007-18475.

19 Statutory Decree (Decreto-Lei) no. 147/2008, Regime jurídico da responsabilidade por danos ambientais (Diário da República no. 145/2008, Série I, 29.07.2008), https://diariodarepublica.pt/dr/legislacao-consolidada/decreto-lei/2008-34503075.

20 The original text reads, *'a dificuldade técnica de provar que uma causa é apta a produzir o dano (e, consequentemente, de o imputar ao respectivo autor)'*.

21 Miljöbalk (1998:808), SFS nr: 1998:808, available (in Swedish) at https://www.riksdagen.se/sv/dokument-och-lagar/dokument/svensk-forfattningssamling/miljobalk-1998808_sfs-1998-808/. An official English translation by the Swedish Government can be found at https://www.government.se/legal-documents/2000/08/ds-200061/.

22 Ibid. (32 kap. §3 III). The first paragraph refers to the different types of pollution, such as water pollution, air pollution, etc. The rule is open, since any other 'similar disturbances' *('annan liknande störning')* may trigger liability.

> effects, other possible causes and any other circumstances, the balance of probability indicates that the disturbance was the cause.[23]

However, the truth is that this rule does not say much either, since it merely establishes that the causal link will depend on its probability being greater than the probability of the opposite – what in English law is often called the 'more probable than not' rule. This approach to causation responds to a binary point of view,[24] in which causation either exists or does not, with no possibility in between. Secondly, it is noteworthy that the absence of a general causal rule within the ELD mentioned above allows each national legislature to independently address causal problems: this, perhaps inadvertently, paves the way for the lack of uniformity among national laws.

Indeed, both the Directive and the Spanish LRM merely stipulate that liability for environmental damage caused by diffuse pollution arises when a causal link can be established between the damage and the activities of specific operators (Article 4(5) of the ELD and Article 4.3 of the Spanish LRM). It can be inferred that this causal link is also required in other cases in which contamination is not diffuse, or in which damage is caused by factors other than contamination. Thus, the ELD has dismissed the possibility, proposed by the European Parliament, that environmental liability could be attributed to the party simply having caused, or having had the potential to cause, the damage. A similar solution had already been advanced by the Council of Europe'sLugano Convention,[25] a magnificent statutory text that will go down in history as what could have been but was not, since it has never entered into force, and never will. Pursuant to its Article 10 on 'Causality':

> When considering evidence of the causal link between the incident and the damage or, in the context of a dangerous activity as defined in Article 2, paragraph 1, sub-paragraph d, between the activity and the damage, the court shall take due account of the increased danger of causing such damage inherent in the dangerous activity.[26]

---

23 In its original Swedish original form: '*En skada skall anses ha orsakats genom en störning som avses i första stycket, om det med hänsyn till störningens och skadeverkningarnas art, andra möjliga skadeorsaker samt omständigheterna i övrigt föreligger övervägande sannolikhet för ett sådant orsakssamband.*'.

24 Similarly, see I. Hunt and The Hon Mr Justice Mostyn, 'Probability reasoning in judicial fact-finding', *International Journal of Evidence and Proof*, (2019) (24–4), pp. 75–94, pp. 75 *et seq*. (also available at https://www.judiciary.uk/wp-content/uploads/2019/10/hunt_and_mostyn_2019.pdf), who speak of a 'binary method' regarding causation.

25 Council of Europe Convention no. 150, of 21.06.1993, on Civil Liability for Damage Resulting from Activities Dangerous to the Environment, signed in Lugano in 1993, available at https://rm.coe.int/168007c079.

26 Art. 2 of the Lugano Convention (ibid.) defined 'dangerous activities' as 'one or more of the following activities provided that it is performed professionally, including activities conducted by public authorities: (a) the production, handling, storage, use or discharge of one or more dangerous substances or any operation of a similar nature dealing with such substances;

Thus, the Lugano Convention established a presumption of causation on the basis of a mere increase in danger: something which the EU legislature was not ready to accept.

Certainly, in the case of diffuse pollution, it might not be reasonable to demand a causal link for liability to be established, since, due to its very diffuse nature, proving such a link would be unfeasible in many scenarios: for instance, consider contamination resulting from motorised traffic, agricultural fertilisers, or eutrophication of the sea. In fact, the ELD itself acknowledges that, in the case of widespread and diffuse pollution, it is impossible to attribute so-called 'negative environmental effects' to the actions or omissions of specific individual agents (Recital 13, ELD). Thus, the aforementioned provision in the Directive anticipates a scenario that is essentially laboratory-oriented, where only a few identifiable causes of diffuse pollution exist. However, the ELD fails to provide a clear definition of 'diffuse pollution'. In any case, it leaves the critical matter of the causal link unresolved, thereby inadvertently causing more harm than good (see Art. 4.5 ELD).

The complexity of environmental causation arises primarily from the imperfect understanding that persists regarding the environment. Determining the cause of ecological disruptions is often a near-impossible task, or one fraught with considerable difficulty, given the intricate nature of natural environmental processes, the frequent lack of experimental verifiability for hypotheses, and the simultaneous micro and macro scale of these disruptions. It is not merely a challenge for the victim to establish the causal link. Rather, an actual evidential gap often exists, characterised by general or absolute etiological uncertainty stemming from the limitations of human knowledge. In fact, aspiring to attain complete precision in comprehending environmental phenomena appears unrealistic.[27] These difficulties are exacerbated in the context of climate change, again a rather complex phenomenon which defies human comprehension.

(b) the production, culturing, handling, storage, use, destruction, disposal, release or any other operation dealing with one or more: genetically modified organisms which as a result of the properties of the organism, the genetic modification and the conditions under which the operation is exercised, pose a significant risk for man, the environment or property; micro-organisms which as a result of their properties and the conditions under which the operation is exercised pose a significant risk for man, the environment or property, such as those micro-organisms which are pathogenic or which produce toxins; (c) the operation of an installation or site for the incineration, treatment, handling or recycling of waste, such as those installations or sites specified in Annex II, provided that the quantities involved pose a significant risk for man, the environment or property; (d) the operation of a site for the permanent deposit of waste.' As can be seen, there is a mistake in the reference in Art. 10 to Art. 2, since the definition of dangerous activity in subpara. (d) refers only to the operation of sites for waste deposits.

27 As has already pointed out in A. Ruda González, *El daño ecológico puro: La responsabilidad civil por el deterioro del medio ambiente, con especial atención a la Ley 26/2007, de 23 de octubre, de responsabilidad medioambiental*, Thomson Reuters Aranzadi, 2008, pp. 175 *et seq.*

Moreover, it is evident that the precise mechanisms through which greenhouse gases contribute to climate change remain incompletely understood. Global climate change is a profoundly intricate phenomenon, defying formulation as a straightforward physical law.[28] The challenges inherent in studying small organisms, both in physics and ecology, contribute to this limitation. In these disciplines, given their inherent complexity, mathematical tools, like matrix algebraic calculus, are employed to provide approximate descriptions of reality through models. However, the situation is compounded by the fact that, even with the utilisation of such models, and despite their application in toxicology (specifically toxicokinetics) within an environmental context (ecotoxicology), experts must acknowledge their inability to predict the distribution of chemical substances within an ecosystem.[29]

From this discussion, an apparent absence of a strictly linear, direct or immediate causal connection in nature *(natura facit saltus!)* becomes apparent. This may lead to an intriguing implication for the scope of this chapter. Specifically, the foregoing suggests that attaining scientifically precise knowledge of all natural phenomena is inherently unattainable – an elusive dream; a chimera. The inherent imperfections of scientific understandings of natural phenomena and the element of probability reside within the very essence of these phenomena. Consequently, one must content oneself with a knowledge framework based on probabilities or stochastic processes, which inherently carry the possibility of error.[30]

If the foregoing is true, it may be submitted that a judge – or whoever has to adjudicate environmental liability in general, and climate change liability in particular – can never be expected to achieve absolute certainty in the hypothetical determination of causation. The intrinsic, inherent uncertainty accompanying natural, environmental or climate phenomena makes it challenging to establish not only the existence of damage, but also the purely factual causal link (cause in fact). Any illusion of security or certainty is thereby shattered. Since future consequences cannot be predicted with certainty, the viability of the 'more probable than not' and *conditio sine qua non* tests becomes questionable. In matters related to climate change, where the limitations of scientific knowledge are particularly pronounced, crucial questions arise as to what extent individuals can be held accountable when the causal link is partially uncertain, and whether the law can persist in utilising a notion of causation that has been dismissed by the natural sciences.

---

28 See S.R. Weart, *The Discovery of Global Warming*, Harvard University Press, 2003, p. 195.

29 See C.H. Walker, S.P. Hopkin, R.M. Sibly and D.B. Peakall, *Principles of Ecotoxicology* (2nd ed.), Taylor and Francis, 2001 (reprinted 2002), pp. 59–60.

30 In a similar vein, see C. von Bar, *Gemeineuropäisches Deliktsrecht,* vol. II, C.H. Beck, 1999, p. 461 *Randnummer* (margin number) no. 436.

Ecological damage often entails harm to an ecological balance rather than to a specific entity. In a similar vein, climate change damage has a collective or 'macro' nature, whereby the victim is nature itself, more than a single individual or a group of persons. Even where a specific victim may be identified, the climate has a collective nature which is hardly captured by the perspective of tort law, which focuses on the individual. Climate change law is at odds with this, both where one tries to find an individual victim and an individual culprit – ultimately, all of us pollute. Therefore, attributing environmental and climate damage to specific conduct often poses difficulties, as the number of potential offenders is always high, and the relationships between them are complex. Cases where causation remains monocausal or monofactorial are rare in practice.

Therefore, it may be suggested that, in the climate change arena, the attribution of causation within a framework of absolute certainty must give way to some sort of collective decision-making mechanisms in the face of uncertainty, with epidemiological evidence serving as an illustrative example. An instance of the latter approach can be found in Spanish law, in the case of damage caused by denatured rapeseed oil *(aceite de colza)*. As is well known, the Spanish Supreme Court decided, in this case, that there was no need to establish the individual causal link. According to the Criminal Chamber of the Spanish Supreme Court[31] the causal link between the action of handling and mixing oil, and the resulting poisoning, injuries and deaths of hundreds of people, could be deemed to be established on the basis of a general epidemiological or statistical causality notion. All the people affected by the toxic syndrome (about 15,000) had consumed the oil in question, although not all of those who had consumed it were affected. It was not possible to identify the specific cause (the so-called 'molecule with toxicological significance') that had produced this result, since experiments carried out gave negative results.[32]

Another compelling illustration of the epidemiological approach can be observed in notable environmental lawsuits for mercury poisoning in Japan. Most

---

31 Decision of 23.2.1992. Repertorio Jurisprudencial (RJ) Aranzadi 1992/6783. On the case, see, among others, J.M. Paredes Castañón, 'Caso del aceite de colza' in P. Sánchez-Ostiz Gutierrez (ed.), *Casos que hicieron doctrina en el derecho penal*, La Ley, 2011, pp. 425–439; from a product liability perspective, see T. Rodríguez Montañés, 'Incidencia dogmática de la jurisprudencia del caso de la colza y otros casos en materia de productos defectuosos' in F.J. Boix Reig, R. Campos Cristóbal and A. Bernardi (eds.), *Responsabilidad penal por defectos en productos destinados a los consumidores*, Iustel, 2005, pp. 115–132, with further references. On the long-term effects of the case, see L. Bajatierra, 'Afectados por la colza 25 años después', *Cambio 16*, (2006) 1803, pp. 50–52. On the etiology of so-called 'toxic-oil syndrome', see A. Martínez Cabot, 'La síndrome de l'oli tòxic: contribució a la seva etiologia mitjançant estudis xenobioquímics del 3-(Nfenilamino)-1,2-propandiol', Tesis doctoral dirigida por A. Messeguer Peypoch, Universitat de Barcelona, 2008, https://diposit.ub.edu/dspace/handle/2445/42940.

32 See F. Muñoz Conde, 'La responsabilidad por el producto en el Derecho penal español', *Derecho y Sociedad*, (2017) 49, pp. 253–279, https://dialnet.unirioja.es/descarga/articulo/7792284.pdf, p. 268.

interesting are the so-called *Minamata* and *Itai-Itai* cases. Certainly, in spite of the fact that there were thousands of victims, such cases are largely unknown to Western lawyers, possibly because they were dealt with in a distant jurisdiction, many years ago, and the Japanese language remains an unsurmountable barrier to in-depth information on them.[33] Nevertheless, the disaster (consisting of Mercury pollution) was once again drawn to public attention in the West by the 2020 biographical drama film *Minamata*, by Andrew Levitas,[34] and probably to a lesser extent, but no less importantly, by the signature of the Minamata Convention on the Elimination of Mercury, in Kumamoto (Japan), in 2013.[35] Japanese scientists had to demonstrate associations between fish intake and the Minamata disease, after careful descriptive and analytical epidemiological studies.[36] As a result of these studies, Japanese courts admitted this type of evidence as a means to address catastrophic damage suffered by thousands of victims who would otherwise have struggled to establish a direct causal link. Japanese scientists even clarified symptoms of the Minamata disease by focusing on the degree of exposure to, and duration of, pollution, although the disposition of the individual victim was also concluded to be relevant.[37] Eventually, the Japanese Ministry of the Environment

---

33 The victims were poisoned because of the ingestion of fish and shellfish contaminated with a high concentration of the neurotoxin methylmercury. See M.A. Valera Cerdá, 'Intoxicación por metilmercurio: la enfermedad de Minamata', *MoleQla: revista de Ciencias de la Universidad Pablo de Olavide*, (2013) 9, pp. 122–124, https://www.upo.es/cms1/export/sites/upo/moleqla/documentos/numero_9.pdf. On the role of the Japanese state in these cases, see P. Jobin, 'L'État, c'est personne ! Ou l'État (japonais) à l'épreuve des catastrophes industrielles', *Quaderni: la revue de la communication*, (2012) 78, pp. 45–66, https://journals.openedition.org/quaderni/577. From a cultural perspective, see M. Matzeu, 'Il Giappone e le sue contraddizioni. Attorno alla sua politica ambientale, ruotano i concetti di natura, territorio, tecnologia e shintoismo, concetti cardine che fanno parte dell' identitá giapponese', *Revista HMiC: història moderna i contemporània*, (2006) 4, pp. 75–96, https://ddd.uab.cat/record/15094.

34 The film is based on the homonymous book by W.E. Smith (played by Johnny Depp in the film) and A.M. Smith, published by Holt, Rinehart and Winston, in 1975.

35 See Minamata Convention on Mercury, adopted on 10 October 2013 at Kumamoto (Japan) on the occasion of the Conference of Plenipotentiaries on the Minamata Convention on Mercury held from 7 to 11 October 2013 and entered into force on 16 August 2017; https://mercuryconvention.org/en. In legal scholarship, see L. Vassallo, 'L'adoption de la convention de Minamata, ou la longue marche vers un instrument international juridiquement contraignant sur le mercure', *Revue Juridique de l'Environnement*, (2013) (38–2), pp. 237–246; B. Lozano Cutanda and A. Lago Candeira, 'Hacia la progresiva eliminación del mercurio: Adopción del Convenio de Minamata' in F. López Ramón (ed.), *Observatorio de Políticas Ambientales 2014*, Thomson Reuters Aranzadi, 2014, pp. 61–86. For a more cinematographic approach, see A. Gutiérrez Bermejo, 'El fotógrafo del pánico', *Cinemanía*, (2021) 308, p. 18.

36 See T. Yorifuji, 'Lessons from an Early-stage Epidemiological Study of Minamata Disease', *Journal of Epidemiology*, (2020) 30(1), pp. 12–14, https://www.ncbi.nlm.nih.gov/pmc/articles/PMC6908841/pdf/je-30-012.pdf, p. 13.

37 See A. Igata, 'Epidemiological and Clinical Features of Minamata Disease', *Environmental Research*, (1993) 63(1), pp. 157–169, https://www.sciencedirect.com/science/article/abs/pii/S0013935183711370?via%3Dihub.

laid out medical criteria for the certification of the Minamata disease, to be conducted by official certification boards.[38]

In one of these cases, the victims, who suffered from respiratory tract disorders, obtained compensation from the defendant companies, emitters of sulphur dioxide (SO2), based on the statistical correlation test between the concentration of this substance in the air and the respiratory illnesses they experienced. In another case, victims received compensation from mining companies in a particular region, after demonstrating a statistical relationship between the incidence of a specific disease resulting from excessive cadmium exposure and the spills caused by the defendants. Therefore, the Japanese courts have accepted the epidemiological test where the hazardous factor increased the plaintiffs' risk of contracting a particular disease.[39]

Of course, one could ask what these cases have to do with climate change. As stated above, in climate change the good affected or harmed is collective, while in cases of pollution or poisoning in which an epidemiological approach has been adopted, there are specific victims who can be identified by their names. Nonetheless, the epidemiological test is important in that it supplements the traditional perspective with regard to causation. Certainly, doubts may still arise, since this approach provides general, typological or statistical information that is never conclusive when applied to a specific case or victim. Epidemiology, for instance, examines disease incidence within groups of individuals, allowing for a better understanding of the causes of such an incidence, rather than the causes of the disease in each individual case. Specifically, epidemiology aims to indicate 'relative risk' (also referred to as etiological probability), which quantifies the risk of individuals exposed to a presumed causative factor (for example, a substance such as colza oil or methylmercury) developing a specific disease, compared with those who have not been so exposed. For example, the epidemiological approach assesses the risk of smokers developing lung cancer, compared with non-smokers, or the risk of oral contraceptive users developing cardiovascular disease, compared with non-users.[40]

---

38 See N. Hachiya, 'The history and the present of Minamata disease – Entering the second half a century', *Japanese Medical Association Journal (JMAJ)*, (2006) 49(3), pp. 112–118, p. 117.

39 For a list of the lawsuits against the polluting company, and other relief measures, see Minamata City, *Minamata Disease: Its History and Lessons*, Minamata City Planning Division, 2007, https://minamata195651.jp/pdf/kyoukun_en/kyoukun_eng_all.pdf, pp. 24 *et seq*. See also (Japanese) Ministry of the Environment, *Lessons from Minamata Disease and Mercury Management in Japan*, Ministry of the Environment (Japan), 2013, https://www.env.go.jp/content/900414989.pdf.

40 See B.W. Stewart and P. Kleihues (eds.), *World Cancer Report*, WHO, 2003, p. 182, https://www.env.go.jp/air/asbestos/commi_hhmd/03/ext01.pdf; S. Franceschi and E. Bidoli, 'The epidemiology of lung cancer', *Annals of Oncology*, (1999) 10, S3–S6, https://www.sciencedirect.com/science/article/pii/S0923753419575159/pdf; A.J. Sasco, M.B. Secretan and K. Strai, 'Tobacco smoking and cancer: a brief review of recent epidemiological evidence', *Lung Cancer*, (2004) 45(2), S3–S9, https://www.lungcancerjournal.info/article/S0169-5002(04)80002-3/pdf.

Therefore, it is true that such an approach may not fully align with the particularistic or atomistic framework of tort liability law, which generally focuses on determining the *specific* cause of damage to individual victims rather than increases in disease incidence. Moreover, while epidemiology may identify a significant statistical *association* between a factor and a particular disease, it does not necessarily establish *causation*, just as the absence of a statistical association does not imply that the factor is not the cause of the disease.[41] Additionally, the epidemiological test is inherently designed for personal injury cases, making it less suitable for litigation involving pure ecological damage, such as climate change litigation. Similar challenges arise with toxicological information, which, while capable of accurately describing substance behaviour in a laboratory setting, may not fully explain the interactions of substances both with one another and also with people in reality. This is particularly true when dealing with carcinogenic substances, where the risk of causal confusion (causal confounding) is a significant concern.[42]

As can be seen, the issue of determining who is responsible for what presents a significant challenge in environmental cases such as the ones under discussion. While some forms of pollution can be attributed to identifiable and distinct sources, such as the smoke from a factory or the vibrations and noises emitted by a music bar, these instances are relatively uncommon, and often draw immediate attention from public authorities. In contrast, cases involving pure ecological damage tend to involve scattered and elusive sources that are difficult to pinpoint. For instance, fertilisers or pesticides from various sources, like farms, golf courses and gardens, can be dispersed through the air by the wind. Much environmental damage is the result of collective activities carried out anonymously within a mass society. As is well known, urban areas, where numerous polluting sources converge, exhibit higher incidences of cancer, compared with rural regions.[43] Consequently, it is improbable for a judge to attribute specific responsibility for environmental deterioration. In this context of organised irresponsibility, attempting to identify a precise causal link would

---

41 See R. Craig, M.D. Green, A. Klein and J. Sanders, *Toxic and Environmental Torts: Cases and Materials*, West Academic Publishing, 2011, pp. 1 *et seq*. Warnings not to confuse association and causation abound in the literature on environmental and toxic torts. Among many others, see A. Bradford Hill, 'The Environment and Disease: Association or Causation?', *Proceedings of the Royal Society of Medicine*, (1965) 58(5), pp. 295–301, https://journals.sagepub.com/doi/10.1177/003591576505800503, p. 295.

42 Among others, see C.H. Hennekens and J.E. Buring, *Epidemiology in Medicine*, Little, Brown and Co., 1987, p. 33.

43 See W. Zheng et al., 'Urban-rural disparity in cancer mortality and changing trend in Tianjin, China, during 1999 and 2016', *BMC Cancer*, (2021) 21, Art no. 1208, https://bmccancer.biomedcentral.com/articles/10.1186/s12885-021-08907-0. In comparison with urban areas, inhabitants of rural areas face disadvantages related to economic deprivation. See National Cancer Institute, GIS Portal for Cancer Research, 'Rural-Urban Disparities in Cancer' (no date), https://gis.cancer.gov/mapstory/rural-urban/.

be akin to engaging in a game of chance. It comes as no surprise, then, that causation has emerged as a formidable barrier to litigation in environmental suits.[44]

From the preceding exposition, it can be deduced that the causal link is fundamentally problematic from the factual or natural point of view, i.e. when it is understood as the cause of the damage. In many cases, it is simply very difficult, if not impossible, to establish the causal link, because the reality is too complex, there is a lack of information, or there are no adequate criteria. It will surprise nobody, then, that some legal scholars advocate for a change in approach. Evidential uncertainty, it is said, is forcing the law to consider a different rule, according to which the defendant would be liable to pay compensation based on the probability that their tortious conduct caused the victim's harm, rather than adhering to liability on an all-or-nothing basis.[45]

3. CAUSATION IN CLIMATE CHANGE LITIGATION CASES: POLLUTION-SHARE LIABILITY AS A PANACEA?

It has already been noted that causation is one of the major conundrums with regard to climate change liability litigation, yet it is hardly discussed in practice. With regard to litigation against states (of which *Urgenda* is one example), there is hardly any doubt that causation may be established. In this case, the Dutch state did not even try to refute the fact that it had polluted. In fact, by arguing that the Netherlands was contributing very little to climate change, compared with bigger countries, the defendant state actually confessed its own liability.

Nevertheless, more issues may arise when the claim is addressed against individual polluters, such as large corporations. In a case pending before the Hamm regional court (Germany),[46] a Peruvian farmer called Saul Lliuya alleges that Germany's largest electricity producer (RWE) bears some measure of responsibility regarding the melting of mountain glaciers near the claimant's town of Huaraz. Therefore, he claims that RWE should reimburse him for a portion of the costs he and the Peruvian authorities will foreseeably have to bear

44 See 'Note: Causation in Environmental Law: Lessons from Toxic Torts', *Harvard Law Review*, (2015) 128, pp. 2256–2278, https://harvardlawreview.org/wp-content/uploads/2015/06/causation_in_environmental_law.pdf, p. 2258. See also see B.M. Zupančič, 'Causation in Cases of Environmental Degradation: The Missing Link in Adjudicating Human Rights', *The Yearbook of Polar Law Online*, (2011) (3–1), pp. 113–128, https://brill.com/view/journals/yplo/3/1/article-p113_9.xml.

45 See M.D. Green, 'The Future of Proportional Liability', Wake Forest University Legal Studies Paper No. 04-14 (2004), https://papers.ssrn.com/sol3/papers.cfm?abstract_id=610563, p. 1.

46 *Luciano Lliuya v. RWE AG*. See the case abstract in http://climatecasechart.com/non-us-case/lliuya-v-rwe-ag/.

as a result of having to set up flood protections. The District Court of Essen swiftly dismissed the claim on the basis of lack of causation.[47] However, the claimant has raised, on appeal, that causation is the very issue which should be analysed.

When hearing about such a case, an obvious question comes to mind: why RWE? Surely the glaciers' melting cannot be caused by RWE alone. What, then, is the criterion upon which such a claim may be grounded?

In this regard, it may be useful to examine a doctrine which has been gaining momentum in recent years, if not decades, first in the US, and later in Europe. This doctrine is a notable example of a legal challenge arising where the victim cannot establish the identity of the manufacturer responsible for the product that caused the harm. A well-known case illustrating this is the situation surrounding the generic drug diethylstilbestrol (DES), in the US. DES, a synthetic oestrogen[48] prescribed to women at risk of miscarriage, was manufactured by multiple companies in the mid twentieth century. The daughters of those who took DES, often referred to as 'DES daughters', experienced significant health issues, or even death. Due to the extended period between exposure and damage, many of these victims were unable to prove which manufacturer's product their mothers had consumed.

In a groundbreaking decision, *Sindell v. Abbott Laboratories*,[49] the Superior Court of California held certain DES manufacturers accountable for compensating victims, based on their respective market shares. This case is usually said to have revolutionised American tort law, in that it deviates from the traditional requirement of causation, and adopts a principle of proportional responsibility, in line with the new proposals referred to above. Such a new approach aimed to strike a Solomon-like balance between full compensation and proportional responsibility.[50]

The *Sindell* case is widely recognised as a groundbreaking application of market-share liability, although the doctrine was not actually created by the

47 An unofficial translation of the Essen decision, *Luciano Lliuya v. RWE AG*, Case No. 2 O 285/15 Essen Regional Court (2015) (issued on 15 December 2016), into English can be found at https://climatecasechart.com/non-us-case/lliuya-v-rwe-ag/.

48 Synthetic oestrogens are used in both hormonal birth control and treatments for menopause symptoms. However, they have been linked to different illnesses, in particular cancer. See L. Hilakivi-Clarke, S. de Assis, and A. Warri, 'Exposures to Synthetic Estrogens at Different Times During the Life, and Their Effect on Breast Cancer Risk', *Journal of Mammary Gland Biology and Neoplasia*, (2013) 18-1, pp. 25–42, https://link.springer.com/article/10.1007/s10911-013-9274-8.

49 26 Cal. 3d 588; 607 P.2d 924; 163 Cal. Rptr. 132 (1980).

50 In legal scholarship, see, among others, W.H. Van Boom, 'Aansprakelijkheid naar rato van het veroorzakingsaandeel' in W.H. Van Boom, C.E.C. Jansen and J.G.A. Linssen (eds.), *Tussen 'Alles' en 'Niets': van toedeling naar verdeling van nadeel*, WEJ Tjeenk Willink, 1997, pp. 135–152, p. 142; O. Ben-Shahar, 'Causation and Forseeability' in B. Bouckaert and G. De Geest (eds.), *Encyclopedia of Law and Economics*, Edward Elgar Publishing, 2000, http://encyclo.findlaw.com/3300book.pdf, p. 652.

California court, but by a student called Naomi Sheiner, in 1978.[51] One of the DES manufacturers involved in the case was Abbott. DES was authorised by the US Food and Drug Administration in 1947, but not identified as posing health risks until 1971. This drug was commonly prescribed as a generic medication, readily available in any pharmacy. Consequently, years later, when damage ensued, many women who had taken DES could not recall the specific brand or brands of tablets they had ingested; in some cases, they could not even remember the ingestion itself. Judith Sindell, the daughter of one of those women, along with other young women who had experienced the adverse effects of DES exposure, initiated a lawsuit against multiple manufacturers involved in its production. It is estimated that between 1.5 and 3 million individuals were exposed to DES. Many manufacturers had failed to conduct adequate tests before introducing the product to the market, instead relying on results obtained by others. The consequences were catastrophic, including death from DES' signature disease,[52] vaginal and uterine adenocarcinoma.[53]

Due to the significant time lapse, of approximately 20 years, since the distribution and consumption of DES, tort liability actions had become time-barred by prescription (or limitation of actions, as it is also called). To enable the victims to seek compensation, legal scholarship advanced several proposals, such as the discovery rule, or state provisions which tolled the statute of limitations for minors.[54] Along these lines, the State of California resorted to an extraordinary measure, by enacting a specific statute that revived these actions and provided a new time frame for the claimants. Throughout the legal process, the connection between DES and the damage suffered by the victims was firmly established through medical studies. However, the claimants were not able to identify the specific manufacturers of the DES tablets consumed by their respective mothers – besides the time issue, the number of manufacturers involved was estimated to be around 200.

---

51 See N. Sheiner, 'DES and a Proposed Theory of Enterprise Liability', *Fordham Law Review*, (1978) 46, pp. 963–1007, also available at *Fordham Law Review*, (2014) 83, pp. 963–1007, https://ir.lawnet.fordham.edu/flr/vol83/iss1/2/.

52 Such diseases are rare under normal circumstances, so it may be assumed that their cause can only be exposure to the substance at stake.

53 See D. Ibarreta and S.H. Swan, 'The DES story: long-term consequences of prenatal exposure' in P. Harremoes et al. (eds.), *The Precautionary Principle in the 20th Century*, Routledge, 2002, pp. 84–94, https://www.eea.europa.eu/publications/environmental_issue_report_2001_22/issue-22-part-08.pdf, p. 85. See also, on the rare occurrence of non-DES-associated adenocarcinoma of the vagina, S.J. Frank et al., 'Primary adenocarcinoma of the vagina not associated with diethylstilbestrol (DES) exposure', *Gynecologic Oncology*, (2007) 105(2), pp. 470–474, https://www.gynecologiconcology-online.net/article/S0090-8258(07)00007-8/pdf.

54 See C.A. Feigin, 'Statutes of limitations: The special problem of DES Suits', *American Journal of Law and Medicine*, (1981) 7(1), pp. 91–106, https://www.cambridge.org/core/journals/american-journal-of-law-and-medicine/article/abs/statutes-of-limitations-the-special-problem-of-des-suits/7A13CC4FB9996C4CDFEDBA2ED83C56EC, pp. 91 *et seq.*

A strict application of the existing law would likely have resulted in the dismissal of the claims, due to lack of a causal link. It was impossible to ascertain with certainty which particular manufacturer's DES tablets had caused harm to each victim. However, the court used so-called 'market-share liability' to set aside these considerations. Under this doctrine, all manufacturers sued were held accountable for each claimant victim, based solely on their presence in the relevant market, and their distribution of a potentially harmful product, even if it could not be determined precisely whether they had caused the harm to a particular plaintiff, or to someone else.

Time and space constraints prevent discussion of the market-share liability doctrine in detail, in this chapter.[55] Suffice it to say, for now, that, for this doctrine to be applicable, the product in question must be fungible, meaning that all units of the same product carry the same risk of causing harm, and, therefore, that the more units a manufacturer puts into circulation, the greater the risk that someone consuming the product will suffer damage. Moreover, the product must result in a specific series of symptoms or a characteristic disease (a 'signature disease', as mentioned above). This criterion, which was fulfilled in the case of DES, does not apply to other substances, such as lead paint, which can cause variable effects depending on the individual exposed to it.

Should this criterion, and the remaining conditions for market-share liability, be met, the defendants will bear the burden of proving that they did not manufacture the product that caused harm to the victim. Should they fail to do so, they will be held liable to the extent of their proportional market share, as determined by the court.

Certainly, market-share liability remains highly problematic, basically because it lacks a clear statutory basis (this is particularly serious in civil law jurisdictions, of course). For instance, it is dubious if and to what extent such a doctrine could be accepted under the EU product liability regime, as transposed by national legislatures.[56] Spanish law, for instance, already addresses the issue of lack of identification of the manufacturer, by holding the provider *(proveedor)* liable (Art. 138 TRLGDCU),[57] which is in line with the EU Directive. If the supplier is also unknown, it may be argued that the concept of market-share

55 For a detailed account of the same, see A. Ruda Gonzalez, 'La responsabilidad por cuota de mercado a juicio', *InDret*, (2003) 3, pp. 1–34, https://indret.com/la-responsabilidad-por-cuota-de-mercado-a-juicio/, pp. 6 *et seq.*

56 For Spain, see the Statutory Royal Decree (*Real Decreto Legislativo*) 1/2007, of 16 November, por el que se aprueba el texto refundido de la Ley General para la Defensa de los Consumidores y Usuarios y otras leyes complementarias (BOE no. 287, of 30.11.2007) (hereinafter 'TRLGDCU'), available (in Spanish) at https://www.boe.es/buscar/act.php?id=BOE-A-2007-20555. In particular, see Art. 135 *et seq.* This statutory instrument supersedes the previous Act 22/1994, of 6 July, de responsabilidad civil por los daños causados por productos defectuosos (BOE no 161, of 07.07.1994).

57 Ibid.

liability still cannot be applied, because the special product liability legislation requires the victim to establish a causal link (Art. 139 TRLGDCU).

Leaving the scholarly discussion on the product liability realm aside for now, and turning to environmental damage, it has been suggested that a variation of market-share liability could be accepted, in the form of a so-called 'pollution-share liability'. According to the same, each polluter could be held liable in proportion to their emissions volume or pollution quota.[58]

Once again, one of the problems with such approaches is that tort law seems to be rather rigid with regard to causation. A basic concern for the equality principle should, in principle, prevent the courts from applying causal criteria differently in one specific area of the law. Any such differences in approach should be justified very carefully. In particular, it seems that tort law generally requires the claimant to pinpoint damage to a specific defendant. In the market-share liability scenario, as may be recalled, the problem is that the individual victims cannot trace their damage to a specific manufacturer. Although it could be established that DES was apt or sufficient to cause the kind of damage suffered by the claimants (general causation), the specific causal link with each defendant could not be established.

Nevertheless, this does not apply to the case of climate change, with which there is just one victim: the climate. Therefore, it is always possible to identify to whom the defendant caused damage. Climate is a collective good, it may be argued. Therefore, one of the major hurdles to accepting some sort of pollution-share approach is removed. In other words, if establishing a specific link between the defendant's conduct and the damage sustained is no longer an issue, establishing general causation may be sufficient to trigger liability. Therefore, in a case such as *Lliuya*,[59] there may be no need to establish that RWE caused damage to the claimant in particular. Since it may be established that RWE have polluted the environment with the kind of emissions that have contributed to climate change, Lliuya – as well as any other person in Earth – could say that he is a victim, and is thus entitled to compensation. In order to establish the compensation amount, which obviously depends on the level of contribution of the defendant to the damage, it may be necessary to apportion damages, since RWE is obviously not the only author of such damage. In this regard, recent scientific developments have elaborated on the science of attribution,[60] which makes it possible to pinpoint the effects of climate change to specific polluters, such as the so-called carbon majors. Therefore, in spite of its many uncertainties

58 See, for instance, G. Díez-Picazo Giménez, 'La responsabilidad civil derivada de los daños al medio ambiente', *Diario La Ley*, (1996), pp. 1419–1421, p. 1420; similarly, see A. Cabanillas Sánchez, *La reparación de los daños al medio ambiente*, Aranzadi, 1996, p. 174.

59 *Luciano Lliuya v. RWE AG*, supra, note 46.

60 On which, see C.A. Banfi del Río, *Responsabilidad Civil por daños climáticos en el Derecho chileno y Comparado*, Tirant lo Blanch (Chile), 2023, pp. 95ª *et seq.*, with further references.

and problems, pollution-share liability may turn out to provide a solution for climate change litigation.

4. CONCLUSION

Climate litigation is filling courts around the world with lawsuits based on the negligent omissions of states, or the active contributions of companies to climate change. This type of claim presents enormous difficulties, which in part explains why such claims tend to suffer very different fates, depending on the jurisdiction in which they are pursued. Alongside notable victories, such as the *Urgenda* case in the Netherlands, there are resounding defeats, such as Greenpeace and others, in Spain.[61]

However, if there is one thing these cases have in common, it is that causation is often paid little or no attention. One of the main criticisms levelled against the District court judgment in the *Urgenda* case is precisely that of not having thoroughly examined causality. Nevertheless, causation was also paid little attention in the review by the Hoge Raad, which ended up sentencing the Dutch state on the basis of a breach of tort liability rules. By contrast, in the Spanish case, the claim filed before the administrative jurisdiction has failed, as mentioned above.[62] In the German case,[63] the causation requirement has doomed the claim to failure for the time being: only the appeal will establish whether damage allegedly suffered by the Peruvian farmer can be pinpointed to an electricity producer based in Germany.

Recent attribution science is beginning to develop criteria for imputing climate change damage to the conduct of specific individuals, especially large corporations. One of the proposals formulated to circumvent the problems of indeterminate causation – the doctrine of market-share liability, or its environmental variant, pollution-share liability – initially had the problem that the causal link, as it is usually understood, presupposes that the damage suffered by a specific victim must also be attributed to a specific defendant. Such a requirement simply disappears in the case of climate change, since this is a global or collective phenomenon. There is, therefore, no such problem in establishing who has been harmed by the defendant's conduct, since, if it is possible to establish that the defendant has contributed to climate change, it is undoubtedly the collective interest that is affected. A different question is whether tort liability is an appropriate technical instrument for all the people on the planet who are going to suffer the consequences of climate change, to start flooding the courts with claims of this type.

---

61 See note 10 above.

62 See note 10, above.

63 See note 47 above.

INDEX

ABOUT THE EDITORS

Endrius Cocciolo is an Administrative and Energy Law Associate Professor at the Public Law Department of Universitat Rovira i Virgili (Tarragona, Catalonia, Spain) and a researcher at the Tarragona Centre for Environmental Law Studies (CEDAT) and at the Research Institute In Sustainability, Climate Change And Energy Transition (IU-RESCAT). He is currently the coordinator of a Horizon MSCA Doctoral Network project (THERESA) on hydrogen regulation and the Principal Investigator of an interdisciplinary project founded by the Spanish Ministry of Innovation on energy communities (ComEnerSys).

Jordi Jaria-Manzano is Serra Húnter Fellow of Constitutional and Environmental Law at the Public Law Department of the Universitat Rovira i Virgili (Tarragona, Catalonia, Spain) and a researcher at the Tarragona Centre for Environmental Law Studies (CEDAT) and at the Research Institute in Sustainability, Climate Change and Energy Transition (IU-RESCAT). He is chief editor of the 'Revista d'Estudis Autonòmics i Federals/Journal of Self-Government) and currently leads a research project on sustainability in the digital domain, funded by the Spanish Ministry of Economic Affairs and Digital Transformation.

Aitana De la Varga-Pastor is an Administrative and Environmental Law Associate Professor at the Public Law Department of the Universitat Rovira i Virgili (Tarragona, Catalonia, Spain) and a researcher at the Tarragona Centre for Environmental Law Studies (CEDAT) and at the Research Institute In Sustainability, Climate Change And Energy Transition (IU-RESCAT). She is the Principal investigator of the R+D+I project "Climate change and plastic waste: legal challenges of the circular economy as a paradigm for the protection of planetary health and justice" (JustCircular).

Maria Marques-Banque is a Criminal Law Associate Professor at the Public Law Department of the Universitat Rovira i Virgili (Tarragona, Catalonia, Spain) and a researcher at the Tarragona Centre for Environmental Law Studies (CEDAT) and at the Research Institute In Sustainability, Climate Change and Energy Transition (IU-RESCAT). Her research focuses on environmental crime, wildlife crime, transnational environmental crime and EU criminal law. She is the Director of the Environmental Law Clinic at Universitat Rovira i Virgili.

www.ingramcontent.com/pod-product-compliance
Ingram Content Group UK Ltd.
Pitfield, Milton Keynes, MK11 3LW, UK
UKHW051847100926
8556IPUK00005B/488